ecpr PRESS

constraints on party policy change

Thomas M. Meyer

ecprPRESS

© Thomas M. Meyer 2013

First published by the ECPR Press in 2013

The ECPR Press is the publishing imprint of the European Consortium for Political Research (ECPR), a scholarly association, which supports and encourages the training, research and cross-national cooperation of political scientists in institutions throughout Europe and beyond.

ECPRPress
University of Essex
Wivenhoe Park
Colchester
CO4 3SQ
UK

Typeset by ECPR Press

Printed and bound by Lightning Source

British Library Cataloguing in Publication Data

A catalogue record for this book is available from the British Library

Paperback ISBN: 978-1-907301-49-0

ECPR – Monographs
Series Editors:
Dario Castiglione (University of Exeter)
Peter Kennealy (European University Institute)
Alexandra Segerberg (Stockholm University)
Peter Triantafillou (Roskilde University)

Other books available in this series
Agents or Bosses?: Patronage and Intra-Party Politics in Argentina and Turkey (ISBN: 9781907301261) Özge Kemahlioğlu

Causes of War: The Struggle for Recognition (ISBN: 9781907301018) Thomas Lindemann

Constraints on Party Policy Change (ISBN:9781907301490) Thomas Meyer

Citizenship: The History of an Idea (ISBN: 9780954796655) Paul Magnette

Civil Society in Communist Eastern Europe: Opposition and Dissent in Totalitarian Regimes (ISBN: 9781907301278) Matt Killingsworth

Coercing, Constraining and Signalling: Explaining UN and EU Sanctions After the Cold War (ISBN: 9781907301209) Francesco Giumelli

Deliberation Behind Closed Doors: Transparency and Lobbying in the European Union (ISBN: 9780955248849) Daniel Naurin

Democratic Institutions and Authoritarian Rule in Southeast Europe (ISBN: 9781907301438) Danijela Dolenec

European Integration and its Limits: Intergovernmental Conflicts and their Domestic Origins (ISBN: 9780955820373) Daniel Finke

Gender and Vote in Britain: Beyond the Gender Gap? (ISBN: 9780954796693) Rosie Campbell

Globalisation: An Overview (ISBN: 9780955248825) Danilo Zolo

Joining Political Organisations: Institutions, Mobilisation and Participation in Western Democracies (ISBN: 9780955248894) Laura Morales

Organising the European Parliament: Committees' Role and Legislative Influence (ISBN: 9781907301391) Nikoleta Yordanova

Parties and Elections in New European Democracies (ISBN: 9780955820328) Neil Munro and Richard Rose

Paying for Democracy: Political Finance and State Funding for Parties (ISBN: 9780954796631) Kevin Casas-Zamora

Policy Making in Multilevel Systems: Federalism, Decentralisation, and Performance in the OECD Countries (ISBN: 9781907301339) Jan Biela, Annika Hennl and André Kaiser

Political Conflict and Political Preferences: Communicative Interaction Between Facts, Norms and Interests (ISBN: 9780955820304) Claudia Landwehr

Political Parties and Interest Groups in Norway (ISBN: 9780955820366) Elin Haugsgjerd Allern

Regulation in Practice: The de facto Independence of Regulatory Agencies (ISBN: 9781907301285) Martino Maggetti

Representing Women?: Female Legislators in West European Parliaments (ISBN: 9780954796648) Mercedes Mateo Diaz

Schools of Democracy: How Ordinary Citizens (Sometimes) Become Competent in Participatory Budgeting Institutions (ISBN: 9781907301186) Julien Talpin

The Personalisation of Politics: A Study of Parliamentary Democracies (ISBN: 9781907301032) Lauri Karvonen

The Politics of Income Taxation: A Comparative Analysis (ISBN: 9780954796686) Steffen Ganghof

The Return of the State of War: A Theoretical Analysis of Operation Iraqi Freedom (ISBN: 9780955248856) Dario Battistella

Urban Foreign Policy and Domestic Dilemmas: Insights from Swiss and EU City-regions (ISBN: 9781907301070) Nico van der Heiden

Why aren't they there?: The Political Representation of Women, Ethnic Groups and Issue Positions in Legislatures (ISBN: 9780955820397) Didier Ruedin

Widen the Market, Narrow the Competition: Banker Interests and the Making of a European Capital Market (ISBN: 9781907301087) Daniel Mügge

Please visit www.ecpr.eu/ecprpress for information about new publications.

To my family

| contents

List of Figures and Tables   ix

Acknowledgements   xiii

Part I. Party Competition and Time

Chapter One: Constraints on Shifting Party Policy Platforms   3

Chapter Two: Linking Parties and Time   15

Chapter Three: Measuring Party Policy Shifts   29

Part II. Voter Perception and Party Policy Shifts

Chapter Four: The Voters' Perception of Party Policy Shifts   57

Chapter Five: Causes and Consequences of Voters' Perceived Party Policy Shifts   75

Chapter Six: Voter Perceptions of Party Policy Shifts: An Empirical Analysis   97

Chapter Seven: How Voter Perceptions Affect Party Policy Shifts: An Empirical Analysis   135

Part III. Parties' Internal Structure and Party Policy Shifts

Chapter Eight: How Parties' Internal Structure Affect Party Policy Shifts   169

Chapter Nine: Parties' Internal Structure and Party Policy Shifts: An Empirical Analysis   179

Part IV. Conclusion

Chapter Ten: Conclusions and Directions for Future Research   209

Appendices   217

Bibliography   233

Index   259

| list of figures and tables

Figures

Figure 1.1: Constraints on party policy shifts: The role of voters' perceptions and intra-party structure   8

Figure 3.1: Comparing additive RILE estimates and log ratio with expert judgements   43

Figure 3.2: Comparing the standard deviation of left-right positions using election manifestos and uncertainty of expert judgements (log-transformed estimates)   50

Figure 4.1: Voters' perception of party policy shifts   58

Figure 6.1: Party left-right placements in Great Britain (October 1974 – 2001)   105

Figure 6.2: Marginal effect of party identification on the perception of 'New Labour' (depending on the direction of the party policy shift)   110

Figure 6.3: The effect of party identification on the acceptance of policy shifts depending on the party shift's direction: Nationalisation   117

Figure 6.4: The effect of party identification on the acceptance of policy shifts depending on the party shift's direction: Taxes vs. Services   121

Figure 6.5: The effect of party identification on the acceptance of policy shifts depending on the party shift's direction: Unemployment vs. Inflation   124

Figure 7.1: Curvilinear effect of leadership tenure on party policy shifts   153

Figure 8.1: Intra-party structure and its effect on party policy shifts   169

Figure 9.1: Mean magnitude of party policy shifts depending on the inclusion of party members in the candidate selection process   197

Figure A.1: The perception of party policy shifts in a two-stage process   219

Figure A.2: Recoding covariates for the analysis   224

Tables

Table 3.1: Measuring party policy shifts using an additive scale and log ratios (Example 1)   42

Table 3.2: Measuring party policy shifts using an additive scale and log ratios (Example 2)   42

Table 3.3: Type I and Type II error for measuring party position shifts   45

Table 3.4: Explaining size of standard errors by centrist party emphasis on left-right issues   48

Table 4.1: Voters and potential voters of party j (holding competitors' policy positions constant)   65

Table 4.2: Voters and potential voters of party j (shifting competitors)   69

Table 4.3: Voter position shifts and incentives for party policy change   71

Table 5.1: Reception and acceptance covariates and their variation across voters, parties, and time   94

Table 6.1: Importance of policy issues for making vote choices (rank-order)   99

Table 6.2: Independent variables for the data analyses   103

Table 6.3: Perception of 'New Labour' in %   106

Table 6.4: Expected effects of covariates for the reception and acceptance of 'New Labour'   107

Table 6.5: Perception of 'New Labour' 1997   108

Table 6.6: Perception of party position shifts in Great Britain 1974–2001 (in %)   113

Table 6.7: Perception of policy shifts – Nationalisation (with clustered SEs)   115

Table 6.8: Perception of policy shifts – Taxes vs. Services (with clustered SEs)   119

Table 6.9: Perception of policy shifts – Unemployment vs. Inflation (with clustered SEs)   122

Table 6.10: Hypotheses and regression results for the reception covariates   125

Table 6.11: Hypotheses and regression results for the acceptance covariates   126

Table 6.12: Using political awareness instead of political interest and the effect on the reception of party policy shifts — 128

Table 6.13: Acceptance models without party identification: Avoiding multi-collinearity — 129

Table 6.14: The acceptance of 'unexpected' party policy shifts — 131

Table 6.15: Summary: Reception and acceptance covariates — 132

Table 7.1: Independent variables for the data analyses — 139

Table 7.2: Independent variables: number of observations and mean values — 143

Table 7.3: Political interest of voters and its effect on party policy shifts — 145

Table 7.4: Political interest and its effect on party policy shifts: Distinguishing directions — 146

Table 7.5: The magnitude of mean voter shifts and its effect on party policy shifts — 147

Table 7.6: Government participation and its effect on party policy shifts — 148

Table 7.7: The effective number of parliamentary parties and its effect on party policy shifts — 150

Table 7.8: Change in party leadership and their effect on party policy shifts — 151

Table 7.9: The magnitude of party policy shifts depending on party leader change and the necessity to shift party policy positions — 154

Table 7.10: Party leader prestige and its effect on party policy shifts — 155

Table 7.11: Party leader prestige and its effect on party policy shifts: Distinguishing directions — 156

Table 7.12: Magnitude of past party policy shifts and their effect on current party policy shifts — 158

Table 7.13: Share of voters with party identification and their effect on party policy shifts — 158

Table 7.14: Voter position shifts and their effect on party policy shifts — 161

Table 7.15: Shifts reacting to voter expectations of party policy positions — 163

Table 7.16: Summary of the findings: How reception and acceptance affect party position shifts — 164

Table 9.1: Independent variables for the data analyses   182

Table 9.2: Independent variables: number of observations and mean values   188

Table 9.3: Mass organisational strength and its effect on party policy shifts   191

Table 9.4: Explaining mass organisational strength   191

Table 9.5: Mass organisational strength and its effect on party policy shifts –
including control variables   192

Table 9.6: Mass organisational strength and its effect on party policy shifts –
depending on public funding   194

Table 9.7: Intra-party decision-making processes and their effect on party policy
shifts   196

Table 9.8: Explaining intra-party decision-making rules – descriptive patterns   198

Table 9.9: Intra-party decision-making processes and their effect on party policy
shifts – including control variables   199

Table 9.10: Public funding and its impact on party policy shifts   200

Table 9.11: Explaining the varying relevance of public funding for party income   202

Table 9.12: Public funding and its impact on party policy shifts – including control
variables   202

Table 9.13: How intra-party structure affects party policy shifts   203

Table 9.14: Explaining mass organisational strength, intra-party decision-making
rules, and sources of income   203

Table A.1: Policy scales used in British panel election studies: 1974 – 2001   217

Table A.2: Number of observations by elections   218

Table A.3: Error structure and model specification   228

Table A.4: Classifying left-wing, right-wing, and centre parties   231

Table A.5: List of niche parties   232

| acknowledgements

This book has begun as a dissertation at the University of Mannheim. It deals with the constraints parties face when shifting policy positions. Yet, without the support and advice of colleagues, friends, and family members the task of carrying out this research project thereby overcoming my restricted knowledge, ability, and motivation would not have been possible.

First and foremost, I am especially grateful to my supervisor Wolfgang C. Müller for his helpful comments, criticism, and suggestions. My research on political parties tremendously benefitted from his support, patience, and good will. It is no exaggeration to say that I cannot think of a better supervisor than him. I am also indebted to Michael J. Laver for his willingness to co-supervise the dissertation project and his helpful comments and suggestions on my research.

Critical comments are essential to develop and improve research ideas, hypotheses, and empirical models. My work benefitted from feedback at international conferences. I thank the participants of the 'Annual European Graduate Conference on Political Parties' (AEGCPP) in Birmingham, February 2009, the 19th ECPR Summer School on 'Political Parties and European Democracy' (directed by Peter Mair) at the EUI in Florence, September 2009, and the 'Comparative Subconstituency Representation Workshop' (organised by Lawrence Ezrow) at the University of Essex, October 2009. This book is also based on work carried out during a visit to the European Centre for Analysis in the Social Sciences (ECASS) at the Institute for Social and Economic Research, University of Essex, supported by the Access to Research Infrastructures Action under the EU Improving Human Potential Programme. I thank these institutions for their financial support.

Furthermore, the University of Mannheim with its associated Graduate School of Economic and Social Sciences (GESS) and the Mannheim Centre for European Social Research (MZES) does provide an excellent and stimulating research environment. Financial support was granted by the German Science Foundation (DFG) which funded my first year at the Center for Doctoral Studies in Social and Behavioural Sciences (CDSS) with a scholarship. Moreover, I am very fortunate to have received comments from my friends and colleagues in those institutes during the last three years. I am especially indebted to Christian Arnold, Hanna Bäck, Patrick Bayer, Tanja Dannwolf, Marc Debus, Gema García Albacete, Thomas Gschwend, Maiko Heller, Oshrat Hochman, Marcelo Jenny, Heike Klüver, Sebastian Köhler, Bernhard Miller, Nicole Seher, Ulrich Sieberer, Michael Stoffel, Stephan Solomon, and Bettina Trüb for their advice, suggestions, and friendship. While these persons deserve full credit for improving my work, I take responsibility for all remaining mistakes.

Finally, I would like to express my gratitude to my family. Without a doubt, my parents, brother, grandma, aunts, uncles, and cousins are the ones who contributed most to my research. Their love and support allowed me to finish this research project. This book is dedicated to them.

Thomas M. Meyer, May 2013

part i. party competition and time

chapter one | constraints on shifting party policy platforms

This book contributes to the literature analysing party position-taking. This line of research answers the question why parties take the positions they do. Parties advocate different policy positions in various policy areas. For example, some parties advocate the use of nuclear power while others argue that nuclear power stations should be shut down. Parties also take different stances whether minimal wages are a good thing or not or whether the national defence should be organised with a professional army or a compulsory military service. On almost every day, parties present their different positions in parliament, to the media and to voters. Parties also defend their policy stances in public debates and defend their position when they bargain with other parties.

Which positions parties take is of crucial importance. Parties are central actors in modern democracies and the policies they pursue affect policy outcomes. Although it is attractive to dispute that 'parties do matter', the overwhelming empirical evidence suggests that the different policies pursued by different parties do affect policy outcomes. From a normative point of view, it is desirable if the policy stands taken by parties represent those of their voters or even the wider electorate. Not only should parties propose different policy solutions to issues such as economic growth, unemployment, inner security or environmental protection but the menu of policy offers (the supply) should reflect the different positions in the electorate (the demand). Meaningful representation is only feasible if this basic condition is fulfilled.

Given the importance of the parties' position-taking, it should not be surprising that political scientists have aimed to explain the parties' choices of policy platforms. All these models depart from the original model proposed by Downs (1957) that parties in two-party systems converge to the median voter's policy preferences. Following Downs, there have been numerous extensions and adaptations in spatial models. Just to mention a few, these models consider different party goals (votes, office or policy), change assumptions about the voters' behaviour and the information voters possess and model party position-taking in two- or multi-party systems. There are various spatial models of party competition and they work from different assumptions, provide various arguments and deliver wide-ranging predictions for party platforms. A unifying feature, however, is that these models focus on the parties' incentive structures. Although the incentives differ starkly, a defining element of each spatial model is that it works from a set of party incentives. Downs, for example, assumes that parties are driven by the incentive to win as many votes as possible. Other scholars have focused on other goals such as power, posts or influencing policies.

It is *not* the aim of this study to add yet another spatial model of party competition. Rather, the purpose of this analysis is to focus on an element which has been neglected in most of the existing research: the constraints parties face when adopting the most preferred policy positions. Consider the following example. In June 2011, the German government led by the Christian Democrats (CDU) announced the end of the use of nuclear power in Germany until 2022. This step was initiated with an 'atomic moratorium' in March 2011 according to which 7 older nuclear plants had been shut down. By these means, the German government reacted to the nuclear disaster in Fukushima where a tsunami hit the nuclear power plant on the 11th March and caused a nuclear meltdown. In polls right after this event, 53 to 60 per cent of the respondents have supported a renunciation of nuclear power (*Spiegel* 2011a). That is not to say that the Fukushima disaster really changed the public opinion on that matter. The issue has been controversial for years (FAZ 2009) and earlier polls also show popular support for a renunciation of nuclear power (Infratest dimap 2000). Yet, it is safe to say that the Fukushima disaster increased the issue's salience and that the CDU's attempt was driven by the aim to gain popular support on this matter.

What seems to be a rational strategy to increase popular support is undermined by the fact that the CDU has advocated a 'pro-nuclear' position before. In 2000, the government coalition of Social Democrats and the Greens initiated the withdrawal from nuclear power. When the bill was in parliament in late 2001, the CDU voted against this withdrawal. The party could not change this status quo in its coalition with the Social Democrats (2005–2009) but when it entered a coalition with the Liberals after the 2009 general election, the coalition contract named nuclear power as a 'bridging technology' (CDU-CSU-FDP coalition contract October 2009: 29) which is necessary to ensure Germany's power supply in the near future. Though this rather cautious formulation considers the general public's scepticism about nuclear power, it was clear that the Christian Democrats and Liberals had a 'pro-nuclear' position while the Social Democrats, and especially the Greens, were at the 'anti- nuclear' pole.

The position shift involves a dilemma for the Christian Democrats. Voters in favour of nuclear energy know that the CDU no longer represents their position and voters against nuclear energy do not believe in the CDU's newly adopted position. Thus, the CDU suffered from its low credibility (*Spiegel* 2011b; *Süddeutsche* 2011) and the opponents of nuclear energy have put more faith in the Social Democrats and especially the Greens. Hence, even if the 'anti-nuclear' position seems to provide higher benefits, it is not necessarily the best strategy for a party that took an 'anti-nuclear' position before.

This book seeks to analyse the feasibility of policy shifts more closely. It provides an analysis of party policy change over time. It is argued that integrating the time dimension in theories of party competition allows for a more realistic perspective on party behaviour. While most spatial models explain *which* positions parties should take, this study is devoted to the question *how* they can actually adopt these positions. The general argument is that parties cannot simply take their most preferred policy position. The reason is that a party does not take a policy position from scratch. It has represented specific positions in the past. If an optimal position differs from that position, it is not always possible to alter the currently pursued position. This is because deviations from the status quo entail some costs and a party may refrain from taking these shifts if the costs are sufficiently high. The following analysis focuses on the consequences of this insight and advocates a dynamic perspective on models of party competition.

The choice of party policy positions and party policy shifts

Tony Blair's 'New Labour' is one of the most prominent party policy shifts in the British post-war era. Between 1992 and 1997, the British Labour party changed in several ways, including a change of leadership, intra-party decision making, the party's image and policy positions. Labour got rid of its 'tax and spend' policies, presenting an election manifesto which was much more moderate than the preceding one. Stating that 'the policies of 1997 cannot be those of 1947 or 1967' (Labour Party 1997), the 1997 election programme emphasises the renewal and the reforms associated with the party policy position and distinguishes the new proposed policies from the previously pursued ones.

Although Labour won the general election in 1997, Blair's strategy to move away from its previous policy platform also entailed risks. Perhaps most important, it was crucial to convince voters that Labour was serious about its newly proposed policies. Blair was very successful in doing so. Being party leader only since 1994, he was not associated with Labour's past policies so that his pledges for party renewal were credible. Similar pledges by leaders who had previously pursued other policies would have been less credible. Blair's charisma helped to convince voters that Labour had changed. But what would have happened if Blair had been responsible for the policies represented in the 1992 general election? And what if Blair's prestige had been worse?

The difficulties associated with changing party policy positions become even more apparent when turning to the British Conservatives after the general election in 2005. The Tories had lost the last three elections to Labour (under Blair) and David Cameron (who became party leader after the electoral defeat in 2005) was in a similar situation as Blair in the mid-1990s. The Tories' policy platform did not attract enough voters to replace Labour in government. Cameron therefore aimed at moderating party policies to win the next general election. Yet, he was less successful than Blair. Although Cameron aimed at changing party policies, he was not able to dissociate the party's image from the Thatcher years (Evans 2008). The resulting mixed messages made voters unsure what the party actually stood for and resulted in an election manifesto for the 2010 general election, which *The Economist* calls 'the longest betting-slip in history' (*The Economist* 2010).

A party's ability to shift policy positions may also be affected by its internal structure. Consider, for example, the situation of Felipe González, leader of the Spanish Social Democrats (PSOE) between 1974 and 1997. After the electoral defeat in 1979, González advocated a new electoral strategy involving more moderate policies to win the votes of the electoral centre but the party congress rejected his proposal to water down the party's Marxist image (see Maravall 2008; Share 1999). As a consequence, González refused to run for re-election and the party congress finally agreed on reforming internal rules, increasing the control of the party leadership over the organisation. With the new party rules, González was able to reform party policies and to win the general election in 1982.

These examples support the major argument from above: parties do not choose policy positions from scratch. Rather, choosing new policy platforms always entails a shift away from the present policy position. This shift of perspectives is unproblematic as long as actors always move away from the status quo to reach an optimal outcome. Yet, this simplifying assumption is unlikely to hold. New policy positions need to be advertised and voters have to believe that a party truly represents the proposed policies. Moreover, a party's internal structure may affect the likelihood of moving away from its policy position. The constraints may lead parties to refrain from choosing optimal policy positions. It is, therefore, necessary to take a closer look at the dominant role of the status quo.

The dominant role of the status quo and party policy shifts

Decision-making research highlights the traps of making rational or 'good' decisions. One important reason for 'bad' decisions is the so-called *status-quo trap*. When making decisions, individuals compare the pros and cons of various alternatives. Yet, they do not devote the same attention to all options. The current state of the world, the status quo, plays a dominant role and shapes future actions. People tend to stick to the status quo because it appears to be the safer option.[1]

Actors may refrain from deviating from the status quo if this involves *costs*. The time it takes to implement changes is perhaps the most prominent example. Actors refrain from taking the costs of comparing the pros and cons of alternative choices if the potential benefits are only marginal. Hence, sticking to the status quo can be rational.

Moving away from the status quo also entails *uncertainty*. The status quo is a 'safe bet' whereas alternative options – including those expected to leave a decision maker better off – entail risks. This is the case because individuals often lack information on the consequences of alternative options. When comparing job offers, for example, the monthly salary is an indicator which is not likely to be affected by uncertainty. Yet, other factors like flexibility in work time, job satisfaction, or collegiality may be harder to evaluate. These factors are well known for the status quo (i.e. the current job) but less so for alternative job offers. If environmental factors are quite satisfactory in the current position, it is questionable whether one would change positions for the sake of marginal salary improvements

---

1. In one experiment (reported in Hammond *et al.* 2006: 121–2), people randomly receive one of two gifts (a Swiss chocolate bar or a mug) of approximately the same value. They are then asked whether they would like to exchange their gift for the other one. Because both items have the same price, one would expect that around 50% of the participants substitute their gifts. In fact, only 10% do. It is also shown (Hammond *et al.* 2006: 122) that the status quo's appeal increases with the number of alternative options.

by taking the risk of higher uncertainty associated with alternative jobs. In other words, people may prefer a sufficient, yet not optimal, status quo they know to an alternative that *could* leave them better off.

This reasoning may be applied to political parties. Reaching optimal policy positions often requires moving away from the status quo so that parties have to consider the costs and the uncertainty when doing so. Suppose that a given (static) model predicts optimal party policy positions. Neglecting the time dimension, the predictions entail that the parties just choose the optimal platforms. Yet, what if 'choosing' a policy platform actually means that parties have to *shift* their policy platforms?

The status-quo trap implies that a party may stick to its policy position even if a different policy platform exists that would leave it better off. Such behaviour is especially likely if the difference in the utilities derived from the status quo and the optimal policy position is negligible. A shift promising to increase a party vote share by, say, 0.2 per cent may not lead parties to shift their policy positions. The potential benefits of the policy shift may simply not outweigh its costs (including time, personnel, and financial resources).

In addition, uncertainty on the consequences of alternative policy positions may affect party policy shifts. Static models usually assume that parties know the effects of policy positions with certainty. Yet, parties typically know more about the consequences of their current policy position than on those entailed in alternative policy platforms. For instance, parties know the electoral consequences their current policy platform generates. Although an alternative policy program *could* leave the party better off than the status quo, uncertainty remains whether the forecasts predicting an increase in the party's vote share really will hold. If the predictions are wrong, parties risk losing traditional voters 'by too-blatant appeals to the new target groups' (Wilson 1994: 271) who, in turn, may not perceive a party's policy change.

Introducing the time dimension modifies models of party competition. First, moving the policy position away from the status quo involves costs because changing policy platforms requires time, personnel and financial resources. Second, policy shifts entail uncertainty because parties lack information on the consequences entailed in moving away from the status quo. If potential new voters do not perceive a party's change of policy positions, the shift may leave it worse off than if it sticks to its original policy position. These insights motivate studying party competition from a different perspective. Rather than explaining where parties should locate to maximise their utilities, it is worthwhile to study how they actually reach optimal positions and which problems they face pursuing this goal. In other words, *what constraints do parties face when shifting their policy positions?*

Time and its consequences: how voters and intra-party structure constrain party policy shifts

The answer provided here emphasises two factors (see Figure 1.1). First, the parties' uncertainty in making policy shifts stems from the electoral market. Voters differ in their perception of party policy shifts. If potential new voters do not perceive party platform changes, a party may be worse off moving away from the status quo. Second, party policy shifts are constrained by the parties' internal structures. The distribution of power within parties, intra-party decision-making rules and the role of party members differ across parties. Whereas some parties are more likely to overcome constraints in adapting their policy positions to new situations, other parties suffer from their organisational 'baggage' and inflexibility. These differences account for different party shift behaviour. Voter and party organisation constraints are discussed in greater detail in the next sections.

Figure 1.1: Constraints on party policy shifts: The role of voters' perceptions and intra-party structure

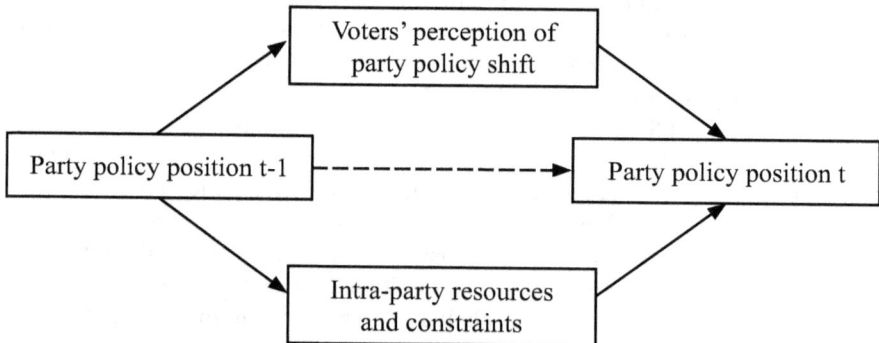

Voters and their perceptions of party policy shifts

> Oceania was at war with Eurasia and in alliance with Eastasia. [...] Actually, as Winston well knew, it was only four years since Oceania had been at war with Eastasia and in alliance with Eurasia. But that was merely a piece of furtive knowledge which he happened to possess because his memory was not satisfactorily under control. Oceania was at war with Eurasia: therefore Oceania had always been at war with Eurasia. (George Orwell, *Nineteen Eighty-Four*: 31–2)

In static models of party competition, political parties take policy positions and voters, in turn, react to the parties' signals casting their ballot for the party maximising their expected utilities. Which policy positions parties have taken in the past is irrelevant because voters neglect all kinds of information on past party policy platforms. In that sense, voters in models of party competition are similar to Winston Smith, the main character in Orwell's *Nineteen Eighty-Four*. Parties change policies (e.g. allies and enemies) and voters soak up the new information completely forgetting about the past.

Can we indeed apply Orwell's reasoning to our models of party competition? In Orwell's dystopia, power is based on a totalitarian system in which a single party (INGSOC) controls citizens' lives. There are no elections, freedom of press, rival parties, and therefore, no opposition. Moreover, thoughts and actions deviating from the party line are 'thoughtcrimes'. Things are different in democratic systems which are the focus of models of party competition. Voters can opt to gather information or prefer to stay uninformed. Moreover, they have various sources of information from which they can pick and choose. By doing so, they may trust some parties and distrust others. Regarding party policy shifts, no party controls voters' memory of the past. Hence, the perception of party policy shifts differs across voters and parties.

In what follows, I specify a theoretical model of how voters perceive party policy shifts. Following research on public opinion (Zaller 1992), it is argued that the perception of party policy shifts is a two-stage process. First, voters *receive* information on party policy shifts. If the reception fails, voters stick to their previous perception of a party's policy position. Second, voters decide whether to *accept* (i.e. consider credible) newly received information. Whereas the reception of a party policy shift is a cognitive task, the decision whether to accept the shift is a matter of beliefs. Only if voters receive and accept a party's shift message, they *perceive* a party position shift away from the status quo. Yet, if the reception or the acceptance fails, voters stick to the status quo.

Testing the proposed two-stage process is difficult because surveys do not contain direct measures for whether voters receive and accept party shift messages. The following analysis hence focuses on the observable implications of the perception process. It leads to hypotheses predicting whether and how covariates affect the reception and the acceptance of party policy shifts and how the hypothesised effects translate into testable predictions for the perception of party policy shifts.

Cognitive aspects of receiving political information are expected to affect the reception of party policy shifts. Here, the focus is on the incentives and the ease of processing relevant information. Specifically, it is argued that voters with lower costs for gathering information, that is, more educated and politically aware individuals, are more likely to receive party position shifts. Moreover, voters changing their preferences have more incentives to track party changes to update their political market information. In addition, party- and party-system specific factors affect the voters' likelihood of receiving information. Government parties are more visible than those in opposition, so their ability to shift policy platforms is higher. Moreover, substantive policy changes (such as 'New Labour') are more likely to draw voters' attention than minor adjustments of a party's policy platform. Finally, party systems differ and the larger the number of relevant parties, the higher the number of actors sending information and hence, the lower the probability that voters receive party policy shifts.

The acceptance of party policy shifts hinges on factors that affect the voters' evaluation of a party's credibility. In particular, this study emphasises the effect of party leader changes and party leader prestige. It is argued that changes in the party leadership and high prestige make the acceptance of party policy shifts more likely. Furthermore, parties are expected to be constrained by their past behaviour because constantly shifting the policy position reduces a party's credibility. In addition, it is postulated that a voter's party identification affects the acceptance of party policy shifts. Identification with a party increases a voter's likelihood of accepting the party policy shift if it is towards his or her personal policy preferences. In contrast, voters who identify with a party are less likely to accept platform changes away from their personal policy position. Moreover, party policy shifts are more likely to get accepted if they are in line with shifts of a voter's policy position. In contrast, voters are less likely to accept party platform changes running counter to shifts in public opinion. Finally, party ideology and the party system generate voter expectations on where parties should locate relative to each other. In the United Kingdom, for instance, Labour's ideological territory is expected to be left of the Conservatives. It is hypothesised that party policy shifts away from these expectations are less likely to be accepted. In that sense, parties are constrained by the ideological expectations voters attribute to them.

The outlined mechanisms help us to understand the political behaviour of voters. Yet, this analysis focuses on the effects of voters' perception on party policy changes. In general, parties benefit from higher reception and acceptance values and are thus more likely to shift their policy platforms. In case the reception or acceptance differs across voters, a party benefits most if voters being worse off by its policy shift do not perceive the party change while potential new voters do receive and accept the party's shift message. This leads to hypotheses about how the covariates influencing the voters' reception and acceptance of party policy shifts also affect the likelihood that parties change their policy platforms. The postulated hypotheses are then tested based on a sample of party position shifts in ten West European countries.

Intra-party structure

A leader in the Democratic Party is a boss, in the Republican Party he is a leader. (Harry S. Truman)

Remember the difference between a boss and a leader; a boss says 'Go!' – a leader says 'Let's go!' (E. M. Kelly) [2]

In addition to the voters' perceptions of party policy changes, parties are also constrained by their respective intra-party structure. Parties are organisations representing members, sometimes from regions with diverse interests, occasionally

---

2. Truman in Safire, W. (2008) Safire's Political Dictionary, Oxford: OUP, p.77. E. M. Kelley, www. worldofquotes.com/author/E.+M.+Kelly/1 (accessed 17 October 2012).

also driven by intra-party factions. Whether parties are able to shift their policy positions hinges on intra-party factors such as the role of party members in the party's decision-making process.

The postulated model distinguishes two types of actors within parties: a party elite and the party members on the ground (Katz and Mair 1993).[3] It is argued that party members provide resources and manpower helping the organisation to change its policy position. In particular, party members provide information on voter preferences and which party policy shifts they accept (or even expect). Moreover, members represent the party on the ground and therefore help with advertising party policy shifts. In addition, financial contributions of their members allow parties to run costly campaigns thereby increasing the likelihood of getting a policy shift heard. Thus, from the resources perspective, parties with a substantial mass organisation are more able to shift their policy positions.

Yet, the importance of mass membership has been decreasing over time. Not only do parties lose members, it is also the role of members that has changed. The emergence of mass media, capital-intensive campaigning and professional advisors diminish the advantage of parties with mass organisational strength. Public funding is a crucial factor allowing parties with lower membership figures to pay for TV and radio commercials, pollsters, and capital-intensive election campaigns, without drawing on resources derived from membership organisations. Nowadays, public subsidies allow parties without mass organisational resources to catch up with their well-organised rivals.

Parties also differ in their formal decision-making processes. The intra-party structure can be modelled as a principal-agent relationship in which party members delegate competences to the party leadership. Party leaders, in turn, are accountable to the party's rank-and-file. In some parties, decision-making processes are hierarchical with centralised and exclusive power given to the party leadership. Other parties opt for a more inclusive and decentralised way of making decisions. Both forms have advantages and drawbacks. Whereas party leaders in more hierarchical parties have discretion to make use of their expertise, they are also more likely to shirk moving away from the members' preferences. In contrast, more inclusive and decentralised decision-making processes decrease the risk of shirking, while simultaneously increasing the number of intra-party veto players, and hence, the party's inflexibility. It is therefore hypothesised that the more hierarchical parties are more likely to shift their policy platforms.

The members' role within the party also hinges on the resources the party leadership depends on. Financial means are probably the most important resource because they ensure a party's survival. The higher the leaders' dependence on the financial means provided by party members (i.e. membership fees), the more credible the members' 'exit' option (Hirschmann 1970). Consequently, party leaders depending on their rank-and-file are not likely to move away from the

---

3. For the sake of variability, I use the terms 'party members', 'party activists' and 'rank-and-file' interchangeably.

members' preferences. Conflicts may arise because the two actor types – party elite and members on the ground – differ in their incentives and goals: party members want to see specific policies enacted whereas party elites primarily aim at winning elections. Hence, it is argued that leaders stick to their members' policy preferences if the party income mainly derives from member contributions.

The emergence of public funding reduces the party leaders' dependence on the financial means provided by party members. Therefore, the relative importance of membership fees decreases. Moreover, the amount of public subsidy usually depends on a party's vote share. This, in turn, increases the incentive for vote-seeking behaviour. Hence, parties with the opportunity to hunt for votes will adopt party policy positions maximising the party's vote share. Doing this requires the permanent adaption of a party's policy position which responds to its rivals' policy shifts as well as to the demands of an increasingly volatile electoral market. Therefore, the increasing relevance of public funding should increase the probability of party policy shifts.

The road ahead: structure of the book

The following chapters are devoted to the theoretical arguments and the empirical test of factors constraining party policy shifts. Chapter Two briefly reviews the literature on party position-taking. In particular, it deals with the key actors parties need to take into account – rival parties, voters, and a party's internal structure – and gives a brief overview of how parties are expected to react to their environment. Whenever possible, I highlight the role of time and its consequences on the incentives and constraints parties face when shifting their policy positions. Chapter Three is devoted to the measurement of the dependent variable: party policy shifts. There are various approaches to measuring party policy positions and an extensive literature discusses the strengths and weaknesses of each of them. The aim of this chapter is to highlight the consequences for the analysis of party policy change.

Chapter Four presents a theoretical model of how voters perceive party policy shifts. A two-stage model is postulated in which voters first receive information on party policy platform changes and subsequently decide whether to accept (i.e. consider credible) the information or not. The main results are summarised in three axioms stating: how voters perceive party policy shifts (Axiom 1), how the voters' reception and acceptance affect party policy shifts (Axiom 2) and the effects of public opinion shifts on the parties' ability to shift their policy positions (Axiom 3). Chapter Five breathes life into the theoretical framework stating how covariates affect the voters' likelihood of receiving and accepting party position shifts. The axioms postulated in Chapter Four lead to several hypotheses of how voter-, party- and party system-specific factors affect the voters' probability to perceive party policy shifts and how these perceptions affect party policy shifts.

A first test of the model at the voter level is presented in Chapter Six. It describes the data derived from several British panel election studies as well as the empirical results. The first empirical analysis is devoted to one particularly well known party position shift: 'New Labour' in 1997. Concentrating on one party position shift holds party-specific covariates constant thus simplifying the model. In addition, restricting the model to one party shift allows using data of higher quality. Thereafter, we extend the empirical focus analysing voter perceptions of party policy shifts in various elections. Pooling data from several party position shifts in various elections, allows the inclusion of explanatory factors that vary across parties and elections. Chapter Seven is devoted to the analysis of political parties. It analyses how covariates impacting on voters' perceptions of party policy changes affect party policy shifts. The empirical analyses are based on party policy shifts in ten West European countries between 1945 and 2005.

Chapters Eight and Nine are concerned with the effect of intra-party factors on party policy shifts. Chapter Eight presents hypotheses of how a party's mass organisational strength, internal decision-making rules, and the relevance of public funding affect party behaviour. It is argued that party policy shifts are more likely if a party has sufficient mass-organisational resources, hierarchical decision-making processes and if it mainly depends on income derived from public subsidies. In contrast, policy movement is rather unlikely if a party lacks mass-organisational strength, involves many intra-party veto players and is less dependent on financial resources that hinge on electoral success. Chapter Nine presents the data and the empirical tests of these hypotheses.

Chapter Ten summarises how the results presented here help to improve our understanding of party policy behaviour. Furthermore, it outlines how the findings (and non-findings) of this work can enrich future research. In particular, I deal with potential future research on voter satisfaction with political institutions, dynamic representation, consequences of party leader changes, research on niche parties, and the role of public funding for ensuring fair party competition. Research in these fields will further extend and deepen our knowledge on voters, parties and party systems.

chapter two | linking parties and time

Because of their central role in modern democracies (see e.g. Schattschneider 1942: 1), political parties are in the focus of research on voting, policy outputs and outcomes, legislative behaviour, government formation, governance, termination and the stability of democratic systems. One aim of this chapter is to show that one severe drawback of previous research on parties and party competition is the neglecting of *time*. This book aims at narrowing this gap by studying party *change*, and more specifically, party *policy* change. Hereby I do not mean comparing snap-shots of party history, for instance, comparing modern parties with those of the 1950s. Rather, party policy change is defined as a *process* from one party policy platform at time t to a party platform at time t+1.

As mentioned in Chapter One, this analysis focuses on the *constraints* of party policy change. Hence, it does *not* deal with motivation or incentives for party policy change. As the following discussion will show, recent research acknowl-edges the importance of a dynamic perspective identifying reasons why parties change over time. Yet, what is still missing is research on *how* parties change policy positions and what constraints they face when doing so. If parties (or party leaders) are constrained in their actions, this is likely to be due to other key actors they deal with. Therefore, this study concentrates on the main actors parties face in their environment: rival parties, the electorate, and their party organisations. The following sections provide an overview of how previous research addresses party interaction with rival parties, voters and their own organisations. They also serve to provide an overview of how these key groups affect party behaviour over time. It is shown that recent research on party competition has begun to take the time dimension into account. Yet, this dimension is missing in research that connects parties with voters and studies of party organisations.

Parties and their environment

Defining parties helps to identify the environment they act in and the constraints they face when shifting party policy positions. Before so doing, however, it is important to stress that this analysis focuses on parties in democratic systems and leaves autocratic systems aside. Dahl (1971) characterises political systems along two dimensions, namely with respect to (1) their level of public contestation (i.e. competition) for power and (2) the degree of participation of all full citizens (especially the right to vote, and to join and form organisations). A system with high levels of contestation and participation fulfils the minimal requirements of an (ideal-type) democracy. This (minimal) definition is sufficient for the purpose of the present study.

There is no 'gold standard' definition of what political parties are. Rather, several definitions exist and each of them has its assets and drawbacks. The main reason is, I suppose, that each of them highlights factors that are relevant for the present research project. For example, studies on parties 'from within' use and cite definitions emphasising that parties are organisations. Researchers studying parties in non-democratic countries use definitions highlighting the parties' will to place representatives (with or without elections) in government positions (see e.g. Janda's definition in Sartori 1976: 62–63). In contrast, research focusing on democratic countries often uses definitions emphasising elections and competition for power.

In *Party Government*, Schattschneider (1942: 35) defines parties as an 'organised attempt to get to power'. The definition hence emphasises that parties strive for power and organise themselves to achieve this goal. In contrast, Schattschneider puts no emphasis on elections, party policies or ideologies. Burke's famous definition considers different aspects, stating that a party is 'a body of men united, for promoting by their joint endeavours the national interest, upon some particular principle in which they all agreed' (Burke, cited in Sartori 1976: 9). Burke not only stresses that parties are groups (implicitly in need of rules) but also that parties have (policy) goals on which their members agree. This policy motivation distinguishes Burke's definition from the 'Schumpeterian' one that a party is 'a group whose members propose to act in concert in the competitive struggle for political power' (Schumpeter 1942: 283).

Schumpeter's emphasis on parties as groups competing for power can also be found in Downs's party definition, as a 'team of men seeking to control the governing apparatus by gaining office in a duly constituted election' (Downs 1957: 25). As in Schumpeter's definition, parties seek power and contest in elections. Both criteria are also in place in Sartori's minimal definition. In contrast to Schumpeter and Downs, however, Sartori puts (free or non-free) elections in focus stating that '[a] party is any political group that presents at elections, and is capable of placing through elections, candidates for public office' (Sartori 1976: 64). And Panebianco – although not offering a proper definition of parties – states that, 'whatever else parties are and to whatever other solicitations they respond, they are above all organisations' (Panebianco 1988: xi) which leads back to Schattschneider's party as an 'organised attempt to get to power'.

These definitions from well-known scholars exemplify that there is no 'gold standard' defining political parties (see also Sartori 1976: ch. 3). Each of them highlights specific aspects and neglects others. Collectively, however, they help in identifying the key actors political parties engage with. First, parties in democratic systems compete with *rival parties*. This emphasis is strongest in the party definitions of Schattschneider, Schumpeter and Downs. Second and related, parties in democratic systems run in elections and hence aim to persuade *voters*. Next to Schumpeter and Downs (but not Schattschneider), it is Sartori who emphasises this aspect. Third, parties are organisations thus involving an *internal structure*. Schattschneider, and especially Panebianco, highlight the role of party organisation and power within a party. In addition, Burke's definition stresses the importance of joint opinions and hence, connects parties with party *policies*. In what follows, I focus on these key actors in greater detail with a particular focus on research connected with party *policy* positions and their shifts over time.

Parties and party competition

Democratic systems are characterised by competition for power and modern democracies employ parties to fulfil this task. Competing for power, a party faces other parties that constrain its choices and have an impact on its goals. Parties are first and foremost interested in votes. Winning votes is an 'instrumental goal' (Strøm and Müller 1999: 9) as votes serve as the 'currency' of party competition. A party's vote share affects its bargaining power and its chances of entering government and implementing its preferred policies. These three factors – policy, office, and votes – constitute a party's objectives. Which of the goals prevails in case of goal conflicts, and whether parties strive for office or policy as an end in itself (see Laver and Schofield 1998: ch. 3), differs across parties (for an overview see Müller and Strøm 1999; Strøm 1990). Yet, all of the models presented below assume that parties strive for sometimes conflicting goals (policy, office, or votes) and choose policy positions that are optimal to fulfil their respective objectives.

In the beginning was Downs (1957). Adapting economic thinking to party competition, Downs argued that parties aim at maximising votes just as firms aim at maximising their profit (see also Hotelling 1929: 54–55). In line with his definition of political parties (cited above), parties choose policies as a means to maximise the benefits.[1] Of course, this implies that voters have preferences regarding these policies and vote accordingly. Downs argues that voters choose parties that are closest to their policy preferences. While various researchers have extended (Grofman 1985; Kedar 2005; 2009) or criticised (Macdonald *et al.* 1998; 2001; Rabinowitz and Macdonald 1989) the proximity voting model, the overwhelming empirical evidence suggests that the voters' policy preferences have a significant impact on vote choices.[2] Assuming proximity voting and a two-party system, the result of the Downsian model is the well-known *median voter theorem* stating that two parties in a one-dimensional policy space both choose policy positions identical to the median voter's one (see also Black 1948; Downs 1957: ch. 8).

Scholars illustrate emerging equilibria using terms such as 'converge' with party policy positions or 'shifts' of parties towards the centre of the policy space. Yet, these equilibria are inherently *static*:[3] Parties are in equilibrium if they have no incentive to diverge from their policy position (i.e. the policy position maximises

---

1. For a critique on vote-'maximising' rather than winning elections see Robertson (1976).

2. That is not to say that spatial voting in the only factor that affects vote choice. How voters make their vote choices is a question that has been at the heart of studies on political behaviour and party competition. A comprehensive review of the effect of socio-structural factors, party identification (Campbell *et al.* 1960), and retro- and prospective voting (Fiorina 1981; van der Brug *et al.* 2007) is however, beyond the scope of this chapter.

3. That is not to say that all equilibria are robust. Some rest on very specific assumptions (see e.g. Plott 1967) while others are robust to a number of alternative specifications. In that sense, equilibria differ in their stability. Yet, all equilibria are stable in the sense that – given the current conditions – parties do not alter their policy positions.

their utility function). Although the existence and uniqueness of these equilibria is shown using iterative algorithms of party policy change, the 'convergence' of party policy positions is a pure thought experiment. Researchers are interested in equilibria serving as predictions for their models.

Downs's *Economic Theory of Democracy* not only settled the principle of parties as rational actors but also motivated additional research, extending, criticising and modifying specific model assumptions.[4] A comprehensive review is (if feasible) beyond the scope of this review. Hence, I focus on major developments in spatial models of party competition.

Parties and static party competition

Static models of party competition predict party position-taking for a single election. Summarising the huge body of literature, there are four major developments how scholars have extended and altered Downs' spatial model. These include the consideration of the parties' *policy motivation*, voters' perceived differences across parties for *non-policy reasons* ('valence'), *linking the electoral and the legislative arena* and *stochastic models of vote choice*.

One way to deviate from Downs's model is to drop the assumption that parties are purely vote-maximising actors. Rather, parties are *policy-seeking* and value office as a means to implement their preferred policies (Chappell and Keech 1986; Wittmann 1983, 1990). Because parties are usually assumed to have policy preferences that are not at the centre of the policy space, entering policy motivation usually leads to equilibria with parties located at distinct policy positions closer to the periphery of the policy space (see e.g. Adams *et al.* 2005: chs 11 and 12).

The reasons for parties to value policy goals differ. Previous research highlights the role of party activists on whom the party depends to run their campaigns (see e.g. Schofield and Sened 2006: 22–5). Activists are motivated by policies (Aldrich 1983) and party leaders have to take the activists' preferences into account if their support is crucial for the party's success. In addition to the role of party members, a party may be constrained by voters and their expectations on what policies the party should pursue. A party's ideology shapes its 'image' and the proposed policies should correspond to it. Sánchez-Cuenca (2008) argues that voters only vote for the closest party if the proposed policies are consistent with the party ideology (see also Downs 1957: ch. 7). Yet, if a party's ideology and the proposed policies are inconsistent, voters refrain from voting for the closest party choosing other parties which are more credible. In the model that follows, I resort to the role of activists and voter expectations on party policy positions (and shifts).

Models which assume that voters that do not solely base their vote choice on party polices but also take *non-policy factors* into account lead to different

---

4. In fact, many articles cite Downs in their very first sentence (see e.g. Groseclose 2001; Macdonald and Rabinowitz 1998).

predictions of party policy positions than their policy-oriented rivals. Non-policy factors affecting vote choices can be summarised as a party's valence (see e.g. Clarke *et al.* 2011; Green 2007; Schofield 2005; Stone and Simas 2010). The concept goes back to Stokes (1963, 1992) who differentiates *position* and *valence issues* stating that the latter are 'those that merely involve the linking of the parties with some condition that is positively or negatively valued by the electorate' (see also Adams *et al.* 2005: App. 3.1; Stokes 1963: 373).[5]

Various theoretical (Adams 1998; Adams *et al.* undated; Adams and Merrill 2009; Groseclose 2001; Macdonald and Rabinowitz 1998; Schofield 2003) and empirical (Adams *et al.* 2005; Clark 2009; Erikson and Romero 1990) contributions study the effect of non-policy factors including the concept of party identification (Campbell *et al.* 1960), candidate images and the voters' sociodemographic traits (such as race, gender and class). If the voters' evaluation of parties differ, parties can make use of better evaluations to adjust their party policy positions. Depending on the parties' utility functions (and their policy-seeking behaviour), parties with higher valence values are predicted to represent more centrist (see e.g. Groseclose 2001) or more extreme (see e.g. Adams 1998; Adams and Merrill 2009) policy positions. In any case, the larger a party's valence value, the higher its utility. As shown in the theoretical model (see Chapter Five), a similar argument can be used in a dynamic model studying party position *shifts*: the larger the share of voters with party identification and the higher a party leader's prestige, the higher is a party's ability to shift its policy platform.

The parties' choices of party policy positions may also hinge on factors that are outside the electoral arena. Specifically, parties do not only aim at maximising their vote share but also consider *post-electoral legislative bargaining* and the probability of entering coalition governments (see also Downs 1957: ch. 9; Strøm 1990; Strøm and Müller 1999). As Schofield and Sened (2006: 32) argue, participation in government is most likely if a party is at the core position (Plott 1967). It is argued below, that government parties not only enjoy the (private) benefits of holding public office but also have higher abilities to shift their policy positions.

Finally, models of party competition include probabilistic rather than deterministic voting. Parties are either not fully informed about the voters' preferences (Roemer 1994) or voters place their votes stochastically, that is, they do not always vote for the closest party (Chappell and Keech 1986; Erikson and Romero 1990; Lin *et al.* 1999). Most of the research on *probabilistic voting* aims at answering the question whether equilibria exist and, if so, where parties locate. Including an error term in vote choices makes the parties' predictions on benefits derived from specific policy positions more difficult. As such, models assuming

---

5. Although mostly referring to Stokes (1963), subsequent research is less precise on what exactly valence issues entail. Schofield and Sened (2006) simply define valence as 'the weight given to judgment, rather than to preference' (Schofield and Sened 2006: 15). Groseclose (2001) subsumes several factors using the valence label including incumbency, campaign funds, name recognition, or the party leader's charisma and intelligence (Groseclose 2001: 862).

probabilistic voting are more realistic than their deterministic counterparts. This is especially important for the literature on information and vote choice discussed below.

A dynamic perspective on party competition

All of the models presented so far are static, aiming at finding (Nash) equilibria which serve as predictions for party policy positions. Recently, however, scholars have paid more attention to the dynamics of party competition. Introducing the time dimension in models of party competition allows for studying actions that are shaped and constrained by the past. This idea is closely linked with 'path dependence'. Following Levi (1997: 28), path dependence entails that 'once a country or region has started down a track, the costs of reversal are very high'. Hence, decisions of the past shape actors' present choices and sticking to past decisions becomes more likely, the more often and longer they are used (Pierson 2000). As a result, norms, institutions and choices may prevail although they are known to be inefficient or irrational.[6]

Many spatial models of party competition neglect these constraints. In a recent review of the literature, Adams (2012: 403) notes:

> [V]irtually all spatial models specify parties as unitary actors that announce their position intentions to the electorate, and that can instantly – and costlessly – update these policy promises in response to changes in the political environment. With respect to voters, spatial modelers typically assume that all voters have identical perceptions of each party's policy positions, and that voters instantly update these perceptions – along with their party evaluations – in response to changes in the policy statements issued by the party's elites. [...] Of course, the simplifying assumptions listed above abstract away from the constraints that real-world party elites confront.

Similarly, Budge (1994) argues that '[g]reat costs are incurred in writing programmes, so another document cannot easily be put together immediately afterwards' (Budge 1994: 450). In other words, parties are constrained by their past policy positions and the choice of present policy platforms heavily depends on the policies they represented in the past.

Recent research incorporated time effects in models of party competition, testing theories on party policy change with the help of simulations. Although mostly lacking empirical backing, simulations are particularly suitable to study

---

6. A well-known example of path dependence is the design of computer and typewriter keyboards. The dominance of QWERTY keyboards prevents the evolution of alternative designs. Although these are said to be more efficient and ergonomic, their implementation is hindered by costs involved when deviating from the current standard.

new phenomena because they allow for answering 'what if' questions (Laver and Shepsle 1996: 5–8). As with experiments, researchers are able to manipulate specific factors while holding others constant. This approach is particularly adequate when scholars study the effect of new elements in established models as, for instance, the inclusion of the time dimension in models of party competition. From the early 1990s onwards, scholars applied simulation models to study the behaviour of parties that adapt their policy positions over time (Bendor *et al.* 2006; de Marchi 1999; Fowler and Laver 2008; Kollman *et al.* 1992; 2003; Laver 2005; Miller and Stadler 1998; Smirnov and Fowler 2007). Bendor and colleagues (2006), for example, assume that incumbent parties satisfice (i.e. stick to their policy position) while losers search for a platform outperforming the incumbent. Laver (2005) offers four party types with distinct strategies of how to adapt policy platforms. Parties may aim at satisfying their present party supporters' preferences, hunt for votes, adapt policy positions to rival parties, or stick to their policy positions. Various scholars have proposed more algorithms to model party behaviour (Fowler and Laver 2008).

All the above are theoretical models. A second strand of research analyses party policy shifts empirically.. Rival parties (Adams and Merrill 2006; Adams and Somer-Topcu 2009a), election results (Adams and Somer-Topcu 2009b; Janda *et al.* 1995; Somer-Topcu 2009a, b), the economic performance (Hellwig 2012) and shifts in public opinion (Adams *et al.* 2004; Adams *et al.* 2009; Ezrow *et al.* 2010; Somer-Topcu 2009a; Stimson 1999; Stimson *et al.* 1995) make parties adapt their policy platforms. Tavits (2007) argues that parties are more likely to shift their position on 'pragmatic issues' while changing policies on 'principled issues' is more difficult. In addition, Adams and colleagues (Adams *et al.* 2006a; see also Ezrow 2010) argue that 'niche' parties differ from mainstream parties and that the latter are more likely to respond to shifts in public opinion. Similarly, intra-party factors like factional dominance, leadership changes, and organisational patterns affect party position shifts (Budge *et al.* 2010; Evans 2008; Harmel *et al.* 1995; Harmel and Janda 1994; Walgrave and Nuytemans 2009).

Note that most of the factors mentioned here focus on the parties' *incentives* to shift their policy platforms. Hence, parties adapt new policy positions to follow shifts in public opinion, to increase their vote share (after electoral defeat) or because of a change in the dominant faction within a party. Yet, previous research does not focus on the *constraints* parties face when shifting policy positions. There are notable exceptions, for example, Walgrave and Nuytemans's (2009) study on organisational factors influencing party policy shifts (see the discussion below) and Wickham-Jones's study (2005) on the British Labour Party transformation between 1979 and 1997. Wickham-Jones highlights the role of credibility and argues that parties performing policy changes run the risk of losing credibility with voters (see also Laver 1997: 115–116). Similarly, Wuffle *et al.* (1989) argue that candidates choose policy positions that allow them to react to *any* challenger position by taking a position *nearby*, this so called 'finagle point'. The need for minimal adaption is justified because,

[T]here are costs to a candidate in attempting to shift his or her location in the policy space. The greater the shift the less likely it will be credible. The greater the shift the more effort it may take for candidates to sell it to the voters as reflecting a genuine change. Moreover, too great a shift may lead to accusations that a candidate lacks principles or is incompetent or wishy-washy. (Wuffle *et al.* 1989: 351)

Similar arguments can be made for policy shifts of parties instead of candidates. In fact, that policy shifts are not always feasible was already observed by Downs (1957). He argues that parties are constrained by their past and that party actions have to be consistent with their past behaviour: 'If a party frequently adopts new policies inconsistent with its old ones, voters will suspect that it cannot be trusted to carry out any long-range policies at all' (Downs 1957: 109). Thus, the parties' credibility hinges on the voters' acceptance of party policy shifts.

Voters and party policy shifts

This leads to the question how voters perceive party policy platforms. The existing empirical evidence suggests that voters differ in their perceptions of party policy platforms and, as a consequence, in their perceptions of party policy shifts. This is partly due to the fact that voters differ in their level of attention and information about politics. Schumpeter's (1942: 262) statement that 'the typical citizen drops down to a lower level of mental performance as soon as he enters the political field' nicely makes the point that assuming completely informed voters is inappropriate. As a consequence, it is unlikely that all voters perceive party policy positions equally because (correctly) locating candidates requires costly information. Even if parties and candidates make clear statements what they stand for, voters have to invest resources (e.g. time) to get informed about their policy platforms. The less information voters have, the higher the 'perceptual uncertainty' (Enelow and Hinich 1984: 122–125) of the candidates' policy platforms. Because voters 'prefer the devil they know more about to the devil they know less about' (Alvarez 1997: 109), increasing uncertainty on a candidate's policy platform decreases the probability that a voter votes for the respective candidate.

Various scholars (Alvarez 1997; Alvarez and Brehm 2002; Alvarez and Franklin 1994; Bartels 1986) have studied the voters' uncertainty of candidate platforms. Referring to Downs (1957: 209–210), the authors argue that voters have different 'information costs' in gathering information. More educated voters, for example, have lower costs understanding political messages. Consequently, they are more likely to place candidate and party policy platforms accurately. Another crucial factor is the voters' political knowledge. Political awareness 'refers to the extent to which an individual pays attention to politics *and* understands what he or she has encountered' (Zaller 1992: 21; emphasis in the original). The more informed voters are, the lower their uncertainty on candidate and party policy platforms. This is in line with Zaller's (1992) research on *The Nature and Origins of Mass Opinion.* Zaller argues that individuals are more likely to receive political messages if their level of cognitive engagement (i.e. their political awareness) is high (Zaller 1992: 42). Less informed individuals are less likely to be exposed to, or understand political messages so that their uncertainty on party and candidate platforms is higher.

Although the role of information is crucial for locating party policy positions, there is almost no research on how voters perceive party policy *shifts*. Only a recent study by Adams and colleagues (2011) shows that the majority of voters do *not* perceive party position shifts. This lack of research is surprising because the non-perception of party policy shifts has severe consequences for the voter's vote choices. Based on biased information of outdated party policy positions, voters may make suboptimal vote choices and have wrong expectations of the parties' behaviour in parliament (and government). Proposing a model how voters perceive party policy shifts, the present study discusses these consequences in greater detail.

Placing parties on policy dimensions is also a matter of beliefs. Sánchez-Cuenca (2008) shows that voters do not necessarily vote for the party closest to their policy preferences. If they doubt that a party's proposed policy platform is consistent with its ideological stance, voters refrain from voting for it (see also Downs 1957: ch. 7). Sceptical voters may hence make parties take policy positions closer to their respective ideologies, thus creating a centrifugal trend. Similarly, Zaller (1992) and Alvarez and Brehm (2002) argue that predispositions shape how individuals cope with political information. If newly received information is not in line with the dominant predispositions, individuals resist accepting it (Zaller 1992: 44) and are less coherent in answering survey questions (Alvarez and Brehm 2002: 57–58). Applied to party policy positions, voters linking a party and its ideology are less likely to accept policy platforms that are too far away from its ideological territory, so that voters perceive parties as being located closer to their ideologically 'expected' position (see also Rahn 1993). Regarding party policy *shifts*, it may be argued that voters doubt candidate or party policy shifts (Enelow and Hinich 1984: 115–117). Platform changes induce uncertainty as it is not clear whether voters believe the shift or not. If not, candidates lose credibility with voters. Thus, parties and candidates have incentives to avoid shifting their platforms or to restrain the magnitude of these shifts (Wuffle *et al.* 1989). Again, more systematic research on how parties suffer from, and can counteract, losing credibility when shifting policy platforms is missing. This research project aims at narrowing this gap.

Parties and their organisations

Another factor that may affect a party's ability to shift its policy platform is its inner working: How hierarchical are the decision-making processes? How many resources are at its disposal? And who provides the recourses that are crucial for a party's survival? In general, the distribution of power within the party both in ways of formal rules and 'actual' dependencies, affect the behaviour of party leaders and the decisions of whether or not to shift a party's policy platform. One way to account for the varying internal structures of political parties is to classify different party types. The most common distinction separates the classic cadre or elite party from Duverger's (1954) mass party and Kirchheimer's (1966; Krouwel 1999, 2003) catch-all party. Newer party types entail Panebianco's (1988) electoral-professional party, Katz and Mair's (1995) cartel party, and Carty's (2004) franchise party. Each party type implies a specific type of intra-party structure that, in turn, shapes the relationship between party members and elite.

The role and power of party members

Formal rules are one way to describe a party's internal structure. Intra-party decision-making processes include the formal rules of selecting (and dismissing) party leaders and parliamentary candidates, passing election programs and making key decisions (such as whether or not to take part in a coalition government). Party organisations entail principal-agent relationships in which a party's rank-and-file delegates competences to the party elite. The more hierarchical a party's organisation, the higher is the leader's ability to act. Yet, limited control mechanisms involve the risk that party leaders move away from the members' preferences. Hence, as in all delegation relationships there is a trade-off between the agent's discretion and the risk of shirking (for an overview see Epstein and O'Halloran 1994, 2006; Kiewiet and McCubbins 1991).

Parties differ in the way they deal with this trade-off: some parties have very centralised decision-making processes and powerful leaders while others rely on direct control mechanisms and a higher inclusion of the party's rank-and-file. Because of its importance for intra-party decision making (Crotty 1968: 260; Gallagher and Marsh 1988: 1–4; Ranney 1981: 103; Schattschneider 1942: 64), most research on party organisations studies the selection of candidates and party elites to measure the distribution of power within parties.[7] Parties differ according to the centralisation of the selection rules with decisions being made at the national, regional or local levels. Moreover, the inclusiveness of the selection process varies: whereas US American parties partly rely on primaries open to non-members, the European counterparts mostly rely on intra-party selections. In its most exclusive form, a party's leader decides on the selection of parliamentary candidates (Hazan and Rahat 2010; Hazan and Voerman 2006; Rahat 2007; Rahat and Hazan 2001).

Formal decision-making rules affect the role of party members. Simply put, the more inclusive and decentralised a party's decision-making process, the more power party members have. Including a party's rank-and-file in decision-making processes has several advantages. It provides a selective benefit to reward the members for their efforts. Granting party members influence on personnel or policy decisions may be necessary because parties produce public goods from which voters benefit, irrespective of their participation in parties (Schlesinger 1984). Providing selective benefits may hence help in keeping and motivating

---

7. For the weaknesses associated with formal decision-making rules see Katz (2001) and Shaw (2002).

party activists (Strøm 1990: 576–579). The inclusion furthermore leads members to articulate dissatisfaction rather than taking the 'exit' option (Hirschmann 1970). Therefore, incorporating party members is a strategy to react to, or prevent, membership losses (Scarrow 1996) which have affected most West European parties in recent years (Mair and van Biezen 2001).

However, the inclusion of party members also has drawbacks. As Kitschelt (1994a, b: ch. 5) argues, (Social Democratic) parties are less likely to react to new challenges if their leaders are constrained by their respective party organisations. In contrast, autonomous leaders are more successful in reacting to challenges coming from the electoral market. Hence, the inclusion of party members increases the members' satisfaction but simultaneously increases the number of intra-party veto players (Tsebelis 2002) and may hence lead to inflexibility.

Studies on intra-party decision-making processes find that parties become more inclusive over time (Bille 2001; Hopkin 2001) and that various institutional factors such as federalism and the electoral system affect the rules for selecting party elites (see e.g. Lundell 2004; Thorlakson 2009). Turning to the consequences, intra-party decision-making rules are likely to affect the composition of parliamentary groups and their behaviour in parliament (see e.g. Gallagher and Marsh 1988; Norris 1997; Obler 1973, 1974). Only a few studies look at the consequences of the distribution of intra-party power on party policy changes. Bille (1997) and Harmel and colleagues (Harmel *et al.* 1995; Harmel and Janda 1994) study the effect of leadership changes and turnovers of dominant factions within parties. Yet, the authors focus on changing *preferences* and do not take the formal decision-making rules into account (for notable exceptions see Maravall 2008; Schumacher *et al.* 2012; Share 1999).

Research on party organisations and intra-party decision-making processes is still fragmentary. This is mainly due to the lack of data and the low number of cases. As a consequence, scholars attribute differences in the decision-making processes to the parties' membership figures or institutional factors (such as the electoral system) without specifying and testing the mechanisms that link the phenomena. Hence, previous research on intra-party decision making first and foremost provides descriptive in-depth insights into intra-party decision-making processes.

Sources of income

Apart from formal rules, the distribution of power within parties also hinges on the provision of financial means: party leaders depend on actors providing the party's financial backbone and should therefore take their preferences into account. Even if the financiers cannot formally dismiss the party elite, withdrawing their resources from the party can put the party leadership at risk. This is the argument of the resource dependence theory (Pfeffer and Salancik 1978).

Political parties mainly rely on three sources of income: membership fees, donations (from patrons and interest groups), and public funding.[8] Mass parties typically draw mainly on the members' contributions (Duverger 1954; see also Scarrow 1996: ch. 2; Ware 1996: 298–9). Other parties heavily rely on the funding of political patrons (as, e.g. Silvio Berlusconi) or contributions coming from interest groups such as labour unions, employer associations and companies. This 'plutocratic' financing (Nassmacher 2001b: 22–6)[9] makes parties dependent on the donors' preferences. Finally, parties also draw on public money. Because public subsidies are linked to a party's vote share, they increase the incentives for vote-seeking party behaviour (van Biezen 2003, 2004, 2008).

The relevance of the main sources of party income varies over time. In the West European context, membership fees and donations were predominant until the 1960s. With decreasing membership figures, the role of members' donations diminished. From a normative perspective, contributions coming from patrons and interest groups put the party image and credibility at risk because the donors might expect something in return (Wiberg 1991a: 9). In fact, the fear that corruption could undermine parties which, in turn, are needed in modern democracies is a major justification for the adoption of public funding. If modern democracies build on political parties, they should also be willing to support them (Nassmacher 2001b: 16; Ware 1996: 302). Nowadays, in most countries public subsidies provide the lion's share of party income (Pierre et al. 2000).

The decreasing role of membership fees, accompanied by the increasing significance of public subsidies, has severe consequences for party behaviour. If a party leader's behaviour aims at satisfying the preferences of the actors providing financial resources, the attention turns away from a party's rank-and-file (Strøm 1990: 579–581; Strøm and Müller 1999: 19–21). As a consequence, the 'exit' option for party members is no longer a credible threat because party leaders can substitute their losses of membership fees by other means. In turn, decreasing membership figures force party leaders to concentrate on alternative sources of income. Apart from donors, party leaders are most likely to allocate financial resources by drawing on public money. Because the amount of public funding usually hinges on a party's vote share, incentives coming from the electoral market (rather than the party members' preferences) are becoming the key factor steering party behaviour.

The consequences of public funding for party behaviour are best illustrated in the literature on cartel parties (see e.g. Bolleyer 2008; Detterbeck 2005; Katz and Mair 1995, 2009). As Katz and Mair (1995) argue, public subsidies are a key indicator for the growing interpenetration of parties and the state. As a consequence, long-established links between political parties and their represented

---

8. In addition, parties can also rely on the salaries of their office holders, candidates contributing to campaigns, and investment incomes and sales. Yet, I argue that the lion's share of party income stems from membership fees, donations, and public subsidies (see Ware 1996: 298–303).

9. Nassmacher attributes the term 'plutocratic financing' to Gullan Gidlund (see also Gidlund and Koole 2001).

societal segment lose importance (van Biezen 2003: 40) and parties increasingly turn their attention to the electoral arena. As a consequence, parties become more 'coalitionable' and less partisan (Mair 2008: 216). The fact that they face voters who are also becoming less partisan and more likely to vote for different parties enforces this trend (Dalton and Wattenberg 2000; Mair *et al.* 2004).

In sum, monetary incentives and the increasing number of floating voters (associated with the drop in voters with party identification) makes parties react to electoral market signals. Testing the expected (but undesired) consequences of public funding is part of this book.

Summary

In what follows, I argue that party competition involves a time component. Parties do not simply choose party policy positions from scratch. Rather, choosing a policy position always implies a shift away from the former one. Hence, choosing party platforms is a *process* that cannot be captured in static models of party competition treating each election in isolation.

Introducing the time dimension in models of party competition leads to two questions. First, what are the incentives for parties to change policy platforms? And second, what are the constraints when so doing? As this brief literature review reveals, scholars devote more attention to the first question. In line with static models, recent research on the dynamics of party competition focuses on factors (such as rival party (policy) behaviour, electoral defeats, and shifts in public opinion) that make parties shift their policy platforms. Yet, there is far less research on the constraints parties face when adapting their policy positions over time.

Drawing on various party definitions, I identify three major groups of actors with which parties interact: rival parties, voters and their own organisation. Rival parties are the competitors a party has to cope with. The policy platforms competitors take, and the vote shares they hold, provide incentives for party policy change. In contrast, the constraints when doing so are most likely to come from the voters' willingness and ability to perceive party policy shifts. The research reviewed in this chapter highlights the importance of the voter's information for locating party policy positions. Moreover, voters differ in their evaluation of a party's credibility. In what follows, similar arguments are made for the voter's perception of party position shifts and the consequences for party policy behaviour (Chapter Five). These hypotheses are then tested at the voter (Chapters Six) and the party level (Chapter Seven).

Another factor affecting a party's ability to shift its policy platform is its internal structure. I have reviewed previous research on the distribution of power within parties, distinguishing formal decision-making rules and the actual dependence on actors who provide the financial resources. Various types of intra-party structure affect the role and the power of party members. Their effect on party policy shifts are outlined (Chapter Eight) and tested (Chapter Nine) later in this book. Before turning to the factors constraining party policy change, however, I first turn to the measurement of party policy changes in the next chapter.

chapter three | measuring party policy shifts

The following chapters are devoted to the factors constraining party policy shifts. However, it is useful to say a few words on the key variable of interest *party policy shifts*, before turning to these analyses. Analysing policy shifts requires data on party policy positions or, more precisely, *dynamic* data on party policy positions. This chapter, which partly builds on arguments and analyses presented elsewhere (Budge and Meyer 2012b; a; Meyer and Jenny 2012), will deal with the dependent variable and its measurement.

There are various ways to derive these data and a substantive literature analyses the strengths and weaknesses of each of these approaches. The aim of this chapter is twofold. First, it is argued that one approach, content analysis of political texts, is particularly suited to derive data on party policy shifts. The most comprehensive analysis of political texts to date is the data derived by the Comparative Manifestos Project (CMP). It provides party policy positions based on content analyses of party manifestos in about 50 countries and over 60 years. Yet, the CMP data also has its critics and there is an on-going debate on the data's quality and how these estimates should be used (if to be used at all). This leads to the second aim of this chapter. While I agree that these data have their weaknesses and researchers should take these concerns seriously, I show that the proposed modifications are themselves far from costless. They add additional assumptions that are seldom testable and some of them have unintuitive (and mostly unobserved) consequences. Thus, adding additional assumptions does not necessarily improve data quality. This is not to say that the CMP data are free of any noise or bias. As all datasets and estimates, they certainly carry some error. Yet, the aim is to show that there is no 'gold standard' how CMP estimates have to be used.

Approaches to derive party position estimates

It is in principle possible to measure party policy shifts directly, for example by asking survey respondents (i.e. party elites, experts, or the electorate) whether a party's policy platform has changed over a defined time period (e.g. since the last election). Yet, the predominant way to measure policy *shifts* is to compare party policy *positions* at two points in time. A policy shift is then defined as a (significant) change of party policy positions between two points in time.

There are various ways to derive estimates of party policy positions. Party policy positions can be inferred from their MPs' voting behaviour in parliament. Roll call analyses originate from the US-American context where the major goal is to map the policy positions in the U.S. Congress (Clinton *et al.* 2004; Jackman 2001; Poole and Rosenthal 1991). The idea is to derive estimates for the similarity of policy preferences based on the actors' voting behaviour. All else being equal, the more similar the voting patterns, the closer the policy preferences of political actors. This approach has also been used outside the American context (see e.g. Curini and Zucchini 2012; Hansen 2009; Hug and Schulz 2007; Rosenthal and Voeten 2004), especially in the European Parliament (see e.g. Hix *et al.* 2005; 2006). Estimates for party policy positions are then inferred by aggregating scores for individual MPs or by focussing on the voting behaviour of the party elite (e.g. the party leader).

Another approach, the survey-based approach, uses questionnaires asking respondents to place parties on policy scales. One common way to phrase such a question is to ask: 'On a left-right scale where 0 means the left and 10 means the right, where would you place X?'[1] where X indicates a political actor. The answers are then aggregated over all respondents and the mean position indicates the estimate of a party's policy position. Surveys differ in their target groups. Elite surveys focus on party elites, for example parliamentary candidates or MPs (see e.g. Best *et al.* 2012a; Saiegh 2009). In contrast, expert surveys, perhaps the most prominent approach (Benoit and Laver 2006; Castles and Mair 1984; Hooghe *et al.* 2010; Huber and Inglehart 1995; Laver and Hunt 1992; Rohrschneider and Whitefield 2009; Steenbergen and Marks 2007), address close observers of politics, notably political scientists but also journalists or other specialists. Respondents of mass surveys constitute the largest sample, namely the wider electorate. These data can be gathered from national election studies and cross-national projects such as the Comparative Study of Electoral Systems (CSES).

Yet another approach is to derive information about party policy positions from political texts (Holsti 1969; Krippendorff 2003; Neuendorf 2002; Riffe *et al.* 2005). These analyses are based on different text types such as speeches of party elites and party press releases. Yet, the most common text sources are party manifestos because they are 'uniquely authoritative as a statement of the party' (Budge and Klingemann 2001: 8). One could add that party manifestos usually address various issue areas and are thus comprehensive overviews of a party's policy platform. Yet, this does not hold true for all parties and all countries as some parties publish no 'real', comprehensive election programme (Gemenis 2012). There is also variation in how information is retrieved from the documents. One major distinction being made is between 'qualitative' and 'quantitative' forms of text analysis. Here, the focus is on the latter. The 'classic' approach is hand coding where human coders allocate text subunits (e.g. sentences) into one of the categories of a given coding scheme. While coding was literally done in the past 'by hand', it is nowadays assisted by computers that help to reduce coding error. This approach differs from automated forms of text analysis where computers do the actual coding process. In this approach, the human input is minimal and usually restricted to data input on how the textual information relates to policy positions. This input might be by a dictionary containing words or terms that are, for example, classified as 'left' or 'right' (see e.g. Pennings 2011). Another way is to provide a text with position estimates to which a text can be compared to (Laver *et al.* 2003). It is also

---

1.   This is the wording of the question on the elite surveys in the IntUne project (Best *et al.* 2012a).

possible to build on assumptions of word frequencies and to search for expressions that discriminate among different texts (Slapin and Proksch 2008).

There is an extensive debate about which of the approaches is best able to provide valid and reliable estimates of party policy positions (see e.g. Benoit and Laver 2007; Budge 2001; Budge and Pennings 2007; Dinas and Gemenis 2010; Hooghe *et al.* 2010; Klemmensen *et al.* 2007; McDonald *et al.* 2007; Mikhaylov *et al.* 2012; Pennings 2011; Volkens 2007; Whitefield *et al.* 2007). For example, roll call analyses originate from the US context and it is difficult to transfer this technique to parliamentary systems where party cohesion is the rule (Laver 2006). They may also suffer from a selection bias, as not all votes are recorded and the use of roll calls itself is due to strategic party behaviour (Carrubba *et al.* 2008). It may also be argued that content analyses, elite surveys and roll call analyses measure party behaviour while expert and mass surveys rather indicate *perceptions* of party policy positions. Furthermore, proponents of computerised content analysis approaches also highlight the high reliability of their approach *vis-à-vis* classic hand-coding involving human coders. In turn, hand-coding has been said to provide higher validity (see e.g. Pennings 2011).

These comparisons imply that the various approaches measure the same underlying concept. Yet, there is good reason to believe that votes, texts and surveys contain information on different facets of party behaviour (Ray 2007). For example, expert and mass survey respondents can build on various information sources including the parties' actual behaviour in parliament, party communication and reports in the news media. In contrast, content analyses and roll call analyses are based on more limited empirical evidence. The approaches also differ in their focus on policy claims and actual behaviour. Roll call analyses only consider the actual behaviour of MPs in parliament while content analyses only focus on the parties' intentions and pledges as expressed in political texts. It is also likely that the messages differ between text types and the target groups that parties aim to address. Hence, attempts to validate estimates from one approach with those derived from another are necessarily limited.

What can we infer from this comparison for the analysis of party policy shifts? While all the differences and limitations of the various approaches also hold for the analysis of policy shifts, there are two further aspects that need to be considered. First, analysing policy shifts requires time-series data of party policy positions. For some of the approaches mentioned above, it is difficult to gather these data. As a consequence, they are not available for the analysis of policy shifts. Second, analysing shifts requires that policy positions measured at different points in time are comparable. If policy positions are not measured on the same policy scale, it is impossible to say whether a party shifted its policy position. In addition, with cross-temporal comparability, it is preferable to have a measure that allows for cross-national comparison. While this is not a necessary condition, it certainly simplifies the analysis if policy distances have the same meaning across different party systems.

The various approaches differ in terms of data availability. While content and roll call data analyses can be done in retrospect, this is certainly more difficult for survey-based estimates of party policy positions. The reason is that respondents have difficulties in making retrospective judgements about past policy positions (Steenbergen and Marks 2007). This means that the survey-based approach hinges on a contemporaneous measurement of party policy positions. Periods where no such data is available (mostly the post-war period) are 'lost' and cannot be analysed using the survey-based approach. Moreover, some surveys are only conducted at one point in time. At least this holds true for most expert surveys (Benoit and Laver 2006; Castles and Mair 1984; Huber and Inglehart 1995; Laver and Hunt 1992).[2] The analyses based on roll call data are also plagued by problems of data availability. For one, the number of roll call votes differs dramatically (Hug 2010). There is temporal variation (Hug 2006) as well as variation across political systems. For comparable time periods, roll call votes in the European Parliament are much more frequent than for national parliaments in Ireland (Hansen 2009), Italy (Curini and Zucchini 2012) and Switzerland (Hug and Schulz 2007). Moreover, the rules for publishing the results of roll call votes differ (Hug 2010) which may lead to biased estimates of MP policy positions. Even if these data are in the public domain, they need to be collected and prepared for their use in statistical analyses. Although there are some attempts to solve this data problem[3], these data bases are to date not available for most countries.

Another concern for the study of party policy shifts is the comparability of party position data. In particular, a necessary condition for the comparison of party policy positions is that they are measured in the same policy space. All approaches mentioned above map empirical data (respondents, parliamentary votes or texts) onto the issue dimensions of a policy space. The survey-based approach, for example, locates parties on a policy scale with pre-defined ends (e.g. 0 and 10). In roll call analyses and some computerised content analyses, the policy space is identified by 'normalising' the distribution of policy positions (e.g. with a mean of zero and a standard deviation of one). Other approaches, in turn, define the policy space by the theoretical minimum and maximum in the parties' issue emphasis of 'left' or 'right' issues.

Because the definition of 'policy space' differs across the various approaches, it is not possible to compare policy positions in different policy spaces without defining an 'anchor' that links the two metrics (see e.g. Benoit and Laver 2007). Yet, similar problems may arise for comparisons using the same measurement approach. For example, it is hardly possible to compare policy positions from two separate analyses of roll call data because the definition of the underlying policy

2. Some expert surveys provide time-series data of party policy positions (Hooghe *et al.* 2010; Rohrschneider and Whitefield 2010; Steenbergen and Marks 2007). Yet, there are additional methodological challenges with these data because policy scales are usually interpreted in a national, contemporaneous context (discussed below).

3. See, for example, the VoteWorld project (http://ucdata32.berkeley.edu/voteworld/home/).

space differs. To illustrate this, think of a parliament in which *all* MPs shift their policy positions further to the left. Using two separate analyses (i.e. one before, one after the shift) would create the illusion of perfect stability although the whole system has shifted to the left. Policy scales used in survey research are quite similar in this respect. Individuals interpret survey questions in different ways (King *et al.* 2004). For party policy positions, it is likely that respondents take *current context in the political system* into account. To the extent that this holds true, this also means that survey-based position estimates (of parties and voters) omit a lot of cross-national variation (Best *et al.* 2012b). It also means that survey-based position estimates omit cross-temporal variation (McDonald and Mendes 2001). As McDonald *et al.* (2007: 65) observe '[t]his is troubling because it presents us with the possibility that expert scores are operating as if they describe general left-right tendencies across time, a mean position for each party'. While it is certainly valuable to have such estimates, they are not well suited for analysing party policy change.

In toto, the data requirements for the analysis of party policy shifts are relatively high. Analysing such data requires time-series data of party policy platforms that are consistently measured in the same policy space. These data characteristics are far from trivial and most approaches fail to achieve them. Some measures based on content analyses escape much of this criticism. Texts can be coded *ex post* and these data sources are mostly freely available (Benoit *et al.* 2009a; Manifesto Project Database 2012). This also allows for a relatively long time-series of party policy position data. Using content analyses, it is also possible to work around the problem of defining a common policy space. In fact, it is possible to achieve cross-temporal and cross-national comparability. These are the biggest advantages of the Comparative Manifestos Project (CMP) data that is presented in greater detail in the next section.

The Comparative Manifestos Project (CMP) data and its critics

The CMP research project analyses party election programmes to gather data on issue emphasis and party policy positions. Its history ranges back to the 1970s where a group of party scholars founded the Manifesto Research Group (MRG). Their goal was to answer research questions derived from various theoretical models (e.g. Downs 1957) but back then no data was available to test these claims. The project has endured over several decades and the data collection and coding is still going on. Since 2009, the project operates under the MARPOR label ('Manifesto Research on Political Representation') and the current data base covers approximately 3,500 party manifestos from 850 parties in over 50 countries (Manifesto Project Database 2012). The MRG/CMP/MARPOR data have led to several hundred publications and working papers.[4]

---

4. In summer 2012, Google Scholar lists about 1,200 citations of 'Mapping Policy Preferences'.

Data for party policy positions are derived from party manifestos or substitutes that are considered as close equivalents. The coding process is based on hand coding. Human coders first divide the content of texts into single statements, the quasi-sentences. These statements are the basic coding unit. Each sentence is then allocated to one of the 56 issue categories (or coded as 'uncoded'). These scores represent the emphasis a party puts on a specific issue such as 'decentralisation'. To derive estimates for party policy positions, 26 of these categories are classified as 'left' and 'right' issues. The difference in the relative issue emphasis of 'left' and 'right' issues leads to the estimated party policy position (for more details see Laver and Budge 1992).

There are many advantages of using these data. For one, they constitute the only comparative database on party policy platforms that is readily usable. Other approaches have been used to create time-series data on party policy positions. Yet, these attempts are limited to individual parties or countries (see e.g. Hansen 2009; Klemmensen *et al.* 2007) or cover rather short time periods (Hooghe *et al.* 2010; Rohrschneider and Whitefield 2010; Steenbergen and Marks 2007). Another major advantage of the CMP approach is the use of a common coding scheme across countries which allows for cross-national comparisons. In particular, magnitudes of party policy shifts are comparable across countries. This allows for pooling the data from various party systems which is more problematic for other measurement approaches that use different metrics across party systems.

Yet, there are also problems involved in using these data. Many scholars have raised valuable points that researchers should keep in mind when using these data. Researchers tested the validity of the data (Benoit and Laver 2007), criticised the scaling procedure of the parties' left-right positions (Franzmann and Kaiser 2006; Lowe *et al.* 2011; Pelizzo 2003), and produced estimates for systematic (Mikhaylov *et al.* 2012) and non-systematic (Benoit *et al.* 2009b) error in the data. Moreover, there are problems involved in the text selection (Benoit *et al.* 2012; Dinas and Gemenis 2010; Gemenis 2012; Hansen 2008; Proksch and Slapin 2009; Proksch *et al.* 2011). Researchers contributing to the CMP project have sometimes selected wrong documents or chosen flyers, speeches and newspaper articles as the nearest equivalents for comprehensive party manifestos. Yet, using these substitutes may lead to a severe bias in the position estimates.

In my eyes, most of the criticism raised in these papers is justified: There are cases for which CMP data lacks validity. Moreover, using a common left-right scale over time and across space may be inappropriate in some instances. Furthermore, researchers should indeed aim at providing estimates for the uncertainty of their inferences (see also King *et al.* 1994: 152). In the following discussion, my aim is twofold. First, I aim to demonstrate that most concerns (especially regarding the data's validity) are at least only of moderate concern for the sample chosen in this empirical analysis. Second, I emphasise that the use of fixes proposed for the CMP data come at a cost. All of the papers discussed below, which aim at improving the data quality, add additional assumptions. These, in turn, are themselves seldom testable. It is, for example, preferable to have uncertainty estimates for the party policy positions derived from the party manifestos. However, nearly all manifestos have only been coded *once*. Avoiding costly additional hand-coding, uncertainty estimates can only be based on additional assumptions about the data-generating process. If the assumptions are correct, the modifications lead to more precise estimates of party policy positions. Yet, wrong assumptions lead to estimates that are worse than the initial CMP 'raw data'. Thus, there is no 'gold standard' on how CMP estimates have to be used.

I now turn to various critics in greater detail. Specifically, the critical review includes Benoit and Laver's (2007) comparison of CMP left-right positions and expert judgements, three studies which argue for a different interpretation (Pelizzo 2003) and measurement of party left-right positions (Franzmann and Kaiser 2006; Lowe *et al.* 2011) and finally research introducing estimates for systematic (Mikhaylov *et al.* 2012) and non-systematic (Benoit *et al.* 2009b) measurement error.

CMP estimates and expert judgements on party positions

There are several critiques arguing that expert judgements provide more valid estimates of party policy positions than manifesto estimates. For example, Benoit and Laver (2007) compare party policy positions derived from the CMP project with data gathered from expert judgements. Although the estimates on average concur, there are cases where CMP estimates and expert judgements differ. The authors argue that expert judgements are more accurate than CMP estimates (Benoit and Laver 2007: 103). Using data from their expert survey, Benoit and Laver (2006) show that left-right scales have different meanings in different countries. One problem is that there is no systematic way to account for this. Attempts to create time-variant left-right scales that also differ across space have several problems (see below). Fortunately, the varying meanings of left-right scales are less of a problem for my sample of party policy shifts in Western Europe: Benoit and Laver (2007: 92–93) state that differences in the meaning of left-right scales is most crucial between Western and Eastern Europe. Thus, restricting the sample to ten West European countries, the problem is, at least, kept at bay.

Regarding the concurrence of CMP estimates and expert judgements, CMP estimates are likely to be more error-prone than expert judgements. This is particularly so because they are more likely to capture variation across elections than estimates based on expert judgements. As mentioned above, expert estimates of party policy positions do not contain much cross-temporal variation. Hence, they may be more likely to indicate general left-right tendencies, or ideological territories, than policy positions at a given point in time (McDonald *et al.* 2007). For example, the Chapel Hill expert survey provides time-series data of party policy positions (Hooghe *et al.* 2010; Steenbergen and Marks 2007). Using data from three waves (1999, 2002 and 2006), we find that the magnitude of the average party policy shift is about 0.6 units on the 0–10 left-right scale (N = 250) and about 80 per cent of the estimated policy shifts are smaller than one unit. Hence, perceptions of party policy platforms are rather stable. Yet, some of this variation also reflects measurement error in the position estimates. The given party policy positions are the experts' mean perceived positions and reflect some degree of disagreement. One can use the information about this disagreement (or uncertainty) to calculate an estimator for the probability that the observed deviation reflects a 'true' policy shift. To compare two policy platforms, use, say, 1,000 draws from normal distributions with means and standard deviations as given in the expert data. If pairwise comparisons reveal that all draws from one distribution are consistently larger or smaller than those of the other distribution, then the shift is likely to be true. In contrast, if there is no consistent pattern, then the deviation is likely to reflect a random deviation.[5] This leads to estimates for the probability that an observed deviation reflects a 'true' policy change. Discounting all changes with a probability smaller than 0.5 to reflect random variation, then parties *do not* shift their policy platforms in about 80 per cent (208/250) of all cases. This is a remarkably high estimate of party stability.

Party manifesto estimates are more vulnerable to measurement error because they aim to reflect variation over time. Moreover, these estimates are only based on the information provided in texts while experts can draw on various information sources. Manifestos can be misleading, exaggerating or understating 'true' policy positions. They may also contain blunt lies.[6] This should lead to a higher variation in the parties' estimated party policy positions than those we get from expert surveys. Once again, this reminds us that the various approaches do not necessarily compare like with like (Budge 2000; McDonald *et al.* 2007).

Nevertheless, cross-validation can be used to test the data validity of CMP left-right estimates. Users may refrain from using CMP data if the estimates have low face validity and do not match with expert judgements.[7] In their analysis, Benoit and Laver (2007: 98) name parties for which CMP and expert surveys diverge most (i.e. one estimator places the party being 'left', the other one as 'right'). In total, 20 per cent of their sample (23 out of 114) falls in this category. The number is considerably smaller (9 per cent; 5 out of 56) in my sample of ten West European countries. In addition, four of the five 'deviant cases' can be explained by the different yardsticks experts and hand-coders of party manifestos use. Country experts compare party policy platforms *within* countries whereas the CMP left-right scale is cross-national. For example, Benoit and Laver (2007: 97) report that two Austrian parties – the Greens and the Social Democrats – are deviant in the sense that experts place them on the left while CMP places both parties on the right. Yet, the CMP placements of both parties (19.7 and 20.8, respectively) are only right

---

5. More precisely, I used | ('shift left' – 'shift right') | /1000 to estimate the probability for a 'true' policy shift.

6. For instance, in a private party speech given in May 2006 that was leaked to the public, the former Hungarian prime minister Gyurcsány admitted: 'We did whatever was possible to do in secret in the preceding months, making sure that papers on what we were preparing for would not surface in the last weeks of the election campaign.' For an English translation of this speech see http://news.bbc.co.uk/2/hi/europe/5359546.stm.

7. In fact, this is one reason for excluding Italy from my sample.

of the CMP zero point. Their national rivals, the Christian Democrats (40.4) and the Freedom Party (55.7), hold policy positions right of the two left-wing parties. Hence, the CMP rank-order of party positions is plausible. In fact, CMP party placements and expert judgements of party positions on an ordinal scale match perfectly (see Benoit and Laver 2007: Table 3). For the countries under consideration, Kendall's tau ranges from 0.52 (Finland) to 1 (Austria, the Netherlands, and the United Kingdom) therefore revealing quite similar results of party rankings. Only Belgium (Kendall's tau = 0) stands out which is, however, only due to *one* misperceived party placement (*Ecolo*) while the ranking among the remaining parties is consistent.

CMP data indicates direction of policy change rather than policy positions

Another critique comes from Riccardo Pelizzo (2003) who argues that CMP left-right scores do not indicate party policy positions. Rather, the scores signal party policy *change*. For instance, parties which aim at shifting their positions to the left emphasise 'left' issues. Pelizzo's research is motivated by the flawed estimates of Italian parties' policy positions. I agree that the Italian party policy positions lack face validity and Pelizzo's suggestions are worthwhile. Yet, the position comparisons of CMP estimates and expert judgements (see e.g. the Laver/Benoit comparison discussed above) show that his proposed interpretation of manifestos as signals for policy position *change* does not travel across countries. Pelizzo himself compares voters' left-right estimates of political parties and CMP left-right scores. The data matches quite well: for five of the ten elections (in Germany and the Netherlands), the rankings match perfectly. Deviations are mainly due to *one* party for which the rank-order of the respective other scale does not fit (Pelizzo 2003: Tables 6A and 6B). Hence, Italian data should be treated as an outlier rather than generalising the odd Italian estimates for a new interpretation of party policy positions.

Pelizzo's theoretical reasoning that manifestos indicate directions of policy change is interesting. Parties are indeed likely to use their manifestos as signals for voters. But could manifestos really indicate the *direction* of policy change? Consider the following example: imagine a party (with a party policy position) that wants to shift its policy platform. Following Pelizzo, a party drafts a manifesto containing 'left' issues if the intended shift is to the left. In the next election, it drafts another manifesto to indicate another shift. But what if parties use identical claims in two subsequent elections? Pelizzo's logic implies that a party makes two successive shifts in the same direction. They do so, however, using the *same* signals, content, claims, and perhaps even wording, as they did in the last election. If the *same* claims (e.g. income tax reforms or the endorsement of minimum wages) are raised in the next election, does the party shift its position *further* in the respective direction? Or do repetition and re-emphasis of a party's postulates signal that its claims are still valid? The hypothetical example rather supports the latter conclusion.

The meaning of 'left' and 'right' over time and across space

The CMP left-right scale is based on 13 issue categories classified as 'left' and 13 issue categories classified as 'right' issues. Party policy positions are then calculated as the deviation in the emphasis of left and right issues. This approach has the advantage that all policy positions are measured on the same underlying policy space which, in turn, allows for comparing the position estimates. Yet, it also assumes that the meaning of 'left' and 'right' issues is stable over time and travels across various party systems. If their meaning differs over time and across space, assuming a fixed meaning of 'left' and 'right' reduces data validity. Thus, there is a potential trade-off between higher validity using flexible left and right categories and the use of a common left-right scale that allows for comparing policy position over time and across space.

How serious is the thread of losing validity by assuming fixed 'left' and 'right' categories? At least for the Western European context, there is some evidence that these concerns are not justified. Analysing voter perceptions, Huber (1989) finds that the meaning of left and right are indeed comparable across eight Western European countries. And in their analysis based on party manifestos, Gabel and Huber (2000) find a higher correspondence of manifesto-based policy positions, with those derived from expert surveys if the left-right scales are based on a pooled data including various countries and decades. Alternative measures with country- and time-specific scaling approaches show a lower fit. This suggests that using the same scale over time and across space is justified.

Nevertheless, assuming that 'left' and 'right' means the same across time and space is a simplifying assumption and it has been relaxed in previous research. Franzmann and Kaiser (2006) propose a re-analysis of the 56 CMP categories distinguishing 'left', 'right' and 'valence' issues. In essence, their approach works as follows: to distinguish valence and position issues, they use regressions with party fixed effects to explain differences in the usage of policy issues. The authors argue that significant differences across parties indicate position issues.[8] These issues are then classified as being 'left' or 'right'. This decision is based on the party with the highest issue emphasis. If the respective party is a party on the right (e.g. Liberals), the issue is coded as being a 'right' issue. Vice versa, if an issue is emphasised by a party on the left (e.g. Social Democrats), then it falls in the 'left' category. This results in classifications of left and right issue categories that vary across countries and potentially over time. These issue classifications can then be used to estimate party policy positions taking the varying meaning of 'left' and 'right' into account.

This is an innovative approach to derive party policy positions but it also rests on various assumptions. If these assumptions are reasonable, using the approach improves the quality. In contrast, if the assumptions are wrong, then the resulting policy scales are biased. One crucial aspect of their analysis is the distinction of

---

8. That may not be necessarily the case. Taking the logic of valence issues (Stokes 1963), parties could only differ in the emphasis they put on, for example, environmental topics. In other words, differences across parties do not have to be positional in nature.

position issues ('left' and 'right') and 'valence' issues. Franzmann and Kaiser (2006) use significant differences in issue emphasis as their criterion to separate these two groups of issues. The underlying assumption is that parties do not differ in the emphasis of valence issues but this may well be the case especially if there are huge differences in the voters' perceptions of party competence, parties with higher competence evaluations have higher incentives to emphasise valence issues than disadvantaged parties. Another characteristic of this approach is that it restricts the sample of position issues to those where the parties' issue emphasis differs. This clearly helps in separating party policy positions because the measure of positional differences is based on issues where the party issue emphasis differs dramatically. Yet, it also risks overestimating the positional differences because consensual issues are not considered as position issues.

Whether or not an issue is a 'valence' or a 'position' issue, according to the Franzmann and Kaiser approach, also depends on the selected reference category. The more 'extreme' the selected reference party, the higher the likelihood of significant differences in the parties' policy platforms. In contrast, the same policy differences between parties may not reveal significant regression coefficients when being compared to a moderate party. Being aware of this, Franzmann and Kaiser aim for cross-national consistency and use a country's major left-wing party as a reference category. Yet, even this approach involves substantial variation in the chosen reference parties, including centre-left Social Democrats (as in Austria or Germany) as well as Communist parties (as in France or Italy). All else being equal, countries with more centrist reference parties (such as Germany) have less position issues than countries with more extreme reference points. Moreover, the number of valence and position issues also differs across party systems, and hence, across countries. *Ceteris paribus*, the higher the number of parties, the more likely are significant differences between them and therefore, the higher the number of position issues. The empirical data provided by the authors support this statement. The United Kingdom with three major parties shows 31 valence issues but only 22 position issues. For Germany, the number of position issues raises to 28 (28 valence issues). Sweden with slightly more parties shows 34 position issues and 22 valence issues. Finally, Italy with its numerous parties reveals 34 position issues and only 20 valence issues.

Another concern is the distinction between 'left' and 'right' issues. Franzmann and Kaiser assume that 'a party to the right of the ideological centre will emphasise certain right position issues and vice versa for parties on the left' (Franzmann and Kaiser 2006: 171). For that purpose, they distinguish *ex ante* parties as being 'left' and 'right'. Position issues which are emphasised by left-wing parties are 'left' issues and vice versa for 'right' issues and parties. The identification of left and right parties is based on the parties' ideology or external data (e.g. using voter surveys). This approach ensures that parties from 'left' party families (e.g. Social Democrats) have left policy positions and vice versa for parties from 'right' party families (e.g. Liberals). Thus, the resulting left-right estimates are at least in part induced by the assumptions for the estimation process.

In sum, Franzmann and Kaiser (2006) provide an interesting approach to measure party policy positions that takes variation in the meaning of 'left' and 'right' issues into account. Yet, it also shows the problems involved in such an approach: it necessarily involves additional assumptions to identify 'left' and 'right' issues and these assumptions do not necessarily hold true. And if the assumptions are wrong, then the resulting policy scales are biased. These risks have to be considered when aiming for country- and time-specific left-right policy scales, particularly so because they run counter to the cross-national comparability of these scales. Considering variation in the meaning of 'left' and 'right' is worthwhile, but in light of the problems involved in such attempts and the confirming evidence that the left-right scale is comparable (Gabel and Huber 2000; Huber 1989), I refrain from pursuing them.

CMP left-right estimates using odds ratios

Lowe, Benoit, Mikhaylov and Laver (2011) advocate another way to measure party policy positions. The authors advocate a log ratio of 'left' and 'right' sentences. Instead of using additive scales (such as the CMP left-right scale), the resulting scale hinges on the relative balance of 'left' versus 'right' sentences. In order to demonstrate the plausibility of their scale, the authors present the following example:

> If the party's previous platform contained 50 sentences in favour of increased European integration, and 20 emphasising its disadvantages, then a new manifesto containing 50 sentences in favour and 21 against would barely register as an indicator of policy change. But if the previous platform had contained 10 and 4 sentences for and against the EU, and the new platform 10 and 5 then a policy change is more plausible. (Lowe *et al.* 2011: 130)

In other words, the effect of one additional sentence in the 'against' category should depend on what the manifesto entailed so far. The more information an additional sentence entails (compared to the information which is already given in the party's manifesto), the larger the marginal effect of the additional sentence should be.

This is indeed plausible but it is worth noting that the additive CMP left-right scale (RILE) already takes this characteristic into account. It calculates the difference between 'right' (R) and 'left' (L) sentences and divides the result by the total number of sentences (i.e. 'left' and 'right' sentences and those 'neutral' (N) ones that are neither left nor right). If all sentences either deal with 'left' or with 'right' issues, the formula is given by

$$100 \cdot (R-L)/(R+L+N) \tag{1}$$

The marginal effect of adding one 'left' (or 'right') sentence depends on the number of already existing 'right' and 'left' sentences: the higher the number of already existing 'left' or 'right' sentences, the smaller the effect of adding an additional one. This can be seen in the derivatives of (1) given by

$$\frac{\partial Pos}{\partial L} = 100 \cdot \frac{-(2R+N)}{(R+L+N)^2} \tag{2}$$

and

$$\frac{\partial Pos}{\partial R} = 100 \cdot \frac{2L+N}{(R+L+N)^2} \tag{3}$$

Holding the number of 'right' ('left') sentences constant, the effect of adding one additional 'left' ('right') sentences decreases (and converges to zero), as the number of already existing coded as 'left' ('right') increases. In addition, the marginal effect of one additional 'left' or 'right' sentence depends on the number of sentences in the respective other category. To take an extreme example, the marginal effect of 'left' sentences (L) is zero if the number of 'right' sentences (R) equals zero. With regard to equation (1), this results in parties with left policy positions irrespective of the number of 'left' sentences in the manifesto (see also Lowe *et al.* 2011: 130).

The authors state that this characteristic of the additive scale is problematic. As an alternative, they propose a measure of party policy positions using the logarithmized ratio of 'left' and 'right' sentences. Table 3.1 shows an example comparing policy shifts of two parties, P_1 and P_2, on the additive CMP scale and the authors' proposed log ratio of 'left' and 'right' sentences (see also Budge and Meyer 2012b). Party P_1's manifesto at time t is considerably longer (30 sentences) than the one of party P_2 (3 sentences). Yet, both parties have moderate right-wing positions with twice as much 'right' than 'left' sentences. Both parties are modelled as shifting their policy positions towards the centre of the policy space. So doing, both parties keep the number of 'right' sentences constant and increase the number of 'left' sentences. Yet, party P_1's manifesto is longer so more sentences are needed to outweigh its emphasis of 'right' issues at time t. Therefore, party P_1 increases its number of 'left' sentences by 10 while party P_2 only adds one additional 'left' sentence. Both parties shifted their right-wing policy positions with a 2 to 1 ratio in favour of 'right' sentences at time t to a balanced relation between 'left' and 'right' sentences at time t+1.

Table 3.1 shows that the authors' proposed log ratio scale assigns the same values to the parties' policy shifts. Both parties shifted their policy positions from a policy position on the right (with a 2 to 1 ratio in favour of 'right' sentences) to a centrist policy platform with a balanced allocation to 'left' and 'right' issues so

Table 3.1: Measuring party policy shifts using an additive scale and log ratios (Example 1)

	P_1		P_2	
Time	t	t+1	t	t+1
R	20	20	2	2
L	10	20	1	2
RILE	33.3	0	33.3	0
log (R/L)	log(2)	log(1)	log(2)	log(1)
Shift(RILE)	**-33.3**		**-33.3**	
Shift(log ratio)	**-log(2)**		**-log(2)**	

that both policy shifts are equally large (log(2)). In other words, party P_2's manifesto is shorter so that adding one additional 'left' sentence has the same effect than adding 10 'left' sentences in party P_1's manifesto. Yet, the same holds for the additive RILE scale so that both measures produce similar results.

Table 3.2 shows additional examples of party policy shifts and the measurement using the additive RILE scale and the authors' proposed log ratio of 'left' and 'right' sentences. The first party policy shift is identical to the one of party P_2 in Table 3.1 (i.e. P_2 increases the number of 'left' sentences from 1 to 2). Its manifesto is very short with only two 'right' sentences so that we would expect to see a rather large effect of the additional 'left' sentence on its policy shift. In contrast, the effect of adding one additional 'left' sentence should be lower if a party puts more emphasis on right-wing issues. Table 3.2 shows two additional parties emphasising 'right' issues in 20 (party P_2') and 2000 sentences (party P_2'') in their manifestos

Table 3.2: Measuring party policy shifts using an additive scale and log ratios (Example 2)

	P_2		P_2'		P_2''	
Time	t	t+1	t	t+1	t	t+1
R	2	2	20	20	2000	2000
L	1	2	1	2	1	2
RILE	33.3	0	90.5	90.9	99.9	99.8
log (R/L)	log(2)	log(1)	log(20)	log(10)	log(2000)	log(1000)
Shift(RILE)	**-33.3**		**-0.5**		**-0.1**	
Shift(log ratio)	**-log(2)**		**-log(2)**		**-log(2)**	

The examples presented in Table 3.2 show that the log ratio fails to account for its proposed property: independent on how many sentences are dedicated to 'right' issues (ranging from 2 to 2000), the marginal effect of one additional 'left' sentence is constant (= log(2)). This is due to the fact that the effect of increasing the

Figure 3.1: Comparing additive RILE estimates and log ratio with expert judgements

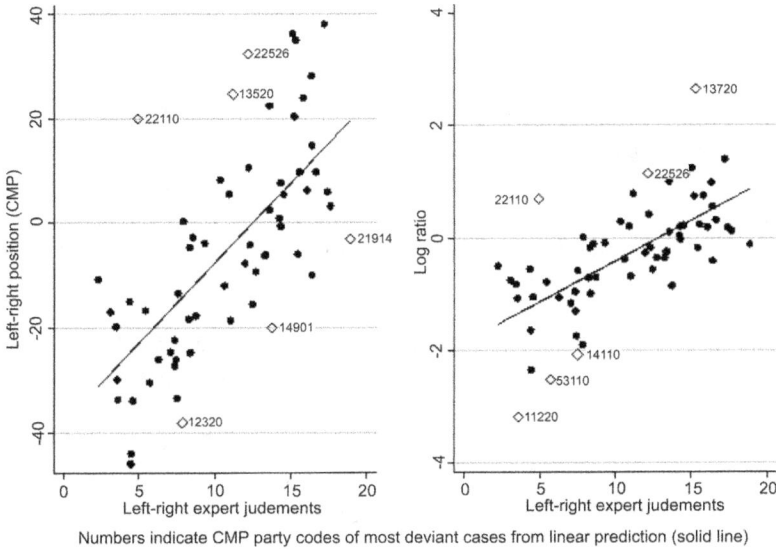

Numbers indicate CMP party codes of most deviant cases from linear prediction (solid line)

number of 'left' ('right') sentences in the manifesto only depends on the number of already existing 'left' ('right') sentences but not on the number of 'right' ('left') sentences. Thus, the effect of one additional sentence on the left, for example, is independent on the number of 'right' sentences in the manifesto. This is not intended (see the example presented above) and may lead to odd results. In contrast, the additive RILE scale takes the decreasing shift effect into account: the effect is large for short manifestos (party P_2), diminishing for right-wing manifestos of moderate length (party P_2'), and is practically zero if the manifesto contains many sentences which are overwhelmingly 'right' (party P_2'').

So far, the discussion has focused on the theoretical properties of the two measures. We may also want to know which of them empirically outperforms the other in measuring party left-right positions. For that purpose, Figure 3.1 displays comparisons of expert judgements (Benoit and Laver 2006) and the CMP estimates of party left-right positions using the additive scale (left) and the log ratio proposed by Lowe and his colleagues (right).[9] The solid line indicates the linear prediction. The hollow diamonds indicate the most deviant cases (and their CMP party codes).

At first sight, the left-right placements of RILE (left) and the log ratio (right) do not differ substantially. Readers who claim that the observations in the right-hand graph are closer to the regression line should note that the adjusted R-squared of

---

9. Specifically, I match the expert judgements with the CMP party positions in the most recent election as indicated in Benoit and Laver's dataset.

the OLS regression is slightly higher for the additive RILE scale (0.45 compared to 0.42 for the log ratio). At least for the left-right scale and the sample presented here, the log-transformed ratio does not outperform the additive RILE scale.

Uncertainty estimates for CMP data

Benoit, Laver, and Mikhaylov rightfully emphasise a major shortcoming of CMP data: Although social scientists should always aim at providing uncertainty measures for their inferences (see also King *et al.* 1994: ch.5), the CMP data does not provide such information. Most of the party manifestos were only coded once so that there is no information on the uncertainty of the derived saliencies and policy positions. Neglecting measurement error may result in measuring policy 'shifts' which are only due to measurement error.

Although I agree with the authors' concern, it should be noted that all attempts to create uncertainty estimates *ex post* involve costs: indicators for the researcher's uncertainty can be obtained by repeating the measurement several times. One or several coders repeat the coding process so that researchers can calculate means and standard deviations of the coding process. The larger the standard deviation, the less precise is the measurement. However, repeating the coding procedure increases the costs in terms of time and required financial resources. Moreover, repeating the coding process *ex post* entails unequal coding conditions because previous research has already highlighted the most likely cases for coding errors (see e.g. Pelizzo 2003 for Italy).

Benoit and colleagues propose an alternative approach. Instead of re-coding the manifestos, the authors make additional assumptions on the data-generating process. So doing, it allows for estimating standard errors for each of the 56 issues in the CMP coding scheme[10] and additive scales like the CMP left-right scale. Specifically, the authors assume that the data-generating process is stochastic following a multinomial distribution (Benoit *et al.* 2009b: 500). Although plausible, this approach also involves costs because we cannot test whether the assumptions hold true. If they are correct, the process increases the data quality. If they are wrong, researchers add additional error to the data.

Assume for a moment that these assumptions are correct. In this case, the uncertainty estimates improve the quality of the data. However, it is not entirely clear how the uncertainty estimates can be used when studying party policy *shifts*.[11] Table 3.3 helps to illustrate this point. Let H_0 indicate the null hypothesis that a party shifts its policy position. There is a true (and unobserved) value whether a party sticks to (H_0: false) or shifts (H_0: true) its policy position and a measure indicating whether we observe a policy shift or not. If the measure correctly captures party position shifts, there is no measurement problem. Yet, two types of error may

---

10. In addition, the authors also provide uncertainty estimates for the uncoded sentences leading to 57 categories.

11. I am aware of the SIMEX algorithm discussed by the authors. Yet, my concern is more fundamental.

occur. First, the measure may reject the null hypothesis although it actually holds (familiar as the Type I error). For party policy shifts, that means that we measure a party sticking to its policy position although it has actually shifted away from its prior platform. In addition, researchers may measure policy shifts although the party in fact sticks to its policy position (known as Type II error). Good measures minimise both Type I and Type II errors.

Table 3.3: Type I and Type II error for measuring party position shifts

		True value	
		H_0: false	H_0: true
Observed party behaviour	No shift	Correct	Type I error
	Shift	Type II error	Correct

Using CMP left-right positions to indicate party policy shifts clearly risks making Type II errors because changes in the parties' policy platforms may also be due to measurement error. This is the point the authors criticise. Using the estimated standard errors, they show that only 38 per cent of the policy shifts reported in CMP data are substantive policy shifts (Benoit *et al.* 2009b: 504). Yet, these estimates risk making a Type I error (i.e. underestimating the true proportion of party policy shifts): the authors aim at a 95 per cent probability that a party really shifts its policy platform ending up with critical cases coded as parties sticking to their policy platforms. In other words, they reduce a Type II error (common in CMP data) but simultaneously increase a Type I error.

This raises two questions. First, which method can be used to obtain 'appropriate' estimates of party position shifts which minimise both errors of Type I and Type II? And second, how large is the error using the original CMP left-right estimates? To answer the first question, I propose a 'mixing strategy': coding policy shifts as statistically significant if the probability of having a real party position shift is larger than 0.5. So doing, coding errors are randomly distributed between Type I and Type II errors. For my sample of ten West European countries, the number of significant changes using the method proposed by Benoit et al. (2009b) is 38 per cent and hence, similar to the authors' estimate based on a larger sample. Using the 'mixing strategy' leads to different results: 72 per cent of all policy shifts are coded as substantive shifts of party policy positions. Therefore, the Type II error of the CMP estimates to measure party policy shifts is much smaller than the authors suggested.

How crucial is the error using CMP estimates as well as neglecting the estimates' uncertainty? With the 'mixing strategy' to distinguish insignificant from significant party policy shifts, the average magnitude of insignificant shifts is 2.3 while significant shifts are considerably larger (about 17.0 points on the CMP left-right scale). In other words, insignificant shifts have values close to zero, indicating that the results of linear models using the magnitude of party policy shifts as dependent or independent variable are not very likely to be error-prone. Assuming that the authors' proposed data-generating process is correct, the Type II error of the initial CMP estimates is arguably rather small.

Unintended consequences of the assumed data-generating process

Apart from the question of how the proposed error estimates should be used (and how large the benefits are compared to the costs of using additional assumptions), it is also valuable to study the consequences of the assumptions entailed in this approach (see also Meyer and Jenny 2012). Specifically, which elements impact on the size of the uncertainty estimates? For individual issue categories, the error variance depends on two factors: (1) the number of (quasi-)sentences in the manifesto and (2) the (observed) probability that a (quasi-)sentence falls in the selected issue category (Benoit *et al.* 2009b: 502). The first property is intended by the authors who argue that additional information (i.e. sentences) reduces the uncertainty of the estimates. The second property states that errors are least likely if the issue category covers no or all sentences in the manifesto. In contrast, the uncertainty is highest if a category covers 50 per cent of all sentences. Although this property has severe consequences for the uncertainty estimates, the authors devote no attention to it. Let me therefore elaborate on it.

Assume a fixed number of quasi-sentences and a coding scheme which only distinguishes three issue categories: 'left', 'right' and 'neither left nor right'. The first two categories are used to build a left-right scale. Let further p_l and p_r denote the share of sentences coded as 'left' or 'right'. According to the data-generating process, the error variance depends on p_l and p_r: the closer p_l (p_r) to 0.5, the higher the error variance within each category. Combining both categories has two implications:[12]

1. Parties with extreme policy positions to the left or the right have smaller uncertainty estimates than centrist parties *if* the centrist parties emphasise topics on the left-right dimension.

2. Centrist parties emphasising left-right issues have *larger* standard errors than centrist parties putting less emphasis on the left-right dimension.

---

12. The following discussion is rather illustrative and therefore not mathematically correct. Yet, the reasoning only serves to come up with observable implications that can be tested afterwards.

Note that both conclusions derive from the assumed data-generating process and have no theoretical backing. Yet, the first expectation theoretically makes sense: centrist parties mix 'left' and 'right' issues and hence coding is more difficult than for 'extreme' parties mainly expressing their preferences in either the 'left' or the 'right' category. I therefore concentrate on the second property: the standard errors of parties with centrist policy positions differ according to the emphasis they put on 'left' and 'right' issues. Yet, the stated direction is somewhat odd: the more (quasi-)sentences centrist parties use for left-right issues, the larger are the standard errors of a party's left-right position. This expectation is counterintuitive and – as I suppose – unintended by the authors. I therefore test whether the standard errors (as derived by the authors) also have empirical repercussions for the estimates of the additive left-right scale.

Table 3.4 shows the regression results of several regression models predicting the (simulated) standard deviation of CMP left-right positions.[13] The key variable of interest is the percentage of a party manifesto devoted to 'left' and 'right' issues. Because the length of a manifesto negatively affects the size of the uncertainty estimates, it is necessary to control for the number of quasi-sentences. In models 1 to 3, centrist parties are those with policy platforms between the 40th and 60th percentile of the CMP left-right positions. Models 4 to 6 use a broader (30th to 70th percentile) measurement leading to a higher number of observations. To show the robustness of the results, three different model specifications are used including OLS regressions (models 1 and 4), OLS regressions with clustered standard errors (by elections; models 2 and 5), and linear two-level regressions using countries at the second level (models 3 and 6). The sample consists of party policy shifts in ten West European countries in Chapters Seven and Nine.

The results show the odd effect that the supposed data-generating process entails. The more emphasis centrist parties put on issues on the left-right scale, the *higher* the uncertainty of its estimated policy position. The result is robust and statistically significant in all model specifications. The counterintuitive implication derived from the assumed data-generating process hence indeed has empirical repercussions. But because this property is not intended, it adds (systematic) error to the data. Instead of improving the data quality, researchers thus end up with even more error-prone estimates.

Challenging the assumed data-generating process

Finally, we may also ask whether the assumptions of the data-generating process are correct. Specifically, sentences in party manifestos are modelled as draws from a multinomial distribution, assuming that longer manifestos provide more information and hence more confidence on the party position estimates (Benoit *et al.* 2009b: 502). The assumption that longer texts entail more information is plausible and also used in previous research (see e.g. Huber *et al.* 2001). Yet, longer

---

13. I use a log transformation of the dependent variable.

Table 3.4: Explaining size of standard errors by centrist party emphasis on left-right issues

	(1) OLS regression	(2) OLS regression (clustered SEs)	(3) Two-level regression	(4) OLS regression	(5) OLS regression (clustered SEs)	(6) Two-level regression
	Centrist parties: 40th to 60th percentile			Centrist parties: 30th to 70th percentile		
% of manifesto dealing with l-r issues	0.0563**	0.0563**	0.0523**	0.0582**	0.0582**	0.0575**
	(3.62)	(2.85)	(3.31)	(6.42)	(5.24)	(6.14)
# of (quasi-)sentences	-0.00169**	-0.00169*	-0.00138**	-0.00211**	-0.00211**	-0.00165**
	(-7.47)	(-2.20)	(-6.02)	(-12.95)	(-2.90)	(-9.66)
Constant	3.277**	3.277**	3.350**	3.261**	3.261**	3.031**
	(4.52)	(3.15)	(4.01)	(7.71)	(5.48)	(5.51)
Observations	184	184	184	367	367	367

t and *z* statistics in parentheses

$^{+} p < 0.1$, $^{*} p < 0.05$, $^{**} p < 0.01$

manifestos may also mirror divergent intra-party policy stances.[14] Manifestos express a party's policy goals. Intra-party factions representing divergent policy preferences want to see their policy goals in the party manifesto and cohesive parties face fewer difficulties to express these statements than incoherent ones. Thus, the length of party manifestos increases with the number of groups with divergent policy preferences to be represented by the party label.[15]

As noted above, there is no direct way to test the contradicting hypotheses because researchers do not know the 'true' uncertainty of party policy positions. It is, however, reasonable to argue that parties use the manifestos to signal their policy stands. Experts on parties can therefore use a party's manifesto to assess its policy position on the left-right scale. The more precise the party manifesto, the less problems experts should face when estimating party policy positions. Because experts can rely on various sources to obtain information (such as news stories, law proposals, and speeches), vague manifestos do not necessarily lead to imprecise expert judgements. Precise manifestos hence decrease the uncertainty of the experts' judgements while imprecise party manifestos do not necessarily lead to imprecise expert judgements.

Figure 3.2 compares the uncertainty estimates of the CMP left-right scale using the authors' proposed method (x-axis) with the deviation of expert judgements when placing party policy positions (y-axis) using data from Benoit and Laver's (2006) expert survey.[16] If the authors' assumptions on the data-generating process are correct and if experts use information derived from party manifestos, we expect to see a lower triangular scatter plot. Manifestos with smaller measurement error (i.e. low values on the x-axis) lead to precise expert judgements. In contrast, imprecise party manifestos (i.e. large values on the x-axis) *may* lead to imprecise expert judgements or they are compensated by additional information sources.

The scatter plot shown in Figure 3.2 does not support the statement. There is no lower triangular form indicating less deviation for smaller values on the x-axis. The correlation ($r = 0.07$; $N = 62$; $p=0.58$) is practically zero, which means that the uncertainty involved in expert judgements, and the authors' derived standard deviation, are independent of each other. This is, of course, no direct evidence that the authors' assumptions are wrong. Yet, the negative findings cast doubts whether their derived uncertainty estimates are correct.

In sum, this discussion shows the problems involved in deriving uncertainty estimates for CMP party position estimates. While it is preferable to measure the uncertainty associated with CMP data, proposals to derive such estimates are

---

14. I owe this potential explanation to Ulrich Sieberer.

15. Empirical evidence that the length of a party manifesto does not necessarily lead to more precise policy positions comes from the British Conservatives' 2010 election manifesto which *The Economist* calls the 'longest betting-slip in history' (*The Economist* 2010). Despite its length, the stated policy goals are too vague to predict the party's government policies.

16. Note that the standard *deviation* (not the standard *error*) is shown which does not depend on the number of observations.

Figure 3.2: Comparing the standard deviation of left-right positions using election manifestos and uncertainty of expert judgements (log-transformed estimates)

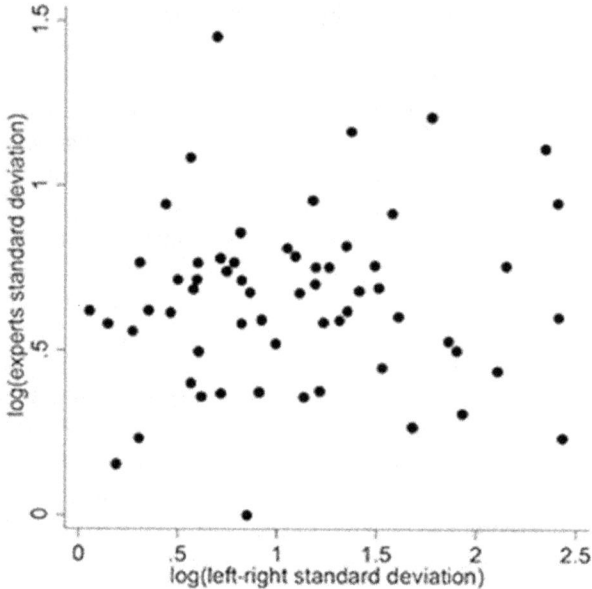

based on additional assumptions. If these assumptions do not hold, the resulting uncertainty estimates stand on shaky grounds. Given these difficulties, the suggested modifications should be treated as an alternative to, rather than improvements of, the original CMP data.

Coder reliability and systematic bias in CMP position estimates

Apart from unsystematic sources of error, CMP estimates may suffer from systematic coding errors (Mikhaylov *et al.* 2012). Using a coding experiment where participants were asked to recode two CMP 'gold standard' texts, Mikhaylov, Laver and Benoit demonstrate that the overall reliability (i.e. the probability of classifying a quasi-sentence in one category) is rather low.

Regarding party policy positions on the CMP left-right scale, the authors show two things. First, low reliability increases the (unsystematic) noise in the data. Second, the systematic error component is more critical for parties with extreme policy positions. Systematic miscoding is less severe for centrist parties because they balance 'left' and 'right' topics. In contrast, extreme parties mainly put their emphasis on either 'left' or 'right' issues. Thus, incorrect coding leads to 'centrist bias' with more moderate policy positions than the 'true' value. Let P* denote a party's 'true' policy position, then the erroneous measure P is given by

$$P = a \cdot P^* + c + \varepsilon \qquad (4)$$

with $0<a<1$ (because of the 'centrist bias') and ε reflecting non-systematic 'noise'. Let P^*_t and P^*_{t-1} the 'true' policy positions of party P at time points t and t-1. With

$$P_t = a \cdot P^*_t + c + \varepsilon_t \qquad (5)$$

and

$$P_{t-1} = a \cdot P^*_{t-1} + c + \varepsilon_{t-1} \qquad (6)$$

we get the observed policy *shift*:

$$P_t - P_{t-1} = a \cdot (P^*_t - P^*_{t-1}) + (\varepsilon_t - \varepsilon_{t-1}) \qquad (7)$$

For policy shifts, the constant term c disappears thus cancelling out parts of the systematic error. Yet, the policy shift still hinges on the slope and because of this 'centrist bias', large policy shifts are likely to be underestimated. This finding has consequences for research on party policy shifts because the bias reduces the variance of the dependent variable. With decreasing variation on the dependent variable, however, explaining differences in the dependent variable becomes less likely (see also King *et al.* 1994: 147–149).

This poses two additional questions. First, how large is the systematic bias? And second, are there reliable estimates which allow correcting for it? To answer the first question, the authors only provide graphs but a = 0.6 seems to be a reasonable estimate. Using that estimate, an 'observed' policy shift of 12 points is, for example, considerably smaller than the 'true' values (around 20 points). This leads to the second question: Are there reliable estimates to correct for the systematic bias? In my eyes, the answer is 'not yet'. The authors *demonstrate* that systematic bias exists. But up to now, there is no way to circumvent it: the authors use coding experiments based on a mixed sample of former CMP coders and inexperienced ones. The authors contact a (biased) sample[17] of 172 subjects and get a response rate of roughly 23 per cent. To be fair with the CMP estimates, the authors discard the least reliable coding results leading to a sample of 24 coders and 2 texts with (in total) 144 quasi-sentences. Yet, the very small sample of coders, lacking incentives (which were in place for the original coding), and the non-random selection of subjects, may bias the reliability estimates. Lacewell and Werner (2012) make similar experiments based on a sample of trained CMP coders. They also find systematic error in the coding of issue categories but their results differ from those of Mikhaylov and colleagues (2012). For one, the coding error is smaller or, vice versa, their sample of coders provides more reliable estimates. Another difference is that Lacewell and Werner (2012) find *asymmetric* coding mistakes for left and right issues: coding error is much more likely for 'left' than for 'right' issues. 'Left'

---

17. The research team was not able to obtain contact information for all coders.

issues are (falsely) classified as 'right' ones in only 6 of 100 cases while 'right' issues are coded as 'left' ones in 24 of 100 cases. What accounts for this difference? Although I only speculate here, the text selection may account for this variation. The coding experiment is based on a manifesto of the Republican Party. Coders know this, and if they are not sure, tend to code issues as 'right' issues to account for the party's ideology. While this reflects additional coding error, the irony is that it cancels out the 'centrist bias' observed by Mikhaylov et al. (2012). Based on these considerations, there is no clearly valid and reliable way to correct for biased CMP estimates. Future research may, however, solve this problem.

Summary

Analysing party policy change requires data on the parties' policy platforms. Fortunately, there are various approaches to derive these data and their strengths and weaknesses have been discussed extensively in the literature. Yet, the options are more limited when it comes to the analysis of party policy change. It requires time-series data on party policy positions which implies that (1) party policy platforms are measured at various (at least two) points in time and that (2) both position estimates are measured on the same policy scale. It is argued in this chapter that the most suitable approach that fulfils these criteria is the content analysis of political texts.

The Comparative Manifestos Project (CMP) provides the most comprehensive data collection of time-series party position data based on content analyses. The data has many merits but the extensive literature also highlights its weaknesses. In some cases, researchers are right in questioning the data quality of CMP estimates, particularly if the left-right placements raise the doubt of country experts. Yet, I show for my research project and its sample of ten West European countries that measurement problems are kept at bay so that the CMP estimates of party policy positions are fairly valid.

There are also various approaches that modify CMP data with the aim to improve the data quality. This results in various alternative scaling approaches and procedures to derive uncertainty estimates for the position data at hand. The problem for researchers using CMP data is to find the most authoritative or 'best' way to use the manifesto estimates. And while some approaches make claims to provide such estimates[18], my aim is to show that altering the existing data by adding additional assumptions does not necessarily improve data quality. This is most obvious for the uncertainty estimates derived for the CMP position estimates, which are based on the assumption that the text generation is a stochastic process. First, it is not entirely clear how to apply the proposed uncertainty estimates for party policy positions to party policy *shifts* because reducing Type II error in the orig-

---

18. With regard to their uncertainty estimates, for example, Benoit et al. (2009b: 512) state that 'there is no longer any excuse for scholars to use error-prone measures as if these were error free'.

inal CMP estimates may simultaneously add Type I error. Second, the assumed data-generating process has (intended and unintended) consequences on the size of the uncertainty estimates. Third, it is difficult (if not impossible) to test whether the authors' assumptions of the data-generating process hold. In case the assumed data-generating process does hold, the approach provides additional information about the position estimates. Yet, the provided error estimates can also be misleading and lull researchers in a false sense of security if the underlying assumptions are not met. This example suggests that there is no 'gold standard' how CMP estimates have to be used.

part ii. voter perception and party policy shifts

chapter four | the voters' perception of party policy shifts

In this chapter, I outline the first part of my theoretical framework. Specifically, I present a vote choice model assuming that voters vote for the party closest to their policy preferences. An important element in the model is that voters' perceptions of party policy positions are influenced by perceptions of past policy platforms. The degree to which perceptions of prior time periods play a role depends on the voters' ability and willingness to perceive a party's position shift.

Drawing on work by Zaller (1992), it is argued that this perception is a two-stage process: For party policy shifts to be effective, parties have to broadcast their new policy goals and voters have to pay attention. In other words, voters have to *receive* policy shifts of parties (reception criterion). If the transmission fails, voters continue to rely on a party's previous policy stands. Second, voters may not *accept* an announced policy position (acceptance criterion). While the reception of information is a cognitive process, the acceptance of party policy shifts depends much on the trustworthiness of parties and their leaders. The crucial point is whether voters believe in the political message sent to them. If ideological proximity matters for vote choice, then the voters' reception and acceptance of party policy shifts also affects party behaviour. In general, parties benefit from higher reception and acceptance of their party policy shifts. Individual parties benefit most if voters perceive party policy shifts towards their personal preferences, while voters being worse off under these policies do not perceive the policy shift. Regarding voter position shifts, parties react to shifts in public opinion if the shifts move away from the party's policy position.

The voters' reception and acceptance of party position shifts

In what follows, I present a model of how voters perceive party position shifts. Rather than looking at single elections, the proposed model takes the time dimension into account. As shown in Chapter Two, research on public opinion (see e.g. Alvarez 1997; Zaller 1992) highlights the importance of information and predispositions when forming opinion on political issues. For example, political awareness and party identification shape the way voters think about foreign affairs, defence policies, the evaluation of the economic situation, or social issues like abortion.

John R. Zaller (1992) proposes a model of how voters form opinion statements. In his Receive-Accept-Sample (RAS) model, Zaller argues that opinion statements 'are the outcome of a process in which people *receive* new information, decide whether to *accept* it, and then *sample* at the moment of answering questions' (Zaller 1992: 51, emphasis in original). The model states that people differ in their exposure and comprehension of political messages. The higher their cognitive engagement (or political awareness), the more likely they *receive* information on a political issue. Yet, the received political information does not directly transfer

Figure 4.1: Voters' perception of party policy shifts

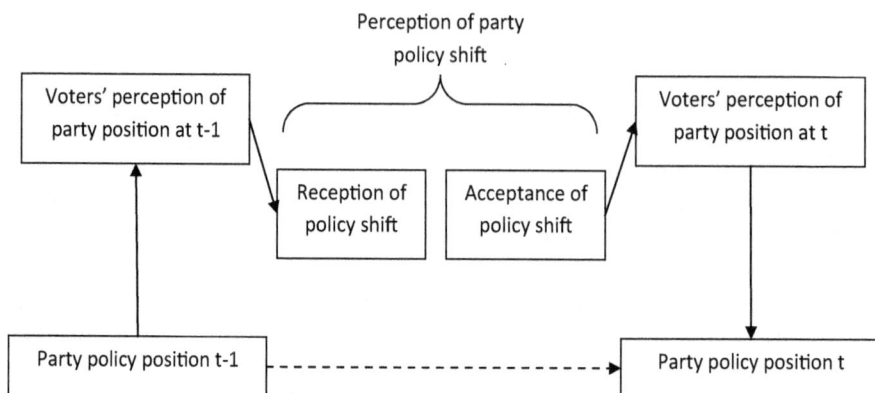

Perception of party
policy shift

| Voters' perception of party position at t-1 | Reception of policy shift | Acceptance of policy shift | Voters' perception of party position at t |

| Party policy position t-1 | ------------------------------> | Party policy position t |

to the formation of a political opinion. Rather, individuals evaluate the received information and resist information contradicting their predispositions. In other words, people may or may not *accept* political messages. Finally, Zaller argues that individuals express their opinions 'at the top of the head'. The more recently a consideration has been called to mind, the more likely people 'remember' it and take it into account when answering survey questions.

I apply Zaller's model to the perception of party policy shifts (see Figure 4.1). It is argued that parties shifting their policy platforms may face voters who do not *receive* the shift message. If voters are not engaged in party politics or face other difficulties in receiving the shift massage, voters do not receive a party's policy shift and, therefore, stick to their previously perceived policy position. Moreover, voters may not *accept* a proposed party policy shift. If voters doubt that a party represents the proposed policies, they resist the received information, thus sticking to the previously perceived policy position. Yet, I refrain from modelling the sampling process. For the specific case of party policy shifts, sampling the various considerations is unlikely to occur because parties advertise their policy positions in the politicised environment of election campaigns. Hence, the parties' new platforms are much more likely to be at the voters' 'top of the head' than the party policies represented in the last election.

I connect Zaller's model with a spatial model of voting. The model is very simple, assuming a one-dimensional policy space. Although policy spaces may sometimes be more complex, the restriction to a single policy dimension has its advantages. First, it reduces the complexity of the model. As can be seen below, introducing the time dimension in a one-dimensional spatial model already has its difficulties. Keeping the model one-dimensional allows keeping the spatial aspects of the model as simple as possible while simultaneously introducing the new elements of reception and acceptance. Another reason for a one-dimensional policy space is provided by the actors involved. Although elites, parties and party leaders may think along several policy dimensions, the complexity of party competition usually boils down to one dimension for voters in the electoral market (Pierce 1999: 30): mass communication requires simplification and all participants aim at reducing complexity. The assumption that voters evaluate parties on several clearly distinguishable and important policy dimensions is unlikely to hold. But even if voters would like to talk about politics in a more complex way, the public discussion on policies concentrates on one-dimensional left-right comparisons. For example, parties present themselves as the 'New Left', and the media constantly talks about 'left', 'centre' and 'right' parties and policies. Moreover, social scientists use the left-right dimension, asking questions on the voters' and the parties' placement on a left-right axis. Hence, although the political space may be more complex, parties and voters interact on one dimension. News media reporting typically reinforces such complexity reductions.

Developing the model: The reception and acceptance of party position shifts

Let us assume that voters are policy-seeking actors deriving benefits from party choices based on the distance between their personal policy preferences and the party's policy platform. For voter i and party j, we may define a utility function based on the quadratic distance[1] of the two policy positions given by

$$U_{ij}(p_j) = -(v_i - p_j)^2 + \varepsilon_{ij} \tag{1}$$

where v_i and p_j are the voter's and the party's policy positions, respectively and ε_{ij} denotes a random error component. If there is just one voter, party j's utility is maximised if the two policy positions are identical. Assume that a party's policy position is different from the voter's ideal position (i.e. $p_j \neq v_i$). I label party j's position at t-1 with $p_{j(t-1)}$. How can party j increase voter i's utility? The simple answer is: by shifting its policy position from $p_{j(t-1)}$, its position at t-1, to voter i's ideal position v_i. However, this implies two assumptions. First, the party's former policy choices do not impact on voter i's perception of the new policy position. There is no path dependency or, put differently, the old policy position $p_{j(t-1)}$ is no longer relevant for voter i to locate party j. Second, all voters form common perceptions of party j's policy position. Yet, empirical evidence suggests that voters differ in their ability to estimate party policy positions (see e.g. Alvarez 1997). In what follows, I refrain from both assumptions presenting a model of how voters perceive party policy shifts.

---

1. Using quadratic utility functions is the most common way to measure distances between two points (Adams *et al.* 2005; Enelow and Hinich 1984: 15; Merrill and Grofman 1999). Alternative norms (like the city block metric or the uniform norm) exist but research on which distance perceptions individuals use is an under-researched area (see Humphreys and Laver 2010). Note, however, that the most common distance perceptions are identical in a one-dimensional policy space.

The reception criterion

Do voters (in our case: voter i) receive the policy shift? Let p_{jt} denote party j's 'intended' new position (i.e. the 'official' new policy position as shown in, for example, the party's manifesto). The reception process can be modelled as

$$rp_{ijt} = r_{ijt} \cdot p_{jt} + (1 - r_{ijt}) \cdot pp_{ij(t-1)} \qquad (2)$$

where rp_{ijt} is voter i's reception of party j's new policy position at time t, $pp_{ij(t-1)}$ is voter i's *perception* of party j's policy position at t-1, and r_{ijt} is the probability that voter i receives party j's policy shift from $pp_{ij(t-1)}$ to p_{jt}. In other words, r_{ijt} is equal to one if voter i receives the new message and equal to zero if the message goes unheard.

If voter i estimates his utility for party j based on the received policy position (and not on the party j's intended position), the utility function U_{ij} can be written as

$$U_{ijt}(rp_{ijt}) = -(v_i - rp_{ijt})^2 + \varepsilon_{ijt}. \qquad (3)$$

In contrast to equation (1), the policy distance in equation (3) depends on the *individually* received party policy position at time t. This creates problems for parties dealing with voters who vary in their ability and willingness to receive party position shifts.

The acceptance criterion

Turning to the second factor, voters may receive party position shifts but they do not necessarily *accept* this new announcement as credible (see also Enelow and Hinich 1984: 117–120). For example, a party may claim to support pro-environmental policies but voters may not believe this policy announcement if the party previously supported the construction of coal power stations. Of course, voters have to receive this policy shift before being able to evaluate its credibility.

In the model presented above, the acceptance can be added using a_{ijt}, the probability that voter i accepts party j's policy shift from perceived position $pp_{ij(t-1)}$ to p_{jt}. If a_{ijt} is large, voter i accepts the policy shift given its reception. If, in contrast, a_{ijt} is small, voter i does not accept party j's announcement and locates party j at its perceived position at t-1.

In more formal terms, the accepted party position is given by

$$pp_{ijt} = a_{ijt} \cdot rp_{ijt} + (1 - a_{ijt}) \cdot pp_{ij(t-1)} \qquad (4)$$

and hence with equation (2)

$$pp_{ijt} = a_{ijt} \cdot [r_{ijt} \cdot p_{jt} + (1 - r_{ijt}) \cdot pp_{ij(t-1)}] + (1 - a_{ijt}) \cdot pp_{ij(t-1)}. \qquad (5)$$

which simplifies to

$$pp_{ijt} = r_{ijt} \cdot a_{ijt} \cdot (p_{jt} - pp_{ij(t-1)}) + pp_{ij(t-1)}. \qquad (6)$$

Equation (6) displays the relation between voter i's perceptions of party j's policy position at time t-1 and t. If party j does not shift its policy position away from voter i's perceived position $pp_{ij(t-1)}$, the two perceived positions are identical. In this case, the reception and acceptance of party policy shifts are redundant. If, however, party j moves away from the position initially observed by voter i, the perception of this party policy shift hinges on its reception r_{ijt} and acceptance a_{ijt}. Only if both factors are equal to 1, voter i's perception of party j's policy position is identical to the party's intended policy position p_{jt}.

From equation (6), we can derive

> Axiom 1: Voters' perception of party position shifts is a two-stage process of (i) receiving and (ii) accepting a party's policy shifts. Voters who do not receive or accept a party's shift message continue to locate the party at its previously perceived policy position.

Voters' reception and acceptance and vote choices

I argue that parties face voters with varying abilities and willingness to receive and to accept announced policy position shifts. As a result, the party's intended policy position p_{jt} is not necessarily equal to the voters' perceived position of party j at time t. Voters base their vote choice on available information (i.e. on the perceived and accepted policy position) instead of the party's intended policy position. Hence, voter i's utility for voting for party j is given by

$$U_{ijt}(pp_{ijt}) = -(v_i - pp_{ijt})^2 + \varepsilon_{ijt} \tag{7}$$

To study the effect of party position shifts on voter i's utility of party j (and hence, voter i's vote choice), compare the utility of the perceived party positions at t-1 and t. Using the equations (6) and (7), some maths reveals that

$$U_{ijt}(pp_{ijt}) = -(v_i - pp_{ijt})^2 + \varepsilon_{ijt}$$

$$= -(v_i - (r_{ijt} \cdot a_{ijt} \cdot (p_{jt} - pp_{ij(t-1)}) + pp_{ij(t-1)}))^2 + \varepsilon_{ijt}$$

$$= -(v_i - pp_{ij(t-1)})^2 + r_{ijt} \cdot a_{ijt} \cdot (p_{jt} - pp_{ij(t-1)}) \cdot [(v_i - pp_{ij(t-1)}) + (v_i - pp_{ijt})] + \varepsilon_{ijt}$$

$$= U_{ijt}(pp_{ij(t-1)}) + r_{ijt} \cdot a_{ijt} \cdot (p_{jt} - pp_{ij(t-1)}) \cdot [(v_i - pp_{ij(t-1)}) + (v_i - pp_{ijt})] \tag{8}$$

The second addend of the right-hand equation contains information about when voters are indifferent between the two perceived party positions at t-1 and time t. The utilities derived from the perceived party positions are equal if

1. voter i's reception r_{ijt} of party j's policy shift equals zero,
2. voter i's acceptance a_{ijt} of party j's policy shift equals zero,

3. party j chooses a policy platform p_{jt} similar to voter i's perception at t-1, or if

4. the two perceptions are equidistant mirror images left and right of voter i's policy position v_i.

For which of these conditions is voter i's vote choice based on biased information? And when do party policy shifts lead to 'inappropriate' vote choices in the sense that voters do not vote for the party maximising their utility? Turning to the first question, only condition 3 is unproblematic: if party j's policy position at time t equals voter i's perception $pp_{ij(t-1)}$, voter i's utility is unbiased in the sense that voter i's utility is based on party j's official policy position. For all other cases, however, not perceiving party j's policy shift leads to biased expectations because party j's official policy position does not correspond to voter i's expectation. The reasons are manifold. Voter i may not receive (condition 1) or accept (condition 2) party j's policy shift. As a consequence, the perception of party j's policy position does not change although party j moves its policy position away from $pp_{ij(t-1)}$. Alternatively, voter i may perceive a policy shift from t-1 to t but constraints on the voter's reception or acceptance lead to a biased perceived policy position pp_{ijt} not identical with the party's official policy position p_{jt}. As a consequence, voter i perceives party j's policy positions at t-1 and t as equidistant although party j's official position p_{jt} does not match with voter i's perception (condition 4).

The misperceived party policy position has severe consequences for the accountability of parties *vis-à-vis* voters. Party platforms differing from the corresponding voter perceptions create dissent on a party's mandate (Manin et al. 1999; Stokes 1999), thus complicating the evaluation of party policies. Clearly, voters are still able to 'throw the rascals out' (Riker 1982) if parties do not fulfil the voters' expectations. Yet, the parties may have outlined their policy plans beforehand but voters just may not have perceived this message. Hence, party policy shifts not perceived by voters may have negative consequences such as (1) dissatisfaction with the vote choice, (2) low popularity scores of government, parties and politicians, (3) decreasing satisfaction and trust in political parties and, as a consequence, party democracy, and (4) high turnover rates in government and parliament.

Moreover, misperceived party policy shifts also affect vote choices. A voter not perceiving changes in party policy platforms may vote a party that does not maximize his or her utility. Assume for a moment a very simple party environment: all parties except party j stick to their policy platforms held at t-1. Furthermore, assume that voter i's perception of party j's policy platform at t-1 was correct so that $p_{j(t-1)}$ equals $pp_{ij(t-1)}$. If party j turns away from voter i's policy preferences, not perceiving the policy shift is most severe if voter i voted for party j at t-1. Assuming that at t-1 party j was the best policy option for voter i, not perceiving the policy shift away from personal preferences may lead voter i to continue voting for party j although competing parties may offer policy platforms closer to the voter's preferences. In other words, voter i continues to vote for party j although better options may exist. In a similar manner, not perceiving shifts towards voter i's policy preferences may also affect vote choice if voter i did not vote for party j at t-1. In this case, party j responds to the policy preferences of voter i and shifts its policy platform closer to the voter's policy preferences. If voter i does not perceive this policy shift, the vote choice is still based on information of party j's policy platform at t-1. In the worst case, voter i does not maximise his or her utility by voting for an inappropriate party with policy preferences further away from the voter's policy preference v_i.

In sum, not perceiving party policy shifts has severe consequences for voters. Because party policy positions and the corresponding voter perceptions do not match, the link connecting voters and parties is weakened. In such situations voters are inclined to think that parties have not observed their mandate as the parties' record in parliament and government does not correspond to the voters' initial expectations. Thus, the perception of party policy shifts is crucial for optimal vote choices on policy grounds. Not perceiving party policy shifts may lead voters to vote for parties which no longer represent their best policy choice. All these issues would merit further attention. Yet, this book concentrates on parties and their reactions to the voters' reception and acceptance of party policy shifts. I hence leave the implications of the (mis-)perception of party policy shifts for voter attitudes and their systematic effects for future research.

Party reactions to the voters' reception and acceptance

So far, I have focused on voters and the consequences the perception of party policy shifts has on vote choices and the evaluation of individual parties and system effects. I now turn to political parties and their reactions to the voters' reception and acceptance of party policy shifts. In what way are parties constrained by voters being uninformed or critical towards the policy shifts of their parties? Under which circumstances are parties most likely to shift their policy positions? And when do they refrain from doing so?

I argue that parties are mainly maximising their expected vote share. In politics, votes are the currency for bargaining power in parliament, government participation, and the distribution of offices among cabinet parties. In other words, office and policy chances of parties are based on their electoral strength. Therefore, parties first and foremost aim to win as many votes as possible. As we will see later on, policy motivations enter into the model in two different ways. First, it is argued that voters form policy 'images' of party positions and these expectations on where parties should locate relative to their competitors affect the parties' policy behaviour (see Chapter Five). Second, party members are primarily interested in policy goals. While party leaders may be driven by their ambition for cabinet office or other perks of office, the party's rank and file is primarily interested in policy gains resulting from governmental and parliamentary decision-making. Party leaders have to take the policy concerns of their voters and members into account (see Chapter Eight). However, in my model party leaders do not value 'policy as an end in itself' (Laver and Schofield 1998: 45).

When do parties shift their policy platforms? Provided that parties aim at maximising their vote share, in a time perspective this means that they try to (1) keep their present voters and (2) attract new ones who did not vote for the party in the last election. On policy grounds, parties attract new voters by shifting their policy positions closer to the voters' policy preferences. If voters do not receive or accept a party's policy shift, they continue to locate the party at the perceived position at t-1. Hence, a party policy shifts brings no benefit at all. On the contrary, shifting the party's platform is costly. Just as changes in institutions and rules, moves away from the policy status quo involve costs. This is partly due to organisational constraints (Walgrave and Nuytemans 2009: 193). Election programs and deviations from past positions need approval by party conventions or other intra-party decision-making bodies. For this process, time for deliberation and decision-making is required. In other words, parties suffer from transaction costs (Kreps 1990: 743; Lupia and Strøm 2008: 60) when shifting policy positions. Of course, these decision-making costs differ across parties. The parties' size, the number of intra-party factions and official party bodies and the decision rules for making such policy shifts determine to what extent parties are able to change their policy positions. Put differently, the combination of the number and preferences of intra-party veto players (Tsebelis 2002) and the decision rules determine the degree of policy stability. These factors alone may not be sufficient to explain stability or changes of party policy positions. Party leaders may also depend on the good will of a party's rank-and-file as providers of voluntary labour and finance (see Chapter Eight). Notwithstanding these inter-party differences, all parties suffer from some costs when shifting policy positions. I use a simple cost-benefit argument stating that parties only shift their policy positions if the benefits (i.e. the vote gains) outweigh the costs involved. In other words, parties only move away from the status quo if potential new voters are expected to perceive party policy shifts.

For a better understanding, I next present a simplified version of the model, studying one party while holding its competitors' and the voters' policy positions constant. Subsequently, these assumptions are relaxed providing a more general model.

Holding competitors' and voters' positions constant

To keep the argument as simple as possible, assume that all parties, except for party j, keep their policy positions constant. Further, assume for a moment that all voters do not shift their policy positions over time. All else being equal, party j's decision to shift its policy platform hinges on the question whether a shift increases its vote share in the next general election. Table 4.1 classifies four voter groups that are necessary to distinguish when making this decision.

First, it is necessary to distinguish between party j's voters at t-1 and the remaining electorate. Because the voters' and the competitors' policy preferences are held constant, the first group involves the voters party j keeps when sticking to its policy position. The latter group contains the share of the electorate which party j can attract by shifting its policy position. Now think of any desired policy position p_{jt} being different from voter i's perception of party j's platform $pp_{ij(t-1)}$ at time t-1. We can identify two groups of voters: those for which the party's new policy position is closer to the personal preferences and those who gain a higher utility from party j's perceived position at t-1.

Table 4.1 combines the two categories creating four voter groups. Those voters who voted for party j in the previous election may be divided in two groups distinguishing whether party j shifts its policy position towards (group 1) or away from (group 2) voters' preferences. If voters and competing parties stick to their previous policy positions, voters belonging to group 1 are *safe voters*: they voted for party j before, and party j's policy shift is favourable to its pre-shift position. In contrast, the party policy shift leaves voters in group 2 worse off so that voters belonging to this group are *potential vote losses* for party j. As *potential new voters*, we can further identify those voters who did not vote for party j in the last election but for which the party policy shift puts party j's policy position closer to personal preferences (group 3). Finally, group 4 covers voters who did not vote for party j in the last election and who are worse off by its policy shift compared to the previous party policy position. Because the party shifts its policy position further away from these voters' preferences, I label this group *unattractive voters*.

Table 4.1: Voters and potential voters of party j (holding competitors' policy positions constant)

	Party policy shift towards voters' policy preferences	Party policy shift away from voters' policy preferences
Party j's voters at t-1	Group 1: Safe voters	Group 2: Potential vote losses
Voters not voting for party j at t-1	Group 3: Potential new voters	Group 4: Unattractive voters

With voters and competing parties sticking to their policy preferences, party j's strategy is straightforward: it aims at winning new voters while keeping old ones. Concerning the former, potential new voters belong to group 3. Therefore, party j has to make sure that these voters perceive its policy shift. In the simplified version with constant policy preferences of competing parties and voters, group 4 is unattractive for party j. They did not vote for party j before and will not change their decision given the direction of party j's policy shift. In contrast, party j can count on those voters in group 1 because these voted for party j before and they benefit from the party's policy shift. Hence, party j can concentrate on the potential vote losses in group 2. The situation is best, of course, if voters in group 2 *do not* perceive the party shift away from their policy preferences.

When does party j shift its policy position? Using the simplified setting presented in Table 4.1, it keeps the 'safe voters' in group 1 and never reaches those in group 4. The two target groups are therefore the voters in groups 2 and 3. Because parties only shift policy positions if shifts are expected to increase their vote share, a necessary condition for vote gains is that voters in the target group (group 3) perceive their policy shift. Hence, the parties' abilities, in general, increase with the voters' increasing reception and acceptance. Ideally, parties also want voters in group 2 who do not perceive the shift away from their own preferences. In this case, party j may profit from winning new votes in group 3 while avoiding vote losses in group 2. Such a scenario is indeed possible if reception and acceptance vary across voters. In that case, the parties' abilities for position shifts only increase with the voters' reception and acceptance in group 3. Specifically, parties benefit from voters with higher degrees of reception and acceptance *if* the party shifts its policy position towards their policy preferences. Next, I disentangle the perception effects.

I stick to the simplified version presented in Table 4.1 assuming that voters and competing parties have fixed policy positions and that party j is the sole actor moving its policy platform. Further, the focus is on the voters' reception of party j's policy shift. Let, therefore, the acceptance of party policy shifts only vary across groups. In other words, the acceptance a_{ijt} is the same for voters within the four voter groups displayed in Table 4.1. In formulas,

$$a_{jlt} = a_{ijt} \text{ for all } i \in \text{group } l \tag{9}$$

Further, assuming that the perceived party policy position $pp_{ij(t-1)}$ of party j at time t-1 is identical in group l

$$pp_{jl(t-1)} = pp_{ij(t-1)} \text{ for all } i \in \text{group } l, \tag{10}$$

the mean perceived policy position of party j in group l is given by

$$pp_{jlt} = \frac{1}{n_l} \sum_{i=1}^{n_l} pp_{ijt} = \frac{1}{n_l} \sum_{i=1}^{n_l} r_{ijt} \cdot a_{ijt} \cdot \left(p_{jt} - pp_{ij(t-1)} \right) + pp_{ij(t-1)}$$

$$= \frac{1}{n_l} \sum_{i=1}^{n_l} \left(r_{ijt} \cdot a_{ijt} \cdot p_{jt} \right) - \frac{1}{n_l} \sum_{i=1}^{n_l} \left(r_{ijt} \cdot a_{ijt} \cdot pp_{ij(t-1)} \right) + \frac{1}{n_l} \sum_{i=1}^{n_l} \left(pp_{ij(t-1)} \right)$$

$$= a_{jlt} \cdot p_{jt} \cdot \frac{1}{n_l} \sum_{i=1}^{n_l} \left(r_{ijt} \right) - a_{jlt} \cdot pp_{jl(t-1)} \cdot \frac{1}{n_l} \sum_{i=1}^{n_l} \left(r_{ijt} \right) + pp_{jl(t-1)}$$

$$= a_{jlt} \cdot p_{jt} \cdot r_{jlt} - a_{jlt} \cdot pp_{jl(t-1)} \cdot r_{jlt} + pp_{jl(t-1)}$$

$$= r_{jlt} \cdot a_{jlt} \cdot \left(p_{jt} - pp_{jl(t-1)} \right) + pp_{jl(t-1)}$$

$$r_{jlt} = \frac{1}{n_l} \sum_{i=1}^{n_l} r_{ijt}$$

Equation (11) shows that party j's mean perceived position of voters in group l depends on the mean reception r_{jlt} and acceptance a_{jlt}. Keeping the acceptance constant, the higher the mean reception r_{jlt}, the more voters perceive party j's policy shift. Referring to the different groups in Table 4.1, party j focuses on the target groups 2 and 3. Party j is likely to keep its voters and win new ones simultaneously if r_{j2t} is small and r_{j3t} is large. In other words, party j benefits most if its previous voters do not receive the shift moving away from their personal preferences, while potential new voters do receive party j's shift message.

If the reception does not vary across voters, the reception r_{jt} of party policy shifts is a necessary condition for parties to shift their policy positions: party j only shifts its policy position if shifts result in an increase of its vote share. Potential new voters in group 3 only receive the party policy shift if the reception r_{jt} is high. Because the reception is constant for all voters i, party j cannot hope for unaware voters in group 2. Hence, it is only able to shift its policy position if the electorate, in general, is able to receive the shift message. If the reception is low, party j sticks to its policy position.

In a similar manner, we can study the effect of the voters' acceptance on the perception of party policy shifts. As above, I assume that the perceived party position $pp_{ij(t-1)}$ at time t-1 only varies across groups but is constant within the four groups in Table 4.1. But now we are interested in the effect of the voters' acceptance a_{ijt} of party j's policy shift. Therefore, I set the reception r_{ijt} to be the same for all voters within group l. A calculation similar to equation (11) reveals that

$$pp_{jlt} = \frac{1}{n_l}\sum_{i=1}^{n_l} pp_{ijt} = \frac{1}{n_l}\sum_{i=1}^{n_l} r_{ijt} \cdot a_{ijt} \cdot \left(p_{jt} - pp_{ij(t-1)}\right) + pp_{ij(t-1)}$$

$$= \frac{1}{n_l}\sum_{i=1}^{n_l}\left(r_{ijt} \cdot a_{ijt} \cdot p_{jt}\right) - \frac{1}{n_l}\sum_{i=1}^{n_l}\left(r_{ijt} \cdot a_{ijt} \cdot pp_{ij(t-1)}\right) + \frac{1}{n_l}\sum_{i=1}^{n_l}\left(pp_{ij(t-1)}\right)$$

$$= r_{jlt} \cdot p_{jt} \cdot \frac{1}{n_l}\sum_{i=1}^{n_l}\left(a_{ijt}\right) - r_{jlt} \cdot pp_{jl(t-1)} \cdot \frac{1}{n_l}\sum_{i=1}^{n_l}\left(a_{ijt}\right) + pp_{jl(t-1)}$$

$$= r_{jlt} \cdot p_{jt} \cdot a_{jlt} - r_{jlt} \cdot pp_{jl(t-1)} \cdot a_{jlt} + pp_{jl(t-1)}$$

$$= r_{jlt} \cdot a_{jlt} \cdot \left(p_{jt} - pp_{jl(t-1)}\right) + pp_{jl(t-1)}$$

As can be seen from equation (13) the result is similar to equation (11). Holding the reception constant across groups studying the acceptance of policy shifts hence reveals the same implications as for the reception of party policy shifts. Recall that party j is mainly interested in the potential vote losses (group 2) and potential gains of new voters (group 3). Party j is most likely to shift its policy position if potential new voters (group 3) accept the party's policy shift towards their position while voters disadvantaged by the shift (group 2) do not accept it. Therefore, party j is most likely to shift its policy platform if a_{j2t} is small and a_{j3t} is large. The larger the difference between both groups, the more likely the policy shift.

In case the acceptance does not differ across voters (and therefore, across voter groups), the acceptance of party policy shifts of party j is given by a_{jt}. Again, the acceptance of party policy shifts is a necessary condition for party j to shift its position so that party j only shifts its policy position if its acceptance is high.

For the perception of party policy shifts, we can thus summarise

> Axiom 2: The parties' abilities to shift their policy platforms increase with the voters' reception and acceptance of party position shifts.
> If the reception and acceptance varies across voters, parties benefit most if voters perceive party policy shifts towards their personal preferences while voters being worse off under the new policies no not perceive the policy shift. The larger the share of voters benefiting from a party's platform change, the more the party wants the voters to perceive its policy shift.

A dynamic model: party position shifts of all parties

So far, I assumed that party j is the only actor shifting policy positions. The competing parties stick to their respective policy position. How does the model change when we relax this assumption allowing all parties to shift their policy positions? As one might expect, the situation gets less comfortable for party j: so far, party j enjoyed the mover advantage and could therefore act in a relatively simple competitive environment. As illustrated in Table 4.1, party j could count on a share of safe voters (group 1) who voted for party j before and who benefited from the party's policy shift. Group 4 consisted of unattractive voters, that means, voters who cast a ballot for another party and for whom the policy shift puts the party's platform further away from their own preferences. Party j could therefore concentrate on two target groups: party voters who are disadvantaged by the party's policy shift and those potential new voters who would benefit from party j's position shift.

The implications change once competing parties start to shift. Although the characterisation of the groups 2 (potential vote losses) and 3 (potential vote gains) still holds, there are no longer safe voters (group 1) or voters unappealing for party j (group 4). Rather, party j has to consider all four voter groups. The new situation is shown in Table 4.2. As can be seen, party j is worried about potential losses from all voters in the previous election. The situation is known for the voters in group 2 because party j *abandons* those voters by shifting away from their personal policy preferences. But the so-far safe voters are also at risk because competing parties may attract these voters by shifting in their direction. Although party j shifts its policy position towards these voters' preferences, the voters belonging to this group may, nevertheless, become *disloyal* to party j by voting for one of the competing parties.

The situation is also more complex for potential new voters of party j. So far, party j concentrated on voters who might be attracted by the party policy shift and group 3 remains the *target* for party j, even when other parties also shift their positions. Yet, under the new conditions even group 4 is no longer unattractive for party j. Although it shifts away from these voters (who voted for another party before), they nevertheless may vote for party j in the next election. That might occur when a party shifts its policy position away from these voters' preferences (i.e. these voters belong to group 2 of another party j' ≠ j). Because all political parties abandon these voters, I label this voter group *orphan voters*. Although these voters are potential new voters for party j, their vote choice leaves them worse off compared to the previous election.

Table 4.2: Voters and potential voters of party j (shifting competitors)

	Party policy shift towards voters' policy preferences	Party policy shift away from voters' policy preferences
Party j's voters at t-1	Group 1: Potential vote losses (disloyal)	Group 2: Potential vote losses (abandoned)
Voters not voting for party j at t-1	Group 3: Potential new voters (target)	Group 4: Potential new voters (orphans)

How does this new situation affect party policy shifts? Although the competitive environment is more complex when rival parties also shift their policy positions, party j still has an incentive to emphasise policy shifts towards the voters' preferences (groups 1 and 3) while masking its shifts away from the preferences of other voters (groups 2 and 4). Using the notation introduced above, party j profits most if r_{j1t} and r_{j3t} are large while r_{j2t} and r_{j4t} are small. The same holds for the acceptance parameters a_{jlt}. Although the choice may be more complex when rival parties shift as well, the general idea remains the same: parties benefit from voters receiving and accepting policy shifts towards their policy preferences. To the same extent, parties want voters being worse off by the platform shift not to perceive the position change. In other words, parties only benefit from the voters' reception and acceptance if the policy shift is towards their policy preferences. The larger the share of voters benefiting from a party's position shift, the more the party wants the electorate to receive and to accept its platform change.

If the reception and acceptance does not differ across voters and voter groups, higher reception and acceptance give parties the capacity to shift their policy positions. In other words, the parties' leeway for policy shifts is larger. Although the competitive environment may not allow party j to increase its vote share, position shifts may help by minimising vote losses.[2] Hence, Axiom 2 still holds.

---

2.   This situation could not occur in the simplified version holding the rival parties' policy positions

Voter position shifts and their effects on party position shifts

I now turn to the effect of voter position shifts and their effects on party position shifts. So far, voters are constrained to stick to their policy positions. I now relax this assumption, studying the implications of voter position shifts on the parties' incentives to shift their policy platforms.

Consider again the situation of party j. We can subdivide party j's electorate in the previous election t-1 into voters shifting towards the party's perceived position $pp_{ij(t-1)}$ and those moving away from it. To hold previous voters who are shifting towards party j's policy position, no policy shifts are necessary. If voters who voted for party j in the previous election shift away from the perceived party policy position $pp_{ij(t-1)}$, party j has an incentive to follow these voter shifts to hold the voters. Whether to hold voters who are shifting towards the party's position or to follow previous voters who are moving away from the party's perceived position, hence, depends on the *size* of the respective groups. If the number of party voters shifting away from the party's perceived position exceeds the number of voters shifting towards the party's policy platform, party j has an incentive to shift its policy position following its voters' position shift.

In a similar vein, we can distinguish voter position shifts of the remaining electorate. Party j's strategy for winning new voters also depends on the direction of voter policy shifts. Hence, we may subdivide the remaining electorate (i.e. those voters who did not cast a ballot for party j at t-1) into those voters shifting their policy positions closer to the party's perceived policy position, and those shifting away from it. While party j has no incentive to shift to convince the former, party position shifts are in place to hunt for potential voters whose preferences move away from the party's platform. A strategy for winning new voters again depends on the relative size of the relevant groups. If a majority of voters shifts towards party j's platform, party policy shifts are not necessary. If, in contrast, the majority of voters shift away from the party position, party j may aim at following the voters' position shifts.

For the ease of interpretation, I follow Adams and colleagues (2004) distinguishing 'benign' and 'harmful' shifts in public opinion. Harmful public opinion shifts are characterised by shifts of the mean voter away from a party's policy position. Benign shifts, in contrast, are in the direction of the party's policy position (Adams *et al.* 2004: 598). Using this notation for the two voter groups discussed above, we can tabulate harmful and benign shifts for party j's voters (at t-1) and potential future voters. The combinations and the resulting incentives for party policy shifts are shown in Table 4.3.

Depending on the direction of position shifts of former party voters and potential new voters, parties are more or less interested in the perception of their policy position shifts. If both voter groups shift towards party j's perceived policy

constant. With competing parties shifting their policy positions, party j may find itself in a situation where vote losses are inevitable. Nevertheless, policy shifts may help to minimise these losses.

Table 4.3: Voter position shifts and incentives for party policy change

	Benign shift of party voters at t-1	Harmful shift of party voters at t-1
Benign shift of potential voters at t-1	No incentive for party position shift	For party voters (t-1): High perception For remaining voters: Low perception
Harmful shift of potential voters at t-1	For party voters (t-1): Low perception For remaining voters: High perception	Both groups shift in same direction: High perception (all voters) If not: ambiguous

position, party j has no incentive to shifts its policy position. Consequently, the voters' reception and acceptance should not affect the party's behaviour. The situation is different if potential new voters shift towards party j's policy position while its former voters move away from the party's perceived policy position at t-1. In this case, party j faces two (contradicting) incentives. To hold its voters, party j should follow the harmful public opinion shift. Yet, at the same time, party j should stay put to attract potential new voters who shifted towards its policy position. For the perception of party policy shifts, the consequences are two-fold. First, party j is interested in the perception of its policy shift by its former voters who the party is trailing. At the same time, party j is not interested in the perception of its position shifts by potential new voters attracted by its policy position at t-1. Hence, party j's policy shifts are most likely if the perception of party voters is high while potential voters are not likely to perceive the party's position shift.

The party's strategic challenges are in many ways similar if party j's voters shift towards its policy platform while potential new voters shift their policy positions away from it. Party j wants its potential new voters to perceive its party policy shift following them. At the same time, the present voters should not perceive shifts away from the party policy platform. Hence, party position shifts are most likely if the perception of party j's shift is low for party voters at t-1 while being high for potential new voters moving away from party j's perceived platform.

Finally, it may occur that both party j's voters at t-1 and potential new voters move from the party's perceived party position at t-1. In this case, party j has a high incentive to follow these harmful public opinion shifts. In case party voters and potential new voters shift in the same direction, party j benefits from the perception of a policy shift following both voter groups. In other words, party position shifts are most likely if the perception is high among both groups. The situation is different if both groups move away from the party's policy position but in different directions. To take an example, think of the majority of party j's voters placed left of their perceived policy position of party j. Furthermore, the majority of potential new voters hold policy preferences right of their perceived policy position of party j. If party j's present voters shift to the left while potential new voters shift to the right, both groups move away from party j's policy position. It is an open question what party j's incentives are in an unlikely situation like this.[3] Without further assumptions (e.g. on the size of the two groups) forming expectations is rather difficult. Party j could follow its party voters at t-1 counting on the low reception of potential new voters. Similarly, party j could hunt for new voters on the right relying on the low perception of party voters who shifted to the left. It is also reasonable to argue that party j reacts to the contradicting incentives by staying put. Hence, I do not formulate a specific expectation.

In sum, voter position shifts affect the parties' incentives for party policy shifts. Voter shifts towards the parties' perceived position (i.e. benign public opinion shifts) decrease the incentives for moving away from the platform. In contrast, harmful shifts in public shifting away from the parties' perceived policy positions increase the incentives for party policy shifts. Concerning the perception of party policy shifts, parties benefit from (1) voters shifting towards the party's policy position not perceiving party shifts away from it and (2) voters moving away from the party's policy position perceiving the party's shift following them. Distinguishing these two groups for former party voters and potential new voters (see Table 4.3), parties face different incentives for platform changes. Summarising the arguments presented above, I postulate

> Axiom 3: Party policy shifts are most likely if the perception of voters shifting towards the party's perceived platform is low, while the voters moving away from the party's position receive and accept the party shift trailing their own opinion shift.

Summary

This chapter presented the theoretical model which provides the basis for the analyses presented in the Chapters Six and Seven. While standard spatial models treat elections in isolation, I argue that focusing on the challenges of relocation over time reveals important insights into the dynamics of party systems. According to the model presented here, voters have to receive and accept parties' shift messages so that party policy shifts are much more complicated than established spatial models suggest.

Following Zaller (1992), it is argued that the perception of party policy shifts is a two-stage process. First, voters have to receive the party's policy shift. If voters

---

3. In the sample of ten West European countries used for the empirical analysis (see Chapter Seven) public opinion shifts of both groups, moving away from a party's platform in different directions, only occur in 6 out of 196 cases.

are not aware of the parties' actions or if parties do not broadcast the shifts of their policy platforms, voters do not perceive the party position shifts and hence the vote choice is based on outdated perceptions of policy platforms. Second, voters receiving the party policy shifts are not forced to accept (i.e. consider credible) the proposed policy positions. While the reception of party shifts is a cognitive process, the acceptance step is a political one, related to trust and other feelings towards parties and their leaders. Put differently, voters have to believe in the party's policy turn.

I present a simple spatial model defining voter utility functions as the negative of the squared distances between voter positions and the voters' individual perceptions of party policy positions. To keep the model as simple as possible, the analysis is restricted to a one-dimensional policy space. Another assumption is that parties are first and foremost interested in maximising their vote share. Hence, they shift their policy platforms only if this shift from the status quo leaves the party better off. However, because party policy shifts involve costs, parties refrain from implementing them if they do not expect a net benefit. In that sense, voters not receiving or accepting party position shifts constrain party policy options.

I postulate two axioms on the effect of reception and acceptance on voters (Axiom 1) and political parties (Axiom 2). Furthermore, I present the effects of public opinion shifts on the parties' incentives and their ability for party position shifts (Axiom 3). Axiom 1 states that the perception of party policy shifts is a two-stage process of (1) receiving and (2) accepting the party's new policy position. If one of the two steps fails, then voters stick to their previously perceived policy position of the respective party. I hint at potential consequences of non-perception on the trust in institutions, elites, and political parties, as well as its meaning for the delegation of powers in democratic regimes. Yet, my main interest lies in the parties' reactions to the challenges of voters' reception and acceptance. Axiom 2 states the expectations for the reception and the acceptance of party policy shifts. It postulates that parties benefit from higher reception and acceptance of their policy shifts. If the reception and acceptance varies across voters, parties may furthermore profit from varying reception and acceptance in the electorate. Parties benefit most if voters receive and accept party policy shifts towards their personal preferences, while those being worse off by the policy shift ignore or reject the move away from their personal preferences. In this case, the positive effect of the voters' perception only holds for voters being better off by the party's policy shift.

Finally, I study the effects of public opinion shifts on the incentives for party position shifts. Distinguishing benign (i.e. shifts towards) and harmful (i.e. shifts away from the party's policy position) voter shifts, it is argued that parties have incentives to shift their platform in the latter but not in the former case. Parties benefit most if voters perceive party shifts following voter position shifts. At the same time, parties also benefit from low reception and acceptance of their policy shifts by voters who, in turn, shift towards the party's pre-shift position. Effects of the reception and acceptance of party policy shifts hence hinge on the parties' incentives for policy shifts indicated by changing preferences of present and potential new voters.

Chapter Five is dedicated to the covariates affecting the reception and acceptance of party position shifts. So far, the reception and acceptance of party policy shifts are rather abstract and not measurable as such. In the next chapter, we turn to specific covariates that increase or decrease the probability of receiving and accepting the parties' policy shifts. I formulate hypotheses how these covariates affect the voters' perception of party policy shifts and the parties' reactions. The subsequent empirical chapters test these expectations at the voter (Chapter Six) and the party level (Chapter Seven).

This chapter breathes life into the previously introduced model of party policy shifts. So far, the discussion focused on two concepts, the voters' reception and acceptance of party policy shifts, which are neither directly observable nor measurable. For that reason, I posited axioms rather than hypotheses. They explicate expectations of how voters receive and accept party policy shifts and how these perceptions affect the parties' abilities to shift policy platforms. This chapter adds more flesh to these bones, discussing factors expected to affect the voters' reception and acceptance. These covariates provide observable implications of the theory stated above (King *et al.*1994): I argue that these covariates impact on the reception and acceptance of party policy shifts and test their overall effect on the voters' perception of party policy shifts. Moreover, the covariates affecting voters' perception of party policy shifts also affect the parties' abilities to shift their policy positions. The main goal of this chapter hence is to derive testable predictions for voters and parties.

I start with presenting covariates expected to affect the voters' reception of party policy shifts. As mentioned earlier, the reception of party policy shifts is a cognitive process. Hence, the covariates need to include factors measuring the voters' ability to receive party policy shifts and factors measuring the complexity of the political market. Drawing on the axioms presented in the previous chapter, I derive hypotheses about how these factors impact on voters' reception and the parties' reactions to it.[1] In contrast to their reception, the acceptance of party policy shifts is a political matter. As a result, factors measuring the parties' persuasiveness and the voters' willingness to believe in parties' messages play a role here. These factors also lead to hypotheses on the consequences for parties when changing their policy platforms.

Impacts on the reception of party position shifts

In total, I identify six factors that affect the reception of party policy shifts. Three of them are voter-specific. First, it is argued that voters' political awareness affects the reception of party policy shifts. Drawing on Zaller (1992), the reception of political messages should be more likely if a respondent's political awareness is high. Second and related, I use a similar argument stating that the voters' level of education affects the reception of shifts in the party policy platform. Third, voter position shifts should lead voters to update their information on party platforms. Voters shifting their policy positions update the information about the appropriate

---

1. For simplicity, I use the capital letters V for voter-specific and P for party-specific hypotheses.

party choice. Hence, the reception should be more likely if voters move away from prior policy positions.

In addition, party and party system-specific factors affect voters' reception of party policy shifts. I differentiate between different levels of media exposure. While some parties enjoy a higher level of media coverage, other parties do not. Simply put, increased media attention should make the reception of party policy shifts more likely. Furthermore, the complexity of the political market affects the voters' reception of party position shifts. Two-party systems are less complex than multi-party ones with more 'relevant' parties. All else equal, the higher the complexity of the party system, the less likely voters are to receive parties' shift messages. Finally, it is argued that the magnitude of the party policy shifts affects their reception. Incremental changes are less likely to be perceived. In contrast, large policy position shifts cause a stir in the public, improving the chances of the policy shift's reception. Next, I present all these arguments in greater detail and formulate hypotheses for the voters' reception and how the parties, in turn, react to the voters' behaviour.

Political awareness

Zaller defines political awareness as 'the extent to which an individual pays attention to politics *and* understands what he or she has encountered' (Zaller 1992: 21, emphasis in the original). In other words, political awareness captures whether voters are informed and comprehend political information. Therefore, awareness captures more than pure interest. Following Zaller, political awareness increases the probability that respondents receive political messages. In Zaller's own words, the reception axiom states that 'the greater a person's level of cognitive engagement with an issue, the more likely he or she is to be exposed to and comprehend – in a word, to receive – political messages concerning this issue' (Zaller 1992: 42). I argue that his argument is also applicable to party position shifts. Parties shifting their policy position spread political messages and political awareness increases the probability that voters receive these messages.

For voters, the implications of political awareness are straightforward: the higher their political awareness, the higher the likelihood of receiving party policy shifts. All else being equal, higher reception increases the probability of perceiving party policy shifts. Hence, I formulate

> Hypothesis V1: The higher a voter's political awareness, the more likely is the perception of party policy shifts.

Evaluating the effect of political awareness for political parties is slightly more complex. The reception of party policy shifts is a necessary condition for voters to perceive party policy shifts. Without perception of policy shifts, parties would shift their policy platform without being heard. But because shifts involve costs, parties refrain from shifting their platforms without a chance of attracting new voters. This leads to

Hypothesis P1a: The higher voters' mean political awareness, the more likely are shifts of parties' policy positions.

In fact, Axiom 2 states that parties benefit most from voters receiving party policy shifts towards their personal policy preferences. Yet, the situation is even better if voters do not receive the party's policy shift away from their preferences. The larger the share of voters benefiting from the party's policy shift, the higher is the party's incentive that voters perceive its platform change. Attracting voters, parties should therefore build on aware voters if the policy shift is towards the majority of the voters' preferences. In contrast, political awareness does not motivate parties to shift their policy positions and move away from the majority of the voters' preferences. Hence, the slightly more detailed hypothesis reads as follows:

Hypothesis P1b: The higher the voters' mean political awareness, the more likely parties shift their policy positions if the party shifts its platform towards the majority of the voters' policy preferences. In contrast, political awareness does not motivate party position shifts away from the majority of the voters' preferences.

Education

Similar to political awareness, I argue that voters' level of education affects the reception of policy shifts. The argument is connected to costs of information considerations going back to Downs (see also Alvarez and Brehm 2002: 33; Downs 1957: 208–210). Downs argues that obtaining information entails costs. He distinguishes two kinds of information costs: transferable and non-transferable information costs. While voters may transfer some of the information costs to elites or the mass media, other costs are non-transferable: selecting data sources, updating information, and using information to make a decision are payable by the voters themselves. Information costs are, however, not distributed equally in a democratic society (Alvarez and Brehm 2002: 33). Voters with higher costs of obtaining information are less likely to acquire it. Hence, voters with higher information costs face higher uncertainty. Voter uncertainty and information costs have been subject to various studies of public opinion and electoral behaviour (Alvarez 1997; Alvarez and Brehm 2002; Alvarez and Franklin 1994; Bartels 1986). Studying the uncertainty of voters in placing presidential candidates, for example, Alvarez (1997: 94) argues that voters with higher information costs are more uncertain about the candidates' policy positions. I make a similar argument here: voters with higher information costs are more uncertain about parties' behaviour. Hence, they are less likely to receive information about party policy shifts.

Information costs may be measured in different ways. Most commonly, researchers use data on voters' political awareness and education. As the former was discussed before, I can focus on the level of education as an indicator for varying information costs. In line with previous research, it is argued that more highly educated individuals have a greater ability to acquire information so that their information costs are lower. Therefore, education should increase the probability of receiving party policy shifts. As a consequence, the perception of party policy shifts increases. Therefore, I state

Hypothesis V2: The higher a voter's level of education, the more likely is the perception of party policy shifts.

Turning to the effect of voters' education on the policy shifts of political parties, we can make the same general argument as for political awareness: party position shifts involve costs and parties only take this burden if the benefits (i.e. the increase in vote share) outweigh the costs. For voters to react to party position shifts, their reception is a necessary condition. Hence, parties are more likely to shift their policy positions if potential new voters receive the party's shift. This leads to

Hypothesis P2a: The higher voters' mean level of education, the more likely it is that parties shift their policy positions.

Axiom 2 allows for a more fine-grained version of Hypothesis P2a. Specifically, parties benefit most if voters receive party policy shifts towards their personal policy preferences while voters being worse off by the party's policy shift do not receive the platform shift. Higher education levels therefore increase the party's ability to shift its policy platform if the shift is towards the voter's policy preferences. The larger the share of voters being better off with the party's policy shift, the more the party benefits from highly educated voters. Hence, the voters' mean level of education should depend on the direction of the party position shift *vis-à-vis* the voters' policy positions. As for political awareness, I formulate a modified

Hypothesis P2b: The higher the voters' mean level of education, the more likely it is that parties shift their policy positions *if* the party shifts its platform towards the majority of the voters' policy preferences. In contrast, the level of education does not motivate party position shifts moving away from the majority of the voters' preferences.

Updating information following voter position shifts

Voters' policy position shifts also affect the perception of party platform changes. I argue that voters have a higher need for updating their information on party positions once they alter their personal policy preferences. The reason is that voters changing their personal policy preferences have to consider whether their previous vote choice is still appropriate. As a consequence, voter policy shifts increase their probability of receiving a party's shift message.

According to the model presented so far, updating information on political parties is not necessary for all voter groups. Assuming a one-dimensional policy space, voters with policy preferences left of (or right of) all major parties in a given system further shifting to the left (to the right), have no incentive for renewing their information on party policy positions. Based on policy grounds, their only reasonable vote choice was the leftmost (rightmost) party so that respective voters do not benefit from updating their information. Hence, voters with extreme preferences shifting their positions further to the respective boundaries of the policy space should face no incentive to update available information on political parties.[2] Yet, this argument does not consider that voters with extreme preferences further shifting to the respective boundary are voters which are not well represented by the existing party alternatives. Although one (extreme) party is closest to their policy position, the distance towards the closest party is rather large. Because 'no candidate is sufficiently attractive to merit [the voter's] support' (Adams *et al.* 2005: 120), these voters are likely to abstain due to alienation (Adams *et al.* 2006b; Downs 1957; Enelow and Hinich 1984: 90; Riker and Ordeshook 1968). Hence, extreme voters also face incentives to update their information on party position shifts in order to be able to evaluate the policy distance to the closest party. Instead of deciding which party to vote for after shifting their personal policy preferences, these voters choose whether to vote at all.

Hence, voters shifting their policy positions update their information on political parties and are thus more likely to receive party policy shifts. Holding the acceptance of party policy shifts constant, I summarise:

Hypothesis V3: The larger a voter's shift in policy positions, the more likely is the perception of party policy shifts.

Axiom 3 identifies the parties' incentives to shift their policy positions as reactions to voter position shifts. A party benefits from a low perception of voters shifting their policy preferences towards its policy position. Simultaneously, it benefits from the reception of its shift by voters performing harmful public opinion shifts. Hence, the voters' updating leads parties to shift their policy positions if public opinion moves away from its prior position. The larger the share of voters moving away from a party's policy position, the higher its incentive to shift the policy platform. Hence, I formulate

Hypothesis P3: The larger the shifts in public opinion *moving away* from a party's platform, the more likely it is that the party shifts its policy positions. In contrast, large public opinion shifts *towards* the party's platform make it refrain from party position shifts.

---

2. The situation is different for extreme voters shifting their policy positions towards the centre and for voters already located at the centre of the policy space: they can choose between several parties and shifting the policy positions may lead to a new evaluation of the policy distances. Hence, shifting the policy position to the left or the right requires an information update of the new environment.

Media exposure

On average, voters do not actively search for party information by collecting election manifestos or other party documents. It is safe to assume that most voters rely on what they can extract from media reporting. Parties' visibility in the public sphere should positively affect voters' probability of receiving party policy shifts. Some parties are more likely to be on the media agenda than others. Of course, a party may be in the media's focus because its leading figures are involved in political scandals or because intra-party dissent is made public. But even this kind of exposure to media attention with no, or only indirect, connections to a party's policies is more likely to hit 'relevant' or 'important' parties rather than small ones and those without any say in politics. With regard to more policy-related issues, newspapers, TV and radio stations are also more likely to cover news stories and to conduct interviews with leading politicians rather than irrelevant outsiders.

How can the 'relevance' of political parties for the media be measured? The size of parties may serve as a proxy. Large parties have more weight in politics than small parties because they have more seats in parliament and may, moreover, cover more experts in various policy areas. In addition, size is a good proxy for a 'fair' allocation of media attention: newspapers, magazines, TV and radio stations may have incentives to allocate their time and space to various parties and split their resources according to the parties' relative importance. In addition to party size, a party's policy positions *vis-à-vis* its competitors is relevant. If media reports aim at capturing 'public opinion', the media is more likely to report mainstream opinions than preferences of radical parties on the left or the right of the political spectrum.

Both the parties' size and their policy positions *vis-à-vis* their competitors are connected to the probability that parties enter government (coalitions). The argument is immediately apparent for two-party systems where the party winning the plurality of votes usually also enters a single-party majority government (Lijphart 1999; Powell 2000). But the same argument also applies for minority situations in parliament. For coalitions to form, a party's size (Lupia and Strøm 2008) matters as well as its ideological position *vis-à-vis* its competitors (Axelrod 1970; de Swaan 1973). In their book on *Making and Breaking Governments*, Laver and Shepsle argue that so-called 'strong parties' are likely to participate in cabinets (Laver and Shepsle 1996: 73). Because strong parties are also likely to be large and centrist (Laver and Shepsle 1996: ch. 5), parties are more likely to participate in (coalition) cabinets if their seat share in parliament is high and if they hold a centrist policy position. Hence, it is useful to study government parties as a proxy for media attention to political parties.

But even more important, parties in government have more policy influence than opposition parties and are, hence, more likely to be a target of media attention.[3] Using a case study of Ross Perot's bid in the 1992 US presidential campaign,

---

3. Note that I am primarily interested in media attention and not in the content of media reports.

Zaller and Hunt argue that media attention is a necessary condition for electoral success (Zaller and Hunt 1994, 1995). Moreover, there is research studying the news media's dependence on information provided by government officials (Bennett 1990; Zaller and Chiu 1996). The basic idea is that journalists depend on 'official' sources within government. The more divergent the opinions in government, the higher the variance in news reports. However, the American findings do not travel easily across the Atlantic. Bennett, as well as Zaller and Chiu, use the term 'government' with a wide definition including legislative actors, while I am interested in the government-opposition divide using 'government' in its narrower sense of 'being in office'. Moreover, the studies are restricted to a specific policy field, namely foreign affairs. Finally, the situation is different in parliamentary systems with governments depending on the majority in parliament and more cohesive parties.

Empirical research on European parties is only anecdotal. Transferring Bennett's argument to parliamentary systems, Sheafer and Wolfsfeld (2009: 149) state that

> anyone familiar with coalition politics knows that some of the fiercest arguments can be found *within* a governing coalition. This is important because some of these oppositional voices are ministers with political power who have better access to the news media than leaders from the opposition (emphasis in the original).

However, they provide no evidence supporting this claim. Similarly, Jenkins (1999: 432) states that 'the literature suggests that major parties can expect to receive the majority of attention in the news media, with incumbents possibly benefiting from a greater share of coverage because of an office-holding advantage' but, again, as the word 'possibly' indicates there are no empirical sources to back up the argument. In the only relevant empirical study I am aware of (Koopmans 2007), the author finds that the Europeanisation of public debates favours government and executive actors compared to legislative and party actors. While heads of states and governments and cabinet ministers are overrepresented in the public sphere, legislative actors are less visible. At least for the European level, we may hence conclude that media attention is biased towards government actors.

If government actors are more visible than opposition parties, the likelihood of receiving their party policy shifts is higher. Holding the acceptance functions constant, Axiom 1 states that a higher reception increases the likelihood of perceiving the parties' platform changes. This leads to

Hypothesis V4: Voters are more likely to perceive party policy shifts of parties in government than shifts of opposition parties.

Since I am currently discussing effects for the reception of policy shifts, the contents of the media exposure is irrelevant.

Turning to the effects of the parties' governmental status on party position shifts, government parties benefit from higher media attention. In contrast to the factors discussed earlier, however, governmental status is a party-specific variable and hence its effect on voters' reception does not vary across voters. As a consequence, parties cannot hope for winning those voters who receive party policy shifts towards their personal preferences while at the same time counting on the ignorance of voters from whom the party moves away (see Axiom 2). Rather, parties will shift policy positions if the vote gains outweigh the vote losses. Because a higher reception increases a party's ability to shift its policy position, I postulate

> Hypothesis P4: Government parties have a higher ability to shift their policy positions than opposition parties.

The complexity of the political market

The reception of party position shifts also hinges on the complexity of the political market. Casting a ballot, voters choose from the menu of available alternatives. A decision between two alternatives may be difficult in some cases but is even more challenging with an increasing number of (vote) choices. Moreover, decisions get more complex if new alternatives enter from time to time while others disappear. I argue that the complexity of the political market negatively affects the probability of voters receiving party policy shifts.

A change in the menu of political parties suggests that a political market is complex. The situation is most challenging for voters if political parties enter and leave the political market in rapid succession. Moreover, parties changing their 'brand names' (Aldrich 1995) make it increasingly difficult for voters to follow their behaviour. Hence, I expect that changing party alternatives increases the complexity of the political market and reduces the likelihood of receiving parties' policy shifts. But whereas party systems are rather fluid in Eastern Europe, their West European counterparts are rather durable: parties seldom change their names and the composition of parliaments is fairly stable. The stability of West European party systems led Lipset and Rokkan (1967) to conclude that the party systems are 'frozen'. Although new parties and party families have entered West European Parliaments since the 1960s (see Kitschelt 1989), these changes are rather evolutionary. Because my sample only contains West European countries, I refrain from using changes in party names and the creation and death of parties as factors indicating the complexity of the political market.

But although the suppliers of policies have not changed substantially over time, party systems differ according to the number of actors involved. Clearly, political markets are easiest to understand if only two parties compete for votes. Voters are faced with clear-cut alternatives, one in government and one in opposition, and (except for those who abstain) either vote for the former or the latter. The more parties, the more difficult it gets to receive party policy shifts. The higher the number of 'relevant' parties, the lower the likelihood that voters are able to perceive the parties' position shifts. The number of major parties may be calculated using a classical measure like the effective number of relevant parties (Laakso and Taagepera 1979) or variants thereof (Dumont and Caulier 2005). Sartori (1976: 121–125) combines arguments on the parties' size with their ideological position, counting parties as 'relevant' if they have the potential to enter government (coalition potential) or the power to influence the tactics of party competition (blackmail potential).

Irrespective of how we count 'major' or 'relevant' parties, the higher the number, the more complex the political market and hence the more difficult it is for voters to receive party policy shifts of individual parties. Again, holding acceptance of party policy shifts constant, voters' reception (and hence perception) of party policy shifts is lower in complex political markets. I postulate

Hypothesis V5: The larger the number of political actors, the less likely is the perception of party policy shifts.

The number of rival parties also affects the likelihood of observing party policy shifts. The more complex the political market, the less likely are voters to receive individual party's policy shifts. As stated in Axiom 2, low reception precludes party policy shifts. Hence, the following hypothesis is deduced:

Hypothesis P5: Parties are more likely to shift their policy positions if the number of competitors is low.

Magnitude of party position shifts

As a final factor influencing voters' reception, I discuss the magnitude of party position shifts. Voters should be more likely to receive major or 'historic' policy shifts than minor or incremental adjustments. This intuitive argument is at least valid in the world of science: political scientists are much more interested in punctuated changes of policy platforms than in minor adjustments. Given that significant platform changes may have tremendous repercussions for party systems and government participation and options, this bias is not surprising. To take an example, much scientific attention was paid to the moderating policy shift of the German Social Democrats in 1959 (Klotzbach 1996; Miller 1974). The basic program agreed on in Bad Godesberg differs in many respects from its predecessor. Perhaps most important, the SPD transformed into a catch-all party and explicitly accepted the necessity of a market economy. This moderating shift paved the way for winning new (moderate) voters and finally led the way to government in 1966. Perhaps even more prominent, 'New Labour' attracted much attention of party researchers (see e.g. Heath et al.2001; Seyd 1998; Shaw 2002; Wickham-Jones 2005). Between 1992 and 1997, the British Labour Party moderated its policy platform in several ways. These policy changes were accompanied by a new party image and a new language distinguishing these reforms of 'New Labour' from the former period. Because of the relevance of the 1997 'New Labour' policy shift for the British political landscape, I discuss voters' reception and acceptance of party position shifts explicitly focusing on the Labour Party 1997 in Chapter Six.

I argue that the effect of punctuated party policy shifts does not only arouse the interest of scholars. Rather, voters are also more likely to receive drastic and 'loud' shift messages rather than incremental and 'quiet' ones. In addition, large policy shifts are also more likely to attract the attention of the media. Hence, the significance of the party's policy shift is likely to affect its reception. All else being equal, the voters' probability to receive (and hence, to perceive) party policy shifts increases with the magnitude of the shift. Put differently:

> Hypothesis V6: The larger party policy shifts, the more likely it is that voters perceive them.[4]

Impacts on the acceptance of party position shifts

Reception of party policy shifts is a cognitive process. Thus, the covariates affecting the reception focus on the ability of voters to perceive policy shifts. In contrast, the acceptance of party policy shifts depends on voters believing in the parties' commitment to their claims. Specifically, I discuss six factors affecting the acceptance of party policy shifts. The first two focus on party leaders. In line with previous research, it is argued that policy and personnel changes often go hand in hand. New personnel may have different visions and goals than their predecessors. Moreover, new leaders do not suffer from decisions they made in the past committing them to specific paths. In other words, new party leaders may have the incentives and the ability to do things differently. I argue that voters are more likely to accept changes in the parties' platforms if the party leadership is not tied to the past. In addition, it is argued that party leaders' prestige affects the acceptance of party policy shifts. Simply put, if voters like the party elites, they are more willing to accept their proposed policy goals.

I also discuss the role of parties' past behaviour. Voters' acceptance of party policy positions depends on position shifts in the past. Parties constantly changing their position endanger voter support for further policy shifts. Because voters cannot rely on the persistence of the party's policy claims, large policy shifts in the past constrain parties: only minor adjustments are possible in the near future. As a fourth factor, I introduce voters' party identification. Whether a voter believes

---

4. Naturally, the magnitude of party policy shifts can only affect the voters' reception and not the parties' shifting options. I therefore refrain to postulate a party-specific hypothesis P6. It may only be stated that parties refrain from 'smooth' policy shifts rather aiming at less frequent large policy changes (see Walgrave and Nuytemans 2009). To be consistent with the voter-specific hypotheses, however, I continue with hypothesis P7 (instead of P6).

in party policy shifts depends on the feeling towards the political parties. Voters feeling attached to a specific party are, in general, more likely to accept its pledges. However, acceptance also hinges on the direction of the party position shift *vis-à-vis* the voters: For party shifts towards a voter's preferences, being identified with that party increases the acceptance of the shift. Because shifts away from the voters' preferences do not conform to the image of 'their' party, identifiers are, in contrast, less likely to accept these.

Furthermore, I study the effect of voter position shifts on the acceptance of party position shifts. In contrast to the effect of voter position shifts on reception, the direction of the voters' shifts is crucial: voters should be more likely to accept a party's policy shift in line with shifts of their personal preferences, and parties follow public opinion shifts moving away from their policy platforms. Finally, the analysis also focuses on the constraints of a party's ideology. It is argued that voters expect parties to hold policy positions within an ideological territory on the left-right axis. Social Democratic parties should, for example, always pursue policies left of Liberal or Conservative parties. Once party position shifts deviate from these expectations, voters are less likely to accept the moves. In that sense, parties are constrained by their ideology and refrain from shifts deviating from 'expected' policy areas. Next, I discuss these factors in greater detail.

Changes in party leadership

The argument that party position shifts follow leadership changes is not new. For organisations in general, Gilmore (1988: 10–11) states that

[l]eadership transitions represent a 'natural entry point' [...] for change [because] [t]he transition is an occasion to rethink the commitment to the present agenda, to reflect on roads not taken in the past, and to review future choices [...] Many significant changes – in policy, people, organisational structure, procedures – are more easily introduced simultaneously with a leadership change.

Harmel and colleagues (Harmel *et al.*1995; Harmel and Janda 1994) transfer this general theory to political parties. They state that party leader changes and party position shifts go hand in hand. Newly elected party leaders are often expected to accomplish modifications compared to their predecessors. Voters should be more likely to accept changes of party policy positions once the party leadership changes. In contrast, long-term party leaders will have a hard time 'selling' shifts in the face of their previous policies. As Downs puts it: 'Because individual men become identified with certain policies it is often necessary for a party to shift its leadership before it can shift its platform' (Downs 1957: 111).

Turning to the model presented above, changes in leadership affect the acceptance function for party position shifts. If a party changes its leader, voters are more likely to accept (i.e. consider credible) policy position changes. Holding the reception function constant, increasing the acceptance means that the probability of voters' perception of party policy shifts increases. Hence, I postulate

Hypothesis V7: Voters' perception of party policy shifts increases after changes in the party leadership.

For political parties, the effect of party leader changes is straightforward: if the party leadership changes, voters are more likely to perceive party position shifts. A higher acceptance allows parties to shift their policy positions because potential new voters perceive the party's policy shift (Axiom 2). This leads to:

Hypothesis P7: Parties are more likely to shift their policy positions if the party leadership has changed.

Prestige of political leaders

The idea that voters are also interested in non-policy factors goes back to Donald Stokes. In his well-known review of Downs's *Economic Theory of Democracy*, Stokes (1963, 1992) develops the idea that some issues may not be placed on policy dimensions. Stokes argues that there are 'valence issues' involving the linking of the parties 'with some condition that is positively or negatively valued by the electorate' (Stokes 1963: 373). All voters dislike corruption and economic crises. Choosing between different parties means judging which party is best in fighting crime, keeping inflation low, and bringing people back to work. In contrast to policy issues, all parties and voters take the same 'position' on valence issues but voters distinguish which party or candidate is best to achieve these goals. Following Stokes, numerous studies focused on the theoretical and empirical consequences of valence effects for voting and party competition (see e.g. Abney *et al.*undated; Adams *et al.*undated; Adams and Merrill 2009; Clark 2009; Groseclose 2001; Schofield 2003; Schofield and Sened 2006; Stone and Simas 2007). There is empirical evidence that voters take valence issues seriously and that a party's 'image' affects its electoral results (Abney *et al.*undated; Clark 2009; Stone and Simas 2007). For parties, higher valence scores allows the choice of superior policy positions, usually located closer to the electoral centre (Groseclose 2001; Schofield 2003; Schofield and Sened 2006).

I argue that valence issues affect the acceptance of party policy shifts. The higher a party's competence with regard to valence issues, the more voters believe in its competence and ability to 'get things done'. A positive party image hence leads to higher acceptance of party action on policy grounds. Instead of using media reports to measure valence (see Abney *et al.*undated; Clark 2009), I rely on voter-specific evaluations of party leaders. Simply put, the higher the party leader's prestige, the more likely voters are to accept the announced party policy platform. Holding the reception of party position shifts constant, the larger the acceptance, the higher the probability of perceiving policy shifts. This leads to

Hypothesis V8: The higher the party leader's prestige, the more likely is the perception of party policy shifts.

Regarding the consequences for political parties, we know from Axiom 2 that the acceptance of party position shifts is a necessary condition for policy change shifts. Because high valence increases the probability of acceptance, skilful, sympathetic and charismatic leaders should face fewer difficulties 'selling' their party's policy position to potential new voters.

Hypothesis P8a: The higher a party leader's mean evaluation, the more likely it is that a party shifts its policy position.

Because the party leader's prestige is a voter-specific factor, we can also derive a more fine-grained expectation: following Axiom 2, a party's ability to shift policy positions increases if voters benefiting from the party shift perceive the party's change of policy positions, while voters being worse off do not perceive the position shift. As a consequence, we can refine Hypothesis 8a, restricting the positive effect of a party leader's evaluation on party position shifts to cases where a majority of voters benefit from the platform change. Hence, I formulate a modified

Hypothesis P8b: The higher a party leader's mean evaluation, the more likely it is that a party shifts its policy positions *if* the party shifts its platform towards the majority of the voters' policy preferences.

Party past behaviour

Voters also take the parties' past behaviour into account. The idea that decisions made in the past constrain actors in the present is well known as 'path dependence' (for an overview see Peters 2005). Margaret Levi argues that path dependence means that 'once a country or region has started down a track, the costs of reversal are very high' (Levi 1997: 28). Pierson connects the notion of path dependence with increasing returns so that 'the costs of exit – of switching to some previously plausible alternative – rise' (Pierson 2000: 252). Exploring examples from government, Peters (2005: 72) notes that

a particular programme addressing a policy problem may not be the best in the abstract but once it has been shown to produce some positive results it will dominate other solutions that may, in principle, be superior but which will require movement from an existing and seemingly functional programme.

And for party policy programs, Budge makes the point that a 'party having authoritatively endorsed a programme as the correct one for society, can hardly produce another the week afterwards' (Budge 1994: 450). In that sense, parties are indeed constrained by policy choices of the past. Reconsidering 'New Labour' in 1997, how would voters have reacted if Blair would have withdrawn 'New Labour', reintroducing 'Old Labour' in 2001? Clearly, a voter observing permanent party shifting may have doubts whether yet another shift has anything to say about the future. In other words, on-going policy shifts convey the impression that a party is not sure what it wants, and consequently voters will doubt its credibility.

In the terms of the model introduced in the previous chapter, large past party policy shifts reduce voters' acceptance for further shifts of the party platform. If a party only made minor adjustments in their policy programs, voters are more likely to accept a major shift. Hence, I postulate

> Hypothesis V9: The smaller a party's policy shifts in the past, the more likely are voters to perceive its platform change.

When voters do not accept party position shifts, parties refrain from pursuing them. Hence, parties are constrained by their past policy shifts and stay put if they recently made major adjustments of their party platform. This expectation is in line with 'frictional change' of institutions in general (Baumgartner and Jones 1993) and its application to political parties (Walgrave and Nuytemans 2009). In that view, party policy positions are 'punctuated equilibria' (Krasner 1984) staying relatively stable after reforms are introduced. In the words of the model introduced above, voters are less likely to accept party policy shifts if there have already been major position changes in the party's recent history. Because the voters' acceptance is necessary for parties to adapt their policy positions (Axiom 2), we can formulate

> Hypothesis P9: Parties are more likely to shift their policy positions if their position shifts in the recent past were small.

Party identification

The idea that voters identify with specific parties is based on the 'Michigan model' of voting (Campbell *et al.* 1960). Due to their socialisation, voters differ in their (long-term) perception of parties. Partisanship 'represents long-term, affective, psychological identification with one's preferred party' (Adams *et al.* 2005: 248) and these feelings towards parties influence vote choices.

Although the actual effect of party identification on vote choice is subject to discussions (for an overview see Adams *et al.* 2005: Appendix 2.2), party identification is one of the major findings in public opinion research. The idea that voters do not only consider 'factual data' (like party positions) but also use information shortcuts such as party identification is also emphasised by research on social cognition. Studying the effects of political information and information shortcuts, Rahn (1993) distinguishes two strategies of how voters make decisions: the 'theory-driven' mode emphasises prior beliefs and draws attention to information in line with a subject's beliefs while discounting information contradicting the conception of the world. In other words, beliefs bias the information process and favour confirmative over contradicting news. In contrast, the 'data-driven' mode suggests that voters are able to process information in a neutral way without being taken hostage by stereotypes like biased party images. In experiments using information on party labels as a treatment, the author shows that (1) in the absence of party labels, individuals use the candidates' messages as information sources but that (2) voters prefer the heuristic processing (i.e. party labels) over policy information once these information shortcuts are available (Rahn 1993: 491–2). Overall, then, party identification leads voters to use biased information in line with their beliefs.

How can these findings be used in the present model? I adapt Rahn's findings arguing that party identification has a positive impact on the perception of policy shifts if these shifts are in line with a voter's beliefs. If the shift conforms to a voter's expectations, that is, if the party shifts towards his or her policy position, party identification has a positive effect on the acceptance of party policy shifts. In contrast, if the party policy shift contradicts the expectations of voters with party identification (i.e. if the party moves away from their preferences), voters discount information that contradicts their beliefs and are therefore less likely to accept the platform shift. Holding the reception of party policy shifts constant, party identification hence positively (negatively) affects the perception of party policy shifts if the party platform shifts towards (moves away from) the voter's policy preferences. This leads to

Hypothesis V10: Party identification positively affects the perception of party policy shifts towards the voter's personal preferences. For party shifts moving away from the voter's preferences, identifying with the party decreases the likelihood of perceiving the party position shift.

Although the effect of party identification on the perception of party policy shifts is quite complex at the individual level, the implications for the aggregate level are rather straightforward. According to Axiom 2, parties are most likely to shift their policy positions if voters accept (i.e. consider credible) party policy shifts towards their personal preferences while rejecting those moving away from the voters' personal preferences. Voters identifying with a party fulfill both conditions: they are less likely to perceive policy shifts away from their individual preferences and more likely to accept such shifts towards these preferences. Hence, parties benefit from voters identified with them no matter which direction their policy shift has gone. In sum, I hypothesise

Hypothesis P10: A party is more likely to shift its policy position if the share of voters being identified with that party is large.

Public opinion shifts

Changing voter preferences also affect the acceptance of party policy shifts. The idea that parties react to voter position shifts leans on research by James Stimson and colleagues (Stimson 1991, 1999; Stimson *et al.* 1995). For democratic regimes, we would like to see that public policy responds to changing preferences in the electorate. That is what Stimson and collaborators label 'dynamic representation' (Stimson *et al.* 1995). Political parties are the main actors linking the voters' preferences with the policy output in modern democracies (see e.g. Schattschneider 1942). Changing preferences in the electorate should lead parties to respond to the changing demands by adapting their policy platforms. In fact, previous research has shown that parties do respond to these incentives (Adams *et al.* 2004; Adams *et al.* 2009) although they may listen and respond to different subconstituencies (Ezrow *et al.* 2010).

At the micro-level, the concept of 'dynamic representation' suggests that voters expect a party to follow their respective individual policy shifts: a voter shifting to the right (left) expects parties to respond by shifting to the right (left) and is therefore more likely to accept party policy shifts in line with his position shift. Parties shifting in the opposite direction may find their shift rejected. Holding the reception function constant, the perception of party policy shifts increases if parties respond to voter positions shifts. This leads to

> Hypothesis V11: Voters are more likely to perceive party policy shifts which are in the same direction as shifts in the voters' personal preferences.

Because party position shifts in line with public opinion shifts increase voters' acceptance (and hence the perception) of party policy shifts, parties follow voter position shifts if these preferences move away from their party platforms. The larger the share of voters moving away from a party's platform, the more likely a party follows this shift in public opinion. In contrast, parties are not likely to respond to public opinion shifts that move towards the party's policy position. This leads to

> Hypothesis P11: Parties follow public opinion shifts if these shifts move voters away from their position. In contrast, parties do not respond to public opinion shifts towards their policy position.[5]

---

5. Note that Hypotheses P3 and P11 differ: For the reception of party policy shifts (Hypothesis P3), parties are expected to shift their policy positions if public opinion shifts move away from the parties' pre-shift policy positions. Yet, there is no direction involved in the parties' policy shifts. In that sense, Hypothesis P11 is a refinement stating that parties react to changing voter preferences by shifting *in the same direction* as the majority of the voters. Hypothesis P11 matches with Adams and colleagues' 'Dynamics of Disadvantaged Parties Hypothesis' (Adams *et al.* 2004: 593) and the empirical results presented below may also be interpreted as a replication analysis using different data sources and a slightly different sample.

Party ideology

So far I have argued that party leaders are solely interested in votes. In that sense, they are free to choose policy positions on the left-right axis. Yet, omitting ideological factors is rather implausible. Therefore, I introduce the idea that party leaders are constrained in their vote-maximising ambitions by voters with specific expectations or beliefs about where parties should place themselves relative to each other. Simply put, we expect that Social Democratic parties choose platforms left of Liberal or Conservative parties. In its simplest form, these rank-orders of ideological territories entail the three varieties of parties: left-, centre, and right-wing. Such 'expectations' are widely used in academic writings, newspapers, and political discussions without considering the actual party policy stands indicated in party manifestos or parliamentary speeches. In other words, without knowing where a Social Democratic party would place itself on a particular policy issue on the left-right axis, we expect its policy position to be left of Liberal or Conservative parties. Although such 'expectations' are widely used without deeper theoretical thought or justification, I spend some time explaining how expectations on party policy positions are derived.

The left-right axis is used to describe party systems assigning (ordinal) policy positions to the major parties in the system. To take an example, Damgaard (2000: 233) describes the Danish party system distinguishing five major groupings.

> First, there is a group of relatively small left-wing parties. [...] Second, there is the Social Democratic Party [...] Third, there is a group of relatively small centre parties. [...] Fourth, the two old moderate centre-right parties, the Liberals and the Conservative People's Party [...] Finally, a right-wing Independent Party was represented in the early 1960s. At the remarkable 1973-election a new Progress Party obtained surprisingly strong support of what was called a protest party. (Damgaard 2000: 233)

Although Damgaard distinguishes groups rather than individual parties, readers get first insights into the Danish party system. From left to right, the parties can be placed as small left-wing parties, Social Democrats, small centre parties, moderate right-wing parties (Liberals and Conservatives), and finally the far right (Independence Party and Progress Party, respectively). In other words, the readers expect that the Social Democrats choose policy positions further to the left than those of the Liberals or the Conservative Party. Furthermore, the Progress Party should choose policy positions further to the right than those of the Liberals, for example.

Similarly, some expert surveys designed to obtain party left-right placements (Benoit and Laver 2006; Castles and Mair 1984; Huber and Inglehart 1995; Laver and Hunt 1992) do not use question wordings such as 'in the most recent election'. Rather, the questions are more general asking about 'political parties today' (Huber and Inglehart 1995), or do not mention the time dimension at all (Benoit and Laver 2006; Castles and Mair 1984). Hence, experts do not rate specific policy programs but rather draw a more general picture of the party positions. In other words, country experts state the general expectations of party policy positions. Moreover, these expert judgements (i.e. the expectations) correlate highly although the surveys are conducted over a period of 20 years (see e.g. McDonald and Mendes 2001). The expert judgements' stability over time indicates that these judgements measure general expectations rather than policy issue positions in specific elections.

In essence, then, it is quite clear what expectations of party policy positions are. We expect that Communist parties pursue policies left of Liberal or Conservative parties. Moreover, Social Democrats should be more moderate (i.e. further to the right) than Communist or Socialist parties. However, such expectations are not uniform across countries. This is especially true for some party families. Liberal parties, for example, may be centre parties in some party systems (e.g. Great Britain) but may be located more to the right in others (e.g. the Netherlands). Hence, generalised left-right expectations based on party families (as e.g. in Adams *et al.* 2004; 2006a) are likely to be inappropriate measures. Rather, country-specific expectations of left-right placements should be used.

I argue that the parties' 'expected' policy positions relate to three factors. First and most important, parties' ideologies shape left-right expectations. Most parties hint at their ideology in their official name. In so doing, parties connect their respective ideologies with their 'brand names' (Aldrich 1995). Given the common wisdom about party ideologies (see above), voters develop specific expectations of what policies the parties pursue. Thus, Conservative parties are expected to pursue policies on the right, Socialist or Green parties represent policies on the left of the policy space. However, ideologies create different expectations across countries. As mentioned above, Liberal parties may be centre parties in some countries and right-wing parties in others.

Second, the nature of the dominant left-right dimension differs across countries. Talking about 'left' and 'right' does not determine what issue dimensions map on this general policy dimension (Huber 1989; Knutsen 1995). Although economic issues are most likely to reflect left-right mappings in most West European countries, other issues may also affect party placements on this dimension. While a country's policy space may include other relevant policy dimensions (e.g. economic, social policy, religious or linguistic), placing parties on the left-right dimension economises voter considerations. For example, German voters (and country experts) often place the FDP (Liberals) between the SPD (Social Democrats) and the CDU/CSU (Christian Democrats) on the left-right scale (Benoit and Laver 2006; Castles and Mair 1984; Huber and Inglehart 1995; Thomassen 2005). In so doing, voters (and country experts) mix policy positions from the two dominant policy dimensions (Shikano and Pappi 2004). On economic, social and fiscal policy, the Liberals are right of the Christian Democrats. On the second major policy dimension (domestic, legal, and socio-political issues), however, the Liberals are more moderate than the Christian Democrats. Hence, economic factors are not the sole driving force when voters and country experts place the German parties on a left-right axis.

Third, the respective countries' party systems affect expectations of party left-right placements. Bipolar systems (as the British system) often 'generate' left-right explanations. The Liberal Democrats are just expected to have policy views located in between. The German FDP (Liberals) often built coalitions 'to the left' (with the SPD) and 'to the right' (with the CDU/CSU) – another reason to place them in between the Social Democrats and the Christian Democrats. In Sweden, governments have either been 'socialist' or 'non-socialist' (Bergman 2000). Hence, voters place the 'socialist' parties (Communist Party, Left Party, and the Social Democrats) on the left. The bourgeois parties (Centre Party, The Liberals, and the Conservatives) are placed on the right. Distinguishing within these blocs is much less relevant than the socialist-non-socialist divide. For example, the Centre Party and the Liberals occupy the centre of the policy space. Experts do not distinguish whether the Centre Party is left of the Liberals or vice versa (in Huber and Inglehart 1995 the parties get exactly the same value on the left-right dimension). In other party systems, we distinguish three, four or five groups of parties. This holds for example for Denmark where Damgaard (2000) distinguishes five party groups but, again, there are no expectations where parties within these groups are located.

In sum, we can define voter expectations of party positions as ordinal party placements on a left-right scale arising from the parties' ideologies, the nature of the left-right scale (i.e. the main dimension of the party competition), and the respective country's party system.

I argue that voters are likely to accept party position shifts as long as parties maintain (or reassume) their ideological territories relative to the other parties. In contrast, voters are less likely to accept policy shifts away from the parties' placement relative to their competitors. Holding the reception of party policy shifts constant, this leads to

Hypothesis V12: Voters are less likely to perceive party policy shifts if these shifts move the parties away from their ideological territories.

Voter expectations of relative party placements also affect the parties' decisions with regard to pursuing policy changes. Winning new votes requires that voters accept their policy shifts (Axiom 2). Hence, parties have incentives to maintain (or reassume) their placement relative to other parties according to the voters' expectations. This leads to

Hypothesis P12: If party placements do not match with the voters' expectations, parties shift their positions to locate themselves relative to their competitors according to voter expectations.

Summary

This chapter added flesh to the bones of the theoretical model presented in the previous chapter. Because the reception and acceptance of party policy shifts are latent factors which are not directly observable, I introduce a set of covariates likely to affect the two perception factors. In total, I introduce 12 covariates expected to affect the reception and acceptance of party position shifts. Table 5.1 summarises the variables and indicates their variation across voters, parties, or time.

I argue that the reception of party policy shifts is a cognitive process which is therefore driven by factors affecting the costs of information-gathering. Political awareness, education, and the updating motivated by individual policy position shifts are voter-specific factors that are expected to have a positive effect on the reception function. The parties' governmental status and the magnitude of the party policy shift are party-specific variables that should also increase the probability of receiving party policy shifts. Finally, the complexity of the political market (indicated by the number of relevant parties) negatively affects the reception of party position shifts.

Table 5.1: Reception and acceptance covariates and their variation across voters, parties, and time

	Variation across...		
	Voters	**Parties**	**Elections**
Political awareness	X		X
Education	X		X
Magnitude of voter position shifts	X		X
Party in government		X	X
Number of parties			X
Magnitude of party policy shift		X	X
Change in party leadership		X	X
Party leader prestige	X	X	X
Magnitude of past policy shifts		X	X
Party identification	X	X	X
Direction of voter position shifts	X		X
Ideological territories		X	

In contrast to their reception, acceptance of party position shifts is a political issue. It depends on whether voters trust in or believe a party's claims. Party leadership changes and the leaders' prestige should positively affect the acceptance of party policy shifts. Moreover, party policy shifts are less likely to get accepted if the party's previous policy shift was large. Concerning the role of party identification, I expect a positive effect for party policy shifts towards a voter's policy preferences. In contrast, party identification negatively affects the perception of party policy shifts away from a voter's policy preferences. It is also argued that voters are more likely to accept party shifts that are in line with public opinion shifts. Furthermore, voters care about ideology and do not accept parties 'leapfrogging' (Budge 1994) their competitors.

As indicated in Axioms 2 and 3 in the previous chapter, the consequences of the voters' reception and acceptance are somewhat more complex. In general, parties benefit from increasing reception and acceptance. If the reception and acceptance differs across voters, however, parties benefit most if voters perceive shifts towards their policy position while voters being worse off from the platform shift do not perceive it. Therefore, hypotheses involving voter-specific covariates (Hypotheses P1b, P2b, and P8b) hinge on the direction of the party policy shifts. The voters' party identification (Hypothesis P10) is the sole exception. For hypotheses involving voter position shifts (Hypotheses P3 and P11), parties are most likely to respond to voter shifts away from their policy position while staying put if voters shift towards it.

The following chapters test the hypotheses for voters (Chapter Six) and political parties (Chapters Seven). Although both analyses suffer from restrictions in data availability, they provide first insights supporting the plausibility of the model developed here.

chapter six | voter perceptions of party policy shifts: an empirical analysis

There are a number of studies analysing voter perceptions of party platforms, including cross-national surveys (e.g. Eurobarometer) and national election studies. Unfortunately, most of these studies are cross-sectional, asking a sample of respondents at one point in time. It is therefore difficult (if not impossible) to measure perceptions of party policy changes on the level of individual voters. Yet, these data have been used to measure changes in public opinion and aggregate perceptions of parties (Green and Jennings 2012; Stimson 1991). Panel studies that interview the same respondents at least twice are rare and mostly restricted to election campaigns. Although these studies are well suited to analyse campaign effects on voters, they are of limited use for analysing changes in the voters' perceptions of party platforms. Of course, parties may adapt their positions over the course of a single election campaign. Yet, these changes are likely to be small and 'covered' by changes in issue emphasis or by 're-framing' issues (Chong and Druckman 2007), not least due to the problems of shifting party policy platforms outlined above. Most changes in party policy positions are likely to happen over longer time periods. In these longer time spans, parties can also perform gradual changes that, in the long run, result in major party change. Moreover, party elites may need time to convince fellow party members of the need for major party change and possibly their approval at a party conference. This is why this study analyses party policy change over several years or specifically, the shift in party policy positions between two elections.

The British panel election studies (Crewe *et al.* 1981; Heath *et al.* 1998; 1999a; 2002; Heath *et al.* 1993) are particularly well suited to study the voters' perceptions of party policy shifts. Here, panels cover various years and respondents are interviewed twice at two subsequent elections. This allows us to observe the voters' changing perceptions of party policy positions. Moreover, the hypotheses presented in the previous chapters involve variables which vary across voters (e.g. party identification) and across parties (e.g. party leader changes). Testing the model hence requires data allowing for variation for both types of variables. The British panel studies allow for this because panel data are available for several elections, dating back to the 1970s. Although some question items have changed, there are reasonably good data to test most of the hypotheses stated above.

The empirical analyses are based on different sets of data. First, the first analysis is based on the voters' perceptions of Labour's policy shift in 1997. In addition to the relevance of 'New Labour' in British history, the case selection is also guided by measurement considerations. Studying only one party position shift at one point in time (i.e. one election) also allows for a coherent measurement of the concepts.[1] Holding party-specific covariates constant also simplifies the model and allows for focusing on the voter-specific covariates. Second, I study the pooled sample looking at British general elections from October 1974 onwards. In addition to voter-specific covariates, these models also contain variables which only vary across parties. Hence, pooling the data of several elections allows for testing most of the hypotheses postulated in Chapter Five. Extending the sample size, it is moreover possible to check and to generalise the findings of the 'New Labour' analysis. As the empirical results show, however, the compromises involved in the pooling of the election studies and multicollinearity of the measures lead to mixed results. Therefore, two additional regression analyses are employed to discuss the effects of two covariates in greater detail. I also provide potential explanations for findings that contradict the hypotheses presented above and briefly discuss the effect of parties moving away from their ideological territories.

The data analysis is based on a statistical model which considers the theoretically assumed perception process. Recall that I conceptualise the perception of policy shifts as a two-stage process. Voters have to *receive* the party's shift message. Given reception, voters then decide in a second step whether to *accept* (i.e. consider credible) the party's announced policy shift. A basic approach is to use logistic regression models to estimate the covariates' impact on the reception and acceptance of party policy shifts. However, there are three problems involved. First, given that the data describes the voters' perceptions of policy position shifts of different parties in several elections, heteroscedasticity exists. Second, we are not able to observe voters' reception or acceptance of party position shifts as separate events. Rather, it is only possible to observe the overall process, that is, whether voters *perceive* policy shifts. Calculating logistic regressions with the perception of policy shifts as the dependent variable may bias the results. Third and related, the reception and acceptance of policy shifts is a two-stage process. The reception and acceptance of party policy shifts depend on each other. The acceptance of a policy position shift requires its reception. Vice versa, receiving a party's shift message is not sufficient for the voters to perceive (i.e. also consider credible) the policy shift.

Estimating regression models with clustered standard errors corrects for the first problem (see e.g. Wooldridge 2002). The second, and the related third, problem require a specific regression model deviating from standard regression models. To account for this, I use a two-stage logistic regression with stage one modelling reception, and stage two the acceptance of party policy shifts (for more information see Appendix A).

---

1. Pooling several panel election studies sometimes requires tough coding decisions and compromises in the selection of measures for the underlying concepts. Using only one panel election study avoids these problems and allows for more precise measures.

Data: The British panel election studies, 1974 – 2001

With the exception of the general elections in 1983 and 2005, the British panel election studies were conducted at every British general election since February 1974. To study voter- and party-specific covariates, it is necessary to pool these data files so that the variables at both levels vary. Pooling data from several election years requires making coding decisions which are described in the next two sections. More information on the data and the statistical methods can be retrieved from Appendix A.

The dependent variable

In British election surveys, voters are asked to locate parties on issue-specific left-right dimensions. In general to classical left-right questions, voters locate themselves and the parties by answering questions on topics such as the nationalisation of industries, the priorities of parties in fighting unemployment and inflation, and questions on EU affairs. Mirroring political debate, the issues asked changed over time. The same holds for the wording for some of the questions.

Table 6.1: Importance of policy issues for making vote choices (rank-order)

	Oct. 1974	1979	1987	1992	1997
1st	Common market/EC	Taxes vs. Services	Taxes vs. Services	Unemploy-ment	Taxes vs. Services
2nd	Nationalis-ation	Common market/EC Nationalis-ation	Unemploy-ment	Taxes vs. Services	Unemploy-ment
3rd			Nationalis-ation		Common market/EC
NA		Unemploy-ment		Nationalis-ation	

There is no panel data for the 1983 general election. In 2001, voters were asked to place parties on the four policy scales but no question quantifies the importance for their vote choices.

NA: Policy scale used but no indicator for importance of policy for vote choice.

For the selection of policy dimensions to measure the perception of party policy shifts, it is useful to consider those policy dimensions that (1) were asked in several election studies and (2) were important for making vote choices. Concerning the former, I consider policy scales used in at least four election studies. The policy scales on 'European integration', 'Nationalisation', 'Taxes vs. Services' and 'Unemployment vs. Inflation' fall in this category. Regarding the importance for making vote choices, Table 6.1 shows the issues' salience across several election studies using rank-orders.

'Taxes vs. services' and 'Unemployment' (from 1987 onwards) are the two most important issues to voters. I will therefore use them in the following analyses, although they are not covered over the whole period. Because there is no measure for the 'Taxes vs. Services' scale for the election in 1974, the social service scale is used as an equivalent in this election. Furthermore, I add the 'Nationalisation vs. Privatisation' scale. Although its importance for making voting decisions is decreasing over time, the scale is covered in all available election studies and hence allows for larger sample sizes covering several elections.

The reasons for not using the questions on European integration are manifold. First, this question was not asked in 1987 and in 1992, leading to missing values in the time series. Second, the parties' policy positions on European integration become less likely to influence vote choices. While being the most important policy issue in the 1970s, EU integration only ranks third place in the 1997 general election. Finally, questions on European affairs differ from the 'classical' left-right scale on which I have concentrated so far. Whereas party policy positions correlate highly between economic scales (Nationalisation, Taxes vs. Services, Unemployment), there are no high correlations between those scales and party policy positions on European integration (see also Green 2007; Heath *et al.* 1999b). Additionally, 'official' party position shifts are measured using the CMP's left-right scale (see below) which does not cover European issues. Although it is possible to adapt the model to more policy-specific areas like European affairs, the analyses are restricted to left-right issues. In what follows, I hence use the three policy scales 'Nationalisation', 'Taxes vs. Services', and 'Unemployment'.

Covariates

Most of the independent variables are taken from the British panel election studies ranging from October 1974 to the general election in 2001 (Crewe *et al.* 1981; Heath *et al.* 1993, 1998, 1999a, 2002).[2] All variables related to voters (e.g. political awareness, education, party identification) are drawn from these election studies. Additional sources were used to collect data for (party-specific) covariates.

---

2. For the general elections in 1983 and 2005, only cross-sectional studies are available.

Table 6.2 summarises the independent variables used in the models below. *Political awareness* is measured using two different variables. In 1979 and 1997, respondents were asked to answer political quizzes. Voters answered questions testing their political knowledge on political figures (like party leaders) and institutions (e.g. number of MPs, maximal time between two elections). Political awareness is measured as the number of correct answers. This is perhaps the best approach to measure political awareness (Zaller 1992: 333–336). Unfortunately, the same measure does not exist for the remaining elections. As an alternative, I rely on political interest. Questions on political interest are asked regularly in various forms including interest in politics in general, and the attention to newspaper articles, TV and radio shows dealing with politics and election campaigns. Political interest as substitute for political quizzes suffers, however, from a major shortcoming: people tend to exaggerate their political interest. Because interest is desirable, voters report more political interest than they actually have. The social desirability may therefore bias the results (Schnell *et al.* 2005: 335). For example, Zaller (1992: 334) reports that, according to a survey, 40 per cent of the American public listens to National Public Radio several times a week which is implausibly high and far above the radio's own estimates (by factor 10). Although the measure has its weaknesses, it is the only available measure for political awareness over time. The correlation between the scores in political quizzes (in 1979 and 1997) and the reported political awareness is 0.39 indicating that the measures (at least) tend to measure the same underlying concept.[3]

The variable *education* categorises the voter's education in three categories: basic, moderate, and advanced. Basic education is the educational level reached when getting the O level or the CSE certificate. Moderate education captures qualifications obtained following the obligatory time in school (until the age of 16) either with the A level (or equivalents) or further education (e.g. BTEC ordinary national diploma). Finally, advanced education covers academic degrees from the Bachelor degrees onwards or equivalents. The coding follows the British National Qualifications Framework (NQF) for the comparison of degrees and qualifications.

Voter position shifts are derived from the same policy scales that are used to measure party policy shifts. Voters place themselves on the 'Nationalisation', 'Taxes vs. Services', and the 'Unemployment vs. Inflation' scales. Making use of the panel data structure, it is possible to measure voter position shifts between two subsequent elections. For the reception of party policy shifts, I use the absolute values of these policy shifts to measure the need for updating the parties' policy positions.

The remaining covariates for the reception of party policy shifts are party-specific and not taken from the British panel election studies. First, a dummy vari-

---

3. However, the following analysis reveals that using political interest and political quizzes to measure a voter's political knowledge leads to different empirical results. At least on the micro level, interest in politics is therefore no appropriate measure for political awareness.

able measures whether the *party was in government* before the current election or not. For obvious reasons, it is not possible to include the *number of parties*. The British party system consists of two major parties competing for government and the Liberal Democrats (Liberals and the Alliance, respectively) as a third force. Because the mechanics of the party system did not alter over time, it is not possible to include this variable in the analysis. Finally, the *magnitude of party policy shifts* is obtained from the parties' left-right position changes from the last to the current election using the CMP party positions (Budge *et al.* 2001).[4]

Turning to the covariates for the acceptance function, I hypothesised above that *changes in the party leadership* make the acceptance of party position shifts more likely. The data for leadership changes of the major British parties are drawn from different sources (Butler and Butler 2000; Zárate 2009). The variable is zero if the same party leader is in office and one if the party leadership changed since the last election.

The British panel election studies also measure the *party leaders' prestige*. The measures changed, however, over the years. In the 1970s, voters were asked to grade party leaders on a scale from 0 to 10. From the '80s onwards, respondents answered questions concerning the party leaders' attributes (e.g. whether they are capable of being a strong leader, able to unite the nation, or keep their promises). To obtain a comparable measure over time, I use a similar technique as applied by the European Voter project (Thomassen 2005) and transform the variables used in several election studies to a scale ranging from 0 (low prestige) to 4 (high prestige).

I also argued above that parties may not permanently change their policy positions. Parties with large *past policy shifts* are less likely to shift their policy platforms for the following election: voters simply might get the impression that the party does not know what it wants to do. As for the magnitude of the party policy shifts, data for past policy shifts is obtained from the Comparative Manifestos Project (Budge *et al.* 2001). The variable measures the magnitude of the party's former policy shift on the CMP's left-right scale ranging from -100 to +100.

The British panel election studies contain a question measuring the voters' *party identification*. Voters are asked whether they think of themselves as Conservative, Labour, Liberal Democrat, or another party. For voters not thinking of themselves as identified with any party, a follow-up question asks to which party the respondent feels 'a little closer to'. Therefore, there are two possibilities to measure the voters' party identification: a narrow measure only considers those voters who think of themselves as Conservatives, Labour, or Liberal Democrats. A broader concept also captures those who just feel closer to one of the parties. In the empirical analysis, I use the narrow concept. It should be noted, however, that the two variables correlate highly.

---

4. CMP data on left-right positions mainly deals with economic issues. The policy scales on 'Nationalization', 'Taxes vs. Services', and 'Unemployment vs. Inflation' address specific issues on that dimension so that it is reasonable to assume that the scales are comparable. Criticism and weaknesses of CMP data is more thoroughly discussed in Chapter Three.

Table 6.2: Independent variables for the data analyses

Variable name	Indicators and measurement
Political awareness	Political quizzes (1979 and 1997) or political interest (10-point scales)
Education	Ordinal variable with three categories (basic, moderate, advanced)
Voter position shift (absolute value)	Voter shift on respective scale (Nationalisation, Taxes vs. Services, Unemployment vs. Inflation)
Government party	In opposition (0) or in government (1) before current election
Number of parties	Not used
Magnitude of party policy shift	Absolute distance of the party policy shift from previous to current election (CMP data)
Leadership change	Same party leader as in previous election (0) or leader change (1)
Party leader prestige	Evaluation of party leaders with standardised scores ranging from 0 to 4 using party leader evaluations in marks (1970s) and attributes (from 1987 onwards)
Past party policy shifts	Magnitude of past policy shift (at previous election) using CMP data
Party identification	'think of yourself as (party)' questions in all election studies
Voter shift (with direction)	Party and voter shift in same (1) or different (0) directions
Policy shifts deviating from ideological territory	Party position shift conforming to (0) or deviating from (1) ideological territory (i.e. policy position relative to other parties)
Age	Age of respondent
Sex	Sex of respondent

The first group of variables (Political awareness through Magnitude of party policy shift) is labelled **Reception**; the second group (Leadership change through Policy shifts deviating from ideological territory) is labelled **Acceptance**.

For the acceptance of party policy shifts, it is also important whether the party's and the voter's policy shift are in the same direction. I argued above that party position shifts following *voter position shifts* are more likely to get accepted. This is captured using a dummy variable with value 0 if the voter's policy position shift (on the respective policy scale) runs counter to the party's official policy shift (taken from the CMP data) and value 1 if the two actors shift their policy positions in the same direction.

Finally, I measure whether parties perform policy shifts that are not in line with their *ideological territory*. The measurement of these ideological territories is a sensitive issue which I discuss in greater detail below (see Chapter Seven). For the British case, voters should expect the Labour party on the left, the Conservatives on the right, and the Liberal Democrats (the Liberals and the Alliance, respectively) in the centre of the policy space. To code parties deviating from their ideological territory, a party's *current* party platform is compared with its rivals' policy positions at the *former* election. I use the *former* rather than the *current* policy positions of competitors, as these are known by parties so that they can adapt their policy platforms accordingly. This would be less the case for the competing parties' *current* positions as party programs are written at roughly the same time.[5] If the platform is left of or right of its expected position, the policy shift is coded as deviating from the party's ideological territory.

Figure 6.1 shows the party policy positions of the three major parties according to the CMP left-right scale. The grey-shaded areas indicate 95 per cent confidence intervals obtained using the algorithm developed by Kenneth Benoit, Michael Laver, and Slava Mikhaylov (Benoit *et al.* 2009b).[6] Until 1987, the policy positions most of the time correspond to the ideological territories most of the time with Labour on the left, the Conservatives on the right, and the Liberals in between. The merging of the Alliance of Liberals and Social Democrats into the Liberal Democrats from 1987 to 1992 led to a policy shift to the left, taking a policy position left of that of Labour in the 1987 elections. This is the first unexpected policy shift. The second is 'New Labour' in 1997. Compared to its 1992 position, Labour shifted to the right, 'leapfrogging' (Budge 1994) the Liberal Democrats. Finally, party position shifts were not in line with the voters' expectations in 2001: both Labour and the Liberal Democrats did not sufficiently correct for the unexpected policy positions caused by 'New Labour'. Compared to 1997, both parties are still in inappropriate or 'unexpected' policy positions.

In total, we have four instances of party shifts with are not in line with voter expectations: Liberal Democrats (1992), Labour (1997), Labour (2001), and again the Liberal Democrats (2001). Only the Conservatives 'behave well', having

---

5. Moreover, even if parties would be fully informed about their competitors' intentions, it would be unclear whether voters perceive these shifts. Indeed, insisting that a competing party has not changed may help to undermine its strategy and freeze it at its former position in the eyes of the voters.

6. For a more detailed discussion see Chapter Three.

Figure 6.1: Party left-right placements in Great Britain (October 1974 – 2001)

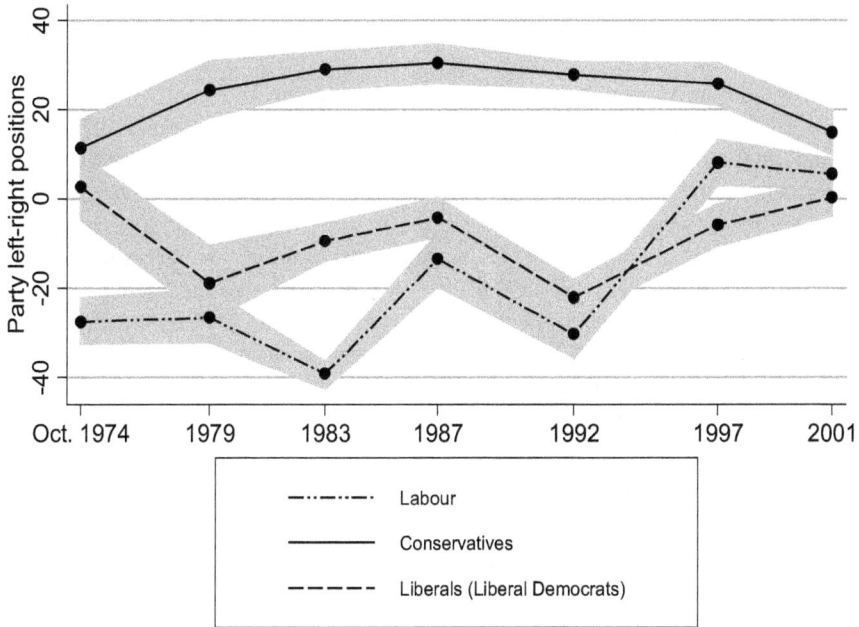

Grey bars indicate 95% confidence intervals

chosen policy positions in line with the ideological expectations in all elections under consideration. Due to missing data, we have no information on the voters' perceptions of the policy shift of the Liberal Democrats in 2001. Therefore, the analysis is confined to three cases of policy shifts leading parties to assume 'unexpected' policy positions relative to those of their competitors. Because the variable does not entail enough variance for a thorough statistical analysis, it is excluded from the multivariate analysis. I will analyse its effect on the perception of party policy shifts separately. Although these results are not as robust as those of the multivariate analysis, they allow for a first test of the plausibility of the arguments presented above.

As control variables, I include the voters' *age* and *sex*. Although not having any specific expectations, it is common to control for these covariates. The voters' age is measured in years and the dummy variable 'female' indicates whether the respondent is male (0) or female (1).

The 'New Labour' policy shift

Between 1992 and 1997, Labour's appearance changed in several ways. The 1993 Labour conference accepted the 'one member, one vote' idea, significantly reducing the trade unions' influence on the selection of the party leader, the parliamentary candidates and the decisions made at the annual party conference (Butler and Kavanagh 1997: 49). In addition to these institutional changes, the Labour Party moderated its policy platform in several ways. It abandoned Clause IV of the party's constitution which committed the party to the 'common ownership of the means of production, distribution, and exchange' (from Seyd and Whiteley 2004: 46). Moreover, Labour abandoned its Keynesian policy views. Instead of aiming for low unemployment, the party committed itself to the goal of low inflation (Heath *et al.* 2001: 104). Finally, the party aimed at getting rid of its 'tax and spend' image promising that a Labour government would not increase the rates of income tax during the next parliament's lifetime (Seyd 1998: 60–62).

These policy changes helped to create a new party image and a new language, distinguishing these reforms of 'New Labour' from the former period. The policy program, for example, explicitly broke up with 'old' Labour stating that '[w]e have changed the way we make policy, and put our relations with the trade unions on a modern footing where they accept they can get fairness but no favours from a Labour government' (Labour Party 1997). Gordon Brown, at that time shadow chancellor, stated in 1994 that

> [i]t is equally clear that the old Labour language, tax, spend and borrow, nationalisation, state planning, isolationism, full jobs for life for men while women stay at home – is equally inappropriate to the future as it was to the needs of the past. (Gordon Brown in the *Financial Times*, 1994 cited in Wickham-Jones 2005: 667)

In sum, the party's institutional design, its image and its policy program differed in many respects from that in preceding time periods. Compared to 1992, the party's image and policies were much more moderate.

Table 6.3: Perception of 'New Labour' in %

	Nationalisation vs. Privatisation	Taxes vs. Services	Unemployment vs. Inflation
Shift to the left	22.4	18.7	29.0
No shift	15.8	21.5	28.5
Shift to the right	61.8	59.7	42.6
N	804	817	815

Given the importance of 'New Labour', it is remarkable that the share of voters perceiving the policy position shift is rather small (see Table 6.3). Taking the 'Nationalisation vs. Privatisation' scale as a yardstick, only 60 per cent of the electorate perceived this moderating policy shift to the right. In other words, 40 per cent of the survey respondents stated that Labour did not moderate its policy position compared to 1992. More specifically, around 20 per cent of the voters asked in 1992, and the subsequent 1997 election, perceived no policy shift. Even more surprising, 20 per cent of the electorate perceived a Labour policy shift to the left.

The same pattern emerges for the 'Taxes vs. Services' scale. In contrast, the share of voters perceiving a rightward policy shift for 'Unemployment vs. Inflation' is even smaller covering roughly 40 per cent of the electorate. Six out of ten respondents stated that Labour made no shift, or a shift to the left, on this policy scale.

Table 6.4: Expected effects of covariates for the reception and acceptance of 'New Labour'

	Variable	Expectation
Reception	Political awareness	+
	Education	+
	Magnitude of voter policy shift	+
Acceptance	Party leader's prestige	+
	Party identification: party shifts towards voter	+
	Party identification: party shifts way from voter	-
	Party shift similar to voter shift?	+

The main goal is to analyse the differences between those voters perceiving the shift to the right and those perceiving Labour's shift or even a shift to the left. Studying only one party policy shift, party-specific factors of the model presented in Chapter Five are held constant. Table 6.4 summarises the remaining voter-specific expectations. Recall that I expect to see positive and significant coefficients for the voters' political awareness, education, and the magnitude of the voters' policy shifts. Moreover, voters should be more likely to perceive party policy shifts if they positively evaluate the party leader (Tony Blair) and if the shift is in line with their personal policy shift. Finally, party identification has a positive effect for voters being better off with Labour's policy shift. In contrast, the effect of party identification is negative for party policy shifts moving away from the respective voter's policy preferences.

Table 6.5 shows the regression results for the 'New Labour' policy shift. The first two models are logistic regressions for the reception (model 1) and acceptance (model 2) covariates. The third model presents the results of a two-stage logistic regression (see Appendix A). Studying the effects of the first model, political awareness has a positive impact on the reception of policy shifts: voters are more likely to receive the 'New Labour' policy shift if they are able to answer questions on political topics correctly. This finding conforms to the theoretical expectation. Moreover, the effect of political awareness on the reception of policy shifts is quite large. Politically unaware voters answering none of the questions correctly have a 46 per cent probability of receiving the party's shift message. This probability increases to 76 per cent if the respondent is able to answer all questions correctly.[7]

---

7. Probabilities computed using *Clarify* (King *et al.* 2000). The difference in the reported probabilities is highly significant at the 1 per cent level. Other variables held at their mean (voter shift and age)

Table 6.5: Perception of 'New Labour' 1997

	(1)	(2)	(3)
	Reception (logistic regression)	**Acceptance (logistic regression)**	**Two-stage logistic regression**
Political awareness	0.139**		0.167[+]
	(0.045)		(0.091)
Moderate education	0.271		0.077
	(0.208)		(0.447)
Advanced education	0.730*		0.845
	(0.304)		(0.761)
Magnitude of voter policy shift	-0.040		-0.029
	(0.057)		(0.114)
Age	-0.005		-0.038*
	(0.006)		(0.019)
Female	-0.066		1.418[+]
	(0.185)		(0.796)
Constant	-0.137		2.263[+]
	(0.401)		(1.304)
Party leader's prestige		0.099	0.147
		(0.103)	(0.153)
Party identification		0.409	0.952
		(0.296)	(0.736)
Party shift away from voter preferences		-1.784**	-2.495**
		(0.258)	(0.476)
Party id – Party shift away from voter preferences		-1.209**	-1.926*
		(0.432)	(0.820)
Party shift in line with voter shift?		-0.064	0.053
		(0.214)	(0.333)
Age		-0.003	0.025[+]
		(0.006)	(0.014)
Female		-0.164	-1.180**
		(0.202)	(0.435)
Constant		1.187*	1.224
		(0.530)	(1.057)
Observations	581	581	581
Log likelihood	-370.9	-307.7	-296.3

+ p < 0.1, * p < 0.05, ** p < 0.01   Standard errors in parentheses

or set to zero (female). The education is set to be moderate.

The impact of education on the reception of party policy shifts is also positive. In comparison to voters with a basic education (i.e. O level or CSE, for example), voters with further or higher education are more likely to receive the Labour position shift. Again, this finding conforms to the theory arguing that more educated voters have less difficulty receiving party policy shifts. In comparison to the effect size of political awareness, the effect of education on the reception is slightly smaller. Whereas voters with a basic education receive policy shifts in 59 per cent of the cases, voters with higher education receive the Labour shift with a probability of 74 per cent.[8]

In contrast, the magnitude of a voter policy shift does not affect on the perception of the 'New Labour' policy shift. Although not conforming to the theory described above, these negative findings could also be due to specific patterns of the 'New Labour' policy shift. In fact, Labour's policy shift in 1997 is not representative for British party policy shifts. For example, approximately 60 per cent of the voters perceived this party policy shift. Although surprisingly low, this figure is much higher than the reception of other party policy shifts. In general, voters only perceive approximately one third of all party policy shifts from the 1970s onwards (see below). Hence, the negative finding may not hold for party policy shifts in general.

Turning to the acceptance of the Labour shift in 1997 (model 2), Tony Blair's prestige as a party leader has a positive effect on the acceptance of 'New Labour': If Tony Blair's image is positive, voters are more likely to accept the proposed policy shift. Holding all other variables constant, voters with a negative view of Tony Blair accepted the party policy shift with a probability of 73 per cent. Voters evaluating Tony Blair's prestige as high do so with a probability of 80 per cent.[9]

---

8. As before, the probabilities are calculated using *Clarify* and the difference is also highly significant at the 1 per cent level. The remaining variables are set as above with political awareness set to its mean value.

9. As before, the size of the effect is calculated using *Clarify*. The probabilities reported hold for middle-aged male voters with no positive party identification for the Labour Party. Furthermore, the voter's policy shift is not in line with Labour's shift to the right and 'New Labour' deviates from the voter's preferences. The probabilities are not statistically significant at conventional levels (p=0.18)

Figure 6.2: Marginal effect of party identification on the perception of 'New Labour' (depending on the direction of the party policy shift)[10]

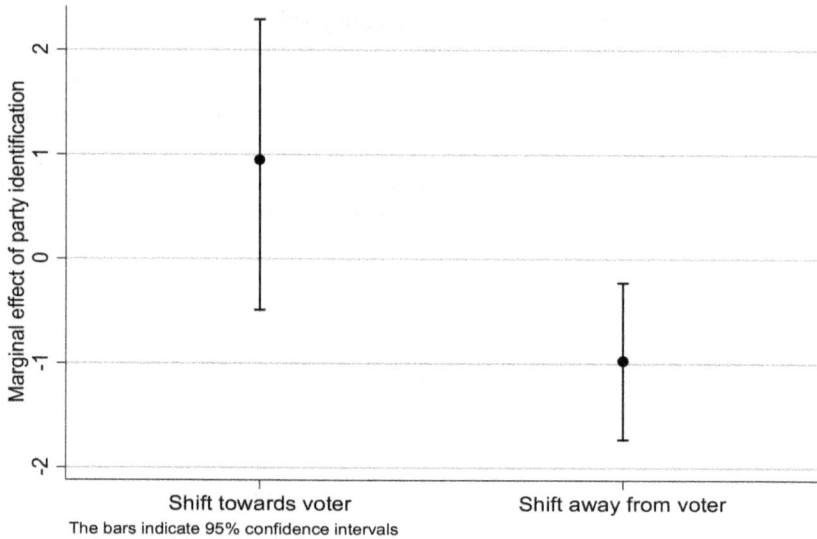

Shift towards voter   Shift away from voter

The bars indicate 95% confidence intervals

However, neither the regression coefficient nor the reported probabilities are statistically significant.

I argued above that the effect of the voters' party identification on the acceptance of party policy shifts depends on the direction of the party policy shift – voters with party identification are more likely to accept party policy shifts towards their policy preferences. In contrast, voters feeling close to Labour are less likely to accept shifts moving away from their personal policy preferences. Because interpreting the interacting regression coefficients is difficult, I illustrate the effect of the voter's party identification on the acceptance of policy shifts in Figure 6.2.

I expect a positive (and significant) effect of party identification for party policy shifts towards the voters' policy positions and a negative effect for shifts that are moving away from the voters' preferences. As can be seen, the point estimates show the expected patterns. The confidence intervals indicate, however, that the effect is only significant for party policy shifts moving away from the voters' preferences. Note that the confidence intervals on the right are much smaller than those on the left indicating that 'New Labour' was a shift away from the preferences of most voters identified with Labour. This is reasonable because voters identified with Labour most often have left-leaning preferences and are worse off by Labour's centrist shift. Substantially, Labour leader Tony

---

10. The estimates are taken from model 3.

Blair benefitted most from left-leaning voters identified with Labour not accepting the party's moderating policy shift. The positive effect of voters with Labour identification appreciating the party's moderating shift towards their personal policy preferences was much smaller. The effect of party identification also differs substantially across the two groups. For voters witnessing 'New Labour' as a policy shift towards their preferences, the probability of accepting the party policy shift increases from 80 per cent (no party identification) to roughly 85 per cent (for voters identified with Labour). Compared to the estimates presented above, the increase of about 5 percentage points is rather weak. For voters being worse off by Labour's policy shift, the probability of accepting this platform change decreases from 40 per cent (no party identification) to 23 per cent (positive party identification). Hence, the negative effect of party identification on the acceptance of party position shifts moving away from the voters' positions is substantially larger (17 percentage points).[11]

Finally, I also argued that voters are more likely to accept party position shifts in line with their personal policy shifts. For 'New Labour', voters turning to the right should hence be more likely to accept Labour's rightward shift. However, the estimate in model 2 does not show the expected positive effect. Rather, the coefficient is practically zero with no substantial effect. It should be noted, however, that voter position shifts correlate with the direction of Labour's policy shift. Voters shifting to the right are more likely to observe Labour's policy shift as a shift towards their policy preferences. The multicollinearity of the covariates may hence bias the results. As shown below, this is indeed the case. Dropping the party identification effect and its interaction terms, voter position shifts have a strong positive and significant effect on the acceptance of 'New Labour'.

So far, I calculated separate logistic regressions for the reception (model 1) and the acceptance (model 2) of Labour's policy shift in 1997. However, according to the theoretical model presented above (see Chapter Four), the perception of policy shifts is a two-stage process. Estimating separate models for the reception and the acceptance assumes that these steps are independent from each other which contradicts my theoretical expectation. Therefore, we analyse to what extent the estimates differ from a two-stage model.

The last column in Table 6.5 shows the estimates of the two-stage model. Note that the model contains two regression equations, one for the reception and one for the acceptance of the party policy shift. Comparing the results of the two-stage models with the reception (model 1) and acceptance (model 2) of 'New Labour', most of the (significant) effects in the separate models stay significant. Hence, the two-stage regression and the ordinary logistic regressions reveal similar estimates.

---

11. As before, the size of the effect is calculated using *Clarify*. The probabilities reported hold for middle-aged male voters perceiving Tony Blair as an average party leader and the voter's policy shift is not in line with Labour's shift to the right. The difference of the reported probabilities is statistically significant at the 10 per cent level (party shifts towards a voter's policy position) and the 1 per cent level (for 'New Labour' moving away from a voter's policy position).

However, two things are noteworthy. First, the effect sizes differ. For most of the covariates, the estimated coefficients of the reception and the acceptance part of the model equation are substantially larger than their separated counterparts presented in the separate analyses for reception (model 1) and acceptance (model 2). Hence, the findings indicate that the covariates of the acceptance function depend on the reception of policy shifts – as expected theoretically. Second, the standard errors of the two-stage model are larger than those of the separated logistic regressions. The increasing uncertainty of the model estimates is partly due to 'noise' introduced by the inclusion of further covariates. Moreover, the interacting nature of the two combined model equations leads to an increase of the size of the standard errors. But although the increasing number of covariates and the complex model structure increase the estimates' uncertainty, it is remarkable that most of the effects presented in models 1 and 2 remain statistically significant.

In sum, voters vary to the extent to which they perceive Labour's centrist policy shift in 1997. First, political awareness and the voter's education impact on the perception of 'New Labour'. Less educated or political unaware voters are less likely to receive the party's shift message. I also find empirical evidence for the voters' party identification affecting the acceptance of 'New Labour'. For party identifiers perceiving 'New Labour' as a shift towards their policy preferences, being identified with Labour increases the changes of accepting the policy shift. The positive effect is, however, not statistically significant at conventional levels. In contrast, being identified with Labour has a strong negative effect on the perception of Labour's shift away from the respective voters' preferences. For those voters, Labour's centrist shift contradicts the party's image formed by their party identification. Because the party identification and the party's announced policy position do not match, those voters are less likely to accept Labour's 1997 policy shift.

The perception of party policy shifts in Great Britain 1974–2001

Labour's position shift in 1997 is rather exceptional in the British history of party competition. Moreover, I argued above that several party-specific covariates impact on the perception of party policy shifts. Testing these propositions is not possible studying only one party position shift. The following analysis makes use of data from multiple elections in Great Britain between 1974 and 2001. The pooled sample allows for testing the theory outlined above on a larger sample including party-specific covariates.

Table 6.6 gives a first overview of the perception of party policy shifts for different parties and policy scales. Taking the CMP left-right positions as a reference point, Table 6.6 indicates how many voters correctly perceive the parties' policy shifts. For all three policy scales the figures indicate that only one third of the electorate perceives party policy shifts. In other words, two-thirds of the parties'

Table 6.6: Perception of party position shifts in Great Britain 1974–2001 (in %)

		Conservatives	Labour	Lib Dems	Total
Nationalisation vs. Privatisation	not perceived	60	71	68	66
	perceived	40	29	32	34
	N	7,535	7,547	5,392	20,474
Taxes vs. Services	not perceived	53	65	62	60
	perceived	47	35	38	40
	N	6,038	6,059	4,882	16,979
Unemployment vs. Inflation	not perceived	59	72	61	64
	perceived	41	28	39	36
	N	5,399	5,407	4,922	15,728

position shifts go unnoticed by voters. Moreover, there is not much variation across parties and across scales.[12] These numbers are even lower than those reported above, showing that the relatively high perception rate for 'New Labour' (around 60 per cent) is the exception rather than the rule.

What factors impact on the perception of party policy shifts? As for the Labour position shift in 1997, I first estimate logistic regressions predicting the reception and the acceptance of policy shifts. Then, I present the results of two-stage regression models distinguishing the reception and the acceptance stages of perceiving party policy shifts. I estimate these regressions for all three policy scales beginning with the 'Nationalisation vs. Privatisation' scale.

Nationalisation vs. Privatisation

Table 6.7 reports the regression results for the reception (1), the acceptance (2), and the two-stage regression model (3) using the 'Nationalisation vs. Privatisation' scale. For the ease of interpretation, the theoretical expectations are summarised in the last column. Regarding the reception of policy shifts, the results do not support most of the theoretical expectations presented above. The strong predictor for the reception of 'New Labour', political awareness, shows a different pattern in the pooled sample. The higher the voters' political awareness, the lower the probability that voters accept the parties' policy shifts. The finding hence

---

12. Note that Table 6.6 is based on respondents being able to locate party policy positions at two time points. In general, British voters are less likely to identify policy positions of the Liberal Democrats. Hence, voters are less likely to perceive their party position shifts.

contradicts the theoretical expectation and the positive finding for 'New Labour'. Note, however, that the reception model in Table 6.7 uses political interest instead of political awareness because political quizzes were only used in the 1979 and 1997 election studies. Calculating regression models for those two elections using political awareness instead of political interest (see below), the effect is positive and highly significant. This suggests argue that this negative finding is due to the unsatisfying measurement of the concept.

The effects of voter's education are in the predicted direction. Voters with moderate or higher education are more likely to receive party position shifts than voters with basic education. At least for voters with moderate education, the estimate is statistically significant at the 10 per cent level. The remaining substantial covariates do not reach conventional significance levels: As in the case of 'New Labour', voters do not update party policy placements when shifting their personal policy preferences. Furthermore, the two party-specific covariates (i.e. governmental status and the magnitude of the party policy shifts) also do not affect the voters' reception in this model specification.

The second model in Table 6.7 puts the acceptance covariates of party policy shifts to an empirical test. In addition to the control variables, five variables are of substantive interest. I expect that the acceptance of policy shifts increases with a change in the party leadership, higher prestige of the respective party leader, smaller party policy shifts in the past, and if the direction of party and voter policy shifts coincide. Moreover, I expect a positive effect of party identification if the party policy shift is towards the voters' preferences. In contrast, the effect should be negative for party platform shifts away from the voters' policy preferences.

The results show that the acceptance of party policy shifts increases if the leadership has changed. In the logistic regression model omitting the two-stage process, however, the finding does not reach statistical significance. Moreover, voters are more likely to accept party policy shifts if the party leader's prestige is high. The coefficient is statistically significant at the 5 per cent level and is in the expected direction. Furthermore, the magnitude of past party policy shifts does not have a significant effect on the acceptance of party policy shifts. In contrast, the empirical results support the theoretical expectations for voter party identification. To ease interpretation, Figure 6.3 shows the marginal effect of party identification on the acceptance of party policy shifts depending on the direction of the party policy shift. For party policy shifts towards the voter's policy position, party identification shows the expected positive effect: voters with party identification are indeed more likely to accept party position shifts towards their personal policy preferences. In contrast, the effect of party identification is negative for party shifts away from the voters' policy preferences. Voters identifying with a particular party are hence less likely to accept (i.e. consider credible) policy shifts of 'their' party away from their policy positions.

Table 6.7: Perception of policy shifts – Nationalisation (with clustered SEs)

	(1) Reception (logistic regression)	(2) Acceptance (logistic regression)	(3) Two-stage logistic regression	Exp.
Political interest	-0.015*		-0.058**	+
	(0.007)		(0.017)	
Moderate education	0.172+		-0.007	+
	(0.089)		(0.165)	
Advanced education	0.053		0.031	+
	(0.098)		(0.115)	
Magnitude of voter policy shift	-0.014		0.162+	+
	(0.030)		(0.085)	
Party in government	-0.273		-11.604**	+
	(0.456)		(1.043)	
Magnitude of party policy shift	0.016		-0.100**	+
	(0.025)		(0.020)	
Conservatives	0.701**		11.075**	
	(0.135)		(0.792)	
Labour	0.231		9.515**	
	(0.372)		(0.731)	
Age	0.003		0.003	
	(0.002)		(0.009)	
Female	0.020		0.403+	
	(0.039)		(0.215)	
Constant	-1.040*		2.286**	
	(0.416)		(0.757)	
Party leader change		0.263	0.293*	+
		(0.210)	(0.143)	
Party leader's prestige		0.108*	0.151**	+
		(0.048)	(0.038)	
Magnitude of past party policy shift		-0.016	0.042**	-
		(0.022)	(0.013)	
Party identification		0.482**	0.552**	+

(cont'd overleaf)

	(1)	(2)	(3)	
	Reception (logistic regression)	Acceptance (logistic regression)	Two-stage logistic regression	Exp.
		(0.302)	(0.305)	
Interaction: Party id · Party shift away from voter preferences		-1.043** (0.125)	-1.158** (0.120)	-
Party shift similar to voter shift?		-0.093	-0.200*	+
		(-0.089)	(0.100)	
Conservatives		0.054	0.105	
		(0.307)	(0.285)	
Labour		-0.050	-0.670	
		(0.292)	(0.410)	
Age		0.0007	-0.001	
		(0.004)	(0.003)	
Female		0.077	-0.079	
		(0.056)	(0.095)	
Constant		-0.049	0.117	
		(0.215)	(0.207)	
Observations	9689	9689	9689	
Log likelihood	-6295.5	-5370.6	-5174.0	

$+ p < 0.1$, $* p < 0.05$, $** p < 0.01$
Clustered standard errors in parentheses

I do not find any effect for a higher acceptance of party policy shifts in line with voter position shifts. As for the 'New Labour' case, however, voter position shifts show a high (negative) correlation with party shifts away from the voters' preferences: voters shifting in the same direction as their respective political parties are more likely to benefit from these party policy shifts. Hence, the insignificant effect may be partly due to multicollinearity of the two covariates. In fact, omitting party identification and the related direction variables from the model (see below), the coefficient for the voters' direction of policy shifts has the expected positive effect: voters are more likely to accept party policy shifts in line with their personal policy shifts.

Combining the reception (1) and the acceptance model (2), the two-stage logistic regression in model (3) considers the covariates of both models and the theoretically assumed perception process. It turns out that the model estimates differ in some respects from their one-stage predecessors. In the reception part of the model, educational variables no longer reach significance. In contrast, the regression results show the expected positive (and significant) effect of the voters'

Figure 6.3: The effect of party identification on the acceptance of policy shifts depending on the party shift's direction: Nationalisation[13]

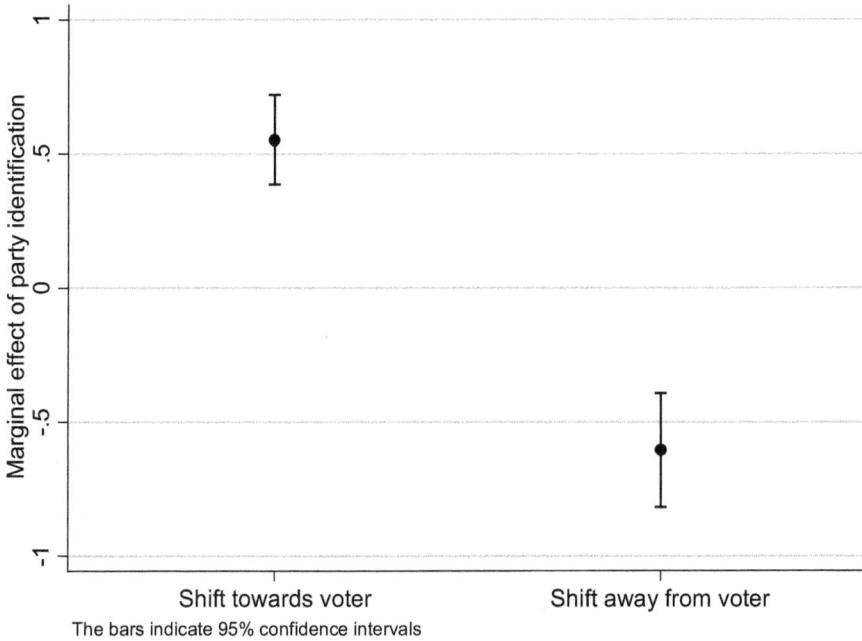

Shift towards voter   Shift away from voter

The bars indicate 95% confidence intervals

updating process: The larger the voters' policy shifts, the more likely voters receive the parties' shift messages. Furthermore, the party-specific covariates of the reception function are statistically significant but both effects are against my theoretical expectation: voters are less likely to receive party policy shifts of government parties. Moreover, the magnitude of the parties' platform changes negatively affects their reception. While the former counterintuitive result may be due to specificities of the British party system (discussed below), the latter result is not replicable in the remaining analyses.

The results of the acceptance part of the model are more in line with those of the pure acceptance model (model 2). For three of the five effects, the coefficients of the two-stage model point in the expected direction: voters are more likely to accept party position shifts if the party leadership changed and if the party leader's prestige is high. Moreover, voters with party identification are more likely (less likely) to accept policy shifts towards (away from) their personal preferences. All regression coefficients are statistically significant. Yet, two effects are against my theoretical expectations. First, the larger a party's previous policy shift, the more

---

13. The estimates are taken from model 3.

likely it is that voters accept another party policy shift. Moreover, voters are less likely to accept party policy shifts in line with voter position shifts. While the former result has substantive consequences for the theoretical model, the latter is likely to be due to multicollinearity of the model covariates.

Taxes vs. Services

This section applies the same covariates to another dependent variable: the perceived party position shifts on the 'Taxes vs. Services' scale. Compared to the analysis of the 'Nationalisation vs. Privatisation' scale, the number of observations is smaller because the question was not asked before 1979. I proceed as before. I first estimate logistic regressions for the reception (1) and the acceptance (2) of party policy shifts. Then, I estimate a two-stage regression combining the covariates of the first and the second model (3). The regression results are displayed in Table 6.8.

Most of the estimates of the reception function are insignificant. The voters' political interest does not affect the reception of party position shifts. As for the 'Nationalisation vs. Privatisation' scale, the negative result maybe due to the measurement of the concept: Restricting the sample to the 1979 and 1997 elections allows for using political quizzes instead of political interest. Calculating the same reception regression with this reduced sample leads to a highly significant, positive coefficient (see below). The coefficients for the voters' education point in the right direction without reaching statistical significance. Moreover, the magnitude of the voters' position shifts does not affect the reception of party policy shifts. Except for the control variables, only one covariate has a statistically significant effect on the reception of party policy shifts: the larger the party's position shift, the higher the likelihood that voters receive the message. Hence, the effect is in the expected direction.

Turning to the acceptance of party policy shifts, model 2 in Table 6.8 reveals only one significant effect. The voters' party identification has the expected effect on the acceptance of party policy shifts. Figure 6.4 plots the marginal effect of party identification depending on the direction of party policy shifts *vis-à-vis* the voters' policy positions. As expected, voters feeling close to a particular party are more likely to accept policy shifts of their party if the policy shifts are towards their own policy preferences. In contrast, party identification negatively affects the acceptance of party policy shifts away from the voters' preferences.

The final model reported in Table 6.8 combines the reception and acceptance covariates in a two-stage logistic regression. The regression results are quite similar to the separate models of reception (model 1) and acceptance (model 2). Both the magnitude of the party policy shifts and the interacting effect of the voters' party identification keep their expected and significant coefficients. In addition, the magnitude of the voters' policy shift positively affects the reception of party policy shifts. As expected, voters 'update' their information on political parties when shifting policy positions. In the acceptance part of the model, the party leader's prestige affects the perception of party policy shifts. Conforming to the theoretical expectations, voters are more likely to accept party policy shifts if they evaluate the party leader positively.

Table 6.8: Perception of policy shifts – Taxes vs. Services (with clustered SEs)

	(1) Reception (logistic regression)	(2) Acceptance (logistic regression)	(3) Two-stage logistic regression	Exp.
Political interest	-0.018		-0.0313	+
	(0.015)		(0.020)	
Moderate education	0.026		-0.117	+
	(0.045)		(0.080)	
Advanced education	0.049		-0.133	+
	(0.076)		(0.155)	
Magnitude of voter policy shift	0.026		0.148$^+$	+
	(0.021)		(0.076)	
Party in government	0.037		-0.333	+
	(0.154)		(0.350)	
Magnitude of party policy shift	0.029*		0.039*	+
	(0.014)		(0.012)	
Conservatives	0.585**		0.475	
	(0.195)		(0.338)	
Labour	-0.114		0.245	
	(0.243)		(0.526)	
Age	0.002		0.013$^+$	
	(0.002)		(0.008)	
Female	0.043		0.309*	
	(0.039)		(0.153)	
Constant	-0.982**		-0.244	
	(0.287)		(0.397)	
Party leader change		0.161	-0.073	+
		(0.357)	(0.382)	
Party leader's prestige		0.081	0.108$^+$	+
		(0.057)	(0.063)	
Magnitude of past party policy shift		0.007	0.017	-
		(0.014)	(0.016)	
Party identification		0.532**	1.150**	+
		(0.0876)	(0.286)	

(cont'd overleaf)

	(1) Reception (logistic regression)	(2) Acceptance (logistic regression)	(3) Two-stage logistic regression	Exp.
Party shift similar to voter shift?		0.083	0.126	+
		(0.123)	(0.130)	
Conservatives		0.137	0.308	
		(0.313)	(0.449)	
Labour		-0.278	-0.521	
		(0.446)	(0.426)	
Age		0.0002	-0.009**	
		(0.002)	(0.003)	
Female		0.124**	-0.077	
		(0.040)	(0.116)	
Constant		-0.133	1.212+	
		(0.303)	(0.721)	
Observations	8253	8253	8253	
Log likelihood	-5482.2	-4769.3	-4712.5	

+ $p < 0.1$, * $p < 0.05$, ** $p < 0.01$
Clustered standard errors in parentheses

Unemployment vs. Inflation

In this section, I use perceived party position shifts on the 'Unemployment vs. Inflation' scale as the dependent variable. Compared to the former two scales, the number of observations is smaller as the questions are available only from 1987 onwards. The models are presented as above. First, I calculate a logistic regression containing the reception variables. The second logistic regression covers the variables expected to impact on the acceptance of party policy shifts. Then, a two-stage logistic regression combines these covariates taking the data-generating process into account. The estimates of these models are presented in Table 6.9.

In the reception function, the magnitude of the party's policy shift has a positive effect on the voters' perception. The effect is positive and statistically significant at the 5 per cent level. The remaining coefficients are insignificant and hence most of the hypotheses are not supported using policy shifts on the 'Unemployment vs. Inflation' scale as the dependent variable. Specifically, political awareness does not affect the voters' reception of party policy shifts. This negative result is – once again – likely to be due to the measurement of the concept. As for the other two scales, restricting the model to elections for which political quizzes were conducted, the effect becomes positive and significant (see below).

Figure 6.4: The effect of party identification on the acceptance of policy shifts depending on the party shift's direction: Taxes vs. Services [14]

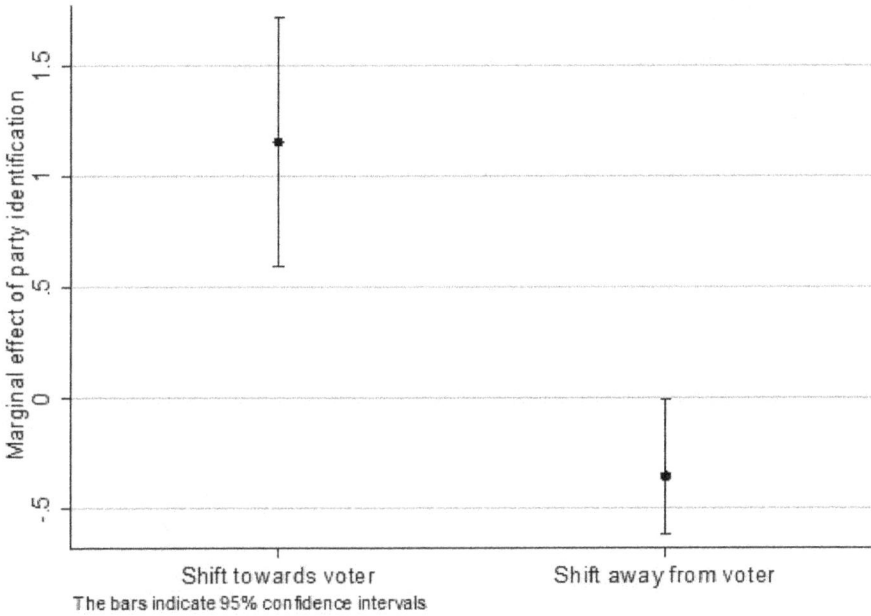

Shift towards voter   Shift away from voter

The bars indicate 95% confidence intervals

Turning to the second model, the effect of the voters' party identification conforms to the theoretical expectation. As for the previous models, I display the marginal effect graphically.

Figure 6.5 shows the expected pattern: Party identification positively affects the acceptance of party policy shifts if the party shift is towards the voter's policy position. In case the party moves away from the voter, however, voters with party identification are less likely to accept the party's new policy position. For the remaining substantial covariates, the effects are insignificant. Note, however, that multicollinearity between the voter's policy shifts and the direction of the party shifts, prevents statistically significant effects of the former. Omitting party identification and its interaction terms from the model, leads to the expected positive effect (see below).

Model 3 in Table 6.9 combines the reception (1) and the acceptance (2) models in a two-stage logistic regression. In the reception part of the model, political awareness has the expected positive effect on the reception of party policy shifts. Hence, the voters' reception of party policy shifts increases with their political interest. The magnitude of the party's policy shift no longer has a

---

14. The estimates are taken from model 3.

statistical significant effect on the voters' reception function. Although the size of the effect increases from model 1 (0.023) to model 3 (0.032), the coefficient no longer reaches a significant level in the two-stage model. The remaining covariates remain insignificant.

Turning to the acceptance function, the voters' party identification still shows the expected pattern. As in the previous models, voters are more likely to accept party policy shifts towards their preferences if they also feel close to that party. In contrast, the effect of party identification is negative for party shifts away from the voters' policy preferences. In addition, the coefficient of the party leaders' prestige becomes significant. As expected, voters are more likely to accept party policy shifts if they rate the leaders' skills highly. The remaining substantial covariates do not reach conventional levels of statistical significance.

Table 6.9: Perception of policy shifts – Unemployment vs. Inflation (with clustered SEs)

	(1)	(2)	(3)	
	Reception (logistic regression)	Acceptance (logistic regression)	Two-stage logistic regression	Exp.
Political interest	0.015		0.065**	+
	(0.014)		(0.018)	
Moderate education	0.012		-0.127	+
	(0.048)		(0.105)	
Advanced education	-0.021		-0.187	+
	(0.048)		(0.142)	
Magnitude of voter policy shift	-0.015		0.078	+
	(0.011)		(0.156)	
Party in government	-0.0007		-0.317	+
	(0.252)		(0.375)	
Magnitude of party policy shift	0.023*		0.032	+
	(0.010)		(0.024)	
Conservatives	0.335*		0.070	
	(0.135)		(0.532)	
Labour	-0.289*		1.149[+]	
	(0.116)		(0.641)	
Age	0.004[+]		0.027[+]	
	(0.002)		(0.015)	

(cont'd overleaf)

	(1) Reception (logistic regression)	(2) Acceptance (logistic regression)	(3) Two-stage logistic regression	Exp.
Party leader change		-0.065	-0.287	+
		(0.232)	(0.197)	
Party leader's prestige		0.031	0.045*	+
		(0.029)	(0.019)	
Magnitude of past party policy shift		0.003	0.004	-
		(0.004)	(0.005)	
Party identification		0.714**	1.017**	+
		(0.098)	(0.195)	
Party shift away from voter preferences		-1.907**	-2.227**	
		(0.191)	(0.169)	
Interaction: Party id · Party shift away from voter preferences		-1.188** (0.096)	-1.532** (0.223)	-
Party shift similar to voter shift?		0.078	0.081	+
		(0.133)	(0.155)	
Conservatives		-0.055	0.222	
		(0.230)	(0.206)	
Labour		-0.229+	-0.502*	
		(0.123)	(0.209)	
Age		0.006	-0.004*	
		(0.003)	(0.002)	
Female		0.054	0.048	
		(0.033)	(0.078)	
Constant		0.003	1.072**	
		(0.186)	(0.292)	
Observations	7160	7160	7160	
Log likelihood	-4657.9	-3770.6	-3745.5	

+ p < 0.1, * p < 0.05, ** p < 0.01

Figure 6.5: The effect of party identification on the acceptance of policy shifts depending on the party shift's direction: Unemployment vs. Inflation [15]

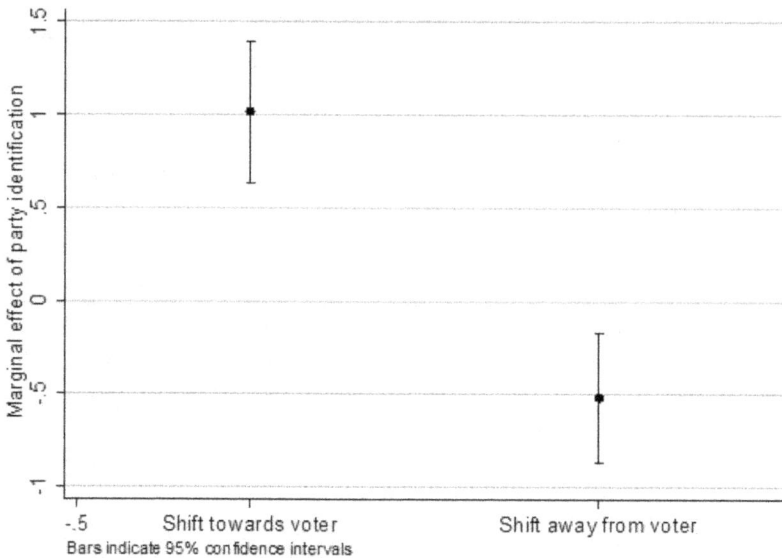

Bars indicate 95% confidence intervals

Summary of the empirical results

The models presented above test the theoretical expectations of how voters perceive party policy shifts using different methods, samples and variables. In this section, I give a short overview of the regression results in the various models. Some of the findings are robust and in line with my theoretical expectations. Other empirical results are rather mixed with contradicting empirical evidence. I argue that some of the insignificant effects are due to the way the concepts are measured while others are the product of multicollinearity of the covariates. Finally, I discuss the effects contradicting the theoretical expectations.

Table 6.10 summarises the regression results for the reception covariates presented above. In two of the four models, the results for the voters' education and the magnitude of the voters' policy shift lend support to my hypotheses. In contrast, the findings contradict the hypothesis that party policy shifts are more visible for government than for opposition parties. In one of the three models capturing party-specific effects, the coefficient is negative and statistically significant. The remaining two covariates provide mixed results: The voters' political awareness and the magnitude of the parties' policy shifts show effects in the expected direction in some models and contradicting findings in others.

---

15. The estimates are taken from model 3.

Table 6.10: Hypotheses and regression results for the reception covariates

	New Labour 1997	Nationalis- ation vs. Privatisation	Taxes vs. Services	Unemploy- ment vs. Inflation
Political awareness (political interest)	✓	✗		✓
Education	(✓)	(✓)		
Magnitude of voter policy shift		✓	✓	
Party in government before election?	NA	✗		
Magnitude of party policy shift	NA	✗	✓	(✓)

✓   Conforms to the hypothesis; significant effect (with at least 90 per cent confidence) in the expected direction.

✗   Contradicts the hypothesis; unexpected, significant (with at least 90 per cent confidence).

(✓) Coefficient significant in the logistic regression but not in the two-stage model.

Turning to the acceptance covariates, Table 6.11 summarises the empirical findings for the analysis of 'New Labour' and the regressions of the pooled sample. The results are more clear-cut than for the reception covariates. Changes in the party leadership positively affect the acceptance in one of the three model specifications. Moreover, the party leader's prestige shows the expected positive effect in three of the four model specifications. In contrast, the parties' credibility is not constrained by large party policy shifts in the past. In three of the four model specifications, the positive effect of the voters' party identification for shifts towards the party's policy position is significant. Furthermore, the hypothesised negative effect of party identification for party shifts away from the voter's policy preferences finds empirical support in all four models. Finally, voters are not more likely to accept party position shifts in the same direction as voter position shifts.

Does political awareness matter?

It is argued above that the mixed results for the voters' political awareness are due to the measurement of awareness using political interest. Using political quizzes for testing the voters' knowledge on political issues is the preferred measure (Zaller 1992: Appendix). Such a measure is unavailable in all but two elections and therefore I have to rely on political interest.

Table 6.11: Hypotheses and regression results for the acceptance covariates

	New Labour 1997	Nationalis- ation vs. Privatisation	Taxes vs. Services	Unemploy- ment vs. Inflation
Change in leadership	NA	✓		
Party leader's prestige		✓	✓	✓
Magnitude of past party policy shift	NA	✗		
Party identification: Shift towards voter's poli- cy position		✓	✓	✓
Party identification: Shift moving away from voter's policy position	✓	✓	✓	✓
Party shift similar to voter shift?		✗		

✓ Conforms to the hypothesis; significant effect (with at least 90 per cent confidence) in the expected direction

✗ Contradicts the hypothesis; unexpected, significant (with at least 90 per cent confidence)

Table 6.12 shows the model estimates of logistic regressions using a restricted sample for which political quizzes, as measures for political awareness, are available. Note that the number of observations drops dramatically as the quizzes are only available for the elections in 1979 (except for the 'Unemployment vs. Inflation' scale) and 1997.[16] The model estimates show that political awareness has a positive and significant effect in all four models. Hence, more aware voters are more likely to receive the parties' policy shift messages, which conforms to my theoretical expectations. I hence conclude that political awareness indeed affects the reception of party policy shifts and that the mixed results in the above regressions are due to the use of weak measures (i.e. using political interest rather than political awareness).

---

16. Because the models only include two election years, I drop the party-specific covariates (governmental status and magnitude of the party's policy shift). Instead of clustered standard errors, the model contains party and election fixed effects.

Are voters more likely to accept party shifts in line with their personal policy shifts?

I hypotheses that voters are more likely to accept party policy shifts in the same direction as their own policy shifts. The empirical results presented so far suggest that the hypothesis does not hold. Yet, the model estimates may be biased by multicollinearity in the regression models: Voters shifting in the same direction as political parties are less likely to perceive the party's policy shift as moving away from their personal policy preferences. Because the two covariates correlate, the standard errors of the estimates increase and the coefficients may hence become insignificant.

To test these considerations, Table 6.13 presents logistic regressions excluding the party identification effect and its interaction terms. A quick look at Table 6.13 reveals that the model estimates of party shifts in line with voter position shifts are positive and statistically significant in all four model specifications. Hence, party shifts in line with voter position shifts are indeed more likely to get accepted.

Explaining contradicting effects

With the regression models presented in Table 6.12 and Table 6.13, two of the odd findings are identified as artefacts of their measurement and multicollinearity. Nevertheless, two covariates show empirical patterns contradicting the hypothesised effects. First, voters are (partly) less likely to receive position shifts of parties in governments. Second, one model shows that voters are more likely to perceive party position shifts if the party made large policy shifts before.

The first finding is rather counterintuitive. Although government parties may not be more likely to get their policy shift message heard, it is curious why government parties should be less visible than their rivals in opposition. It may be that this unexpected pattern is due to characteristics of the British party system. The British party system differs in many respects from many other European party systems. With two major parties, voters are able concentrate on both the party in government and its major rival in opposition. Therefore, the difference between government and opposition parties could be less severe than for systems with three or more parties sending their signals to the electorate. With the increasing number of senders, the voters increasingly focus on action taken by government parties. Thus, the voters' reception differences between government and opposition parties are higher in multiparty systems.

One may also think of situations where opposition parties are more visible than their rivals in office. This is especially likely in party systems with two major rivals, eye-catching slogans in election campaigns of opposition parties, or charismatic party leaders who may get more attention than pale looking prime ministers with low popularity ratings. Particularly if a government party suffers heavily from its time in office and a cabinet turnover is highly likely, voters may concentrate on the promises of the party in opposition rather than the excuses of the government party.[17]

---

17. For party systems covering more than two relevant parties, blame avoidance and credit claiming of coalition partners, turns more attention to cabinet parties. Moreover, losing votes does not

Table 6.12: Using political awareness instead of political interest and the effect on the reception of party policy shifts

	(1) New Labour 1997	(2) Nationalis- ation vs. Privatisation	(3) Taxes vs. Services	(4) Unemploy- ment vs. Inflation
Political awareness	0.139**	0.0533*	0.0548**	0.0656*
	(3.09)	(2.39)	(2.59)	(2.48)
Moderate education	0.271	0.0667	0.0274	-0.170
	(1.30)	(0.61)	(0.26)	(-1.39)
Advanced education	0.730*	0.372**	0.0740	0.00953
	(2.40)	(2.93)	(0.58)	(0.06)
Magnitude of voter policy shift	-0.0403	0.0368	0.00649	0.0114
	(-0.71)	(1.62)	(0.25)	(0.45)
Conservatives		0.518**	0.705**	0.107
		(4.30)	(5.92)	(0.84)
Labour		0.880**	0.858**	0.269*
		(7.26)	(7.19)	(2.12)
1997		0.749**	0.220+	
		(6.53)	(1.85)	
Age	-0.00483	0.0000760	-0.00545+	-0.00152
	(-0.80)	(0.03)	(-1.87)	(-0.43)
Female	-0.0659	-0.0716	0.0662	-0.0591
	(-0.36)	(-0.79)	(0.74)	(-0.54)
Constant	-0.137	-1.797**	-0.992**	-0.626*
	(-0.34)	(-6.35)	(-3.58)	(-2.50)
Observations	581	2290	2319	1557
Log likelihood	-370.9	-1529.5	-1572.0	-1062.0

z statistics in parentheses $+ p < 0.1$, * $p < 0.05$, ** $p < 0.01$

necessarily involve the loss of office. Some government parties may survive in subsequent cabinets either adding new partners to the current coalition, or continuing in government in a coalition with former opposition parties. As a result, multiparty systems are less likely to result in a situation with voters dedicating attention to opposition rather than government parties.

Table 6.13: Acceptance models without party identification: Avoiding multicollinearity

	(1) New Labour 1997	(2) Nationalis- ation vs. Privatisation	(3) Taxes vs. Services	(4) Unemploy- ment vs. Inflation
Change in leadership		0.561**	0.447**	0.303*
		(3.43)	(5.19)	(2.03)
Party leader's prestige	0.0791	0.0823*	0.0721	0.0102
	(0.88)	(2.37)	(1.35)	(0.32)
Magnitude of past party policy shift		-0.0219	-0.000296	-0.00816
		(-1.36)	(-0.02)	(-0.89)
Party shift similar to voter shift?	*0.628**￼*	*0.451**￼*	*0.685**￼*	*0.879**￼*
	(3.57)	*(6.82)*	*(7.42)*	*(11.54)*
Conservatives		0.0721	0.308**	0.0576
		(0.23)	(4.52)	(0.26)
Labour		0.295	-0.0867	-0.0861
		(1.64)	(-0.18)	(-0.54)
Age	-0.00348	0.000385	0.00125	0.00419*
	(-0.61)	(0.15)	(0.60)	(2.03)
Female	-0.326+	0.0417	0.0738**	-0.0115
	(-1.87)	(1.05)	(3.65)	(-0.19)
Constant	0.263	-1.033*	-1.252**	-1.186**
	(0.57)	(-2.44)	(-6.78)	(-3.17)
Observations	581	9689	8253	7160
Log likelihood	-377.4	-6114.8	-5378.6	-4518.9

z statistics in parentheses   + $p < 0.1$, * $p < 0.05$, ** $p < 0.01$

Turning to the second negative finding, it is puzzling why voters are more likely to accept policy shifts if the party's previous policy shift was large. The reason for this odd effect may result from incentives from the party system.[18] In some instances, political parties have to react to changing incentives in their environment.

---

18. For a more detailed discussion see Chapter Seven.

Public opinion shocks, shifts of rival parties and current party positions not in line with their ideological territory may force parties to adapt their policy platform irrespective of past policy shifts. Given that this hypothesised effect is correct, voters may also acknowledge the parties' need to respond to such challenges. If the political market requires parties to shift their policy positions, large party policy shifts of the past may only signal that parties can indeed adapt to changes in their environment. Hence, voters are more likely to accept party policy shifts if the previous shift was large. Yet, this positive effect should only hold in times of political market turbulence. In calm times, however, the hypothesised effect could hold.

Voters' acceptance of party policy shifts deviation from their ideological territory

In the theoretical part (see Chapter Five), I introduce the concept of 'expected' party positions relative to their rivals and argue that voters are less likely to accept party policy shifts deviating from their ideological territory. Due to restrictions of the available data, however, I am not able to include this variable in the multivariate models. For the period between 1979 and 2001, the British party system only witnessed four party shifts not in line with the expected policy positions. Moreover, data is missing for one of those shifts (Liberal Democrats 2001).

We are, therefore, left with three cases of parties shifting to locations that do not conform to their ideological territories: the Liberal Democrats in 1992 and the two Labour party policy shifts in 1997 and 2001. In Table 6.14, I present multivariate analyses regressing these policy shifts on the voters' perception of party policy shifts for the 'Nationalisation' (1), 'Taxes vs. Services' (2), and 'Unemployment' policy scales. Party policy shifts are measured as dummy variables. In addition, I control for the magnitude of party policy shifts. The respondents' age and sex are also captured as control variables. As in the previous models, the standard errors are clustered for the respective elections.

The regression coefficients show the expected negative effects for two of the three party positions shifts (Labour 2001, Liberal Democrats 1992) but the model estimates are positive for 'New Labour' in 1997. Holding the magnitude of the party policy shift constant, voters are hence less likely to perceive the policy shifts of Labour in 2001 and the Liberal Democrats in 1992 but more likely to perceive 'New Labour'. The results suggest that parties may sometimes be able to credibly leave their ideological habitat while voters do not accept (i.e. consider credible) such shifts in other situations.

The two subsequent policy shifts of Labour in 1997 and 2001 are well suited for studying such differences in the perception of party policy shifts. Note that I already control for the magnitude of the party policy shift, indicating that the perception of party policy shifts is not due to the policy distance between the old and the new party policy position. Rather, party policy shifts not in line with the 'expected' policy position should affect the voters' acceptance. Tony Blair's position as a party leader could play a role here. The two policy shifts differ in two respects. First, the 1997 election was the first election for Blair as a party leader. Blair presented himself as a reformer who had

Table 6.14: The acceptance of 'unexpected' party policy shifts

	(1) Nationalisation vs. Privatisation	(2) Taxes vs. Services	(3) Unemployment vs. Inflation
Labour 1997	1.549[+]	1.215[**]	0.376
	(1.87)	(3.28)	(1.04)
Labour 2001	-0.432	-0.574[**]	-0.576[**]
	(-1.54)	(-3.92)	(-4.24)
Liberal Democrats 1992	0.118	0.270	-0.377[*]
	(0.37)	(1.21)	(-2.15)
Magnitude of party policy shift	-0.0178	-0.0142[+]	-0.00175
	(-0.65)	(-1.86)	(-0.16)
Age	0.00171	0.00263	0.00416[+]
	(0.66)	(1.08)	(1.77)
Female	0.0237	0.0707[+]	0.0457
	(0.44)	(1.77)	(0.60)
Constant	-0.417[+]	-0.337[*]	-0.623[**]
	(-1.77)	(-2.56)	(-2.59)
Observations	9689	8253	7160
Log likelihood	-6312.1	-5515.5	-4675.6

z statistics in parentheses

$+ p < 0.1$, $* p < 0.05$, $** p < 0.01$

fundamentally changed Labour's structure, ideas, and policies. Voters may have accepted that these policies and ideas were not in line with the party's ideological territory because Blair was a new leader, expected to handle things differently. In other words, party leader changes may outweigh the negative effects of shifting a party's policy position away from its expected policy location. Moreover, skilful and charismatic party leaders may be one factor reducing the negative consequences of policy shifts moving away from their expected policy position. In 1997, Tony Blair was rather popular and able to 'sell' the party's policy shift in 1997. In the subsequent election in 2001, Blair's mean popularity decreased from 3.4 (1997) to 2.4 (2001) points on a scale ranging from 0 to 4 so that he was no longer able to legitimise policies that were not in line with Labour's image as a left-wing party. Hence, positive party leader evaluations may lead voters to perceive party policy shifts deviating from expected policy locations.

In sum, voters are not likely to accept (i.e. consider credible) a party's position shift moving away from its ideological territory. However, some parties may counteract these negative effects by newly elected and charismatic leaders who are able to 'sell' these policy shifts to the electorate. Although the considerations are plausible, the available data does not allow for testing them empirically. Although British panel election studies are the best data source to study the perception of party position shifts, the number of observations at the party level is insufficient for a detailed analysis of the perception of parties moving away from their 'expected' policy positions.

Table 6.15: Summary: Reception and acceptance covariates

	Variable	Hypothesis	Findings
Reception	Political awareness	V1	✓
	Education	V2	(✓)
	Magnitude of voter policy shift	V3	(✓)
	Party in government before election?	V4	✗
	Magnitude of party policy shift	V6	mixed
Acceptance	Change in leadership	V7	(✓)
	Party leader's prestige	V8	✓
	Magnitude of past party policy shift	V9	✗
	Party identification: Party policy shifts towards voter's policy position	V10	✓
	Party policy shifts away from voter's policy position		✓
	Party shift similar to voter shift?	V11	✓

✓   Strong empirical support.

(✓) Empirical support in some model specifications.

✗   Findings contradicting the theoretical expectations.

Summary and conclusion

This chapter deals with the voters' perceptions of party policy shifts in Great Britain. Drawing on several panel election studies starting from the 1970s onwards, I study (1) how voters perceive the parties' policy shifts and (2) explain why voters differ in their perception of these shifts. For that purpose, several statistical models are applied using different dependent variables.

The first analysis focuses on the Labour Party's policy shift in 1997. Using a single party's policy shift simplifies the model because some (party-specific) covariates are held constant. Using the 'Taxes vs. Services' scale as the dependent variable, I estimate logistic regressions covering the covariates for the reception and acceptance of 'New Labour'. Furthermore, I present a two-stage logistic regression combining the covariates of the reception and the modified acceptance model. To study party-specific covariates I pool several election studies, creating a dataset that covers voter perceptions for party position shifts for several parties and multiple elections. The pooling has several drawbacks including trade-offs between the measurement of key concepts. As dependent variable, the perceptions of party position shifts are used on three policy scales: 'Nationalisation vs. Privatisation', 'Taxes vs. Services', and 'Unemployment vs. Inflation'. For each of them, I estimate several models. Logistic regressions estimate the impact of the reception and acceptance covariates. Finally, a two-stage logistic regression is estimated to combine these effects.

One interesting result is that most voters are largely unaware of most parties' policy shifts. Only about one third of all voters perceive shifts in the parties' policy platforms. Even for a particularly well known policy shift, 'New Labour' in 1997, only about two thirds of all respondents perceived a shift to the centre of the policy space. These estimates, although surprisingly low, correspond to results from previous research based on aggregate level data (Adams *et al.* 2011). Yet, this finding is puzzling as models of party competition build on spatial models of voting. If voters do not perceive the parties' policy shifts, why should parties adjust their positions according to voters' preferences? One possible explanation is that there are always some voters receiving and accepting the parties' position changes. Parties react to these 'subconstituencies' (Adams and Ezrow 2009) and their marginal effect on the election results is large enough for parties to change their policy positions (Adams 2012). As suggested in previous research, the politically knowledgeable voters are particularly relevant in this respect (Converse 1964). But the present analysis also shows that some voters *receive* the parties' information but not necessarily *believe* (i.e. accept) their claims.

In toto, some of the results for the different model specifications presented above strongly conform to the theoretical expectations. For others, the empirical findings contradict the hypothesised effects. For two covariates that provided rather mixed evidence in the analyses, I show that the hybrid effects are due to measurement problems (political awareness) and multicollinearity (direction of voter and party policy shifts). Table 6.15 summarises the regression results distinguishing factors strongly supported by the empirical models, those with predominantly positive results, those showing mixed evidence, and factors contradicting the theoretical expectations.

The voters' political awareness, the prestige of the party leader, the voters' party identification, and the direction of voter shifts relative to parties show the expected patterns in (almost) all model specifications. Voters are more likely to perceive party policy shifts if their political awareness (rather than interest) is high if they positively evaluate the party leader and if the party policy shift is in the same direction as the voter's position shifts. In addition, party identifiers are more likely to perceive party policy shifts towards their policy preferences while not perceiving those moving away from their policy position. The regression results for the voters' education, the magnitude of their policy shifts and changes in the party leadership have the expected effects in some of the regression models. To a certain extent at least, educated voters and those shifting their personal preferences are more likely to perceive party position shifts. In addition, voters are more likely to accept party position shifts following changes in the party leadership.

Three covariates show negative results. While the regression results are rather mixed for the magnitude of the parties' policy shifts, the parties' governmental status and the magnitude of past party policy shifts are not in line with the theoretical expectation. I discuss the covariates in greater detail arguing that (1) the government-opposition divide is not as crucial in two-party systems as it is in multiparty systems and that (2) voters may accept large consecutive party policy shifts if changes in the parties' environment (rival parties or public opinion shifts) require doing so.

I also discuss the implications of party policy shifts which are not in line with the parties' ideological territories. As the data is scarce, the findings have to be treated with caution. Nevertheless, the rare events suggest that voters are less likely to perceive these shifts. A comparison of Labour's policy shift in 1997 and 2001 reveals, however, that parties may outweigh the negative effects if (1) the party leadership changed or (2) the party leader has a good reputation.

chapter seven | how voter perceptions affect party policy shifts: an empirical analysis

The previous chapter dealt with voters and their perceptions of party policy shifts. The empirical results show that variation in the perception of party policy shifts can be explained by differences in their reception and acceptance function. I now turn to the effects of the voters' reception and acceptance on party policy shifts. Are there constraints on party policy shifts resulting from the voters' ability to realise (i.e. to receive) the parties' shift messages? Moreover, are parties constrained by the voters' limited acceptance of party policy shifts? The empirical analysis is based on a sample of ten Western European countries that is presented in greater detail in the next section. I discuss the various covariates one by one starting with covariates derived from the reception of party policy shifts. For each variable, I present several empirical models (i.e. multilevel and PCSE regressions) testing the robustness of the results.

Case selection

The selection of cases is a crucial step in the testing of theoretically hypothesised relationships. One selection strategy is Przeworski and Teune's 'most similar systems design' (see also Mill 1846; Przeworski and Teune 1970). If all 'relevant' control variables are held constant, variation in the dependent variable Y may only be explained by changes of the variable of interest X. In terms of party position shifts, it may be wise to study a single party holding party-specific, time-constant covariates (e.g. party ideology) constant.

Yet, a quantitative research design requires a reasonable number of observations. There are two ways to increase the number of observations. One strategy is to 'dig deeper', studying party policy shifts in several policy areas such as economic, social, foreign, and environmental policies. This approach is, however, not suitable for answering the research question stated here. I argue here that parties face voters who do not receive or accept party position shifts and (consequently) have to react to these challenges. Yet, gathering information of party policy shifts involves costs, and voters are only likely to take these costs for policy dimensions affecting their vote choices. Voters' reception and acceptance of party policy shifts is, therefore, less relevant for policy areas with a limited impact on their vote choices. Studying several policy areas is hence no useful strategy to reach a reasonable number of observations.

Another way to increase the number of observations, is to study party position shifts of several parties within one country. So doing, specific variables (e.g. the parties' ideologies) vary across parties, but at least institutional factors (such as the electoral system) are held constant. Unfortunately, party position shifts within individual countries still do not provide enough cases for statistical tests.[1] Moreover, some of the covariates of interest do not show sufficient variance within countries. As the analysis of the voters' perception of party policy shifts has shown, the complexity of party systems mainly varies across, but rarely within countries. Hence, it is necessary to enlarge the sample studying party position shifts in several countries.

For the selection of cases, we aim at (1) selecting a reasonable number of cases and (2) keeping as many control variables as possible constant. I solve this puzzle by studying party position shifts in West European countries. Due to restrictions on data availability, I omit party position shifts in France, Greece, Portugal, and Spain. Moreover, Italy is excluded because previous research (Pelizzo 2003) doubts the validity of the CMP data (see Chapter Three). The sample, therefore, contains party policy shifts in Austria, Belgium, Denmark, Finland, Germany, Great Britain, Ireland, the Netherlands, Norway, and Sweden.

The sample is sufficiently large to allow for statistical tests. Furthermore and compared with other potential case selections of the same size, the countries offer at least some degree of homogeneity: all the countries in the sample are stable democracies with democratic structures since the post-war period. The long-lasting democratic tradition provides for many elections and thereby reduces the number of countries required to obtain a reasonable sample size. In South America and Southern and Eastern Europe with a much more limited democratic tradition, an equal number of observations may only be achieved by sampling more countries (and hence by increasing variance on potential unobserved further variables).

Moreover, the selected sample only contains parliamentary democracies. The government's dependence on the majority support in the legislature provides incentives for parties to be cohesive (Diermeier and Feddersen 1998; Heidar and Koole 2000: 261) and cohesion results in relatively coherent party policy positions. In contrast, the variety of intra-party policy positions which may emerge in presidential systems makes the evaluation of a party's policy position difficult. Moreover, actors within the same party may move in different directions thus makes the concept of a 'party policy shift' less useful. The case selection focusing on parliamentary systems avoids such problems. Finally, the countries are quite similar with respect to their development (as indicated by the GDP, expectation of life, and the education level). Compared to other samples with an equal number of observations, the selected countries hence share several similarities.

---

1. Using party policy programs to measure party policy positions (and hence party position shifts), we observe around 100 party policy shifts per country in most West European countries over the whole post war period.

The dependent variable

For the following analyses, I use the parties' policy shift on the left-right scale to measure changes in policy positions. To measure party policy shifts, I rely on data collected by the Comparative Manifestos Project (CMP) (Budge *et al.* 2001; Klingemann *et al.* 2006). Using hand-coding, the election manifestos of political parties are subdivided in so-called 'quasi-sentences'. Each of these sentences in then assigned to one of 56 policy categories. Using these categories, it is possible to derive a variable measuring the parties' policy positions on a left-right scale (see also Laver and Budge 1992b: 26–7).

CMP data is widely used in articles appearing in high-ranking journals (e.g. Adams *et al.* 2004; 2006a; Adams and Somer-Topcu 2009b; Budge 1994; Somer-Topcu 2009b; Tavits 2007). It is the only data source measuring party positions over time. Neither other methods using content analysis (Laver *et al.* 2003; Slapin and Proksch 2008) nor expert surveys have been used to systematically measure party policy positions over time. The dataset is often criticised as lacking validity (Pelizzo 2003) and suffering from methodological weaknesses (see e.g. Benoit and Laver 2007; Benoit *et al.* 2009b). Most of these critiques have been discussed in Chapter Three. In what follows, I use CMP left-right positions in two subsequent elections to measure the dependent variable policy shift. Values larger than zero stand for policy shifts to the right. Position shifts to the left are indicated by values smaller than 0.

Most of the hypotheses stated above focus on the magnitude of party policy shifts. The higher the political interest, for example, the larger party policy shifts should be (Hypothesis P1a). Hence, it seems to be appropriate to use the absolute value of the policy shift variable as a dependent variable in the analysis. Nevertheless, the following analyses are based on a dependent variable that captures the direction of policy shifts. I do so for two reasons. First, it allows for using the same dependent variable for all hypotheses. Hypotheses on voter policy shifts and voter expectations of party positions make predictions on the direction of the policy shift so that the dependent variable has to capture the direction of the policy shift. The second reason for using the policy shift variable is methodological. The variable nicely follows a normal distribution and hence fulfils one of the Gauss-Markov assumptions for linear regression models. In contrast, the magnitude of policy shifts (i.e. the absolute value) reveals a different variance structure with asymmetric right-skewed properties. More details about the statistical model are provided in Appendix B.

Covariates

Table 7.1 shows the covariates and the measures used in the subsequent analyses. First, I use survey questions on political interest as a substitute for political awareness. According to the theoretical model, the voters' awareness should affect the reception of policy shifts. In practice, however, surveys rarely contain information on political knowledge. As we have seen in Chapter Six, the British (panel) election studies only asks quizzes on political information in 1979 and 1997. For all other election years, such indicators are missing. Cross-nationally, the situation is even worse. Hence, I rely on a substitute measure: the mean claimed political interest of all survey respondents. Recall that political interest and awareness are conceptually different (Zaller 1992: 333–6) and similar substitutions in individual level data has led to flawed estimates. However, the bias may be diminished by using aggregate survey data. I standardise the political interest scores for each election year in every country and calculate the mean political interest.

For this variable and the following ones based on survey data, I first and foremost rely on the European Voter Database (Thomassen 2005). To allow for comparative electoral research, the European Voter Project compiled data of several national election studies in six West European countries (Denmark, Germany, Great Britain, the Netherlands, Norway and Sweden). National experts compiled data of various variables in election studies until the late 1990s. To extend the time series, additional data are collected to cover more recent elections in Denmark (Andersen *et al.* 2003), Germany (Falter *et al.* 2002), Great Britain (Clarke *et al.* 2005), the Netherlands (Irwin *et al.* 2005) and Norway (Aardal *et al.* 2003). For the remaining countries, I collect data for as many election years as possible using various national election studies, the Eurobarometer trend file and national voter barometers. More specifically, I collected additional data for Belgium (Billiet and Swyngedouw 1995; Billiet *et al.* 1991; Gschwend and Pappi 2003; Swyngedouw *et al.* 1999), Finland (Finnish Voter Barometer 1975, 1979, 1983, 1984, 1986, 1987, 1990, February 1995, January 1999; Karvonen and Paloheimo 2003), and Ireland (Marsh and Sinnott 2002; Schmitt 2006). For Austria, election studies and Eurobarometer data are not available.

Because of serious data constraints with regard to the voters' educational achievements, I refrain from testing my hypothesis on the voters' education and its effect on party position shifts. Because the types and names of educational achievements change over time, comparisons would require the recoding of the data. For the British panel elections studies (see Chapter Six), I have distinguished only three categories (basic, moderate, and higher education). Including a cross-national comparison would lead to further complications because coding requires knowledge on the national training and educational systems in various countries and across time. Although attempts do exist to standardise classifications of education (OECD 1999; UNESCO 1997), the recoding decisions still rest with the individual researcher. Creating a time-consistent, valid and reliable measure of education for several countries from various election studies is simply beyond the scope of this analysis.

I derive data on voter policy position from the surveys mentioned above. First, the left-right self-placements[2] are standardised on a scale ranging from 1 (left) to 11 (right). Next, I estimate the mean voter's policy position at time t. The mean voter's position shift is indicated by the difference in the mean voter's policy position from time point t-1 to t. Values smaller than zero indicate public opinion shifts to the left, values larger than zero stand for shifts to the right. Consequently, the absolute value of mean voter's position shift ranges from 0 to 10.

---

2. The question usually reads as follows: 'In politics, people sometimes talk about parties and politicians as being on the left or right. Using the [scale on card], where the end marked 1 means left and the end marked 11 means right, where would you place yourself on this scale?'

Table 7.1: Independent variables for the data analyses

	Variable	Indicators and measurement
Reception	Political awareness	Mean political interest of the electorate/ party voters per election; standardised to [0;1]
	Voter position shift (absolute value)	Magnitude (0–10) of mean voter position shifts from t-1 to t
	Government party	Share of time spent as party in government since the last election
	Number of parties	Effective number of parties in parliament following Laakso and Taagepera (1979)
Acceptance	Leadership change	Same party leader as in previous election (0) or leader change (1)
	Party leader prestige	Mean party leader prestige; standardised to [0;1]
	Past party policy shifts	Number of consecutive position shifts larger than the mean of previous party position shifts (CMP data)
	Party identification	Share of voters with a positive party identification for the respective party
	Voter shift (with direction)	Mean voter position shifts (-10 to 10) from t-1 to t
	Policy shifts deviating from ideological territory	Party position shift conforming to or deviating from ideological territory (i.e. policy position relative to other parties)

Third, it is hypothesised that government parties are more visible than parties in opposition. Thus, voters are more likely to receive party policy shifts of government parties, and consequently, position shifts of government parties are more likely. I measure the parties' share in governmental office in the last legislative period. Parties in opposition for the full term get the value of 0. In contrast, permanent government parties get the value of 1. In case the government composition changes, parties switching from government and opposition (and vice versa) hold values representing their time share spent in office. Thus, the measurement is more precise than using a simple government dummy variable. Data on government participation is mainly drawn from the *Constitutional Change and Parliamentary Democracies* project (Müller and Strøm 2000b; Strøm *et al.* 2003, 2008). In addition, I update the data using various sources for Austria (Pelinka 2003: 529), Belgium (Hecking 2006: 52), Denmark (Nannestad 2003: 67), Finland (Auffermann 2003: 202), Great Britain (Sturm 2003; Woldendorp *et al.* 1998), Ireland (Elvert 2003: 270), the Netherlands (Lucardie 2006: 345), Norway (Groß and Rothholz 2003: 142), and Sweden (Jahn 2003: 99).

Fourth, I use the *effective number of legislative parties* (Laakso and Taagepera 1979) to indicate the complexity of party competition. The higher the number of (relevant) competitors, the lower the probability that voters observe policy shifts of individual parties. The effective number of parties is calculated for the current (t) and the last (t-1) legislative term. As for parties' share in governmental office, data is drawn from the project on *Constitutional Change and Parliamentary Democracies* (Müller and Strøm 2000b; Strøm *et al.* 2003, 2008). I use own calculations based on additional data for Great Britain (Butler and Butler 2000) and more recent elections (Parties and Elections in Europe 2010).

Turning to the covariates coming from the acceptance function of party policy shifts, I argue that *changes in party leadership* increase the acceptance of party policy shifts. As a result, parties are more likely to shift policy positions if the party leader changed since the last election. Data on party leaders was collected using various sources including data handbooks (Butler and Butler 2000; Feldkamp 2005; Schindler 1999), secondary literature (Arter 1991, 1995), the *World Political Leaders* database (2010), Munzinger online (2010), and various web pages of national governments and parliaments, political parties and politicians. The variable *party leader change* is a dummy variable indicating whether party leadership changed since the last election.

The *party leaders' prestige* is hypothesised to affect the acceptance of party policy shifts. The higher the prestige, the higher is the probability that voters accept shifts away from the status quo. Unfortunately, there is no systematic data on the voters' evaluations of party leaders, especially in older election studies. Moreover, the question formats vary enormously. Some questions ask for the party leaders' competence,[3] sympathy,[4] the voters' feeling about the party leaders[5] and

---

3. 'Using a scale that runs from 0 to 10, where 0 means a very incompetent leader and 10 means a very competent leader, how would you describe X?' (question taken from the British national election survey 2005)

4. 'I would also like to know how sympathetic you find the following politicians. If you don't know a politician, please feel free to say so. First X. Which score would you give him?' (question taken from the Dutch national election survey 2002)

5. 'I'd now like to ask you how you feel about some Irish politicians, using what we call the "feeling thermometer". The feeling thermometer works like this: If you have a favourable feeling (a warm

specific questions on party leaders attributes.[6] In the following, I make use of these data although I am aware that comparing these questions over time and space may be problematic. Nevertheless, all question formats are likely to correlate highly and, on average, the data may hence be comparable. I standardise all scales to a scale ranging from 1 (minimal prestige) to 11 (highest prestige).

The *magnitude of past party policy shifts* should also affect the acceptance of party policy shifts. Parties constantly shifting their policy positions should be less trusted so that parties with large (i.e. visible and memorable) policy shifts in the past are constrained to stick to their policy positions for the next election. The magnitude of party policy shifts may depend on characteristics of the parties (e.g. the size or intra-party decision-making rules) and the party system (e.g. the number of competitors). To control for these effects, I measure the mean magnitude of the parties' past policy shifts at t-2. Party policy shifts at t-1 larger than this threshold are large policy shifts, values smaller are classified as small party policy shifts.[7] Using that information, I calculate the number of subsequent large party policy shifts. The variable takes values ranging from 0 (previous shift is classified as 'small') to 10 (ten subsequent policy shifts larger than their respective preceding mean party shift).

Whether voters accept party position shifts also depends on their party identification. I argue that the larger the share of voters feeling attached to the party, the higher the probability that the party shifts its policy position. Party identification is measured using the standard question for party identification.[8] For each election, I apply the survey data summarised above to estimate the share of party voters with a positive party identification. The indicator varies between 0 and 100.

I also test whether parties shift their policy positions in line with public opinion shifts. It is argued that voters are more likely to accept party policy shifts if they shifted their policy preferences in the same direction. As a consequence, parties follow public opinion shifts if the electorate shifted away from the party's previous policy position. Using the survey data summarised above, I calculate the mean voter's policy position on a left-right scale ranging from 1 to 11. Voter policy shifts are measured as the difference between the mean voter's policy position at time t

feeling) towards a politician you should place him/her somewhere between 50 and 100 degrees; If you have an unfavourable feeling (a cold feeling) towards a politician, you should place him/ her somewhere between 0 and 50 degrees; and If you don't feel particularly warm or cold (have no feeling towards the politician at all) then you should place him/her at 50 degrees. Where would you place these Irish politicians?' (question taken from the Irish national election survey 2002).

6. Such as, whether they are capable of being a strong leader, able to unite the nation, or keep their promises.

7. I rely on the average magnitude of *previous* policy shifts to ensure an exogenous measurement of the covariate.

8. 'Generally speaking, do you think of yourself as Party A, Party B,...?' If possible, I use a narrow measure for party identification avoiding the inclusion of voters who just 'feel a little closer to' a specific party.

and the mean voter's policy position at time t-1. Negative values indicate public policy shifts to the left, positive values stand for public opinion shifts to the right.

Measuring *voter expectations* appropriately is crucial for testing the model. Although left-right expectations are often uncontroversial, in other cases such placements are more difficult. Liberal parties, for example, occupy the centre of the policy space in some countries (e.g. in Great Britain or Norway) whereas they are on the right in others (e.g. in the Netherlands or Belgium). Because of these difficulties, I use different measures for voter expectations to check the robustness of the results. First, I derive country-specific left-right expectations from expert judgements and election surveys for all parties covered in the CMP dataset (Benoit and Laver 2006; Castles and Mair 1984; Huber and Inglehart 1995; see country chapters in Müller and Strøm 2000a; Thomassen 2005). The ordinal party placements are shown in Appendix C. Although most of the party placements are uncontroversial, there are some cases where left-right placements are difficult. This is the case for a number of small and short-lived parties such as DS70 in the Netherlands or small German parties in the 1950s (Zentrum, DP, and GB/BHE). Because the coding of the ideological territories of these parties affects whether other parties are located in their appropriate policy positions, misspecifications may bias the results.

To keep these problems in check, I also code left-right expectations for a sample restricted to major political parties (defined as parties receiving at least 5 per cent of the vote share in two subsequent elections; Appendix C). Whereas this measurement avoids bias due to misspecified voter expectations of small parties, it is at risk of disregarding party reactions to small parties not passing the threshold. In addition, placing parties on an ordinal scale may still be too fine-grained for sceptical readers. Especially expectations on the placement of 'left' parties may be hard to disentangle. Are Green parties expected to be left or right of the Social Democrats? And are the Greens left of the Communists or Socialists? Taking these doubts seriously, I code left-right expectations using a *trichotomous measure distinguishing left-wing, centre, and right-wing parties*. The classification is shown in Appendix D.

Comparing the parties' actual policy positions (measured with CMP scores) with these expected positions, I estimate whether these positions conform to their ideological territory. Using the expected position as a reference category, two dummy variables indicate whether a party is *left of* or *right of its ideological territory*. For the following analysis, the position in the *last* election (i.e. the lagged values) is used to predict a party's position shifts to the left or the right. If several parties hold the same expected positions, parties are coded as having inappropriate policy positions, if no party rank-order exists which places the respective party in its ideological territory. For example, left-wing parties hold inappropriate policy positions only if no centre and right-wing parties exist with policy platforms right of the left-wing party's actual policy platform. Hence, this coding is 'conservative' as it tends to underestimate party policy deviations from their ideological territories.

Table 7.2: Independent variables: number of observations and mean values

Variable	N	Mean
Mean political interest (all voters)	421	0.497
Voter position shift (absolute value)	448	0.252
Governmental share	919	0.385
Effective number of parl. parties (t)	920	4.255
Effective number of parl. parties (t-1)	920	4.205
Leadership change	844	0.404
Party leader prestige	275	6.414
Past party policy shifts	783	0.95
Share of voters with positive party identification	397	59.136
Voter shift (with direction)	448	-0.038
Voter expectations of party policy positions (t-1) (all parties)	871	Left of exp. position: 178 Right of exp. position: 199
Voter expectations of party policy positions (t-1) (restricted selection)	792	Left of exp. position: 154 Right of exp. position: 168
Voter expectations of party policy positions (t-1) (left-wing, centre, and right-wing parties)	792	Left of exp. position: 48 Right of exp. position: 73
Total	920	

Table 7.2 summarises the covariates used in the analysis. In total, the dataset consists of 920 party policy shifts of 99 parties in 10 countries. Note that missing values for the covariates are especially common for data taken from election studies. For voter position shifts, the number of cases drops to roughly 450 cases and data on the voters' party identification and political interest is only available for about 400 party position shifts. Since survey research did not begin before the 1960s or 1970s, missing values mainly occur in the 1940s and 1950s. Across countries, Austrian parties drop out of the analysis because Austrian election studies do not exist for the sample period.[9] The situation is worse for data on the party leaders' prestige. Data is only available for 275 policy position shifts. Although nine out of ten countries are represented, data for Belgian (3) and Irish (6) parties is scarce. Moreover, about 80 per cent of the cases are party position

---

9. Except for voter position shifts between the general elections in 1995 and 1999, no data from the Eurobarometer could be used for measuring public opinion shifts, party identification, political interest, and the party leaders' prestige.

shifts from the 1980s onwards. Only 20 per cent of the cases are party policy shifts in the 1960s and 1970s. Data on government participation, the effective number of parties, leadership changes, prior policy shifts and voter expectations of party policy positions is available for more cases. Missing values are mainly due to cases for which the respective variables are not defined. Past party policy shifts, for example, require data on previous elections. Hence, party position shifts from the first to the second election a party competed in are dropped. In a similar vein, the sample restriction of ideological territories removes small and irrelevant parties from the dataset.

Reception covariates and their effect on party policy shifts

Political interest

As a first hypothesis, I test the effect of the voters' political interest on party position shifts. It is hypothesised that politically aware voters are more likely to receive party policy shifts. Choosing policy positions, parties refrain from shifting policy positions if the voters do not receive the parties' shift message. Hence, the higher the political awareness, the larger party policy shifts should be (Hypothesis P1a). Because questions on political awareness are rare, I take the voters' political interest as a substitute. Table 7.3 reports the regression results of the voters' mean political interest for the magnitude of party policy shifts.

The three models show the results for the different model specifications using the mean political interest of the electorate as a covariate. The regression results are quite similar across the model specifications although the number of observations varies.[10] The higher the voters' political interest at t-1, the larger the parties' policy shifts at time t. The significance levels vary across the models but the size of the effects is quite robust. Increasing the electorate's political interest by one standard deviation increases party policy shifts by about 1 point. From its minimal to its maximal value, political interest positively affects the magnitude of party policy shifts by roughly 4.7 points on the CMP left-right scale.[11] Compared to the average magnitude of party policy shifts (about 12 points on the CMP left right scale), the effect size is moderate.

---

10. Note that the number of observations differs across the model specifications. The reason is that model 1 uses the lagged dependent variable to capture serial correlation. In contrast to the remaining models using the Prais-Winsten transformation, additional information on prior party policy shifts is used. Hence, the number of observations is lower in model 1 containing the lagged dependent variable. Instead of restricting all models to the lowest number of cases (here n=399), I use the additional information given by the additional number of observations used to estimate the coefficients.

11. The estimates are based on the coefficients and the number of cases in model 1.

Table 7.3: Political interest of voters and its effect on party policy shifts

	(1) Multilevel model (Level 2: elections)	(2) Multilevel model (Level 2: parties)	(3) PCSE regression
Political interest (t-1)	11.28[+]	12.64[*]	11.68[+]
	(1.90)	(2.18)	(1.80)
Party policy shifts (t-1)	-0.228[**]		
	(-7.01)		
Constant	5.129[+]	4.378	5.423
	(1.72)	(1.49)	(1.61)
ρ		-0.330	-0.104
Observations	399	421	421

z statistics in parentheses

$+ p < 0.1$, $* p < 0.05$, $** p < 0.01$

ρ capturing serial correlation

In a slightly modified version, I state that the voters' mean political awareness makes party policy shifts more likely if the party position moves towards preferences of the majority of voters. In contrast, politically aware voters do not motivate parties to move away from their preferences. To test the more fine-grained Hypothesis P1b, I differentiate between party position shifts towards the mean voter's policy position and shifts away from it.[12] I expect that the positive relationship only holds for the former but not for the latter.

Table 7.4 reports the regression results. I split the sample for each model specification, distinguishing shifts towards and away from the mean voter's policy preferences. Due to the additional information for the mean voter's policy position and the sample splits, the number of observations decreases from around 400 to about 100 per regression. Nevertheless, we observe the expected patterns: Voters' political interest influences the magnitude of party policy shifts if these shifts are towards the mean voter's policy preferences. For the first two model specifications

---

12. To measure the direction of party position shifts, I rely on survey data and party position shifts using CMP data. Party shifts are moving away from the mean voter's preferences if the mean party placement at t-1 is left of (right of) the mean voter's policy position at t-1 and if the respective party shifts to the left (to the right).

(model 1 vs. model 2; model 3 vs. model 4), the effect sizes differ widely. For policy shifts towards the mean voters' preferences, increasing the political interest by one standard deviation increases the magnitude of party policy shifts by about 1.7 points. In contrast, the effect is substantially smaller for shifts away from the mean voter's preferences (0.8 points).[13] From minimal to maximal values, political interest increases the magnitude of party policy shifts towards the mean voter position by 7.6 points on the CMP scale. For policy shifts away from the mean voter's policy preferences, the effect size (3.7) is considerably smaller. In addition, the effect is only significant if party policy shifts are towards the mean voter's policy position. I hence conclude that the direction of the party policy shift affects the relation between the voters' political interest and the magnitude of party policy shifts.

Table 7.4: Political interest and its effect on party policy shifts: Distinguishing directions

	(1)	(2)	(3)	(4)	(5)	(6)
	Multilevel model (Level 2: elections)		**Multilevel model (Level 2: parties)**		**PCSE regression**	
	Towards mean voter	**Away from mean voter**	**Towards mean voter**	**Away from mean voter**	**Towards mean voter**	**Away from mean voter**
Political interest (t-1)	19.01*	9.165	17.71$^+$	10.57	11.47	9.893
	(2.25)	(0.93)	(1.73)	(1.05)	(0.90)	(0.80)
Party policy shifts (t-1)	-0.162**	-0.155**				
	(-2.68)	(-2.64)				
Constant	-1.693	3.344	0.0993	3.656	3.096	4.005
	(-0.41)	(0.68)	(0.02)	(0.74)	(0.53)	(0.68)
ρ			0.271	-0.169	0.196	-0.050
Observations	95	93	102	95	102	95

z statistics in parentheses

$+ p < 0.1$, $* p < 0.05$, $** p < 0.01$

ρ capturing serial correlation

---

13. The estimates are based on the coefficients and the number of cases in the models 1 and 2.

Table 7.5: The magnitude of mean voter shifts and its effect on party policy shifts

	(1)	(2)	(3)	(4)	(5)	(6)
	Multilevel model (Level 2: elections)		Multilevel model (Level 2: parties)		PCSE regression	
	Benign shift	Harmful shift	Benign shift	Harmful shift	Benign shift	Harmful shift
Voter policy shifts (magnitude)	-2.619 (-0.52)	-2.800 (-0.66)	-0.166 (-0.04)	-7.439[+] (-1.68)	-2.959 (-0.60)	-7.084 (-1.54)
Party policy shifts (t-1)	-0.387**	-0.254**				
	(-5.13)	(-5.06)				
Constant	11.25**	9.649**	9.925**	12.52**	12.09**	12.32**
	(5.97)	(6.90)	(6.79)	(8.60)	(4.74)	(7.47)
ρ			-0.825	0.100	-0.119	0.036
Observations	105	111	111	119	111	119

z statistics in parentheses

+ p < 0.1, * p < 0.05, ** p < 0.01

ρ capturing serial correlation

Size of public policy shifts

Do parties shift policy positions when voters change their policy preferences? I hypothesise that voters are more likely to update information on party policy shifts when they have also shifted their policy preferences. In case the majority of voters shift towards a party's policy position (benign public opinion shift), parties have no incentives to shift their policy platform. If voters move away from the party's policy position (harmful public opinion shift), parties make use of large public policy shifts to change their policy platforms.[14] Table 7.5 reports the regression results using different model specifications and distinguishing voter shifts towards and away from the party's policy platform.

The regression coefficients of voter position shifts are negative, meaning that larger voter position shifts decrease the magnitude of party position shifts. Furthermore, there are only minor differences between voter shifts towards the party's policy position at t-1 and those away from it. The effects hence contradict the theoretical expectation stated in Hypothesis P3. Compared to the findings of

---

14. Public opinion is moving away from a party if its policy position at t-1 is right (left) of the mean voter's position at t-1 and the mean voter's policy position shifts to the left (right) at time t.

political interest, the effect sizes are also rather small.[15] Irrespective of its direction, public opinion changes of one standard deviation make parties shift their policy position about 0.6 points on the CMP left-right scale. The maximal change of the mean voter's policy position in two subsequent elections (~1.2 points on the 1–11 scale) makes parties shift their policy position about 3.3 points on the CMP scale. With one exception (model 4), the effects do not reach a conventional level of statistical significance so I conclude that the magnitude of voter policy shifts does not affect party position shifts.[16]

Government parties

I argue that government parties get higher media attention so that their policy shifts are more visible for the electorate. As a consequence, government parties should be more likely to shift their policy positions (Hypothesis P4). To test this expectation, I regress party policy shifts on the parties' time spent in government since the last election. I expect a positive and significant coefficient.

Table 7.6: Government participation and its effect on party policy shifts

	(1) Multilevel model (Level 2: elections)	(2) Multilevel model (Level 2: parties)	(3) PCSE regression
Government participation	1.651[+]	1.976[*]	2.096[*]
	(1.95)	(2.38)	(2.37)
Party policy shifts (t-1)	-0.217[**]		
	(-9.52)		
Constant	11.04[**]	10.86[**]	11.31[**]
	(20.90)	(21.55)	(21.31)
ρ		-0.244	-0.092
Observations	820	919	919

z statistics in parentheses

+ p < 0.1, * p < 0.05, ** p < 0.01

ρ capturing serial correlation

---

15. Again, the estimates are based on the coefficients and the number of cases in models 1 and 2.

16. Because voter position shifts are usually rather small, the negative finding may be due to measurement error.

The results in Table 7.6 conform to the theoretical expectation. The regression coefficient is positive and reaches significance in all three model specifications. The size of the effect is rather similar for all three model specifications. Its interpretation is straightforward: the policy shifts of parties which took office in the last legislative term are about 1.65 (model 1) or 2 points (models 2 and 3) larger than those of opposition parties. Taking the average 12 point party policy shift as a baseline, the size of the effect is moderate.

The effective number of parliamentary parties

Party policy shifts should also depend on the complexity of the political arena. The higher the number of relevant actors, the lower the probability that voters perceive policy shifts of individual parties. Parties refrain from investing in shifting policy positions if the expected effect (i.e. the perception of the party's new policy position) fails to materialise. As a consequence, party systems with many relevant actors hamper policy changes of individual parties (Hypothesis P5). Using the effective number of parties (Laakso and Taagepera 1979) as a proxy for the complexity of the political arena, Table 7.7 shows the regression results using the current number of parties (models 1 to 3) and the lagged value (models 4 to 6) as covariates.

The regression results show similar patterns across the different models. The effective number of parties has the expected negative effect on party policy shifts. In other words, the higher the number of effective parties, the smaller the parties' policy shifts. The size of the effect is similar across the models and statistically significant in 5 of 6 models. Shifting from the mean number of effective parties (4.28) by one standard deviation (1.54), the magnitude of the parties' policy shifts alters by around 0.75 CMP points.[17] Compared to the legislative term with the lowest number of effective parties (Great Britain 1959, effective number of legislative parties = 1.99), party policy shifts in the most complex term (Belgium 1999, effective number of legislative parties = 9.1) decrease by 3.5 points on the CMP scale. Compared to the other effects discussed so far, the size of the effect is rather small.

Acceptance covariates and their effect on party policy shifts

So far, I discussed the effects of covariates derived from the reception of party policy shifts. The results support three out of four hypotheses. First, the voters' political interest positively affects the magnitude of party policy shifts. Moreover, government parties perform larger policy shifts than opposition parties. Finally, parties are more likely to shift their policy positions if the number of competitors is low. The coefficient for the magnitude of public opinion shifts is insignificant. Next, I turn to the covariates derived from the acceptance of party policy shifts.

---

17. Again, the estimates are based on the coefficients and the number of cases in model 1.

Table 7.7: The effective number of parliamentary parties and its effect on party policy shifts

	(1) Multilevel model (Level 2: elections)	(2) Multilevel model (Level 2: parties)	(3) PCSE regression	(4) Multilevel model (Level 2: elections)	(5) Multilevel model (Level 2: parties)	(6) PCSE ~ regression
Eff. # of parties	-0.494[+] (-1.92)	-0.467[+] (-1.82)	-0.531[*] (-2.09)			
Eff. # of parties (t-1)				-0.508[+] (-1.91)	-0.420 (-1.58)	-0.465[+] (-1.69)
Party policy shifts (t-1)	-0.218[**] (-9.60)			-0.219[**] (-9.61)		
Constant	13.79[**] (11.75)	13.60[**] (11.75)	14.43[**] (12.81)	13.81[**] (11.62)	13.37[**] (11.33)	14.11[**] (11.90)
ρ		-0.243	-0.080		-0.245	-0.085
Observations	821	920	920	821	920	920

z statistics in parentheses

+ p < 0.1, * p < 0.05, ** p < 0.01

ρ capturing serial correlation

Table 7.8: Change in party leadership and their effect on party policy shifts

	(1) Multilevel model (Level 2: elections)	(2) Multilevel model (Level 2: parties)	(3) PCSE regression
Change in party leadership	-1.749[*]	-0.978	-1.126
	(-2.06)	(-1.20)	(-1.33)
Party policy shifts (t-1)	-0.215[**]		
	(-9.13)		
Constant	12.72[**]	12.40[**]	12.95[**]
	(23.05)	(23.20)	(22.07)
ρ		-0.238	-0.098
Observations	763	844	844

z statistics in parentheses

+ p < 0.1, * p < 0.05, ** p < 0.01

ρ capturing serial correlation

Change in party leadership

I argue that long-term party leaders become identified with their previous policies so that voters do not accept (i.e. consider credible) party policy shifts. New party leaders have more leeway to breathe life into a party because voters are more likely to accept party policy shifts introduced by them. Therefore, I expect that parties use leadership changes to shift their policy platforms. Table 7.8 shows the regression estimates for the three model specifications The estimates reported in Table 7.8 show a negative effect of party leader changes on party policy shifts. If the party leadership changed, the magnitude of party policy shifts decreases by 1.7 (model 1) or roughly 1 point (models 2 and 3) on the CMP scale. Although the effect is only significant in the first model, the findings contradict my expectation. If voters are more likely to accept party position shifts of new party leaders, why do new party leaders refrain from using this advantage?

Analysing the causes, newly elected party leaders may lack the resources for policy shifts. For example, party leaders taking office shortly before an election (e.g. because of a scandal the previous party leader was involved in) do not have the time for major policy shifts. Moreover, intra-party resistance may prevent new party leaders from going for significant policy changes. Moving away from the status quo usually requires the discussion and approval of party congresses or, at least, major actors within the party's elite. Some party leaders may be successful in convincing the party's rank-and-file and in getting the support of the major intra-party factions. Yet, others lack this support and face major intra-party actors who are in doubt of the leader's ability to be successful in the next election. In this case, intra-party actors refrain from giving their leader the mandate for party policy changes.

Combining these thoughts with my previous theoretical expectation, we may expect a curvilinear relationship between the tenure of party leaders and the magnitude of party policy shifts. Due to a lack of resources, newly elected party leaders are less likely to shift party policies. With one or two successful election campaigns on the record, party leaders extend their power within the party so that tenure has a positive impact on the magnitude of party policy shifts. The more time party leaders spend in office, however, the more they become identified with prior policies and hence, the less likely are party position shifts.

I test the effect of tenure as party leader on party policy shifts for the three model specifications mentioned above. As for the models reported in Table 7.8, the findings are mixed. Figure 7.1 shows the curvilinear effect of leadership tenure on party position shifts using the estimates of model 1. The model estimates indeed show a curvilinear pattern for leadership tenure on party policy change. Newly elected party leaders shift party policy positions significantly less than more experienced leaders being in office for two or three elections. Thereafter, the trend is negative: the longer party leaders stay in office, the smaller the party position shifts. Yet, the differences are not significant. This is mainly due to the low number of cases with a long-lasting tenure.[18] The findings thus do not fully support the curvilinear relationship.

Instead of using the new party leaders' lack of resources to explain the absence of large party policy shifts, it may also be that newly elected leaders have no incentives to shift the party's policy position. Although missing incentives cannot explain why freshmen shift party policy positions to a significantly lesser extent (model 1 in Table 7.8), they may explain why newly elected leaders do not differ from party leaders which are in office for a longer period (models 2 and 3 in Table 7.8). Leadership turnovers are not always signs of change. Rather, leadership changes may also be a continuation of old policies by a new generation. Newly elected party leaders may have been in the party's wider leadership circle before they took office or they belong to the same intra-party faction as the previous party leader. Both factors are especially likely if newly elected party leaders are foster-sons (and daughters) of the old party elite.

Figure 7.1: Curvilinear effect of leadership tenure on party policy shifts

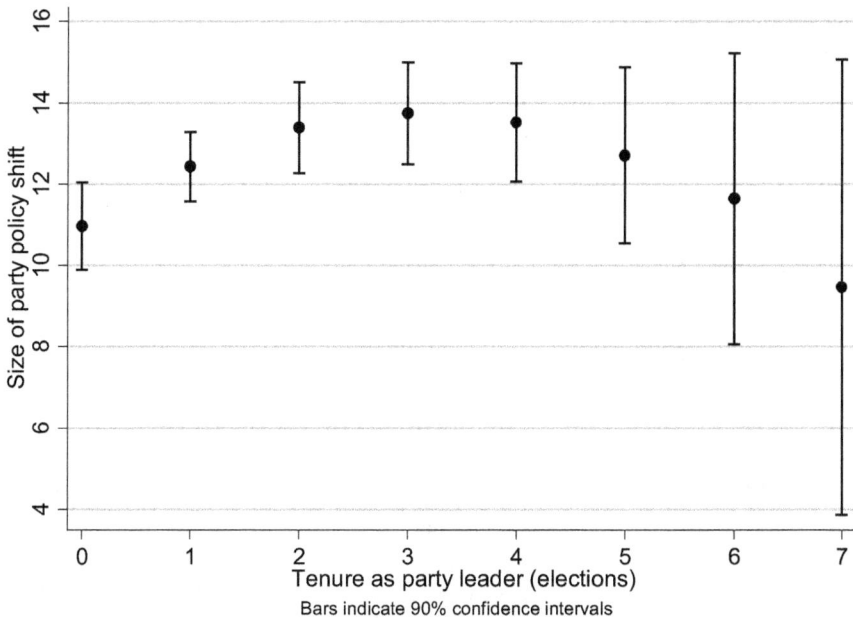

Bars indicate 90% confidence intervals

Note: Model estimates based of model 1 (N=748). Prior policy shifts are kept on their mean value.

18. Out of the 748 cases in the analysis, only 9 party leaders were in office for 7 or more elections. The cases include party leaders in Sweden (Hedlund (CP), Erlander (SAP)), Denmark (Jakobsen (CD), Petersen (SF), Jørgensen (RV), Jespersen (DKP), and Schlüter (KF)), and Germany (Brandt (SPD) and Kohl (CDU)).

Unfortunately, I do not have data on policy preferences or factional member-ship. Neither do I have data on the party leaders' prior membership in the party leadership or whether they are political foster-sons (and daughters) of prior party leaders. Nevertheless, a party leader's willingness to shift the party platform can be measured using the voters' expectations of party policy positions as a substi-tute. If a party's policy position corresponds to its expected position (see below), there is no exogenous need for party policy shifts. However, if the policy position is not in line with its ideological territory, a party leader has incentives to correct that.

If willingness is the main factor explaining smaller policy shifts of new party leaders, party leaders should only differ according to the necessity for party policy shifts. If there is no necessity, party position shifts are rather small. Yet, if the party's policy position is not in line with its ideological territory, party position shifts should be significantly larger. Whether or not the party leadership changed should not affect this relationship.

Table 7.9: The magnitude of party policy shifts depending on party leader change and the necessity to shift party policy positions

	No leader-ship change	New party leader	Significant difference
No necessity	10.91	10.39	
Necessity for policy change	15.92	11.92	✓
Significant difference	✓		

Table 7.9 reports the average magnitude of party policy shifts depending on the party leader's tenure and the necessity to shift party policy positions. The neces-sity for policy change has a positive effect on the magnitude of party policy shift if the party leadership did not change (increasing from roughly 11 to 16 points on the CMP scale) and if a new party leader took office (from 10 to 12 points). However, the difference is only significant for the former group. In other words, while party leaders with a longer tenure react to the necessity for party policy shifts, newly elected party leaders fail to do so. In addition, there is no significant effect of tenure on party policy shifts if there is no necessity for shifting the party's policy position. If the necessity is given, however, newly elected leaders are not more likely to shift the party's policy position. Rather, party leaders who are at least in office since the last election make significantly larger party policy shifts. Both findings do not conform to the 'lacking willingness' hypothesis which may hence be discarded.

In sum, the findings suggest that although voters are more likely to accept party policy shifts of newly elected leaders, leadership changes do not lead to larger party policy shifts. Exploring the reasons, I propose two explanations. First, newly elected party leaders may lack the resources for party policy change. Lacks of time or intra-party support reduce a new party leader's ability to shift the party policies. With one or two successful election campaigns in the past, party leaders' power within the party increases. Combining this effect with the expected negative relation of leadership tenure and the magnitude of party policy shifts, we expect to see a curvilinear relation. As an alternative explanation, newly elected party leaders may have no incentives to shift the party's policy position. If the policy preferences and the factional membership of the old and the new party leader are identical, changes in leadership should have no effect. Although we lack data for testing these theories adequately, preliminary results rather support the first explanation. Controlling for the leaders' willingness for policy change, I still find significant differences between incumbent and newly elected leaders, suggesting that new leaders are not able to act in the same way as party leaders with a longer tenure. The findings encourage further investigation on organisational features and their effect on party policy change to which I turn in Chapter Eight.

Party leader prestige

I now turn to party leader evaluations. I reason that a party leader's prestige affects the acceptance of party policy shifts. If voters evaluate a party leader positively, the acceptance of party policy shifts increases. Hence, parties should be more likely to shift their policy positions if their party leader's prestige is high (Hypothesis 8a). Table 7.10 reports the regression results testing this expectation for the three model specifications.

Table 7.10: Party leader prestige and its effect on party policy shifts

	(1)	(2)	(3)
	Multilevel model (Level 2: elections)	**Multilevel model (Level 2: parties)**	**PCSE regression**
Party leader prestige	0.972*	0.833[+]	0.922
	(2.10)	(1.70)	(1.21)
Party policy shifts (t-1)	-0.324**		
	(-8.42)		
Constant	5.536[+]	6.317[+]	6.874
	(1.80)	(1.94)	(1.36)
ρ		-0.313	-0.040
Observations	261	275	275

z statistics in parentheses
+ p < 0.1, * p < 0.05, ** p < 0.01
ρ capturing serial correlation

All three coefficients point in the expected positive direction: Increasing the party leader's prestige by one standard deviation (SD = 1.5), the policy position shift increases by 1.46 points.[19] Taking the range of all party leader prestige scores from its minimum to its maximum, party policy shifts increase by roughly 9 CMP points. Using the average magnitude for policy position shifts (about 12 points) as a baseline, the effect size is rather large. Although the effect of the party leader evaluation does not reach statistical significance in model 3, I find empirical evidence supporting my hypothesis in two of three model specifications.

Table 7.11: Party leader prestige and its effect on party policy shifts: Distinguishing directions

	(1)	(2)	(3)	(4)	(5)	(6)
	Multilevel model (Level 2: elections)		Multilevel model (Level 2: parties)		PCSE regression	
	Towards mean voter	Away from mean voter	Towards mean voter	Away from mean voter	Towards mean voter	Away from mean voter
Party leader prestige	3.695**	2.090*	3.447**	1.713	4.163**	1.777
	(3.54)	(2.08)	(3.39)	(1.43)	(2.73)	(1.51)
Party policy shifts (t-1)	-0.231**	-0.384**				
	(-3.14)	(-6.58)				
Constant	-13.78*	-4.347	-11.40+	1.050	-16.06+	0.258
	(-1.97)	(-0.64)	(-1.66)	(0.13)	(-1.73)	(0.03)
ρ			0.330	0.247	0.149	0.037
Observations	90	87	97	90	97	90

z statistics in parentheses

+ $p < 0.1$, * $p < 0.05$, ** $p < 0.01$

ρ capturing serial correlation

---

19. The estimates are based on the models and observations of model 1.

In its more fine-grained version, I hypothesise that the positive effect of a party leader's evaluation on the magnitude of party policy shifts only exists if the party shifts its platform towards the mean voter's policy preferences (Hypothesis P8b) and that a party leader's evaluation has no effect if the party shifts its platform away from the majority of the voters. Table 7.11 reports the regression results for the three model specifications splitting the sample in party shifts towards the mean voter's position and those away from it. Note that the sample split and the additional information used for the direction of the party position shifts reduce the number of observations from about 260 to 90 cases for each regression.

Although the number of observations is considerably lower than for the models in Table 7.10, the coefficients indicate that parties are more likely to shift their policy positions if voters evaluate the respective party leaders positively. Moreover, the effect size is larger for party policy shifts towards the mean voter position than for shifts away from the majority of the voters. Taking models 1 and 2 as an example, increasing the party leaders' mean prestige by one standard deviation increases the magnitude of party policy shifts towards the mean voter's policy position by about 4.4 points on the CMP scale. The effect is considerably smaller (2.5 points) for shifts deviating from the mean voter's policy position. All three model specifications report a positive and significant effect for party shifts toward the mean voter's preferences. In contrast, only model 2 shows a statistically significant (but considerably smaller) effect for shifts away from the majority of voters. The findings are hence in line with the theoretical expectations of Hypothesis P8b.

Magnitude of past party policy shifts

I also argue that large policy shifts in the past preclude large policy shifts in the future. The argument is that parties have to conform to party policy reforms of the past to maintain their credibility. Hence, the effect of past policy shifts should have a negative effect on the party's current policy shifts.

Table 7.12 reports the regression results for the three model specifications. All three models reveal a negative, but insignificant, effect of large past policy shifts on the magnitude of policy shifts at time t. Increasing the number of large party policy shifts by one standard deviation (SD = 1.4) decreases the magnitude of party policy shift by about 0.5 points on the CMP left-right scale. Compared to the remaining covariates, this effect is very small. Because the model coefficients are insignificant, I reject Hypothesis P9.

Table 7.13 reports the regression results for the three model specifications. The share of voters identifying with a party has the expected positive effect in all three model specifications. The higher the ratio of voters with party identification, the larger the party position shifts. The size of the effect varies across the models ranging from roughly 0.03 (models 2 and 3) to 0.05 (model 1). Taking the estimates of model 1 as a baseline, the size of the effect is moderate. Increasing the share of identifiers by one standard deviation, the magnitude of party policy shifts increases by 1.11 points on the CMP scale. Although the effect is only statistically significant at conventional levels in the first model, the empirical evidence gives limited support to the expected effect.

Table 7.12: Magnitude of past party policy shifts and their effect on current party policy shifts

	(1)	(2)	(3)
	Multilevel model (Level 2: elections)	Multilevel model (Level 2: parties)[20]	PCSE regression
# of previous policy shifts larger than mean policy shift	-0.352 (-1.21)	-0.310 (-1.06)	-0.00905 (-0.03)
Party policy shifts (t-1)	-0.213** (-8.97)	-0.207** (-8.81)	
Constant	12.08** (24.28)	12.18** (24.72)	12.54** (21.63)
ρ			-0.088
Observations	783	783	733

z statistics in parentheses
+ p < 0.1, * p < 0.05, ** p < 0.01
ρ capturing serial correlation

Table 7.13: Share of voters with party identification and their effect on party policy shifts

	(1)	(2)	(3)
	Multilevel model (Level 2: elections)	Multilevel model (Level 2: parties)	PCSE regression
Share of voters with party identification	0.0519* (2.36)	0.0317 (1.48)	0.0339 (1.40)
Party policy shifts (t-1)	-0.194** (-5.97)		
Constant	6.556** (4.65)	8.116** (6.00)	8.328** (5.35)
ρ		-0.234	-0.058
Observations	376	397	397

z statistics in parentheses
+ p < 0.1, * p < 0.05, ** p < 0.01
ρ capturing serial correlation[20]

---

20. Because model 2 does not converge using a Prais-Winsten transformation, I include the lagged dependent variable.

Critical readers may argue that the parties' advantage of having a large share of identifiers depends on characteristics of the electorate. If most of the voters feel attached to a specific party, 'floating voters' are rare. The higher the number of parties enjoying the advantage of having a large share of identifiers, the less likely it is that party policy shifts result in gains of votes. Hence, the effect of voters with party identification on the magnitude of party policy shifts depends on the share of voters who identify with rival parties. The higher this share, the lower the effect of voters with party identification on party position shifts should be.

Figure 7.2 plots the marginal effect of the share of voters with party identification depending on the share of voters identifying with rival parties. The grey-shaded areas indicate 90 per cent confidence intervals and the model estimates are based on the first model specification presented in Table 7.13. Keep in mind that the overall coefficient for party identification reported in Table 7.13 is 0.05. The marginal effect plotted in Figure 7.2 shows that there is some variation of the effect size, depending on the share of voters identifying with rival parties.[21] If only a small share of voters identify with the competitors, having a large share of identifiers is strong (about 0.09) and statistically significant. The positive effect diminishes as the share of voters who identify with the party's rivals increases. Hence, having identifiers is mainly beneficial if competing parties do not have them.

Figure 7.2: Effect of party identification depending on rival parties' share of voters with party identification[22]

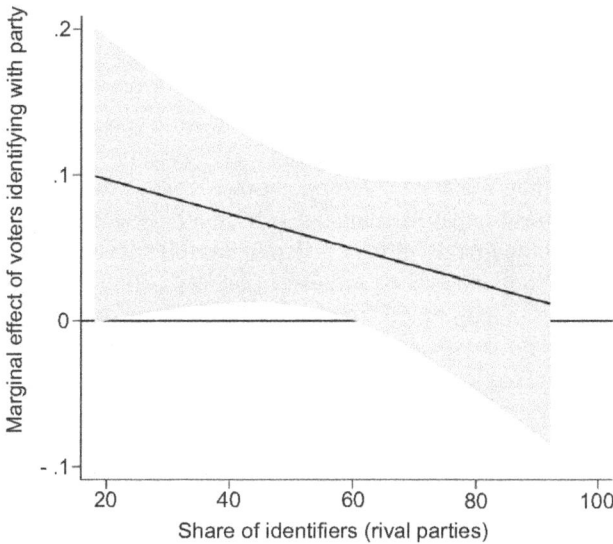

Note: Grey bars indicate 90 per cent confidence intervals.

---

21. Note that the overall interaction effect does not reach a significant level. Nevertheless, the graph shows that the positive effect of the share of voters with party identification on the magnitude of party policy shifts is mainly due to cases where the competing parties only hold a low share of voters with party identification.

22. Estimates based on model specification 1 (N = 376).

Public opinion shifts

Previous research highlights the role of public policy shifts for party position shifts. We expect parties to respond to the changing demands of the public. Previous research by Adams and colleagues (2004) shows that parties indeed react to shifts in the mean voter's policy position. The theoretical model presented in Chapter Five implies the same expectation that parties follow voter position shifts away from their policy position.

Table 7.14 presents regression results distinguishing benign and harmful public opinion shifts. Irrespective of the direction of the voter policy shift and the model specification, the coefficients are statistically insignificant. Moreover, there is no difference in the parties' reactions to benign and harmful public opinion shifts.

The insignificant results are puzzling because they contradict findings from previous research (Adams *et al.* 2004). Exploring the reasons for this discrepancy, I draw on recent research (Ezrow *et al.* 2010; Somer-Topcu 2009c) which emphasises that parties only react to specific voter groups: instead of reacting to shifts in the general public, parties are more responsive to their voters. As a consequence, parties react to shifts of their respective supporters rather than to the whole electorate. For the sample analysed here, however, I do not find a significant effect of party voter shifts. I also test for differences between mainstream and niche parties: Previous research (Ezrow *et al.* 2010) found significant differences in the parties' reactions to shifts in public opinion in that mainstream parties are more likely to adjust their policy positions to shifts of the mean voter than niche parties. Restricting the sample to mainstream parties, however, still leads to insignificant effects. Hence, the question remains why party position shifts seem to be independent of voter position shifts.

The null finding may be due to the fact that most voter position changes are rather small. These deviations in the mean voter positions may reflect measurement error rather than substantial voter position shifts. To distinguish 'noise' from substantial voter position shifts, statistics offer the two-sample t test as an instrument for mean comparisons in two different samples. Using reasonable values for sample sizes and standard deviations in surveys,[23] the test shows that voter position shifts with a magnitude smaller than 0.2 points on the 1 to 11 scale are not statistically significant at the 5 per cent level. For the data used here, about 50 per cent of the observations fall in this category. In other words, in around half of the cases tiny differences in voter positions are interpreted as voter position shifts although they may also be due to measurement error. Additional evidence comes

---

23. I assume equal variances in both samples and test for significant differences (at the 5 per cent level) using the average standard deviation of the voter left-right placements (~2.27). Because data on survey respondents is not included in the dataset, I set the number of respondents in both surveys to 1000. Note that the critical value, roughly 0.2, is an approximate value of what we would expect to see on average and is only used for illustrative purposes.

Table 7.14: Voter position shifts and their effect on party policy shifts

	(1)	(2)	(3)	(4)	(5)	(6)
	Multilevel model (Level 2: elections)		Multilevel model (Level 2: parties)		PCSE regression	
	Benign shift	Harmful shift	Benign shift	Harmful shift	Benign shift	Harmful shift
Voter policy shifts	-0.984	-3.493	-5.444	-4.002	-3.979	-3.245
	(-0.21)	(-0.84)	(-1.43)	(-1.01)	(-1.23)	(-0.77)
Party policy shifts (t-1)	-0.543**	-0.360**				
	(-5.85)	(-5.47)				
Constant	3.203+	1.429	1.328	0.951	1.651	0.720
	(1.78)	(0.99)	(0.71)	(0.73)	(1.02)	(0.48)
ρ			-0.667	-0.137	-0.278	-0.357
Observations	105	111	111	119	111	119

z statistics in parentheses
+ p < 0.1, * p < 0.05, ** p < 0.01
ρ capturing serial correlation

from a comparison of voter positions and voter position shifts from different data sources. For some elections, data coming from national election studies and the Eurobarometer trend file is available (N = 171). The correlation of voter policy positions using the different data sources is rather high (0.55, p<0.001). However, comparing the voter position shifts derived from consecutive national election studies and the Eurobarometer (N = 104) reveals that the correlation is practically zero and insignificant (-0.03, p=0.74). Hence, although left-right placements of mean voters are quite comparable, the shifts (i.e. the differences over time) capture measurement error so that the differences are not statistically significant.

In sum, I do not find evidence that parties follow harmful shifts in public opinion. This negative finding holds for shifts of the whole electorate and shifts of party voters. Moreover, there is no difference between mainstream and niche parties. This may be due to the fact that (mean) voters do not shift their policy positions to a great extent. As a consequence, shifts in public opinion could be fluctuations rather than ideological shifts and the model estimates reflect measurement error.

Voter expectations of party policy positions

I also argue that voters are less likely to accept party position shifts that move the party away from ideological expectations. If a party shifts to the right (to the left) although its actual policy platform is already right of (left of) its ideological territory, voters are less likely to accept the party's policy shift. With voters being less likely to accept party position shifts deviating from ideological expectations, parties avoid those policy shifts that would entail costs (e.g. writing new policy programs) but no potential benefits (i.e. attracting new voters on policy grounds). Hence, parties have incentives to respond to voter expectations correcting for inappropriate policy positions. I expect that parties shift to the left (to the right) if their policy platform is right of (left of) its ideological territory.

Table 7.15 shows the regression results testing this relationship. The regressions test the proposed effect using different measures of voter expectations and model specifications. Models 1 to 3 use voter expectations of all parties and models 4 to 6 report the regression results using a restricted sample of major parties (i.e. those with a minimum of 5 per cent of the vote share in two subsequent elections). Models 7 to 9 capture the effect of voter expectations distinguishing three classes of parties: left, centre, and right-wing parties.

The estimates presented in Table 7.15 strongly support the proposed effect. Compared to parties located at their ideological territories, parties with policy platforms left of their expected policy position shift their policy positions to the right (indicated by a coefficient larger than zero). Similarly, parties right of their ideological territory shift their policy positions to the left (indicated by a coefficient smaller than zero). Both coefficients point in the expected directions and are statistically significant at the 1 per cent level, irrespective of the model specification and the measures of voter expectations. Moreover, the effects are large. Compared to parties with policy positions conforming to the voters' expectations, parties left of their ideological territory shift their policy positions around 5.1 (model 2) to 8.3 points (model 7) further to the right. In a similar vein, parties to the right of their ideological territory are more likely to shift their policies to the left. The policy shifts are 5.2 (model 2) to 7.2 (model 9) points further to the left than those of competitors with ideologically 'appropriate' policy positions. Compared to the average policy shifts, around 12 points on the CMP left-right scale, the effects are large.

In sum, then, the findings conform to the theoretical expectations. If the parties' policy positions deviate from the expectations voters hold about the party's 'appropriate' policy position, parties react by shifting their policy positions. The size of the effects reported in Table 7.15 is also remarkable, given the average magnitude of party position shifts on the CMP left-right scale of about 12 points.

Table 7.15: Shifts reacting to voter expectations of party policy positions

	(1)	(2)	(3)	(4)	(5)	(6)	(7)	(8)	(9)
	Multilevel model (Level 2: elections)	Multilevel model (Level 2: parties)	PCSE regression	Multilevel model (Level 2: elections)	Multilevel model (Level 2: parties)	PCSE regression	Multilevel model (Level 2: elections)	Multilevel model (Level 2: parties)	PCSE regression
	All parties			Restricted to major parties			Distinguishing left, centre, and right-wing parties		
Party left of ideological territory (t-1)	6.169** (4.22)	5.052** (4.07)	5.941** (3.90)	7.235** (4.56)	5.985** (4.50)	7.051** (4.22)	8.294** (3.19)	7.530** (3.59)	8.023** (3.07)
Party right of ideological territory (t-1)	-5.379** (-3.76)	-5.222** (-4.39)	-5.976** (-4.49)	-6.163** (-4.00)	-5.423** (-4.21)	-6.234** (-4.29)	-6.780** (-3.15)	-6.446** (-3.66)	-7.225** (-3.83)
Party policy shifts (t-1)	-0.313** (-9.78)			-0.319** (-9.58)			-0.353** (-10.61)		
Constant	-0.415 (-0.45)	-0.211 (-0.35)	-0.244 (-0.35)	-0.319 (-0.34)	-0.289 (-0.47)	-0.358 (-0.50)	-0.113 (-0.13)	-0.125 (-0.25)	-0.107 (-0.17)
ρ		-0.332	-0.202		-0.341	-0.203		-0.360	-0.261
Observations	783	871	871	722	792	792	722	792	792

z statistics in parentheses + p < 0.1, * p < 0.05, ** p < 0.01

ρ capturing serial correlation

Table 7.16: Summary of the findings: How reception and acceptance affect party position shifts

	Variable	Hypothesis	Findings	Effect size (CMP points)[24]
Reception	Mean political interest	P1a	✓	1
	Mean political interest (direction)	P1b	(✓)	1.71
	Voter position shift (magnitude)	P3	0	-0.60
	Governmental share	P4	✓	1.65
	Effective number of parl. parties	P5	✓	-0.75
Acceptance	Leadership change	P7	(✗)	-1.75
	Party leader prestige (magnitude)	P8a	(✓)	1.46
	Party leader prestige (direction)	P8b	✓	4.40
	Past party policy shifts	P9	0	0.50
	Share of voters with PI	P10	(✓)	1.11
	Voter shift (direction)	P11	0	-1.12
	Ideological territory	P12	✓	5.77

✓   Finding in line with expectation.

0   No significant effect.

✗   Finding contradicts hypothesised effect.

(✓) Mixed findings.

---

24. For continuous variables, the change in the dependent variable is shown if the covariate increases by one standard deviation. For the governmental share, leadership changes, and the voters' expectations of the parties' policy positions, changes from 0 to 1 are reported. For variables distinguishing directions of party policy shifts (P1b and P8b), the effect size for party policy shifts towards the mean voter policy position is shown. For variables measuring voter position shifts, the effect sizes are valid for harmful public opinion shifts. The effect size for the voters' expectations is an average of the expected shifts to the left and the right. Estimates based on the first model specification reported in the previous Tables.

Summary

This chapter presents results of the voters' reception and acceptance of party position shifts and their effects on the parties' shifting options. It is based on empirical data of party policy shifts in ten Western European countries. Calculating a pooled analysis implies losing information on other covariates so that I tested the hypotheses one by one. To show the robustness of the findings and to control for potential model misspecifications, I estimated multilevel models capturing variance between elections (model specification 1) and parties (model specification 2), and a linear regression using panel corrected standard errors (model specification 3)

Table 7.16 summarises the results and indicates whether the empirical results conform to or contradict the theoretical expectations and whether the findings are robust across model specifications. Moreover, the effect size is shown to allow for easy comparison. The empirical results support most of my theoretical expectations: parties are more likely to shift their policy positions if the mean political interest is high, if they have been in government before, and the complexity of the party system is low. All three expectations arise from the voters' reception of party position shifts. Turning to the acceptance of party position shifts, parties are more likely to shift their policy positions if the party leader's prestige is high and if the share of voters identifying with the party is large. Furthermore, a party shifts its policy position if its policy position is outside the ideological territory (defined by the policy positions of its rival parties).

I do not find any effect of public opinion shifts on changes in party positions. These negative findings are surprising given that (1) voters are more likely to accept party position shifts in line with voter position shifts (Chapter Six) and (2) previous research emphasised the normative and empirical links between voter and party position shifts. For the effect of the direction of voter position shifts, I test modified models distinguishing party supporters and the whole electorate. I also consider the distinction between mainstream and niche parties (Ezrow et al. 2010). The regressions do not reveal any significant result. This non-finding is likely to be due to the fact that most public opinion shifts are relatively small. Using reasonable parameters, I show that about 50 per cent of the empirical voter position shifts are not statistically different and hence could be due to measurement error. If these voter position shifts are indeed meaningless, using different data sources[25] leads to different (random) estimates of voter position shifts. Studying the effect of public opinion shifts on party platforms (and hence proposed policy output) requires further research and robustness checks.

Finally, the results for leadership changes and the parties' past policy shifts do not conform to my theoretical expectations. New party leaders are, at least in

---

one model specification, less likely to shift the party's policy position. Instead of giving a new impetus to the party's life, new party leaders shift the party's platform to a lesser extent than party leaders who are in office for a longer time. I suggest that the negative 'newbie' effect may be due to the new party leader's lack of resources for immediate policy shifts. Furthermore, I do not find any significant effect of large past party policy shifts. The incentives to adapt a party's platform to changes in the environment seem to exceed the incentives coming from the acceptance of party position shifts.

Turning to the size of the reported effects (see Table 7.16), the insignificant effects are unsurprisingly among the smallest effect sizes. Increasing the respective variable by one standard deviation, neither the magnitude nor the direction of voter position shifts lead to a party policy shift considerably larger than one CMP point on the left-right scale. Although comparing the effect sizes of continuous and dichotomous variables is problematic, most of the other effects are quite similar in size. Only the effects of the party leader's prestige (including the direction of the party policy shift) and voter expectations stand out. Both effects are in line with the theoretical expectations. The effect is especially large for voter expectations of party position shifts. This finding encourages further research on party position changes as responses to rival parties' policy positions and the need to satisfying the voters' demands.

part iii. parties' internal structure and party policy shifts

chapter | how parties' internal structure
eight | affect party policy shifts

The previous chapters have focused on voters' perceptions of party policy shifts. I emphasise that parties face constraints on the electoral market which they have to take into account when shifting their policy positions. In other words, parties compete under constraints set by the voters' perception process of party policy shifts.

This chapter turns the attention to another factor affecting the parties' abilities to shift their policy positions. I argue that a party's internal structure affects its behaviour. So far, I have treated parties as 'unitary actors'. But although they 'do in practice tend to go into and come out of government as single actors' (Laver and Schofield 1998: 15), parties do not merely consist of a relatively small team seeking votes and office. Rather, parties are more or less complex organisations comprising many – often many thousand – people with various interests. Moreover, organisational rules provide a hierarchical structure. In this chapter, I outline the consequences of intra-party factors on party position shifts.

Figure 8.1: Intra-party structure and its effect on party policy shifts

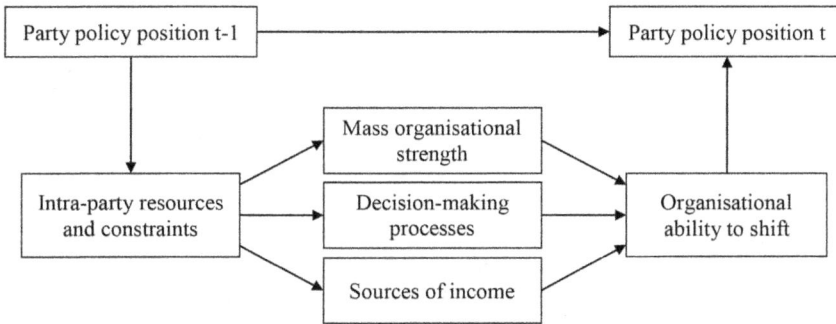

Specifically, I study three factors which are expected to affect a party's ability to shift its policy platform (see Figure 8.1). First, a party's ability to shift its policy positions should hinge on its labour resources it may activate: to advertise a party position shift, activists help to 'spread the word'. Therefore, parties equipped with many activists are more likely to get their message heard. Yet, parties may substitute the lack of rank-and-file by more capital-intensive forms of advertisement. Hence, the positive effect may diminish once public subsidies are in place.

Second, I argue that a party's internal decision-making processes affect its way of making policy reforms. Building on the principal-agent literature, party leaders act as agents of their policy-seeking rank-and-file. As for all principal-agent relationships, delegation entails chances but also risks: the more discretion party leaders have, the more likely they can make use of their expertise. Yet, giving leeway to party leaders also puts the members' representation at risk. Party leaders may be more interested in gaining votes and office spoils than representing the rank-and-file's policy preferences. Parties can counteract such ambitions by creating an intra-party structure with tight control mechanisms. As a major drawback, however, more inclusive party organisations, granting more say to their members, becomes inflexible. Such parties are hence less likely to move away from the status quo. I therefore expect that more hierarchically organised parties involving less veto players are more likely to shift their policy positions.

Third, I address the implications of public party funding for the dynamics of party positions. Drawing on the literature studying public finance accompanied by the emergence of cartel parties (Katz and Mair 1995), parties depending on their members' financial contributions should be more likely to stick to their members' preferences. The emergence of public funding weakens the ties between parties and their rank-and-file, thus decreasing the leader's dependence on the party activists. Hence, public subsidies allow for a higher flexibility when changing the policy programme and make policy shifts more likely.

Mass organisational strength and the consequences for party policy shifts

Labour provided by party members helps party elites to achieve their goals. Strøm (1990) identifies three needs for parties to organise. First, organisations provide information about the electorate and its preferences. Second, party organisations are necessary for election campaigns and the mobilisation of supporters (see also Ware 1996: 64). Third, organisations allow for the implementation of party policy in public office. It may be added that party members provide party and campaign finance (Strøm and Müller 1999: 15) and increase the legitimacy of their party's policy goals. Furthermore, party leaders may not be in the position to choose the basic organisational patterns of their party. Rather, a party's history predisposes how it organises. Elite parties emerged from within the parliaments. Although they adapted to the challenges of mass suffrage, their extra-parliamentary organisations remained rather weak. In contrast, mass parties root in the civil society. Following the bottom-up approach, their extra-parliamentary organisations are stronger (see also Katz and Mair 1995). The same holds for parties emerging from social movements (e.g. Green parties or the Polish Solidarność). If a party builds on such a strong extra-parliamentary pillar, party leaders can rely on a more comprehensive organisation.

Party elites hence need party organisations for various reasons. But how do these factors impact on a party's ability to shift its policy position? I argue that parties benefit from having strong (i.e. sizable) party organisations. For designing favourable policy shifts, parties need information on the citizens' preferences. What issues are crucial for voters? What are the voters' concerns? And what policies do voters prefer? Are the supporters satisfied with a party's performance in parliament and government? Or should the party behave differently? Party activists can help providing answers to these questions by listening to the voters' concerns. To the extent that activists succeed with this task, the party elite gains information on how to react to demands of the electorate. This information is crucial for choosing policy platforms that maximise a party's vote share. In light of the model presented above, parties get information on what voters expect them to do. Without being informed about voter expectations, parties are at risk of making policy shifts which voters do not accept (i.e. consider credible). Uncertainty of the voters' acceptance, and thus the expected benefit, makes parties refrain from taking on the costs of shifting policy positions. Information on the supporters' demands thus increases the acceptance of party policy shifts and makes party position shifts more likely.

Party activists also help parties to get their shift message heard. One of the major advantages of large party organisations is the workforce members provide during election campaigns. Party members organise party rallies and other activities, talk to citizens, provide information on their party's goals, defend their party against criticism and advertise its issues. In short, party activists make voters vote for their party. Regarding policy position shifts, parties with mass organisational strength have more capacity to advertise and to promote these shifts. Parties lacking activist manpower miss this kind of communication channel to the electorate. Consequently, the voters are less likely to receive platform changes.

In addition, party organisations are a recruitment pool for public office. They train future political elites and serve as a screening mechanism for candidates and their abilities to hold higher office (Müller 2000: 327–328). Within parties, candidates for public office learn the rules of political professionalism (e.g. delivering a speech or arguing in a discussion) and parties hence improve the quality of political elites. Parties currently face membership losses both within the core party (Mair and van Biezen 2001) and in their youth organisations (Hooghe *et al.* 2004). Decreasing membership figures have severe consequences for political parties and their recruitment of eligible candidates. The smaller the pool of potential candidates, the less likely is competition for intra-party office. Moreover, the smaller the pool of candidates, the less likely is the recruitment of good candidates for public office. In other words, organisationally weaker parties are less likely to produce competent party elites. In the model presented above (see Chapter Five), it is argued that a party leader's prestige is crucial for the voters' acceptance of party policy shifts. The weaker parties are in organisational terms, the less likely the emergence of competent party leaders and consequently, the less likely it is that voters accept policy shifts.

A party's rank-and-file also serves as a source of income. Higher incomes allow for costly campaigns which, in turn, increase the electoral chances of parties. Prosperous parties are able to hire professional advisors and can afford more expensive election campaigns, including TV commercials and radio spots. In contrast, parties with empty coffers are less likely to run effective campaigns and to attract potential members and voters. This, in turn, decreases their future revenues. While the sources of party income vary between systems and parties, membership fees figure prominently for most parties. Parties also benefit financially from large membership stocks.

In sum, a party's mass organisational strength affects its ability to shift policy positions in several ways. Activists serve as feedback loops that provide information on the voters' demands, advertise policy shifts, increase the pool of potential candidates for higher office and fund election campaigns. So doing, party members provide information on the voters' acceptance of party policy shifts and increase the party's visibility and hence, the reception of party policy shifts. These considerations lead to

> Hypotheses O1: The higher a party's mass organisational strength, the higher is its ability to shift the policy platform.

As a refinement of Hypothesis O1, one may argue that the role of party activists has changed over time. In fact, the outlined mechanisms mainly hold for older forms of political communication. In the classical mass party (Duverger 1954), party members are the central link between a party and the electorate. It is the party members who advertise policies (and policy shifts) and provide the party's campaign funding. But the time has changed and so have parties, party membership and political communication. In the 1950s, Duverger (1954) argued that mass parties are superior to other forms of party organisation. But as Epstein (1967: 257) noted already in the 1960s, Duverger's outlook may have been too hasty. Parties adapted to changes in their environment and transformed from a mass party to a catch-all party (Kirchheimer 1966), an electoral-professional party (Panebianco 1988) and more recently a cartel party type (Katz and Mair 1995). Over the course of time, the role of party members has changed. Once television entered the mass arena, the forms of political communication changed fundamentally (Mancini 1999). Instead of direct contacts, parties now communicate to larger audiences via public mass media (see also Müller 1997). Moreover, parties in Western Europe have recently suffered from decreasing membership figures (Mair and van Biezen 2001) and parties in new democracies in Southern and Eastern Europe show much lower membership levels than their West European counterparts (van Biezen 2003).

These developments affect the role of party members. Parties are able to substitute (lacking) members by other means. Hence, the advantage of parties with organisational resources diminishes. Parties substitute labour-intensive with capital-intensive activities (Strøm 1990; Strøm and Müller 1999). Instead of relying on the 'cheap labour' of their activists, parties use financial means to fulfil functions once performed by mass organisations. Paid professionals and polls substitute the feedback mechanisms of party members. Rather than relying on reports from their rank-and-file, parties consider evaluation and sympathy scores from polling institutes and may react accordingly. Moreover, making public party policy shifts partly passes over to the media. Instead of talking to voters face-to-face, parties build on radio and TV advertisement and their presence in news reports and talk shows. Finally, parties' dependence on financial membership contributions has decreased. On the one hand, the drop in membership figures diminishes the rank-and-file's contribution to party revenues. On the other hand, parties manage to (over-)compensate these losses by generating income from new sources, in particular public party financing.

The state supports political parties in a number of ways: Parties benefit from free time for radio and TV spots during election campaigns, financial aid to youth organisations, means for their parliamentary groups and direct public subsidies to central party organisations. The precise nature of these means and their introduction vary across countries. Moreover, parties differ in the share of their total income coming from public subsidies. In general, however, public subsidies nowadays provide the lion's share of party income. At the end of the 1980s, public money, on average, constituted around 25 per cent of the income of Austrian parties. In Finland and Germany, the parties' share of income from public money accounts for roughly 75 per cent (Pierre *et al.* 2000). It is therefore reasonable to assume that parties receiving public subsidies can substitute the members' contributions in terms of voluntary labour by resorting to capital-intensive means. As a consequence, public subsidies diminish the effect of a party's mass organisational strength on its ability to shift the policy position. I postulate a refinement of Hypothesis O1:

Hypotheses O2: The higher a party's mass organisational strength, the higher is its ability to shift its policy platform *if* public subsidies are not in place.

Intra-party decision making and its effect on party policy shifts

Party activists do not merely work for the party for the joy of activism. As a consequence, party organisations do not only provide cheap labour but also constrain party leaders because members expect to have an impact on the party's policy (Strøm 1990: 574).

The relationship between a party's elite and its rank-and-file may be understood best in terms of a principal-agent relationship (Kiewiet and McCubbins 1991). As Lupia notes, delegation is 'an act where one group or person, called a principal, relies on another person or group, called an agent, to act on the principal's behalf' (Lupia 2003: 33). Within parties, members delegate competences to the party elite. Delegation is useful if the principals do not have the time and the expertise to do the tasks themselves (Epstein and O'Halloran 1994). Yet, delegation also entails risks of adverse selection and moral hazard. Party members may select inappropriate agents (adverse selection) who are unable or unwilling to fulfil their tasks. Moral hazard implies that agents take actions that are unobserved and undesired by their principals (Lupia 2003). Especially if the agent's preferences diverge from his principal's, the latter may be worse off by delegating tasks to the agent. Principals are also able to counteract potential delegation problems within parties (for an overview see Müller 2000; Müller and Meyer 2010). For example, party members screen candidates for higher office to ensure that their agent's interests are in line with their personal preferences. Moreover, a party's rank-and-file monitors the agent's action in office to prevent (or to contain) moral hazard. Most important, however, party members can hold their party leaders accountable by disposing of them from their office if their behaviour is not in line with the members' expectations.

The members' expectations are closely linked to the reasons for participating in their respective party. Whatever drives the members' motivation to become and stay members of a political party: party leaders have to fulfil these needs to keep their jobs. In fact, the question of why people participate in political parties has been subject to vast scholarly attention. Parties produce public goods (Schlesinger 1984) so that all voters are affected by the party's policy output. Hence, participating in parties is a collective action problem because voters can also 'free-ride', taking the benefits without taking the costs (Olson 1965). The problem is solved if side payments exist. Such side payments grant party members private benefits such as patronage and prospects of upward organisational mobility for their participation (Strøm 1990: 577).

Although activists may benefit from party patronage, they are mostly willing to carry the costs of participation because they aim at influencing policy decisions. Hence, activists are policy-seeking actors (Aldrich 1983; Katz and Mair 1993: 598; Robertson 1976: 32). If a party no longer pursues its members' policy preferences, dissatisfied members will not accept these policies. If party leaders nevertheless aim for such policies, the rank-and-file will attempt to veto the proposed policies, remove the leadership or take the 'exit option' (Hirschmann 1970).

To keep and attract party members, party elites may give power to the party's rank-and-file. Party activists are more likely to work for the party (and its leadership) if they have a say in policy and personnel matters. Party leaders may therefore open the party for intra-party democracy by decentralising policy decisions. Furthermore, party leaders may increase their dependence on their members by decentralising the leadership selection. So doing, party leaders stress their accountability *vis-à-vis* the party's rank-and-file (Strøm 1990). Hence, party leaders 'pay' for the manpower of activists by granting access to policy decisions and by linking their fate as party leaders to the good will of their members.

A party's organisational form has various implications on its modus operandi. If a party chooses a decentralised organisational structure, intra-party democracy increases the number of intra-party veto players. Yet, as the number of veto players increases, policy stability does not decrease (Tsebelis 2002: 25). Therefore, parties with more intra-party democracy are less flexible than centralised parties. If (as I argue) party members are policy-seeking actors, their inclusion into decision-making processes hinder party leaders from adapting new challenges to the party. In fact, parties with a high number of intra-party veto players should be most vulnerable to 'friction' (Jones and Baumgartner 2005). In other words, decentralised parties are not likely to adapt to changing environments.

The causal mechanism hence works as follows: a party's history and its dependence on its members' workforce determine the intra-party decision-making processes. Party leaders give more say to the party's rank-and-file (and hence reduce the incentive problems of their members) if they depend on their manpower. Yet, increasing the rank-and-file's say in decision making increases the number of veto players and policy stability does (at least) not decrease. Therefore, decentralised parties are less able to adapt the party's policies.

Several studies show the effect of organisational characteristics on the party's ability to adapt to a changing environment. Comparing Austrian and Swedish Social Democrats, Kitschelt (1994a) argues that classical mass parties face new challenges. If mass parties grant their members a say in policy and personnel decisions, they become inflexible. In contrast, if a party's leadership is rather autonomous, it is more likely to adapt to a changing political market and hence increase its electoral chances. Similarly, Robertson (1976) argues that parties aim at winning elections but they also aim at attracting party members. The two goals may contradict each other and a party's organisational form shapes the emphasis parties put on the one or the other. Giving a say to party members leads to policy positions which are more extreme than vote-maximising policy platforms and hence, 'the less power the members of a party have, and the stronger the leadership, the better its electoral chances' (Robertson 1976: 43). Consequently, more hierarchically organised parties should be able to put more emphasis on the electoral market and be more likely to react to changing environments (see also Walgrave and Nuytemans 2009: 201).

Case studies also prove the plausibility of the argument (see Maravall 2008; Share 1999). In 1979, the leader of the Spanish Social Democrats (PSOE), Felipe González, aimed at abandoning the party's Marxist image because he knew the fear it raised among centrist voters. At that time, the centre-right UCD was the dominant party and González advocated a centrist party position shift to make the PSOE competitive. Yet, the Party Congress rejected his proposal. After González refused to run for re-election as the party's leader, however, the party elite was able to implement new intra-party rules leading to a more centralised party structure. As a consequence, González was able to shift the party's policy position to the right and attracted a sufficient share of voters to win the general election in 1982. In sum, I postulate

Hypotheses O3: The more hierarchical a party's decision-making process, the higher its ability to shift the policy platform.

Sources of income and their effect on party policy shifts

Finally, I consider a party's financial sources as a potential factor in determining its ability to shift policy positions. Financial resources are important for maintaining the party organisation and activities. Actors controlling the party revenues hence constitute 'veto players' whose preferences party leaders are likely to satisfy (Pfeffer and Salancik 1978). Mass parties primarily rely on membership fees and contributions of labour unions. Party leaders not only need to consider the rank-and-file's willingness to provide manpower but also their motivation to supply financial contributions. In the second half of the last century, the parties' sources of income have changed. Instead of private money coming from membership fees and donations of special interests (e.g. churches, labour unions, and employers' associations), parties increasingly draw on public money. Public funding of political parties is one, if not the central indicator of what is called the cartelisation of political parties (Bolleyer 2008; Detterbeck 2005; Katz and Mair 1995; but also Kitschelt 2000; Mair 1997: ch. 6, 2008, 2009; van Biezen 2003, 2004, 2008).

Cartel parties 'become entrenched within the state and employ resources of the state in order to guarantee their own survival' (van Biezen 2004: 706). It is argued that the emergence of cartel parties has many implications for modern democracies. The introduction of public funding made parties more dependent on the state (van Biezen 2008: 346).[1] At the same time, the emergence of cartel parties affects the relationship between parties and their members. Public subsidies reduce the leaders' (financial) dependence on members and hence provide them with the opportunity to disregard their preferences. With public money being available, party leaders can substitute capital for labour inputs and deemphasise policy-seeking (Strøm 1990; see also Strøm and Müller 1999: 21). Instead, parties adopt an electoral strategy. Even from the financial perspective this is a rewarding strategy because maximising a party's vote share is associated with maximising its funding from the public purse (van Biezen 2003: 40; 2004).

As a consequence, public funding reduces the parties' incentive to represent their members' interests. In the words of van Biezen (2003: 40) 'the development of structural and more permanent relationships between party organisation and society' becomes less likely. Moreover, Mair (2008) states that parties nowadays tend to follow a 'mainstream consensus' (2008: 212) and are therefore more 'coalitionable' and less partisan (2008: 216). Hence, parties 'govern but no longer represent' (Mair 2009). The electoral market shows the same pattern. Parties nowadays face an amorphous electorate with decreasing tendencies in turnout, party membership and identification, accompanied by increasing volatility scores. In sum, the emergence of cartel parties and public funding leads to an increasingly volatile political market. Parties refrain from policy-seeking behaviour, pleasing the interests of their members and the 'special interests' on whose contributions they depend. Rather, parties compete for votes because votes ensure public funding and hence the party's survival. The electoral market allows for this because the number of floating voters increases and the share of voters with party identification declines. In maximising their vote share, parties follow the electoral market, that is, they adapt their policy positions to the changing environment. This leads to

Hypotheses O4: The larger the share of public subsidies in a party's income, the higher is its ability to shift its policy platform.

---

1. The drawbacks of this dependence are obvious. In particular, parties have fewer incentives to keep their membership and are hence said to deviate from civil society. But public funding also ensures the survival of political parties, avoids corruption, and protects the independence of political actors (Nassmacher 2001b; van Biezen 2008: 348).

Summary

This chapter is devoted to the theoretical expectations of how intra-party factors affect party position shifts. In deciding on their policy positions, parties do not focus exclusively on rival parties and voters receiving and accepting policy shifts. Rather, they pay tribute to the way they are organised. In particular, I identify three factors shaping a party's ability to shift its policy position.

Parties differ in their membership figures. The better equipped parties are with activists providing information on the electorate's preferences, running electoral campaigns, ensuring vivid intra-party competition for office and safeguarding the party's revenues by contributing membership fees, the higher their abilities for shifting party platforms (Hypothesis O1). Yet, the advantage derived from mass organisational strength diminishes over time. Political competition changes with electoral campaigns becoming more capital-intensive and oriented towards the general mass media. Public funding allows parties to substitute the lack of man-power by the services of professionals such as pollsters and mass media communi-cation. Therefore, I expect that the advantage of parties having strong mass organi-sations for their ability to shift policy platforms diminishes once public funding is in place (Hypothesis O2).

I also expect that a party's internal decision-making processes are relevant. Party members delegate competences to the party elite but parties differ in the level of discretion granted to these selected agents. The more leeway party leaders have, the higher the likelihood of party policy changes. In contrast, less hierarchi-cal parties involve more veto players when making intra-party decisions so that moves away from the status quo are not likely (Hypothesis O3).

Finally, public subsidies should decrease the party leaders' dependence on the rank-and-file. As long as parties raise their funds mainly from donations and fees of their members, party leaders are likely to orient their positions on the members' policy preferences. The emergence of public subsidies introduces a new incen-tive: Because public money is usually tied to vote share, party leaders who aim at maximising their party's vote share are also maximising party income. So doing, parties are more likely to adapt their policy platforms to floating voters rather than sticking to their members' preferences. Consequently, publicly funded parties are thus more likely to shift their policy positions (Hypothesis O4).

chapter nine | parties' internal structure and party policy shifts: an empirical analysis

This chapter is devoted to the empirical analysis of the hypotheses derived in Chapter Eight. I study the effect of mass organisational strength on party platform changes (Hypothesis O1) and whether the introduction of public funding diminished this positive relationship (Hypothesis O2). Then, I turn to intra-party decision-making processes testing whether parties with hierarchically organised decision-making processes are more likely to shift their policy positions (Hypothesis O3). Finally, I turn to public funding and its impact on party position changes (Hypothesis O4).

Case selection, the dependent variable and the statistical model

As for the previous analyses on the effect of voter perceptions on party position shifts (see Chapter Seven), I test my theoretical expectations on a sample of ten West European countries. Specifically, I study the effects of intra-party variables on a party's ability to shift its policy platform for Austria, Belgium, Denmark, Finland, Germany, Ireland, the Netherlands, Norway, Sweden, and the United Kingdom. The reasons for this case selection are discussed in Chapter Seven.

For the analysis of intra-party constraints, there is one more pragmatic reason for this case selection, namely data availability. Systematic data on intra-party factors like membership figures, decision-making rules, and the parties' revenue (including those from direct public funding) is scarce. The first systematic account of collecting intra-party data for several countries is Katz and Mair's (1992) edited data collection on *Party Organizations*. In that, country experts report data on various intra-party characteristics like financial accounts, membership figures, decision-making rules for a period of thirty years (1960–1990). The data is used in a number of publications (see e.g. Bille 2001; Katz and Mair 1994; Krouwel 1999; Mair and van Biezen 2001; Pierre *et al.* 2000) and is, up to now, the only available systematic data collection on political parties. Similar data for other countries and a comparable time span is not available. This also holds for countries serving as alternative cases like newer Southern European and Eastern European democracies. Data on membership figures and public funding are only available for selected countries (van Biezen 2003), only in binary form (for public funding) (Birnir 2005; van Biezen 2004; Walecki 2001) or not at all. I hence rely on the time series data collected by the country experts in Katz and Mair's (1992) *Party Organizations*. Except for the United States (because of its presidential system) and Italy (because of the lacking validity of CMP data), I use all countries for which data on intra-party factors is available. This leads to a sample of party policy shifts in ten West European counties (Austria, Belgium, Denmark, Finland, Germany, Ireland, the Netherlands, Norway, Sweden, and the United Kingdom).

The key variable of interest is the magnitude of a party's policy shift in two consecutive elections. As above (see Chapter Seven), I rely on data collected by the Comparative Manifestos Project (CMP) (Budge *et al.* 2001; Klingemann *et al.* 2006) to measure party policy positions on the left-right scale (see also Laver and Budge 1992b: 26–7). Party policy shifts are measured as the differences in the parties' left-right policy positions in two subsequent elections. This variable is used in a large number of studies dealing with the dynamics of party competition (e.g. Adams *et al.* 2004, 2006a; Adams and Somer-Topcu 2009b; Budge 1994; Somer-Topcu 2009b; Tavits 2007). As above, I refrain from using the absolute values for the party policy shift variable. Rather, I recode the covariates (and the constant) as described in greater detail in Appendix B. I do so because using absolute values of the party policy shift estimates leads to distributions which are skewed to the right and hence violate one of the Gauss-Markov assumptions for linear regression models. Note, however, that the interpretation of the coefficients' direction and size is (due to their transformation) similar to that applied to regression models, including the magnitude of party policy shifts as a dependent variable.

The data structure and the related problems are identical to those already discussed in Chapter Seven. I refer to this chapter (and Appendix B) for a more thorough discussion of the data structure and the statistical model. In brief, there are various problems in the time-series (Beck 2001; Beck and Katz 1995, 1996) and hierarchical data structure (Gelman and Hill 2007; Rabe-Hesketh and Skrondal 2005; Steenbergen and Jones 2002). Unfortunately, there is no statistical model solving all problems at the same time. Hence, I estimate various regression models assuming different structures of the error term: a linear three-level regression clustering party position shifts in countries and elections, a three-level regression clustering party position shifts in countries and parties using the Prais-Winsten transformation, and a linear regression model using panel-corrected standard errors. Robust regression results across all three model specifications strengthen the confidence in the substantial effects.

Covariates

Table 9.1 provides an overview of the concepts and how they are measured in the analyses. Mass organisational strength indicates a party's ability to draw on strong membership organisations. Using a party's membership figures is a simple way to measure organisational resources. Yet, absolute numbers are not comparable across countries because the potential pool of party members hinges on the size of the electorate. In other words, a German party with 50,000 members does not have the same organisational resources as a Danish party with the same membership figures. I opt for a party-specific denominator to measure a party's mass organisational strength. This measure captures a party's mass organisational resources relative to its target electorate. It follows the idea that 'the most obvious single determinant of raw numbers of members is the size of the available membership pool' (Katz *et al.* 1992: 330).[1] Hence, even parties with moderate membership figures may have strong organisations if the number of potential voters is reasonably small. To measure the size of the target electorate, I use the maximal number of party voters in the last two elections as a proxy for a party's voter potential. The maximal number of party voters in the last two elections is a reasonable estimate of what parties aim to achieve. To be sure, the party-specific measure of mass organisational resources does not characterise a party's actual presence in society. Rather, it may be seen as an 'indicator of the respective subcultural implantation of the parties' (Bartolini 1983: 189) and that is what mass organisational strength aims to measure.

Intra-party decision rules may be measured in various ways. Hypothesis O3 states that the more hierarchical a party's way of making decisions, the higher its ability to shift the policy platform. It is therefore necessary to have a measure for intra-party rules indicating the members' say in decision-making processes. In principal, such a measure could deal with the members' intra-party influence studying their effect on policy decisions or – more indirectly – on personnel decisions which, in turn, influence policy choices.

Studying the members' influence on party position shifts, it is preferable to measure the members' involvement in policy decision-making. Specifically, the data should capture the members' role in formulating and deciding on party policies. Members involved in the development of party policies set the agenda for election programs, coalition negotiations, and campaign issues. In contrast, if a party leadership presents proposals which may be amended and finally put to a vote on party congresses, members' influence decreases. But even if party members merely check proposals coming from the party leadership, intra-party rules regarding amendments, voting rules (accepting/rejecting proposed election programs as a whole or in parts) and timing affect the members' effective intra-party power.[2] Unfortunately, systematic research on these intra-party decision-making processes is scarce. Some case studies delve into intra-party affairs showing how manifestos actually emerge. Yet, apart from case studies such as the ones by Shaw (2002) on the British Labour Party and by Pettitt (2007) on the Danish and British left parties at specific points in time, there is not much systematic research on the members' impact on party policy platforms.

---

1. Previous research has also used the size of the national electorate as a denominator (see e.g. Katz *et al.* 1992). The argument is that parties aim at representing the electorate's interests so that the share of organised members, relative to the electorate, is a reasonable estimate for a party's organisational strength. Yet, this usually leads to the conclusion that older and electorally larger parties are better organised than smaller ones.

2. Empirically, members' direct effect on party policies is rather weak (Carty 2004: 19). This is partly due to the parties' organisational structure that typically limits the influence of individual members (see e.g. Michel's (1915) 'iron law of oligarchy'). The perception of party members conforms to this expectation. Surveys show that ordinary party members complain about the lack of influence on intra-party policy decisions (Young and Cross 2002).

Table 9.1: Independent variables for the data analyses

	Variable	Indicators and measurement
Key covariates	Mass organisational strength	Number of members divided by maximal number of party votes in the last two elections
	Intra-party decision making	Inclusion of party members in the selection of candidates - No say: party leader or non-selected agency chooses candidates - Some say: selected party agency decides - Full say: party members personally decide on candidates
	Public subsidies (dichotomous)	Dummy variable (0/1) indicating whether direct public subsidies to a party's central organisation[3] exist
	Public subsidies (continuous)	Share of a party's income from public subsidies
Control variables	Party size	Vote share in per cent – Keman's (1994) threshold for dominant parties
	Time	Number of elections since World War II
	Niche party	Dummy variable measuring whether a party is mainstream (0) or niche (1); Coding following Meguid (2005, 2008)
	Left- and right-wing parties	Dummy variables indicating whether parties are left-wing, centre, or right-wing parties

For data on party membership figures until the end of the 1980s, I mainly rely on Katz and Mair's (1992) data collection on party organisations. For later time periods, several sources are used including literature on party organisations, political yearbooks and financial accounts of parties (including data on their party membership). More specifically, I use data for Austria (Dachs 2006; Liegl 2006; Luther 2006; Mair and van Biezen 2001; Müller 1992, 2006; Ucakar 2006), Belgium (Deschouwer 1992; Res Publica 1988, 1989, 1992, 1993, 1997, 1998, 2001, 2002, 2004, 2005), Denmark (Bille 1992; Mair and van Biezen 2001), Finland (Mair and van Biezen 2001; Sundberg and Gylling 1992), Germany (Niedermayer 2009; Poguntke and Boll 1992; Scarrow 2002), Ireland (Farrell 1992; King and Gillespie 1998; Murphy and Farrell 2002; Totten and MacCárthaigh 2001), the Netherlands (de Boer *et al.* 1999; Deschouwer 2002; Hippe *et al.* 2003, 2004; Koole and van de Welde 1992; Voerman 1996), Norway (Mjelde 2009; Svåsand 1992), Sweden (Pierre and Widfeldt 1992; Widfeldt 1999) and the United Kingdom (Labour Party

---

3. For Ireland and the United Kingdom, data on public subsidies to the parliamentary groups is taken.

2006; Liberal Democrats 2006; Webb 1992, 2002). Data on party votes stem from the country chapters in Katz and Mair (1992). For parties and elections after 1990, I mainly rely on data from online data bases (Election Resources on the Internet 2010; Interparliamentary Union 2010) and secondary literature (Mitchell 1993; Plasser *et al.* 2000).

As an alternative, I use the members' role in making personnel decisions. Like voters in representative democracies, members do not necessarily need to decide on policies in order to have an impact on party policies. Rather, members elect representatives who then formulate the party's policies and remain accountable to the members. Hence, members indirectly affect party policies by electing party leaders or selecting parliamentary candidates (Crotty 1968: 260). Supporting this statement, Schattschneider (1942: 64) states:

> The nominating process [...] has become the crucial process of the party. The nature of the nominating procedure determines the nature of the party; he who can make the nominations is the owner of the party. This is therefore one of the best points at which to observe the distribution of power within the party.

Because personnel decisions are crucial, it is not surprising to observe intra-party conflict over the choice of candidates, signifying conflict over specific policies (Gallagher 1988a: 1–4; Ranney 1981: 103). In that sense, the members' impact on personnel decisions serves as a proxy for their say on policy issues.

There are at least two different dimensions of candidate selection processes. First, inclusiveness indicates which actors are members of the selectorate (see Rahat 2007; Rahat and Hazan 2001; Ranney 1981). On one end of the continuum, party leaders may decide on the selection of candidates. Although rarely observed in Europe, this practice is sometimes applied in parties of the extreme right (Rahat 2007: 160). From that endpoint, the selection process becomes more inclusive as the number of actors deciding on the candidate selection increases. Candidate selection may be made by a (unelected) small group of party elites. Inclusion increases if the selecting party agencies themselves are elected by party members. In that case, party members elect delegates who, in turn, decide on the candidates. Next, party members may directly choose candidates by membership ballots. The most inclusive mechanism to choose candidates for office is primaries. Although practically non-existent in Europe, primaries are used in the United States.[4] In this case, the selectorate entails party members as well as non-members.

Second, the selection of candidates may be distinguished according to its centralisation (see Rahat 2007; Rahat and Hazan 2001; Ranney 1981). In its most centralised form, parties choose candidates at the national level. National

---

4. For more information on the various forms of primaries including open, closed, and blanket primaries, see Ranney (1981: 86).

and sub-national party units may also share in the selection of candidates for higher offices. Usually the process involves one side proposing a list of candidates and the other one deciding on the proposals. Finally, the selection process may be decentralised with sub-national (i.e. regional or local) units deciding on the selection of candidates.

In the following, I use inclusiveness as a measure for the members' say on intra-party decision making. The measurement is closer to the theoretical concept of the (policy motivated) members' say in intra-party decision making than the centralisation of the candidate selection process. Furthermore, the latter may also be due to country-specific factors that are beyond a party's power. For example, a country's size or its nature as either a federal or unitary state may affect the parties' centralisation (Thorlakson 2009). I distinguish three categories to measure the inclusiveness of a party's candidate selection process: First, the selection process is highly exclusive if party members have no (direct) influence in the selection process. In other words, party leaders or unelected party agencies decide on the candidates. Second, the selection process is partly inclusive if party members have an indirect say on the selection process. Party members elect delegates who, in turn, decide on candidates and party lists. Third, the selection process is fully inclusive if party members directly elect their candidates.[5]

For the coding, I mainly rely on secondary literature. For the period until 1990, I use Katz and Mair's (1992) data handbook on party organisations[6] and Gallagher and Marsh's (1988) edited volume on candidate selection.[7] Moreover, I use descriptions of country experts from Katz and Mair's (1994) edited volume for Belgium (Deschouwer 1994), Germany (Poguntke 1994), Ireland (Farrell 1994), the Netherlands (Koole 1994), Norway (Svåsand 1994), and the United Kingdom (Webb 1994). Data on the selection processes also stems from additional journal publications (Hazan and Voerman 2006; Hopkin 2001; Lundell 2004; Obler 1973, 1974; Pennings 1999; Rahat 2007) and book sections in edited volumes (Dachs 2006; Helander 1997; Kuitunen 2002; Leijenaar 1993; Luther 2006; Müller 2006; Müller *et al.* 1999; Pedersen 2002; Sainsbury 1993; Scarrow *et al.* 2000; Ucakar 2006; Valen *et al.* 2002). I also rely on electoral laws and party statutes (Die Grünen 2005; Finnish Ministry of Justice 1998 [amended 2004]; German Federal Elections Act 1993 [amended 2008]).

---

5. Although more fine-grained measurements may be feasible (see Rahat 2007; Rahat and Hazan 2001), it is empirically difficult to distinguish the various selection methods. Put differently, more fine-grained measurements entail a higher risk of coding errors.

6. Specifically, I use data from the various country chapters (Bille 1992; Deschouwer 1992; Farrell 1992; Koole and van de Welde 1992; Müller 1992; Pierre and Widfeldt 1992; Poguntke and Boll 1992; Sundberg and Gylling 1992; Svåsand 1992; Webb 1992).

7. In detail, I draw data from the country chapters on Belgium (De Winter 1988), Germany (Roberts 1988), Ireland (Gallagher 1988b), the Netherlands (Koole and Leijenaar 1988), Norway (Valen 1988), and the United Kingdom (Denver 1988).

I have hypothesised above that public subsidies affect a party's ability to shift its policy platform. Public funding allows for compensating labour by capital-intensive means thus diminishing the effect of a party's mass organisational resources (Hypothesis O2). Moreover, public subsidies decrease the party leaders' dependence on their rank-and-file allowing for an orientation towards the electoral market and more substantial party platform changes (Hypothesis O4). I use two different measures for public subsidies: First, a dichotomous variable indicates whether parties receive public subsidies or not. Specifically, I use the year when public subsidies to the parties' central organisations were introduced. Here, the countries in the sample differ widely (see also Pierre *et al.* 2000). In Germany, political parties already received public finding in 1959. Belgium was rather late introducing public subsidies to the parties' central organisations in 1989. Most of the remaining countries introduced public subsidies in the 1970s.[8] Second, a more fine-grained measure to indicate the importance of public funding for political parties is the relevance of public funding as its share in a party's total income (see e.g. Nassmacher 2001a; Pierre *et al.* 2000; van Biezen 2003; Wiberg 1991b). The higher the share, the lower a party's dependence on other income sources such as donations and membership fees.

Data on party income and the amount of public subsidies is difficult to obtain. In some countries (e.g. Belgium and Germany), parties are obliged to publish their financial accounts on a yearly basis. In others, similar regulations have been implemented lately. In Norway, for example, parties are committed to report their annual incomes since 1999, but precise numbers are only available since the Political Parties Act (The Ministry of Government Administration and Reform 2005) came in force in 2006.[9] In general, these country differences heavily bias the case selection of researchers studying public funding. Most often, researchers concentrate on countries and time periods for which data is available, leaving other countries and time periods aside. The same problems also affect the present study (see above).

For data on party finance until 1990, I mainly rely on Katz and Mair's (1992) data handbook on party organisations. In addition, I collect data on party income and the amount of public subsidies using additional literature, financial accounts of parties, websites of oversight agencies (e.g. statistical bureaus and commissions) and documents from various ministries as well as parliamentary libraries. Specifically, I collect data on party income and the amount of public subsidies for Austria (Sickinger 2000, 2009), Belgium (Belgische Kamer van Volksvertegenwoordigers en Senaat 1997, 2000b, 2000a, 2004c, 2004b, 2004a; Belgische Senaat en Kamer van Volksvertegenwoordigers 1993), Denmark (using financial accounts received from the Folketinget), Germany (Deutscher Bundestag

---

8. For Ireland and the United Kingdom, I take the subsidies to parliamentary groups (the Irish 'Oireachtas grant'; introduced in 1973 and the British 'Short Money'; introduced in 1975) into account.

9. The Norwegian Ministry of Government Reform and Administration, which is responsible for the public funding of political parties, was unable to provide precise numbers on the public subsidies individual parties obtained before 1999 (email response September 2, 2008).

1992, 1995, 2000, 2004), Ireland (Standards in Public Office Commission 2010), the Netherlands (Dutch Ministry of the Interior and Kingdom Relations undated; Gidlund and Koole 2001; Koole 1997), Norway (Statistics Norway [Statistisk sentralbyrå] 2010), Sweden (using financial accounts received from the Riksdag) and the United Kingdom (Gay *et al.* 2007; Koole 2001).[10]

I also use control variables that may affect the relationship between the key covariates and the parties' abilities to shift their policy positions. Party size may affect their mass organisational strength, internal decision-making rules and the share of public funding in the total revenue. One may argue that larger parties aim at representing larger segments of the electorate and face more problems to recruit a reasonable proportion of it than smaller parties with smaller target populations. Moreover, larger parties are also expected to be more hierarchically organised than smaller parties. Party size also affects the effect of public subsidies. Larger parties usually mainly draw on membership fees so that subsidies are less relevant for their revenue than for smaller ones.

Because the estimates for intra-party factors are biased if party policy shifts depend on party size, I include a party's size as a control variable. Yet, simply using a party's vote share is not appropriate because these are not comparable across countries. Whether a vote share of 25 per cent indicates a large or a rather small party, depends on the number of competitors. Therefore, the measure should take the party system's features into account. Following Keman (1994), I use a party system-specific constant (i.e. 100/N with N indicating the number of competing parties) as a parameter for party system-specific party size. A party's size is then indicated by the difference between a party's vote share and Keman's factor (i.e. 100/N). Data on party vote shares and the number of competitors is drawn from the Comparative Manifestos Project (Budge *et al.* 2001; Klingemann *et al.* 2006).

I also control for time effects in the data. Because West European parties are quite resistant to vote changes while simultaneously losing members (Mair and van Biezen 2001), it is reasonable that the parties' mass organisational resources have decreased over time. Furthermore, intra-party decision-making processes may evolve over time and newer parties are likely to choose more inclusive ways of decision-making (Carty 2004; Katz and Mair 1995). Finally, the relevance of public funding has increased over time. If party policy shifts are also time-dependent, these time trends may lead to spurious correlations. In the following analyses, I measure time effects using a count variable indicating the number of post-war parliamentary elections.

Different party types may also drive the results. Niche parties (Meguid 2005, 2008) share characteristics which distinguish them from their mainstream rivals. First, niche parties reject the traditional class-based (left-right) orientation of politics. Second, niche parties raise new issues which are, furthermore, not in line with classical division lines of the political system. Third, niche parties concentrate on specific issues putting emphasis on their core topics, simultaneously neglecting

---

10. I was not able to obtain any data for Finnish parties after 1990.

others (Meguid 2005: 347–8). Using Meguid's notion of niche parties, recent research shows that mainstream and niche parties differ in their reactions to public opinion shifts (Adams *et al.* 2006a; Ezrow 2010; Ezrow *et al.* 2010). In addition, mainstream and niche parties may also differ in their membership organisations, decision-making rules and their sources of income. I expect that niche parties have less mass organisational resources and a larger share of public subsidies in their party's income.[11] A dummy variable indicates whether parties are mainstream or niche parties.[12] For the coding, I mostly rely on Meguid's distinctions (Meguid 2005, 2008). For those parties not mentioned in Meguid's work, coding follows the definition criteria mentioned above. So doing, I avoid coding according to party families as done by Adams and colleagues (Adams *et al.* 2006a; Adams and Somer-Topcu 2009a). A complete list of niche parties in the ten West European democracies under investigation can be found in Appendix E. Note that most of the niche parties have party codes identifying them as Green, nationalist, ethnic, or regional parties.

Finally, I also test whether parties are left-wing or right-wing parties. Previous research (Adams *et al.* 2009) shows that left-wing parties are less likely to respond to public opinion shifts and changes of economic conditions. It may be argued that left-wing parties are ideologically inflexible, relative to centre and right-wing parties (Kitschelt 1994b) and are thus less likely to shift their policy positions. Because left-wing parties are also likely to differ from other parties with respect to their internal decision-making rules, mass organisational resources and the share of their income from public funding, I include two dummy variables in the subsequent analyses indicating whether a party is left- or right-wing. To distinguish left-, centre, and right-wing parties, I use the trichotomous measure introduced in Chapter Seven.

Table 9.2 summarises the covariates used in the analyses and reports their number of observations and summary statistics. In total, the dataset contains 920 party policy shifts of 99 parties in ten West European countries. For the key covariates, data for the parties' mass organisational strength and intra-party decision-making rules, is available for roughly two-thirds of the total sample. There are no missing values when studying public funding using a dichotomous measure. Yet, applying the share of party income from public subsidies, the number of observations drops to 464.

---

11. For the parties' decision-making rules, the expectation is less clear. Some niche parties (especially Green parties) are likely to have more inclusive intra-party decision-making rules. Yet, others (e.g. nationalist parties) are expected to show more hierarchical decision-making processes. In fact, the niche party concept is not appropriate to distinguish niche and mainstream parties on an organisational dimension.

12. I further assume that the mainstream/niche party distinction is dichotomous. Previous research (see e.g. Adams *et al.* 2006a; Adams and Somer-Topcu 2009a) implicitly makes the same assumption coding niche parties using dummy variables. Nevertheless, the niche party definition (Meguid 2005: 347–348) does not explicitly preclude the existence of further party types.

Data on membership resources is available for all ten countries. Due to restrictions in data availability, observations with available data start in the 1950s leading to a small bias across time. Around 85 per cent of the observations with data on party membership are party position shifts from 1970 onwards. In the total sample, only 70 per cent of the observations are placed in that period. In other words, missing values are more likely for earlier time periods and, in fact, around 55 per cent of the missing values are due to party position shifts in the 1940s and 1950s.

Table 9.2: Independent variables: number of observations and mean values

	Variable	N	Mean
Key covariates	Mass organisational strength	639	0.124
	Intra-party decision-making rules	647	– Members have no say: 40 – Members have some say: 248 – Members have full say: 359
	Public subsidies (dichotomous)	920	– No public funding: 436 – Public funding: 484
	Public subsidies (continuous)	464	0.303
Control variables	Party size	920	-0.146
	Time	920	10.8
	Niche party	917	– Mainstream party shifts: 828 – Niche party shifts: 89
	Left- and right-wing parties	791	– Left-wing party shifts: 278 – Centre party shifts: 290 – Right-wing party shifts: 223
	TOTAL	920	

Similarly, data on the parties' internal rules is also more likely to be available after 1960. About 80 per cent of the observed party policy shifts, where data on candidate selection rules is available, stems from 1970 onwards while only 70 per cent of all party position shifts fall in the same period. Again, about 50 per cent of the missing values are due to the lack of data on the parties' candidate selection rules in the 1940s and 1950s. For the remaining time period, the missing values distribute evenly over time, not creating any time gaps.

For data on public subsidies, the number of observations drops to 464. Nevertheless, data is available for parties in all ten countries and across time. The variable also suffers from missing values in the 1940s and 1950s. But the higher number of missing values is mainly due to missing data from the 1960s onwards so that the total sample is more balanced than for mass organisational strength and intra-party decision-making.

Turning to the control variables, data availability is less of a problem. Data on party size over time is available for all observations. The coding of parties as left-, centre, and right-wing and niche parties causes some missing values that are, however, negligible compared to the missing data for the key independent variables.

Mass organisational strength and its effect on party position shifts

I argue that party activists offer important resources for political parties. The more numerous a party's rank-and-file, the better its entrenchment in society and hence, the higher its legitimacy. Parties with strong organisations can draw on their members' manpower to advertise policy shifts. Members also serve as feedback loops, providing information on voter demands (and which policy shifts voters may find acceptable). In addition, party members constitute the main pool of potential candidates. The more members a party has, the better are the chances of recruiting eligible candidates for higher office. Competent candidates and public office holders, in turn, increase the acceptance of party policy shifts. Finally, party members contribute to the funding of election campaigns and other party activities and hence provide the capital necessary to advertise party position shifts. In total, parties with strong organisations have more leeway to shift their policy positions (Hypothesis O1).

Table 9.3 presents the regression results for the proposed positive effect of a party's mass organisational resources on the magnitude of its party policy shifts. As for the following regression analyses, I estimate regression models using the three model specifications described above. The first model is a linear three-level regression using elections at the second level, and a lagged dependent variable to control for serial correlation. Model specification 2 is a three-level regression model with parties at the second level and applying a Prais-Winsten transformation to take the serial error structure into account. The third regression model presented in Table 9.3 is a linear regression with panel-corrected standard errors.

The regression results reported in Table 9.3 support the hypothesised effect. The higher a party's mass organisational resources (i.e. the larger the members per vote ratio), the larger are its policy shifts. The effect is positive and statistically significant for all three model specifications.[13] Increasing a party's membership

---

13. Note that the number of observations differs between the first model specification (N = 603) and the remaining two (N = 639). As in the analyses presented in Chapter Seven, this is due to the different modelling of serial correlation. While the Prais-Winsten transformation allows for keeping all cases with available data, using a lagged dependent variable requires knowledge on

resources by one standard deviation (SD = 0.127) increases a party policy shift by 1.5 points on the CMP left-right scale. From its minimal to its maximal value, party policy shifts increase by 7.7 points.[14] As a reference, the average size of a party's policy shift in the ten West European countries under consideration is about 12 points on the CMP left-right scale. Compared to that (and to the effects presented in Chapter Seven), the effect size is moderate.

For further robustness tests of the effect, I consider additional control variables. I study whether the effect of mass organisational strength on the magnitude of party policy shifts may also be due to party size, the time period in which the position shift takes place, whether a party is a niche party and whether it belongs to the left-, the centre, or the right-wing spectrum of the policy space. I use these covariates to account for differences in the parties' organisational resources. The results are shown in Table 9.4.

Table 9.4 shows the effect of several covariates on the log-transformed membership ratio.[15] As can be seen, party size and time affect a party's mass organisational resources. Moreover, niche parties tend to have smaller members per vote ratios. Yet, a party's status as left-, centre or right-wing party does not affect a party's membership resources.

Small parties tend to have more members per vote than larger ones. A one per cent increase in a party's vote share results in a 1 per cent decrease in the members per vote ratio.[16] The time period is also of importance. Parties have nowadays less members per vote than they had in the post-war period. With each election, the parties' organisational resources decrease by about 6 per cent. Manpower of niche parties also significantly differs from that of mainstream parties. Compared to the latter, niche parties have membership figures which are about 80 per cent smaller than those of comparably sized mainstream parties. The finding suggests that niche parties build less on party members. Even controlling for their later appearance and their smaller party size, niche parties are less organised and should therefore mainly rely on capital-intensive means to run their campaigns. Thus, public funding is expected to be of major importance for niche parties (see Table 9.11).

I include the factors with significant effects on a party's mass organisational resources in the analysis predicting the magnitude of party policy shifts. If a party's size, niche party status or time effects affect the relationship between organisational strength and party policy shifts, the positive and significant effect found in Table 9.3 may disappear. Table 9.5 reports the regression results. For all three

---

previous party position shifts. As a consequence, some cases are dropped from the analysis.

14. Estimates based on model specification 1 (N = 603).

15. I use the log transformation because the membership ratio has a skewed distribution. The resulting probability distribution is closer to the normal one.

16. Because the dependent variable is log-transformed, the regression coefficients cannot be meaningfully compared. Rather, for $y = b \cdot x + c$, a unit increase in x results in a $100 \cdot [\exp(b)-1]$ per cent increase of y.

Table 9.3: Mass organisational strength and its effect on party policy shifts

	(1)	(2)	(3)
	Multilevel model (Level 2: elections)	**Multilevel model (Level 2: parties)**	**PCSE regression**
Mass organisational strength	12.67**	12.19**	13.94**
	(3.21)	(3.09)	(3.36)
Party policy shifts (t-1)	-0.205**		
	(-7.72)		
Constant	10.16**	10.22**	10.57**
	(15.38)	(16.04)	(15.84)
ρ		-0.212	-0.066
Observations	603	639	639

z statistics in parentheses   + p < 0.1, * p < 0.05, ** p < 0.01

Table 9.4: Explaining mass organisational strength

	Multilevel model (Level 2: parties)
Party size	-0.00913**
	(-3.35)
# of national election	-0.0580**
	(-5.53)
Niche party	-1.595**
	(-5.03)
Left-wing party	-0.112
	(-0.45)
Right-wing party	0.0555
	(0.21)
Constant	-1.882**
	(-7.81)
ρ	0.953
Observations	586

z statistics in parentheses   + p < 0.1, * p < 0.05, ** p < 0.01

Table 9.5: Mass organisational strength and its effect on party policy shifts –
including control variables

	(1)	(2)	(3)
	Multilevel model (Level 2: elections)	**Multilevel model (Level 2: parties)**	**PCSE regression**
Mass organisational strength	7.763[+]	7.411[+]	8.708[+]
	(1.76)	(1.67)	(1.85)
Party policy shifts (t-1)	-0.204**		
	(-7.68)		
Party size	0.0433	0.0345	0.0475
	(1.07)	(0.85)	(1.11)
# of national election	-0.183	-0.149	-0.152
	(-1.55)	(-1.29)	(-1.14)
Niche party	-2.169	-2.577[+]	-2.594[+]
	(-1.46)	(-1.77)	(-1.95)
Constant	13.17**	12.91**	13.36**
	(7.65)	(7.60)	(6.86)
Constant		-0.208	-0.057
Observations	603	639	639

z statistics in parentheses $+ p < 0.1$, * $p < 0.05$, ** $p < 0.01$

model specifications, the effect of organisational resources on party position shifts remains positive and statistically significant at conventional levels. Compared to the estimates reported in Table 9.3, the coefficients diminish in size by about 4 points. Using the estimates of model specification 1 as a reference, increasing the member per vote ratio by one standard deviation increases party position shifts by 0.9 points.

From the minimal to the maximum value, the effect size amounts to 4.7 CMP points. Compared to the results excluding control variables, the effect size diminishes by about 50 per cent. Yet, in relation to the average magnitude of party policy shifts (about 12 points on the CMP scale), the effect size is still moderate. I hence conclude that the empirical results support the positive effect postulated in Hypothesis O1.

Note that the control variables are mostly insignificant. Only the coefficient for niche party status reaches a significant level in two of three model specifications: niche parties tend to shift less than mainstream parties. On average, niche party policy shifts are about 2.5 points smaller than those of mainstream parties. This finding holds, although the model considers time effects and party size. This supposes that niche parties are rather dull in the sense that they 'stick' to their policy positions instead of 'hunting' for votes or 'predating' rival parties (Laver 2005). How exactly these differences can be explained is an interesting topic for future research.

As a refinement of Hypothesis O1, I argue that the activists' manpower is especially beneficial if parties cannot substitute it by other means. In former times, parties heavily relied on their members' workforce during campaigns and their financial contributions to ensure the party's revenue. If parties have alternative sources of income, they can also draw on capital-intensive means to fund election campaigns and are, therefore, less dependent on their rank-and-file's good will. The emergence of public funding provides parties access to such alternative sources. As a consequence, the advantage of parties with large mass strong organisations diminishes once public subsidies serve as substitutes for the members' manpower. Table 9.6 reports the regression results testing this expectation. Models 1 to 3 display the results for party policy shifts without public funding for three different model specifications. Models 4 to 6 show the regression results if public funding is in place.

The regression results of models 1 to 3 show a positive effect of a party's mass organisational strength on the magnitude of party policy shifts. If parties cannot substitute lacking organisational resources by public funding, parties with strong organisations have an advantage over less organised parties. In fact, the effect sizes are considerably larger than in the previous (non-interacting) model (see Table 9.5) and statistically significant in two of the three model specifications. Using model specification 1 as a guideline, increasing a party's member per vote ratio by one standard deviation, the magnitude of party position shifts increases by 1.9 points on the CMP scale. This effect is considerably larger than the increase of 0.9 points reported in the linear model (see Table 9.5).

The size of the coefficient decreases once public subsidies are introduced (models 4 to 6). The regression coefficients for party policy shifts without public funding (models 1 to 3) are considerably larger than those for cases where parties can draw on public money (models 4 to 6). Comparing models 1 and 4, the size of the regression coefficient decreases from 18.1 to roughly 4. This is also reflected in the substantive effect size. Increasing the member per vote ratio by one standard deviation increases party policy shifts by 1.9 (without public funding) and 0.5 (with public funding) points on the CMP scale. In addition, none of the regression coefficients in models 4 to 6 reaches statistical significance. In sum, then, party manpower increases a party's ability to shift its policy position but only if parties cannot compensate their lack of resources by public subsidies. The findings hence support the effect postulated in Hypothesis O2.

Table 9.6: Mass organisational strength and its effect on party policy shifts – depending on public funding

	(1)	(2)	(3)	(4)	(5)	(6)
	Multilevel model (Level 2: elections)	Multilevel model (Level 2: parties)	PCSE regression	Multilevel model (Level 2: elections)	Multilevel model (Level 2: parties)	PCSE regression
		Without public funding			Public funding	
Mass organisational strength	18.09*	12.34	14.13[+]	3.974	6.106	7.096
	(2.01)	(1.38)	(1.66)	(0.79)	(1.20)	(1.37)
Party policy shifts (t-1)	-0.190**			-0.218**		
	(-3.81)			(-6.94)		
Party size	-0.0617	-0.0567	-0.0519	0.0864[+]	0.0718	0.0927[+]
	(-0.82)	(-0.75)	(-0.72)	(1.79)	(1.49)	(1.82)
# of national election	-0.120	-0.0847	-0.0558	-0.170	-0.162	-0.178
	(-0.51)	(-0.36)	(-0.25)	(-1.07)	(-1.07)	(-0.94)
Niche party	-4.042[+]	-4.382[+]	-4.452*	-0.947	-0.937	-1.312
	(-1.65)	(-1.77)	(-2.40)	(-0.49)	(-0.50)	(-0.72)
Constant	11.68**	12.19**	12.13**	13.21**	12.96**	13.82**
	(3.73)	(3.88)	(3.98)	(5.68)	(5.78)	(5.03)
ρ		-0.156	-0.042		-0.245	-0.039
Observations	202	216	216	401	423	423

z statistics in parentheses + p < 0.1, * p < 0.05, ** p < 0.01

Intra-party decision-making and its effect on party position shifts

I also argue that a party's internal decision-making rules affect its ability to change policy positions. Simply put, the more veto players are involved in making intra-party decisions, the less likely are shifts away from the status quo. This particularly holds for changes of the policy program. I therefore expect that platform changes are more likely to occur if the intra-party decision-making process is rather hierarchical (Hypothesis O3). Intra-party decision-making processes are measured using the members' voice in the candidate selection for parliament. Specifically, I distinguish whether party members have no say, some say and full say in the selection process. Using the middle category as the reference category, Table 9.7 presents the effect of intra-party decision-making processes on party policy shifts.

In two of the three model specifications, the difference between the most hierarchical party structure (with members having no say in candidate selection) and the moderate inclusion of candidates is significantly different at conventional levels. Party policy shifts of hierarchically organised parties are about 3.5 points larger than those of their most inclusive rivals. Compared to the average magnitude of party policy shifts (about 12 points on the CMP left-right scale), the effect size is considerably large. In contrast, parties granting their members full say in the selection process do not differ significantly from those giving members some decision-making competences in the selection process. Although the coefficients point in the expected negative direction in all three model specifications, the effects are not statistically significant. Moreover, the difference (below 1 point on the CMP left-right scale) is much smaller than the one between moderately inclusive and most exclusive decision-making processes. This can also be seen in Figure 9.1. The graph shows the average magnitude of party policy shifts depending on the members' say in the selection process. The bars indicate 90 per cent confidence intervals.

As can be seen, parties giving their members no say shift more than their rivals with more inclusive internal decision-making rules. Increasing the members' role in the selection of candidates, policy shifts on average decrease from 15.9 over 12.1 to 11.3 points on the CMP left-right scale. The graph also shows that the effect is not monotonically decreasing. Rather, parties granting their members no say in the selection process shift significantly more than their more inclusive rivals. Yet, parties granting some and full say to their members show no significant differences in their shifting patterns.

The differences in the shifting behaviour of parties with different internal decision-making rules may also be due to third factors impacting on the way parties organise, and how they shift their policy positions. Hence, I test for factors that determine the party members' inclusion.

Because internal decision-making rules are rather constant over time, I create a new database with the 99 parties in the sample and their organisational forms.[17]

---

17. In case decision-making processes have changed over time, I use the most frequent type of organisational form over the whole sample period.

Table 9.7: Intra-party decision-making processes and their effect on party policy shifts

	(1) Multilevel model (Level 2: elections)	(2) Multilevel model (Level 2: parties)	(3) PCSE regression
Party members: no say	3.818[+]	3.477[+]	3.506
	(1.94)	(1.76)	(1.55)
Party members: full say	-0.763	-0.408	-0.120
	(-0.81)	(-0.43)	(-0.12)
Party policy shifts (t-1)	-0.212**		
	(-8.27)		
Constant	12.05**	11.79**	12.03**
	(16.54)	(16.24)	(16.41)
ρ		-0.227	-0.105
Observations	610	647	647

z statistics in parentheses

+ p < 0.1, * p < 0.05, ** p < 0.01

The number of observations and the character of the dependent variable do not allow for an appropriate statistical analysis. For the present dataset, an ordered logistic regression (either as a multilevel model or using country fixed effects) would be the appropriate choice. Yet, 99 observations are not sufficient to estimate complex models with the asymptotic model assumptions. I therefore restrict myself to a descriptive analysis. Specifically, Table 9.8 presents the parties' levels of inclusion of party members in the candidate selection process depending on their mean size and age. In addition, I report the share of niche, left- and right-wing parties within each category and for the total sample.

Regarding party size, there is a clear negative trend indicating that small parties (i.e. those with negative values in Table 9.8) are more likely to give their members a say in the selection process. Larger parties, in contrast, tend to rely on more exclusive selection procedures. This finding is hardly surprising because parties that receive more votes also tend to have higher membership figures. Hence, larger

Figure 9.1: Mean magnitude of party policy shifts depending on the inclusion of party members in the candidate selection process

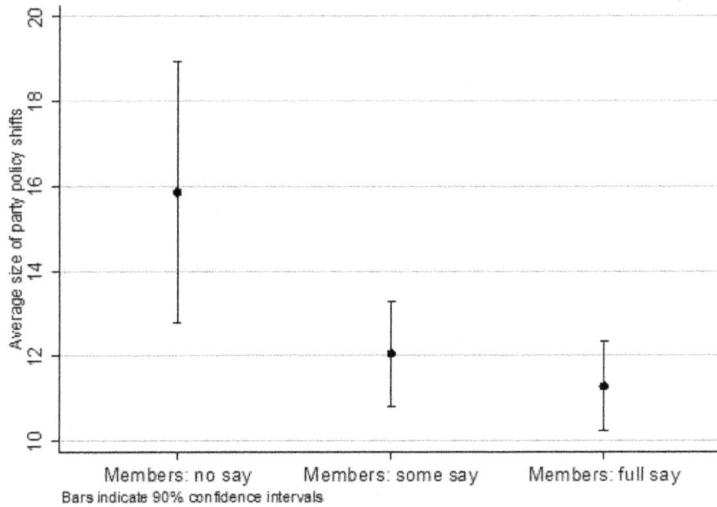

Bars indicate 90% confidence intervals

parties have to deal with more members and consequently, delegate tasks to higher (elected or unelected) party offices. Table 9.8 also reveals a time effect. On average, the most hierarchical form of party organisation emerged in the early 1960s. Parties granting more influence to their members entered party competition later than their more hierarchical rivals.[18]

We can also observe a modest effect of niche parties. On average, 19 per cent of the parties (i.e. 18 out of 97) are coded as niche parties. We find niche parties overrepresented in the group of parties granting their members no say in the selection process (25 per cent). In contrast, niche parties are rather rare in the group of parties being most inclusive (16 per cent). I hence conclude that niche parties tend to organise more hierarchically.[19] In contrast, there is no clear tendency of left- or right-wing parties to organise in particular ways. Their distributions across groups correspond to the total share of left- and right-wing parties.

---

18. Yet, the effect is rather small. In addition, the finding could also be due to alternative factors such as party size or the niche party status. This assumption is, at least, reasonable, thinking of Green, regional, and nationalist parties entering parliament in the 1970s and 1980s. Again, controlling for alternative explanations is desirable, but unfortunately not feasible, with the available (small) number of observations.

19. The result may be surprising for Green niche parties. Yet, it appears reasonable for nationalist parties that are expected to have party organisations which are tailor-made for strong party leaders. The niche party concept, combining various party ideologies, may not show clear-cut divisions to the mainstream party type in terms of the members' role for making decisions. Due to space restrictions, I refrain from a more detailed discussion here. Note, however, that the niche party concept may need some refinement when it comes to explaining differences in intra-party decision making.

Table 9.8: Explaining intra-party decision-making rules – descriptive patterns

	Party members: no say	Party members: some say	Party members: full say	Total	N
Relative party size	1.0	-2.4	-4.8	-3.8	99
Date of first election	November 1961	March 1963	September 1964	February 1964	99
% of niche parties	25	23	16	19	97
% of left-wing parties	33	33	40	37	70
% of right-wing parties	33	25	26	26	70

With those findings at hand, I estimate models predicting the magnitude of party position shifts controlling for party size, time effects and niche party status. The results for the three model specifications are shown in Table 9.9. The differences of the party members' say in the selection process are only statistically significant in one model specification. Compared to the reference category (i.e. some say to party members), models 2 and 3 report that parties giving no or full say to their members do not differ significantly in their shifting patterns.

That is not to say that there are no meaningful differences between parties with varying internal decision-making rules. For models 1 and 2, the differences between parties giving no say to their members and those granting full say is statistically significant even with control variables included in the model. Taking model 2 as a guideline, differences in the organisational form allow more hierarchical parties to make policy shifts which are about 3.5 points larger than their most inclusive rivals ($2.947 + 0.540 = 3.487$; $p = 0.076$). At least for two of the three model specifications, the empirical results therefore support the theoretical expectation put forward in Chapter Eight.

Regarding the control variables, the results in Table 9.9 show that party size and niche party status also affect the magnitude of party policy shifts. In all three model specifications, a party's vote share has a positive effect on its shifting abilities. Large parties also tend to have more hierarchical structures (see Table 9.8) so that party size has a positive impact on both hierarchy in party organisation and party policy shifts. Thus, a party's size soaks up parts of the organisational effect. We also see that niche parties are less likely to change their policy platforms. This finding is in line with the regression results presented in Table 9.5. Again, the finding is a potentially rewarding topic for further research explaining how and why niche party behaviour differs from that of mainstream parties.

Table 9.9: Intra-party decision-making processes and their effect on party policy shifts – including control variables

	(1)	(2)	(3)
	Multilevel model (Level 2: elections)	**Multilevel model (Level 2: parties)**	**PCSE regression**
Party members: no say	3.430[+]	2.947	2.979
	(1.72)	(1.48)	(1.29)
Party members: full say	-0.815	-0.540	-0.281
	(-0.85)	(-0.56)	(-0.28)
Party policy shifts (t-1)	-0.208**		
	(-8.15)		
Party size	0.0730*	0.0721[+]	0.0776*
	(2.00)	(1.93)	(2.06)
# of national election	-0.0859	-0.0555	-0.0643
	(-0.79)	(-0.52)	(-0.60)
Niche party	-2.301	-3.387*	-3.328*
	(-1.24)	(-2.02)	(-2.06)
Constant	13.15**	12.77**	13.11**
	(9.33)	(9.20)	(9.34)
ρ		-0.223	-0.102
Observations	610	647	647

z statistics in parentheses

+ p < 0.1, * p < 0.05, ** p < 0.01

Public funding and its effect on party position shifts

Parties financially dependent on their rank-and-file have incentives to satisfy the needs and preferences of their members. Once this dependence diminishes, party leaders are less likely to take the activists' preferences seriously. Party elites seeking votes and office are hence more flexible because the members' 'exit' option (Hirschmann 1970) is no longer a credible threat. Moreover, the allocation of public money is usually tied to a party's vote or seat share. Therefore, party leaders have incentives to increase a party's vote share even at the price of membership losses. Public subsidies hence increase vote-seeking incentives simultaneously reducing a party's stickiness to its members' policy preferences. I therefore expect that increasing the share of a party's income from public funding increases its ability to shift policy positions (Hypothesis O4).

Table 9.10: Public funding and its impact on party policy shifts

	(1)	(2)	(3)
	Multilevel model (Level 2: elections)	**Multilevel model (Level 2: parties)**	**PCSE regression**
Public subsidies: share of income	-1.041	-0.913	-1.403
	(-0.49)	(-0.44)	(-0.68)
Party policy shifts (t-1)	-0.226**		
	(-6.77)		
Constant	11.93**	12.00**	12.53**
	(13.55)	(13.97)	(14.68)
ρ		-0.210	-0.098
Observations	446	464	464

z statistics in parentheses
+ p < 0.1, * p < 0.05, ** p < 0.01

Table 9.10 presents regression models for the three model specifications test-ing whether public subsidies affect party policy shifts. The empirical results sup-port the postulated effect if the regression coefficient is positive and statistically significant. Yet, the coefficients are negative and insignificant. Increasing the share of revenue from public funding actually decreases the magnitude of party policy shifts. However, the effect is very small: increasing public funding of parties by one standard deviation, the magnitude of party policy shifts decreases by 0.3 points on the CMP left-right scale. From its minimum (0) to its maximum value (0.973), the magnitude of party policy shifts diminishes by about 1 unit.[20] Compared to the effects reported above, and the average magnitude of party policy shifts (around 12 points on the CMP left-right scale), the effect size is rather small. I therefore conclude that the amount of party revenue from public funding does not affect party policy shifts.[21]

---

20. Estimates based on model specification 1 (N = 446).

21. In addition to the regression results reported in Table 9.10, I also calculate additional models (not reported) to test for potential model mis-specifications. Public funding was not in place for various countries and time periods so that its effect on party revenue is often zero. Because this 'zero inflation' may bias the results, I restrict the sample to those policy shifts where public funding is in place. Yet, the effects are still small and insignificant. I also use the alternative dichotomous measure indicating whether public funding exists or not. Again, the findings are insignificant.

Besides the effect of public funding on party policy shifts, I study the factors that impact on the share of a party's income from public subsidies. As for the previous covariates, I aim at ruling out potential third variable effects on both the share of a party's income from public funding and party policy shifts. Specifically, I test whether party size, time, niche party status and its belonging to the left-, the centre, or the right-wing spectrum of the policy space affect the share of public subsidies in a party's income. The regression results are shown in Table 9.11.[22]

The size of parties has no significant effect on the share of party revenue from public subsidies. Put differently, small and big parties equally benefit from the tax-payers' money. Not surprisingly, we see a positive effect of time. Parties increasingly experience income gains from public money while other sources lose significance. Furthermore, the effects of left- and right-wing parties are insignificant.

The niche party effect deserves further attention. Niche parties show a higher share of party income from public subsidies than mainstream parties do. Niche parties emerged in times when party membership figures had already been in decline. In contrast to some of their mainstream rivals, niche parties cannot build on historically large membership organisations and therefore mainly rely on public money. So far, research mainly highlights the perils of public funding for political parties (see e.g. the literature on cartel parties). Yet, the introduction and existence of public subsidies is – among other reasons – justified by the provision of fair competition (see e.g. Nassmacher 2001b). It would therefore be interesting to see whether public subsidies indeed levelled the monetary disadvantages by backing up parties lacking donors and large membership organisations. Yet, the role of public funding for providing a fair basis for competition is not in the focus of this work so I leave it for future research.

Including the significant effects of Table 9.11 (i.e. time and niche party status) into the analysis of party policy shifts leads to the effects reported in Table 9.12. Note that the regression coefficients for public funding remain insignificant for all three model specifications. In addition, the size of the effect further diminishes being practically zero. Using the estimates reported in model 1, increasing the share of public subsidies in the party's income by one standard deviation increases party policy shifts by 0.02 points on the CMP left-right scale. The conclusion that public funding does not affect party policy shifts therefore still holds.

---

22. I also estimate a regression model dropping the cases where public funding is not in place. The number of observations drops from 431 to 332 but the regression results do not substantially differ from the ones reported here.

Table 9.11: Explaining the varying relevance of public funding for party income

	Multilevel model (Level 2: parties)
Party size	0.0000761
	(0.08)
# of national election	0.0303**
	(9.32)
Niche party	0.160**
	(3.08)
Left-wing party	-0.0243
	(-0.76)
Right-wing party	-0.0459
	(-1.30)
Constant	-0.0372
	(-0.46)
ρ	0.514
Observations	431

z statistics in parentheses $+ p < 0.1$, $* p < 0.05$, $** p < 0.01$

Table 9.12: Public funding and its impact on party policy shifts – including control variables

	(1) Multilevel model (Level 2: elections)	(2) Multilevel model (Level 2: parties)	(3) PCSE regression
Public subsidies: share of income	0.0796	0.685	0.266
	(0.04)	(0.32)	(0.13)
Party policy shifts (t-1)	-0.222**		
	(-6.71)		
# of national election	-0.356**	-0.377**	-0.382**
	(-2.66)	(-2.83)	(-2.76)
Niche party	-1.591	-2.277	-2.208
	(-0.69)	(-1.00)	(-1.08)
Constant	16.01**	16.26**	16.80**
	(9.29)	(9.61)	(9.28)
ρ		-0.209	-0.107
Observations	446	464	464

z statistics in parentheses $+ p < 0.1$, $* p < 0.05$, $** p < 0.01$

Table 9.13: How intra-party structure affects party policy shifts

Variable	Hypothesis	Finding	Effect size (CMP points)[23]
Mass organisational strength: Linear effect	O1	✓	0.9
Mass organisational strength: Depending on public funding	O2	✓	Without public funding: 1.9 With public funding: 0.5
Intra-party decision-making process	O3	(✓)	No say for members: 3.4 Some say for members: ref. Full say for members: -0.8
Public funding	O4	0	0.02

✓ Finding in line with expectation.

0 No significant effect.

(✓) Mixed findings.

Table 9.14: Explaining mass organisational strength, intra-party decision-making rules, and sources of income

Variable	Mass organisational strength	Party structure: Hierarchy	Share of public subsidies in party income
Party size	-	+	0
Time	-	-	+
Niche party	-	+	+
Left- and right-wing parties	0	0	0

+ Positive effect.

0 No effect.

- Negative effect.

---

23. For mass organisational strength and public funding, the effect size indicates the change in the magnitude of party policy shifts if the respective covariate increases by one standard deviation. For the candidate selection mechanisms, the reported effects are changes on the CMP left-right scale compared to the reference category 'some say for members'. All estimates based on the first model specification reported in the previous Tables (including control variables).

Summary

In this chapter, I have analysed whether intra-party factors affect the parties' ability and incentive to shift their policy positions. Mass organisational strength, intra-party decision-making processes and the composition of party revenue affect the likelihood of observing party position shifts. Table 9.13 gives an overview reporting the hypotheses as well as the direction and the strength of the effects.

I find moderately strong effects of mass organisational resources on the magnitude of party policy shifts. Organisationally strong parties are better equipped to shift their policy platforms. Increasing the members per vote ratio by one standard deviation increases the magnitude of party policy shifts by 0.9 points on the CMP left-right scale. Moreover, the effect of organisational resources depends on the availability of substitutes for the benefits provided by the party's rank-and-file. If public funding is available allowing for capital-intensive election campaigns and the services of pollsters, less organised parties can compensate lacking man power with public money. Therefore, the effect of mass organisational resources diminishes over time once public party subsidies are introduced. The empirical results support this hypothesis. The effect of mass organisational resources on party position shifts is only significant if public funding is not in place. Increasing organisational resources by one standard deviation entails party position shifts which are 1.9 points larger. In contrast, the effect is insignificant and much smaller (0.5) if public subsidies are present.

Intra-party decision-making rules also show the expected patterns: more hierarchical parties are more likely to shift their policy positions. The more members are involved in intra-party decision making (i.e. the more intra-party veto players exist), the less likely are shifts away from the status quo. I distinguish three levels of members' involvement (no say, some say, and full say for party members in the selection process), showing that the most hierarchically organised parties shift their policy positions by 3.4 points more than their moderately hierarchical rivals. Moreover, there is no significant difference between moderate (some say) and the least hierarchical parties (full say) in their shifting patterns. Yet, not all empirical findings hold when including control variables. The significant effects partly vanish and significant differences occur only in two of the three model specifications. Hence, I conclude that the models show mixed empirical patterns.

Public funding has no significant effect on party policy shifts. Neither in the initial models nor when including control variables does the share of party revenue from public money matter for party policy shifts. This also holds when dichotomous measures are used or if the sample is restricted to instances where public funding is available. In addition, the effects are very small. The effect size for an increase by one standard deviation virtually equals zero. Thus, I conclude that public funding has no effect on party position shifts.

In addition to the core findings connected to party policy shifts, I also show which factors can account for the differences in the parties' mass organisational strength, internal decision-making processes and their sources of income. Although the presented patterns are merely by-products with no intense theoretical backing, they shed light on intra-party politics and point to potentially rewarding topics for future research. Table 9.14 summarises the results of how party size, time, a party's niche party status and its left-, centre or right-wing placement affect intra-party factors.

The findings reveal that larger parties have a lower member per vote ratio than smaller ones and are more hierarchically structured. Yet, a party's size has no effect on the share of its income from public money. Regarding time effects, membership figures decrease over time and parties emerging more recently are likely to choose more inclusive decision-making rules. Not surprisingly, the relevance of public funding increases over time.

Yet, the most interesting results relate to niche parties. Compared to their mainstream rivals, niche parties have a lower member per vote ratio, more hierarchical decision-making rules and show a higher share of income from public money. For mass organisational strength and the significance of public money (for which multivariate analyses were feasible), the findings also hold controlling for party size and time effects. Niche parties differ significantly from their mainstream rivals in several ways. These intra-party differences can actually account for niche party effects found in previous research (see e.g. Adams *et al.* 2006a; Ezrow *et al.* 2010). Hence, the findings suggest a potentially rewarding avenue for further research.

part iv. conclusion

chapter ten | conclusions and directions for future research

The present study differs from previous research on party competition in several ways. Rather than predicting party policy positions, the main goal is to extract how parties can reach optimal policy positions. I highlight that most models of party competition ignore the parties' past policy positions. At each point in time, these static models assume a tabula rasa situation with parties freely choosing policy platforms. Yet in practice, parties do hold policy positions and choosing optimal policy platforms may involve a party policy shift. I therefore consider the time dimension and argue that parties face constraints when moving away from the status quo.

It is also argued that constraints differ systematically across parties. Whereas some parties have severe problems shifting their party platforms, others adapt their policy positions more easily. These systematic differences lead to different party behaviour in terms of position shifting. Neglecting these differences is a form of omitted variable bias that may result in attributing variation across parties to differences in motivation. For instance, scholars may infer that parties sticking to their policy platforms prefer their traditional positions. Yet, a party's stickiness may also stem from constraints preventing it from shifting away from the status quo. Although the parties' lacking willingness and ability to change their party policy platforms lead to the same empirical outcome, the causes for the observed party behaviour are fundamentally different.

Most of the present study identifies factors that account for the differences in the constraints parties face when shifting their policy positions. It is argued that the constraints originate from the key actors with which parties and party leaders interact. I therefore start by deriving these actors from various party definitions. Specifically, I identify three groups of actors: rival parties, voters and a party's rank-and-file. Incentives for party change arise from competition with rival parties and the voters' demands. Recent research has begun to acknowledge the importance of the time dimension and have included it in models of party competition (see e.g. Adams *et al.* 2004, 2006a; Adams and Somer-Topcu 2009b; Kollman *et al.* 1992; Laver 2005; Somer-Topcu 2009b). They study the dynamics of party policy changes resulting from shifts in public opinion, rival parties' shifts, and past election results. Yet, the models mostly assume that parties are not constrained in changing their policy positions. In this study, I analyse two constraints on the parties' ability to shift policy platforms: the voters' perception of political information (such as party policy changes) and the parties' internal structures.

Voters and their perception of party policy changes

The empirical data presented in this study suggests that the average perception of party policy shifts is rather limited. Using a pooled sample of several panel election studies in the United Kingdom, I find that around 40 per cent of the electorate perceived the parties' shift messages. In other words, a majority of voters do not perceive position shifts as signalled in election programmes. As I show for Labour's policy shift in the 1997 election, some party policy shifts are more visible than others. Around 60 per cent of the voters perceived Tony Blair's 'New Labour' shift to the right. Although the perception is around 20 per cent higher than the average of all party position shifts, it is evident that a large share of the electorate did not perceive Labour's shift message. The theoretical model developed in this study aims at explaining whether voters are able and willing to perceive party policy changes.

I adapt Zaller's (1992) Receive-Accept-Sample (RAS) model to party position shifts. It is argued that the perception of party policy shifts is a two-stage process in which voters first receive information on the parties' claims and then decide whether the claims are credible (i.e. whether they accept them). Voters only perceive a party's position shift if they both receive and accept the party's shift message. Whereas the first step is a cognitive process, the latter is a function of the party's credibility. Because surveys typically confine themselves to asking questions on the voters' perception of party policy positions, it is not possible to directly observe the reception and acceptance of party policy shifts. I therefore formulate hypotheses how covariates affect the reception and acceptance of party policy shifts. If the proposed effects hold empirically, then the covariates should also affect the voters' overall perception of party policy shifts.

I test six hypotheses dealing with voters' incentives and difficulties receiving political information, and their effect on the perception of party position shifts. In particular, political awareness, education and the magnitude of voter policy shifts should influence the reception of party position shifts. At the party and party system level, the magnitude of a party's policy shift, the number of relevant parties and their governmental status are expected to affect whether or not voters receive party shift messages. With the sample restricted to British politics, I am not able to test a hypothesis on party system effects (Hypothesis V5). The empirical results are mixed. Only the results of the voters' political awareness conform to the theoretical expectations and reach statistical significance in all model specifications. For the remaining effects, some models support the proposed effects while the hypotheses find no supportive, or even contradicting, empirical evidence in other model specifications.

The empirical results are more in line with the theoretical expectations for the voters' acceptance of party position shifts. I postulate six hypotheses of how changes in party leadership and the leader's prestige, the magnitude of past policy shifts, party identification, voter position shifts and voter expectations of party policy positions affect the perception of party platform changes. With the relatively small sample of British parties, it is not possible to test the hypothesised effect of voter expectations in a multivariate model (Hypothesis V12). Three of the five remaining hypotheses find empirical support in various model specifications. Voters are more likely to accept a party's policy shift if the leader's prestige is high and if the shift is in the same direction as shifts of their personal policy preferences. Moreover, voters with party identification are more likely to accept shifts towards, and less likely to accept shifts away from their individual policy preferences. The results for the magnitude of past party policy shifts and changes in the party leadership show mixed empirical results.

In sum, the analysis of voter perceptions of party policy shifts reveals that there are differences across voters (and parties). These can be explained by covariates that affect the likelihood of receiving and accepting information on party position shifts. Findings contradicting the postulated effects are rare, and solely due to factors located at the party level for which the number of observations is quite low. At the very least, four out of ten tested effects support the hypothesised effect.

How voter perceptions affect party policy shifts

Voters differ in their perception of party policy shifts and the variation can be explained by covariates that affect the voters' reception and acceptance. To study how parties react to the systematic differences, I study party policy shifts in ten West European countries from 1945 until 2005.

Using the two-stage model of how voters perceive party position shifts, I draw conclusions about which parties face more constraints when shifting their policy platforms. The results are summarised in Axioms 2 and 3 outlined in Chapter Four. As for the analysis at the voter level, the proposed effects are not directly testable. I therefore use the covariates expected to affect the voters' perception to formulate hypotheses how these factors affect the parties' abilities to shift their policy positions. Specifically, I postulate fourteen hypotheses of which I test twelve.[1] Five hypotheses deal with covariates derived from the voters' reception of party position shifts. The remaining seven hypotheses relate to acceptance variables. In addition, I formulate modified hypotheses on the direction of party policy shifts for two covariates.

The empirical results support most of the postulated effects. Only one of the proposed effects runs counter to the theoretical expectations. Whereas the regression coefficients are insignificant for three variables, the remaining eight covariates show empirical results supporting the hypothesised relationships in most of the model specifications. The findings are especially robust for the proposed effects of political interest, the parties' status as government parties and the complexity of the political market. In particular, higher political interest increases the likelihood of party policy shifts. As expected, I also find that the effect of political interest depends on the direction of the parties' platform changes: For shifts towards the majority of voters, the positive effect of voters' interest in politics is larger than for shifts away from the majority of voter preferences. In addition, I find that government parties are more visible and hence, more likely to change their policy platforms. The complexity of the political market (as indicated by the number of

---

1. This is due to the fact that I was not able to collect time-consistent data on the voters' education across countries.

effective parties) has a negative impact on the magnitude of party position shifts.

Turning to the variables affecting the voters' acceptance of policy shifts, party leader prestige affects the magnitude of party policy shifts. If voters positively evaluate the leaders' competence, sympathy and skills, parties have a higher ability to shift their policy platforms. In contrast, parties with leaders lacking strong support of the electorate are more likely to stay put. Furthermore, the regression results show a strong effect of voter expectations affecting party policy shifts. If party policy positions are not in line with expectations derived from the parties' ideologies, parties react by shifting their policy platforms to policy locations that conform to the ideological expectations.

In sum, the findings show that voters constrain party policy shifts. Because systematic differences exist in the voters' evaluation of party policy shifts, some parties are more constrained in shifting their party platforms than others.

Intra-party structure and its effect on party policy shifts

Beyond voters and their perceptions of party position shifts, parties are also constrained by their respective intra-party structures. I therefore study the consequences of the members' role within political parties and how the intra-party distribution of power affects party position shifts.

For that purpose, I study three intra-party factors. First, parties should benefit from having members who spread party information and increase the voters' acceptance of party position shifts. The larger a party's workforce, the higher is its ability to shift the policy position. Yet, the benefits derived from party membership decrease once additional means substitute the members' contributions. Public funding allows parties to compensate for the lack of mass organisational resources. The new forms of political communication rely on general news mass media and involve a shift from labour-intensive to capital-intensive campaigning. As a result, the positive effect of mass organisational strength diminishes once public subsidies are in place. Second, the formal decision-making rules determine whether parties can adapt their policies. If important decisions are left to party leaders, parties are more flexible and hence, more likely to shift their policy platforms. In contrast, inclusive parties give their rank-and-file a say in decision-making processes, thus increasing the number of intra-party veto players. As the number of veto players increases, shifting policy positions does not (at least) get more likely. Third, I emphasise the role of financial resources that parties and their leaders depend on. Drawing on resource dependence theory, it is argued that party leaders are likely to serve the interests of actors whose contributions are critical for the party's income. Mass parties hinge on financial contributions from their members and are more likely to stick to their members' policy preferences. In contrast, the increasing significance of public funding enhances the appeals to hunt for votes. Consequently, party leaders have incentives to follow the electoral market. I therefore argue that the increasing relevance of public funding for a party's income makes parties more likely to change their policies.

The empirical results support the hypotheses on the parties' mass organisational strength. Parties are more likely to shift policy positions if they can draw on large membership organisations. Moreover, the results also support the hypothesis that this positive effect diminishes once public funding is in place. Regarding the role of intra-party decision-making rules, the empirical results support the hypothesised effect, although the regression coefficients are not significant in all model specifications. Finally, the statistical models show no significant effect with regard to the share of public subsidies in party income. I hence conclude that party policy shifts are not affected by public funding.

In sum, the relevance of party members as the party workforce and intra-party decision-making rules determine whether parties are able to move away from the status quo. Although I find no empirical evidence that sources of party income affect the parties' policy behaviour, I conclude that a party's internal structure affects its ability to shift policy positions.

Directions for future research

This work has concentrated the parties' constraints when shifting policy positions. Along the way, however, I touched upon several potentially rewarding topics for future research. For example, it is worthwhile to study the consequences of voters not perceiving party position shifts. The present study has shed light on the voters' reception and acceptance of party policy shifts, but only for drawing conclusions at the macro level. Yet, the voters' perceptions also have severe consequences for their evaluations of political parties, governments and politics in general. If voters do not perceive the parties' platform shifts, then official party policy platforms and voter perception of party positions do not match. The mismatch may be due to the lacking reception of voters because voters do not care, or do not understand, what is going on in politics. Moreover, differences in the parties' official policy platforms and voter perceptions may also arise from party policy shifts which are not accepted (i.e. considered credible) by the electorate. In this case, parties have not been able to convince voters of their credibility. Irrespective of whether voters or parties are to blame, the lacking reception and acceptance of party position shifts result in a mismatch of the parties' official policy platforms and the voters' perceived party policy position.

There are severe consequences for misperceived party policy positions. First, voters base their vote choices on biased information. In the worst case, a voter does not vote for the best alternative (e.g. the party closest to his or her policy preferences) but casts the ballot for a party which actually shifted its policy position away from the voter's policy preferences (see also Lau *et al.* 2008; Lau and Redlawsk 1997). As a result, voters not perceiving party policy shifts should be less satisfied with their vote choices. The discrepancy between a voter's perception of his or her vote choice and the official party position should also affect its evaluation of parliament and government. Party policies and the voter's expectations thereof do not match, so that voters misperceiving a party's policy position should be less satisfied with leading politicians, party performance and perhaps even the democratic system.

Turning to political parties, I find that public opinion shifts do not lead to changes in party policy positions. In line with recent research (Adams *et al.* 2004; Ezrow *et al.* 2010; Somer-Topcu 2009c), parties are expected to follow shifts in public opinion. Yet and in contrast to previous research, my empirical findings do not support the hypothesised effect. Measurement error of voters' changing preferences may account for the different results. Rather than measuring substantive shifts of the voters' preferences, the differences are likely to indicate measurement error. A closer look at the data reveals that voter policy shifts are rather small. About 50 per cent of 'shifts' in public opinion have a magnitude smaller than 0.2 on a 1 to 11 scale. Using a two-sample-test and reasonable estimates for the number of voters in the sample, and the standard deviation of the mean voter's policy position, these differences are not statistically significant. The measured 'shifts' in public opinion hence reflect noise rather than substance, and public opinion that is rather stable cannot account for changes of party positions. This finding encourages future research on 'dynamic representation' (Stimson 1999; Stimson *et al.* 1995) to take measurement errors of voter position shifts into account.

In my theoretical model, I also argue that changes in the party leadership affect policy position shifts. Party leaders become identified with policies they have represented in the past. In contrast, new leaders are likely to (and perhaps are also expected to) change policies. Although the argument is in line with previous research (Downs 1957: 111; Gilmore 1988; Harmel *et al.* 1995; Harmel and Janda 1994), the empirical evidence provided here does not support the hypothesised effect. In fact, some model specifications show that new party leaders are less likely to change party policies than leaders who are in office for a longer time.

This result deserves attention in future research. Perhaps new party leaders are not willing to shift the party's platform. Turnovers in party leadership may reflect a generational change rather than a change in policies. Especially if a new party leader belongs to the predecessor's intra-party faction or is a known foster-son or daughter of the previous leader, leadership changes are not likely to result in large-scale party policy changes. It could also be argued that new party leaders lack power to move away from the status quo. Important actors within the party may doubt the new leader's ability to run successful election campaigns and thus hinder him or her from adapting the party's policy position. At the same time, new leaders may refrain from provoking intra-party opposition in their early years in office. Party policy changes hence only occur after a party leader has been in office for some time and thus proven to survive politically. I present some preliminary results indicating that new party leaders lack resources rather than willingness to shift their party's policy platform. Yet, testing more fine-grained models requires better data, especially on the leaders' past career, factional membership and intra-party (s)election processes. Future research which aims at narrowing this data gap is likely to enlighten our understanding of the consequences of party leader changes for party (policy) change.

Previous research (see e.g. Adams *et al.* 2006a; Ezrow *et al.* 2010) also highlights differences in the behaviour of mainstream and niche parties. Yet, 'niche party effects' do not carry a substantive meaning. It is unclear why niche parties differ from their mainstream rivals. They could be different in their behavioural incentives and party goals. Niche parties may, for example, put more emphasis on policy goals and have fewer incentives to enter office than their mainstream rivals. If this is the case, theories on political parties should take the varying motivational assumptions into account. However, the observable differences may also result from different constraints mainstream and niche parties face. In other words, both party types may value the same goals but different environmental factors make parties choose different strategies. This calls for further analyses to identify factors causing differences in party behaviour. In Chapter Nine, I provide a first analysis showing that mainstream and niche parties' intra-party structures differ: Niche parties have fewer members per vote, choose more hierarchical intra-party decision-making processes and rely more heavily on public funding than their mainstream rivals. If intra-party structure affects party behaviour, then differences between mainstream and niche parties are due to differences in intra-party structures. Yet, more research is needed to find further explanations for why mainstream and niche parties differ. Research entailing explanatory factors with a substantive meaning is preferable to 'explanations' based on party 'types'.

Finally, the present study encourages further research on the consequences of public party funding. Research on public funding mainly emphasises the perils of public subsidies. Most prominently, the literature on cartel parties (Katz and Mair 1995, 2009) suggests that modern parties get detached from civil societies and become agents of the state. Yet, there are also arguments in favour of public subsidies for political parties, notably the claim that public party funding ensures fairer competition by providing equal opportunities for all competing parties (Nassmacher 2001b; van Biezen 2008: 348). It is hence worthwhile to study whether party subsidies are capable of decreasing political corruption, facilitating the emergence of new parties and providing opportunities for a fair political competition among otherwise dissimilar rivals. Answering these questions would shed light on relatively neglected research topics. Empirical results giving affirmative answers to the questions above provide a (normative) justification for giving public money to political parties.

Final conclusions

This work contributes to theories of party competition. Introducing the time dimension, I show how voter perceptions and intra-party structures constrain parties when changing their policy platforms. So doing, the present study contributes to research on public opinion, political parties and party systems. It is argued that parties cannot simply choose optimal party platforms but that parties are constrained by their past. Voter-, party- and party system-specific factors systematically affect the parties' likelihood of sticking to the status quo. These results, I claim, deepen and extend our knowledge on political parties and party competition.

| appendices

Appendix A: Supplementary information on data and methods (Chapter Six)

Table A.1 shows the issue-specific questions asked in the British panel election studies from February 1974 onwards. With the exception of 1987 and 1992, voters were frequently asked to place the parties and themselves on scales measuring the policy positions towards 'European integration'. Another policy scale frequently used since the 1970s is the voters' and the parties' policy views on the 'Privatisation and Nationalisation' of British companies. In fact, this is the only policy scale used in all British panel election studies from the 1970s onwards. Since 1979, voters are asked to place parties on a policy scale called 'Taxes vs. Services'. The end points of this policy scale describe the parties' perceived views on the priorities they put on two conflicting policy goals: increasing taxes to spend more on health and social services, or to cut taxes and spend less on these policies.

Table A.1: Policy scales used in British panel election studies: 1974 – 2001

Issue	Feb. 1974	Oct. 1974	1979	1983	1987	1992	1997	2001
Common market/EC	X[1]	X	X[2]				X	X
Nationalisation	X[1]	X	X[2]		X	X	X	X
Taxes vs. Services			X[1 2]		X	X	X	X
Social Service		X	X[2]					
Unemployment			X[1 2 3]		X	X	X	X
Defence					X	X	X[1 4]	
Redistribution								
(income inequality)						X	X	X
Women's rights							X[1]	X[1]

[1] Not asked in previous or current election.
[2] No indicators for Liberals.
[3] In 1979, the question wording was different from the following years. Voters were asked to locate parties on a scale describing the best way to create jobs ('companies keep profits' vs. 'government spending tax money'). In the following years, the question changed. Now, voters were asked to set priorities between the opposed goals of 'keeping the prices down' and 'bringing people back to work'.
[4] Before 1997, the respondents were asked to state the parties' policy positions on the number of nuclear weapons (more or less than the actual number). From 1997 onwards, the question wording changed asking for the amount of money spent on defence.

Note: The Table covers all policy fields covered in at least two election studies. Other policy scales were used occasionally: Parties' and voter's positions on immigration (February 1974), North Sea oil (October 1974), race relations (1979), law and order (1983), and welfare (1992).

Questions on the 'Social Service' provided by the state were already asked in the election of October 1974 but the question changed over time: Voters were asked whether social services should be 'cut back a lot' or 'more are needed' without relating such decisions to increasing or decreasing costs and taxation. Since 1979, voters also place parties on a policy scale measuring the parties' policy positions fighting 'Unemployment'. As for the 'Taxes vs. Services' scale, the question wording changed. In 1979, the question asked whether fighting unemployment can best be achieved if companies keep their profits or if the government spends tax money. From 1987 onwards, the endpoints of the policy scale changed indicating whether the party concentrates on fighting unemployment or the conflicting goal of keeping the prices down (i.e. fighting inflation).

At the end of the 1980s additional policy scales were added. With the end of the Cold War, the question wording on the 'Defence' scale changed, however. Voters were no longer asked to locate parties on a policy scale measuring whether Britain should have more (or less) nuclear weapons. Rather, the question in 1997 asked for the willingness to spend on defence (more or less than the current budget). In addition, questions on 'Redistribution' ask voters to locate parties on a policy scale ranging from putting 'greater efforts to make people's incomes more equal' to 'be much less concerned about how equal people's incomes are'. Finally, voters place parties on a policy scale measuring the parties' views on 'Women's rights' in society (at home vs. equal role with men in running business, industry and government).

Data structure and number of observations

The data file contains the voters' perceptions of party position shifts of the British general election from October 1974 until 2001. Each single case is voter i's perception of party j's policy shift at election t. In other words, at each election t, voter i generates three observations (one for each party $1 \leq j \leq 3$).

Table A.2: Number of observations by elections

	Oct. 1974	1979	1983	1987	1992	1997	2001	Total
Nationalisation	1,468	617		1,571	1,275	1,673	3,085	9,689
Taxes vs. Services		632		1,630	1,285	1,687	3,019	8,253
Unemployment				1,553	1,150	1,557	2,900	7,160

Table A.2 summarises the number of observations for the data analyses. Note that the number of observations is rather small. Except for 'Nationalisation', the policy scales are not used in all elections creating missing values for the elections in October 1974 ('Taxes vs. Services' and 'Unemployment') and 1979 ('Unemployment'). Missing values for the variables (most often in the placement of party policy positions) further reduce the number of observations. Nevertheless, roughly 7,200 to 9,700 observations exist for the pooled analysis. Analysing a single party in one election reduces the sample size drastically. For the analysis of the 'New Labour' policy shift, only 581 observations exist.

Methods: A two-stage logistic regression model

As argued in Chapter Four, the perception of party policy shifts is a two-stage process. Voters receive information on party policy shifts and then decide whether to accept (i.e. consider credible) the parties' shift messages. I model this process denoting voter i's probability of receiving party j's shift message at time t with probability $r_{ijt}(x_{ijt})$, where x_{ijt} is a vector capturing the covariates affecting the reception of party policy shifts. Given the reception of party policy shifts, voter i accepts party j's policy shift at time t with probability $a_{ijt}(y_{ijt})$. Again, y_{ijt} is a vector consisting of variables influencing the acceptance of party position shifts. Because the dependent variable is binary (perceiving/not perceiving party policy shifts), one could calculate two separate logistic regressions for the reception (r_{ijt}) and the acceptance (a_{ijt}) of party position shifts.

However, this approach violates some of the assumptions made by the theoretical model presented above. Specifically, the perception of party policy shifts is a two-stage process in which the acceptance of policy shifts requires their reception. In turn, the reception of policy shifts is not sufficient for their perception. In other words, the logistic regressions depend on each other. A pooled analysis covering the variables x_{ijt} and y_{ijt}, of both functions, is not sufficient to correct for this. Interaction terms between the reception and acceptance covariates are also not appropriate to model the two-level structure. To see this, Figure A.1 maps the two-stage process of perceiving policy position shifts.

Figure A.1: The perception of party policy shifts in a two-stage process

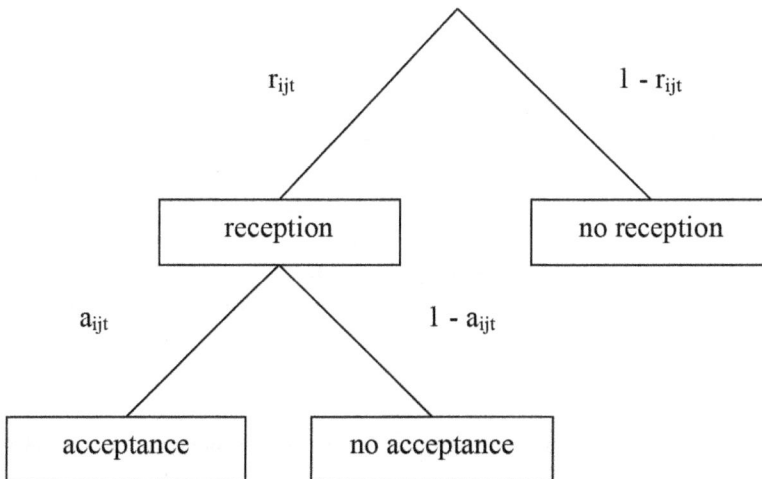

with

$$r_{ijt} = \text{Pr(reception)} = \frac{\exp(\alpha \cdot x_{ijt})}{1 + \exp(\alpha \cdot x_{ijt})} \quad \text{and} \tag{1}$$

$$a_{ijt} = \text{Pr(acceptance)} = \frac{\exp(\beta \cdot y_{ijt})}{1 + \exp(\beta \cdot y_{ijt})} \tag{2}$$

Voters only perceive party policy shifts if they receive and accept the party move. In other words, the probability of perceiving a policy shift is

$$\text{Pr(perception)} = r_{ijt} \, a_{ijt} \tag{3}$$

and

$$\text{Pr(no perception)} = (1 - r_{ijt}) + r_{ijt} \cdot (1 - a_{ijt}) = 1 - r_{ijt} \cdot a_{ijt} \tag{4}$$

Compare this model to logistic regressions only considering either reception or acceptance probabilities. A logistic regression estimating the impact of the reception covariates on the perception of party policy shifts reveals,

$$\text{Pr}_{rec}\text{(perception)} = r_{ijt} \tag{5}$$

and

$$\text{Pr}_{rec}\text{(no perception)} = 1 - r_{ijt} \tag{6}$$

In contrast to the two-stage model in (3) and (4), this model assumes that the acceptance probability of party policy shifts (a_{ijt}) is equal to one. However, if some voters are more sceptical than others, the model yields biased estimates. Similarly, a logistic regression calculation of the acceptance of party policy shifts assumes that the reception probability r_{ijt} is equal to one. Empirical evidence suggests that this is not the case. Alvarez (1997) shows that more educated and more informed voters are more likely to locate presidential candidates' policy positions at their 'true' policy positions.[1]

---

1. A candidate's 'true' policy position is measured using the mean of the voters' perception of the candidate's policy position.

Additionally, Alvarez and Brehm (2002: chs 4 and 6) demonstrate that more informed voters show less response variability answering survey questions. Hence, it is not reasonable to assume that all voters receive party policy shifts.

Estimating a pooled logistic regression covering the covariates for the reception (x_{ijt}) and the acceptance (y_{ijt}) of party policy shifts, is also not appropriate to model the two-stage process. To see this, compare the probabilities of perceiving policy shifts in a pooled model with the same probability of the two-stage model in (3). The comparison reveals that,

$$\text{Pr}_{\text{pooled}}(\text{perception}) = \frac{\exp(\alpha \cdot x_{ijt} + \beta \cdot y_{ijt})}{1 + \exp(\alpha \cdot x_{ijt} + \beta \cdot y_{ijt})}$$

$$\neq \frac{\exp(\alpha \cdot x_{ijt})}{1 + \exp(\alpha \cdot x_{ijt})} \cdot \frac{\exp(\beta \cdot y_{ijt})}{1 + \exp(\beta \cdot y_{ijt})} = r_{ijt} \cdot a_{ijt} = \text{Pr}_{\text{two-stage}}(\text{perception}) \qquad (7)$$

Hence, the pooled model differs from the two-stage model presented above. Moreover, it can be shown that a pooled logistic regression with interaction terms differs from the two-stage model formulation. Furthermore, using interaction terms leads to more complications because all reception covariates would interact with all acceptance covariates. Because of these problems, I deviate from ordinary logistic regression models using a two-stage logistic regression as described in Figure A.1. The likelihood function of this two-stage logistic regression model is given by

$$Likelihood = \prod_{i=1}^{N} [r_{ijt} a_{ijt}]^{y_i} [1 - r_{ijt} a_{ijt}]^{1-y_i}$$

$$(8)$$

With (1) and (2), the logarithm of the likelihood function is equal to
Log likelihood =

$$\sum_{i=1}^{N} y_i \cdot h \left[\frac{\exp(\alpha \cdot x_{ijt})}{1 + \exp(\alpha \cdot x_{ijt})} \cdot \frac{\exp(\beta \cdot y_{ijt})}{1 + \exp(\beta \cdot y_{ijt})} \right] + (1 - y_i) \cdot h \left[1 - \frac{\exp(\alpha \cdot x_{ijt})}{1 + \exp(\alpha \cdot x_{ijt})} \cdot \frac{\exp(\beta \cdot y_{ijt})}{1 + \exp(\beta \cdot y_{ijt})} \right] \qquad (9)$$

For the models presented in Chapter Six, I first calculate logistic regressions for the reception and acceptance of party policy shifts. Although the models have several drawbacks (see above), I estimate the models for two reasons. First, the models contain fewer variables causing less collinearity between the covariates. Logistic regressions may therefore serve as simple preliminary tests of the theory. Second, I estimate the logistic regressions to compare the results with the estimates of the two-stage model. If the estimates are similar, the bias caused by omitting the two-stage structure is small. Different results indicate model mis-specifications of ordinary logistic regressions. Hence, the analyses presented in Chapter Six cover ordinary logistic and two-stage logistic regressions.

Finally, it should be noted that heteroscedasticity exists. Voters perceive party position shifts of several parties at more than one occasion (i.e. elections). Hence, it is reasonable to assume that the observations of one election cluster and, furthermore, the perceptions of individual voters systematically differ from each other. Therefore, I estimate robust standard errors clustered by elections and include party dummy variables to capture party specific effects.[2]

2. The analysis of the 'New Labour' policy shift in 1997 is straightforward. Because the sample only covers one party in one election, ordinary and two-stage logistic regressions without clustering are sufficient.

Appendix B: Supplementary information on data and methods (Chapter Seven)

Measuring the magnitude of party policy shifts

Given data about party policy platforms, one can easily calculate measures for policy shifts by subtracting a party's policy position from its previous one. Values larger than zero indicate shifts to the right (or, in general, to the upper end of the policy scale) while values smaller than zero indicate shifts to the left (i.e. the lower end of the policy scale). Some of the hypotheses stated in Chapter Five deal with these *directions* of party policy changes but most of them make predictions for the *magnitude* of these changes. For the latter, the most intuitive way to measure the magnitude of party policy shifts is to use absolute values.

As mentioned in Chapter Seven, I do not use absolute values for two reasons. First, I aim for using the same dependent variable for hypotheses dealing with the direction and the magnitude of party policy shifts. Second, using absolute values leads to skewed distributions of the dependent variable. Most policy shifts are small and may well be attributed to measurement error (see also Chapter Three). The more considerable policy shifts are equally likely to be shifts to the left or the right. In short, a variable capturing the direction of party policy shifts nicely follows a normal distribution. Given the properties of this distribution, it is preferable to keep it instead of using absolute values. So doing would lead to a dependent variable with asymmetric right-skewed properties.

Instead of transforming the dependent variable, I hence recode the covariates (and the constant term) to allow for correctly testing the hypotheses stated above. Formally, let y denote the variable *policy shift*, then $|y|$ denotes the *magnitude of party policy shifts*. Further, let x be a variable which is expected to affect the magnitude of policy shifts and hence,

$$|y| = a + b{\cdot}x \tag{1}$$

To obtain a recoded variable x_{rec} affecting y, define

$$x_{rec} = \begin{cases} x \text{ if } y \geq 0 \\ -x \text{ if } y < 0 \end{cases} \tag{2}$$

and

$$a_{rec} = \begin{cases} a \text{ if } y \geq 0 \\ -a \text{ if } y < 0 \end{cases} \tag{3}$$

Then

$$|y| = a + b{\cdot}x \longleftrightarrow y = a_{rec} + b{\cdot}x_{rec} \tag{4}$$

holds. Figure A.2 shows the recoding process graphically. The first graph on the upper left (a) shows the expected effect of x on |y|. Given that y is normally distributed, however, the distribution of |y| is skewed to the right (i.e. the mass of the distribution is close to the x-axis). To avoid using the skewed variable |y|, I stick to the variable y. Including the direction of the policy shift, the impact of x on y is twofold (graph b): the effect is positive for y≥0 and negative if y<0. For that reason, I transform x as described above to obtain x_{rec}. Its effect on y is shown in the graph on the lower left (c) in Figure A.2. Note that both regression lines are parallel (i.e. the slope is identical) but the intercept differs. In fact, the intercept of the lower regression line is the negative value of the intercept a of the upper regression line. To obtain valid estimators, it is hence necessary to use a different regression intercept for y≥0 and y<0. For the ease of interpretation, graph d) in Figure A.2 corrects for the different intercepts by shifting the lower regression line upwards (i.e. by adding the intercept's coefficient twice if y<0). Note that the slope and the intercept of the graphs a) and d) are identical.

Figure A.2: Recoding covariates for the analysis

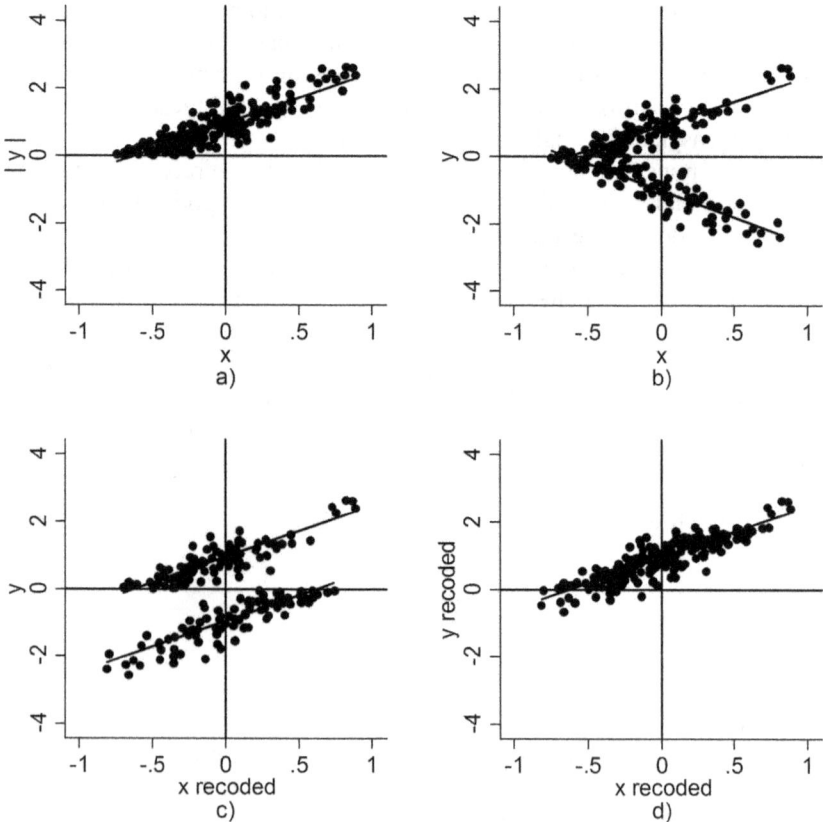

Data structure

The data covers party position shifts of different parties over several elections in various countries. Hence, the observations are not independent and violate the Gauss-Markov assumptions for OLS regressions (Beck 2001; Beck and Katz 1995, 1996). In general, let y_{kjt} denote a party policy shift of party j at time t in country k. With a covariate x_{kjt} the linear regression model reads as follows:

$$y_{kjt} = \alpha_0 + \alpha_1 \cdot x_{kjt} + \xi_{kjt} \tag{5}$$

Beside others, the Gauss-Markov assumptions state that the error terms ξ_{kjt} should be independently distributed and homoscedastic:

$$E(\xi_{kjt} \, \xi_{k'j't'}) = 0 \tag{6}$$

and

$$Var(\xi_{kjt}) = \sigma^2 \tag{7}$$

Using data from different countries, parties, and elections, these assumptions may not hold true. First, there may be unobserved *heteroscedasticity* across countries, parties, and elections. In other words, cases may differ due to (unobserved) factors thereby violating the homoscedasticity assumption. Consequently, the variance of the error term varies across countries, parties, and elections:

$$Var(\xi_{kjt}) = \sigma_k^2 \tag{8}$$

$$Var(\xi_{kjt}) = \sigma_j^2 \tag{9}$$

$$Var(\xi_{kjt}) = \sigma_t^2 \tag{10}$$

Second, parties and their policy positions are not independent of each other. It is unreasonable to assume that parties shift their policy positions independent of their competitors' shifts. During elections, parties interact and are influenced by several election- and country-specific (probably unobserved) factors. Hence, there may be contemporaneous correlation:

$$E(\xi_{kjt} \, \xi_{kj't}) \neq 0$$

$$E(\xi_{kjt} \, \xi_{k'j't'}) = 0 \quad \text{for } k \neq k', t \neq t' \tag{11}$$

Third, observations of parties are not independent over time. Party positions and party position shifts at time t are influenced by party decisions made at t-1. In other words, the serial correlation occurs:

$$\xi_{kjt} = \rho \cdot \xi_{kj(t-1)} + \eta_{kjt} \qquad , \eta_{kjt} \sim N(0, \tau^2) \tag{12}$$

Model choice

Heteroscedasticity at different levels, contemporaneous correlation and autocorrelation are hard to cope with in a single model. Hence, I test the hypotheses using three different model specifications: a three-level random intercept model using elections as a second level, a three-level random intercept model with parties on the second level and a Prais-Winsten regression with panel corrected standard errors. Each specification is best to account for specific violations of the Gauss-Markov assumptions, while none of them controls for all potential errors. Robust results across different model specifications thus increase the confidence in the empirical results.

The first model is a three-level random intercept model clustering cases in countries k and elections t (for an overview see Gelman 2006; Gelman and Hill 2007; Rabe-Hesketh and Skrondal 2005; Steenbergen and Jones 2002). Multilevel models subdivide the error term at different levels allowing for election- and country-specific level differences. In formulas, the model reads as follows:

$$y_{kjt} = \alpha_0 + \alpha_1 \cdot x_{kjt} + \gamma_k + \delta_{kt} + \varepsilon_{kjt} \tag{13}$$

with

$$\gamma_k \sim N(0, \sigma^2)$$

$$\delta_{kt} \sim N(0, \tau^2)$$

$$\varepsilon_{kjt} \sim N(0, \upsilon^2)$$

In contrast to an OLS regression, the error term has three components capturing country-specific errors γ_k, election-specific errors δ_{kj} and a white noise error term ε_{kjt} at the lowest level. This model specification nicely captures heteroscedasticity across countries and elections. Previous analyses using variance components models show that the observations are most likely to differ across elections. This first model specification fits best to take this into account. However, the model also shows deficits. First, we are not able to control for heteroscedasticity across parties. Although the variance is highest across elections, capturing variance across parties may also be worthwhile. Second, the model specification does not allow for using the Prais-Winsten transformation for modelling autocorrelation. Instead, the lagged dependent variable is used to capture time effects. However, lagged dependent variables absorb variance of the dependent variable without actually explaining the variance based on a theoretical explanation.

Moreover, the inclusion of a lagged dependent variable risks a downward bias of the effect of the remaining (and theoretically relevant) covariates (see Plümper *et al.* 2005 for a detailed discussion).[3] Finally, the model does not capture correlations between party position shifts in the same election (i.e. contemporaneous correlation).

The second proposed model corrects for two of these deficits. Instead of clustering parties in elections, it clusters parties at different points in time. The regression equation looks quite similar to equation (13).

$$y_{kjt} = \alpha_0 + \alpha_1 \cdot x_{kjt} + \gamma_k + \delta_{kj} + \varepsilon_{kjt} \tag{14}$$

with

$$\gamma_k \sim N(0,\sigma^2)$$

$$\delta_{kj} \sim N(0,\tau^2)$$

$$\varepsilon_{kjt} \sim N(0,\upsilon^2)$$

Nevertheless, the interpretation is different. This model considers heteroscedasticity across parties to be more important than across elections. In contrast to the first model, however, this model specification does not allow the error variances to vary across elections. I note above, however, that empirically, error variance across elections is more relevant than differences across parties. Apart from this shortcoming, a nice feature of this model specification is that it allows for a Prais-Winsten transformation to capture autocorrelation. Instead of including a lagged dependent variable, serial correlation is estimated taking relevant information from the error term. Assuming an autoregressive process of order 1, we estimate ρ using equation (12).

Whereas both models deal with various forms of heteroscedasticity and serial correlation, both fail in correcting for potential interdependence of party policy shifts in the same election. For that reason, I also calculate a Prais-Winsten regression using panel corrected standard errors (PCSE) (see Beck 2001; Beck and Katz 1995, 1996). Most important, the model takes heteroscedasticity across parties into account and also allows for contemporaneous correlation. Time effects are also covered using the Prais-Winsten transformation. But the PCSE model specification also has its disadvantages. Because error variances are assumed to vary across parties, the observations may also differ across countries. There is, however, no direct measure to account for this. Even more important, the model does not allow for different error variances across elections. As mentioned above, however, the empirical evidence suggests that elections are the most important source for variance across observations.

---

3.   Another reason for using the Prais-Winsten transformation instead of the lagged dependent variable is the modification of the covariates and the intercept described above. Due to the modification, the estimates for the lagged dependent variable are flawed. Note, however, that the effects of the modified covariates are not affected.

Table A.3: Error structure and model specification

		Model specification 1	Model specification 2	Model specification 3
		Multilevel model (Level 2: elections)	Multilevel model (Level 2: parties)	PCSE regression
Heteroscedasticity	across countries	X	X	(X)
	across elections	X		
	across parties		X	X
Contemporaneous correlation			X	
Serial correlation	Lagged dependent variable	Prais-Winsten transformation	Prais-Winsten transformation	

Table A.3 summarises the potential problems arising from the data's error structure and the models' solutions. As can be seen, none of the models accounts for all potential misspecifications. Model specification 1 is best in dealing with heteroscedasticity. The most crucial form is given by heteroscedasticity across elections and neither of the remaining model specifications considers these data characteristics. Model specification 1 does not, however, allow for using a Prais-Winsten transformation which is preferable to using a lagged dependent variable to capture autocorrelation. In that sense, model specification 2 is superior to model specification 1. The major advantage of using a PCSE model (model specification 3) is its inclusion of contemporaneous correlation. Yet, model specification 3 does not capture different error variances across elections. Because none of the model specifications perfectly considers the data structure, I use all models to test my hypotheses. If the coefficients are robust to different model specifications, this provides further backing of the empirical findings.

Appendix C: Ideological territories

Austria:
KPÖ – *GA* – *SPÖ* – *LIF* [4] – *ÖVP* – *FPÖ*

Belgium[5]:
Social Democrats (BSP/PSB, SP, PS) – Green parties (Agalev, Ecolo) – Christian Democrats (*PSC/CVP, CVP, PSC*) – Liberals (*PVV/PLP, VLD, PRL*) – far right (*VB*, FN)

Denmark:
Communists (*DKP, SF*) – *SD* – *RV* – Centre (CD, KrF, *DF, RF*) – Right (*KF, V*)[6] – FP

Finland:
Communists/Socialists (*SKDL, Left Wing Alliance*) – *Greens* – *SSDP* – Centre (*KESK, SMP*) – *LKP* – SKL – *RKP/SFP* – KK

Germany:
Communists (KPD, PDS) – *Greens* – *SPD* – *FDP* – *DZ* – *CDU/CSU* – DSU – GB/BHE – DP

Great Britain:
Labour – Centre (*Liberals, SDP, LibDems*) - *Conservatives*

Ireland:
Socialists (WP, DLP) – Greens – LP – Centre-right (*FF, FG*) – *PD*

Netherlands:
Socialists (*SP*, PPR) – GL – *PvdA* – *D'66* – DS70 – Christian Democrats (*CDA, KVP, ARP, CHU*) – *VVD* – *LPF*[7]

---

4. For the placement of the Liberal Forum see also Jenny (2006).

5. No distinction between Flemish and Walloon parties within party families; no left-right positions for VU, FDF and RW because clear ideological expectations are missing.

6. According to Damgaard (2000: 236), Liberals (V) and Conservatives (KF) switched their policy positions over time. As in other north European countries, party families are not as decisive as in other countries. Rather, party systems are 'best understood in terms of five major groupings of parties' (Damgaard 2000: 233; emphasis added). According to this, I distinguish party groupings rather than party families.

7. List Pim Fortuyn placement according to Laver/Benoit expert study.

Norway:
Communists/Socialists *(NKP, SF)* – *DNA* – *V* – *KrF* – *SP* – *H* – *FrP*

Sweden:
V – *SdaP* - Greens – Centre *(CP, FP)* – *KdS* – *MSP*

Notes:
Party acronyms as indicated in the CMP dataset. Note that not all parties exist at all points in time (e.g. Green parties). *Italic:* Parties with at least 5 per cent of the votes in two subsequent elections. Data from country experts and experts (Benoit and Laver 2006; Huber and Inglehart 1995; see country chapters in Müller and Strøm 2000a).

Appendix D: Classifying left-wing, right-wing, and centre parties

Table A.4: Classifying left-wing, right-wing, and centre parties

Country	Left-wing parties	Centrist parties	Right-wing parties
Austria	Greens SPÖ	ÖVP LIF	FPÖ
Belgium	Social Democrats (BSP/PSB, SP, PS)	Christian Democrats (PSC/CVP, CVP, PSC)	Liberals (PVV/PLP, VLD, PRL) VB
Denmark	DKP SF SD	RV DF RF	KF V FP
Finland	SKDL Left Wing Alliance Greens SSDP	KESK SMP LKP	RKP/SFP KK
Germany	Greens SPD	FDP	CDU/CSU
Great Britain	Labour	Liberals SDP LibDems	Conservatives
Ireland	Labour	FF FG	PD
Netherlands	SP GL PvdA D'66[1]	Christian Democrats (CDA, KVP, ARP, CHU)	VVD LPF
Norway	NKP SF DNA	V SP KrF	H FrP
Sweden	V SdaP	CP FP KdS[2]	MSP

Notes:

Party acronyms as indicated in the CMP dataset. Note that not all parties exist at all points in time (e.g. Green parties). This list is only based on parties with at least 5 per cent of the votes in two subsequent elections.

[1] D66 coded as left-wing party because of party family indicated in the CMP dataset.

[2] The Christian Democrats (KdS) could be classified as a 'centrist' or a 'right-wing' party.

Appendix E: List of niche parties

Table A.5: List of niche parties

Country	Party	CMP party code
Austria	GA Greens	42110
Belgium	Agalev	21112
	Ecolo	21111
	FDF	21912
	RW Walloon rally	21911
	VB Flemish Block	21914
	VU Flemish Peoples Union	21913
	VU-ID21 People's Union-ID21	21915
Denmark	FP Progress Party	13951
	DF People's Party	13720
Finland	VL Greens	41113
	Greens	41111
	Greens-Alliance 90	41112
Ireland	Greens	53110
The Netherlands	GL Greens	22110
	LN Livable Netherlands	22430
	LPF List Pim Fortuyn	22720
Norway	FrP Progress Party	12951
Sweden	Green Ecology Party	11110
	NyD New Democracy	11951
United Kingdom	NA	NA

| bibliography

Aardal, B., Valen, H., Karlsen, R., Kleven, Ø. and Normann, T. M. (2003) *Valgundersøkelsen 2001*, Bergen: Norwegian Social Science Data Services [distributor].

Abney, R., Adams, J., Clark, M., Easton, M., Ezrow, L., Kosmidis, S. and Neundorf, A. (undated) 'When does valence matter? On heightened valence effects for governing parties during election campaigns', Typescript.

Adams, J. (1998) 'Partisan voting and multiparty spatial competition: the pressure for responsible parties', *Journal of Theoretical Politics* 10(1): 5–31.

— (2012) 'Causes and electoral consequences of party policy shifts in multiparty elections: theoretical results and empirical evidence', *Annual Review of Political Science* 15: 401–419.

Adams, J., Clark, M., Ezrow, L. and Glasgow, G. (2004) 'Understanding change and stability in party ideologies: do parties respond to public opinion or to past election results?', *British Journal of Political Science* 34(4): 589–610.

— (2006a) 'Are niche parties fundamentally different from mainstream parties? The causes and the electoral consequences of Western European parties' policy shifts, 1976–1998', *American Journal of Political Science* 50(3): 513–529.

Adams, J., Dow, J. and Merrill, S. III (2006b) 'The political consequences of alienation-based and indifference-based voter abstention: Applications to presidential elections', *Political Behavior* 28(1): 65–86.

Adams, J. and Ezrow, L. (2009) 'Who do European parties represent? How Western European parties represent the policy preferences of opinion leaders', *Journal of Politics* 71(1): 206–223.

Adams, J., Ezrow, L., Merrill, S. III and Somer-Topcu, Z. (undated) 'Policy-seeking parties in proportional systems with valence-related uncertainty: does collective responsibility for performance alter party strategies?', Typescript.

— (2011) 'Is anybody listening? Evidence that voters do not respond to European parties' policy statements during elections', *American Journal of Political Science* 55(2): 370–382.

Adams, J., Haupt, A. B., and Stoll, H. (2009) 'What moves parties? The role of public opinion and global economic conditions in Western Europe', *Comparative Political Studies* 42(5): 611–639.

Adams, J. and Merrill, S., III (2006) 'Why small, centrist third parties motivate policy divergence by major parties', *American Political Science Review* 100(3): 403–417.

— (2009) 'Policy-seeking parties in a parliamentary democracy with proportional representation: a valence-uncertainty model', *British*

Journal of Political Science 39(3): 539–558.

Adams, J., Merrill, S. III and Grofman, B. (2005) *A Unified Theory of Party Competition: A cross-national analysis integrating spatial and behavioral factors*, Cambridge: Cambridge University Press.

Adams, J. and Somer-Topcu, Z. (2009a) 'Policy adjustment by parties in response to rival parties' policy shifts: spatial theory and the dynamics of party competition in twenty-five post-war democracies', *British Journal of Political Science* 39(4): 825–846.

— (2009b) 'Moderate now, win votes later: the electoral consequences of parties' policy shifts in twenty-five postwar democracies', *Journal of Politics* 71(2): 678–692.

Aldrich, J. H. (1983) 'A Downsian spatial model with party activism', *American Political Science Review* 77(4): 974–990.

— (1995) *Why Parties?: The origin and transformation of political parties in America*, Chicago: University of Chicago Press.

Alvarez, R. M. (1997) *Information and Elections*, Ann Arbor: The University of Michigan Press.

Alvarez, R. M., and Brehm, J. (2002) *Hard Choices, Easy Answers: Values, information, and American public opinion*, Princeton: Princeton University Press.

Alvarez, R. M. and Franklin, C. H. (1994) 'Uncertainty and political perceptions', *Journal of Politics* 56(3): 671–688.

Andersen, J. G., Borre, O., Nielsen, H. J., Andersen, J., Thomsen, S. R. and Elklit, J. (2003) *Valgundersøgelsen 2001, hovedundersøgelsen*, Odense: Dansk Data Arkiv [distributor].

Arter, D. (1991) 'The Finnish Election of 17 March 1991: A victory for opposition', *West European Politics* 14(4): 174–180.

— (1995) 'The March 1995 Finnish Election: The Social Democrats storm back', *West European Politics* 18(4): 194–204.

Auffermann, B. (2003) ,Das politische System Finnlands', in W. Ismayr (ed.) *Die politischen Systeme Westeuropas*, Opladen, Leske and Budrich, pp. 187–223.

Axelrod, R. M. (1970) *Conflict of Interest: A theory of divergent goals with applications to politics*, Chicago: Markham.

Bartels, L. M. (1986) 'Issue voting under uncertainty-an empirical-test', *American Journal of Political Science* 30(4): 709–728.

Bartolini, S. (1983) 'The Membership of Mass Parties: The Social Democratic experience, 1889–1978', in H. Daalder and P. Mair (eds), *Western European Party Systems*, London, Sage, pp. 177–220.

Baumgartner, F. R. and Jones, B. D. (1993) *Agendas and Instability in American Politics*, Chicago: University of Chicago Press.

Beck, N. (2001) 'Time-series-cross-section-data: what have we learned in the past few years?', *Annual Review of Political Science* 4: 271–293.

Beck, N. and Katz, J. N. (1995) 'What to do (and not to do) with time-series cross-section data', *American Political Science Review* 89(3): 634–647.

— (1996) 'Nuisance vs. substance: specifying and estimating time-series-cross-section models', *Political Analysis* 6(1): 1–36.

Belgische Kamer van Volksvertegenwoordigers en Senaat (1997) Publicatie van de financiële verslagen van de bedrijfsrevisoren over de boekhouding van de politieke partijen (boekjaar 1996). *1008/1 – 96/97.*

— (2000a) Publicatie van de financiële verslagen over de boekhouding van de politieke partijen en hun componenten (boekjaar 1999). *0671/002.*

— (2000b) Publicatie van de financiële verslagen over de boekhouding van de politieke partijen en hun componenten (boekjaar 1999). *0671/001.*

— (2004a) Publicatie van het financieel verslag over de boekhouding van de politieke partij GROEN! en haar componenten (boekjaar 2003). *1117/003.*

— (2004b) Publicatie van de financiële verslagen over de boekhouding van de politieke partijen en hun componenten (boekjaar 2003). *1117/002.*

— (2004c) Publicatie van de financiële verslagen over de boekhouding van de politieke partijen en hun componenten (boekjaar 2003). *1117/001.*

Belgische Senaat en Kamer van Volksvertegenwoordigers (1993) Publikatie van de financiële verslagen van de bedrijfsrevisoren over de geregistreerde en afgesloten rekeningen von ontvangsten en uitgaven van de krachtens de wet van 4 juli 1989 erkende V.Z.W.'s, alsook over de ontvang sten en uitgaven van de politieke partijen (boekjaar 1992). *993/1 – 92/93.*

Bendor, J., Mookherjee, D. and Ray, D. (2006) 'Satisficing and selection in electoral competition', *Quarterly Journal of Political Science* 1(2): 171–200.

Bennett, W. L. (1990) 'Toward a theory of press-state relations in the United States', *Journal of Communication* 40(2): 103–125.

Benoit, K., Bräuninger, T. and Debus, M. (2009a) 'Challenges for estimating policy preferences: announcing an open access archive of political documents', *German Politics* 18(3): 441–454.

Benoit, K. and Laver, M. (2006) *Party Policy in Modern Democracies*, London, New York: Routledge.

— (2007) 'Estimating party policy positions: comparing expert surveys and hand-coded content analysis', *Electoral Studies* 26(1): 90–107.

Benoit, K., Laver, M., Lowe, W. and Mikhaylov, S. (2012) 'How to scale coded text units without bias', *Electoral Studies* 2012.

Benoit, K., Laver, M. and Mikhaylov, S. (2009b) 'Treating words as data with error: uncertainty in text statements of policy positions', *American Journal of Political Science* 53(2): 495–513.

Bergman, T. (2000) 'Sweden: When minority cabinets are the rule and majority coalitions the exception', in W. C. Müller and K. Strøm (eds) *Coalition Governments in Western Europe*, Oxford, Oxford University Press, pp. 192–230.

Best, H., Lengyel, G. and Verzichelli, L. (eds) (2012a) *The Europe of Elites*, Oxford: Oxford University Press.

Best, R., Budge, I. and McDonald, M. D. (2012b) 'Representation as a median mandate versus bilateralism: taking a cross-national perspective', *European Journal of Political Research* 51(1): 1–23.

Bille, L. (1992) 'Denmark', in R. S. Katz and P. Mair (eds) *Party Organizations: A data handbook on party organizations in Western Democracies, 1960–90*, London, Sage, pp. 199–272.

— (1997) 'Leadership change and party change: the case of the Danish Social Democratic Party, 1960–95', *Party Politics* 3(3): 379–390.

— (2001) 'Democratizing a democratic procedure: myth or reality?: candidate selection in Western European Parties, 1960–1990', *Party Politics* 7(3): 363–380.

Billiet, J., Swyngedouw, M., Carton, A., Beerten, R., Franckx, M., Frognier, A.-P., Aish-Van Vaerenbergh, A.-M., Diest, S. V., Rihoux, B. and De Winter, L. (1991) *General Election Study Belgium 1991*, Amsterdam: Steinmetz Archive [distributor].

Billiet, J., and Swyngedouw, M. (1995) *1995 General Election Study Belgium*, Amsterdam: Steinmetz Archive [distributor].

Birnir, J. K. (2005) 'Public venture capital and party institutionalization', *Comparative Political Studies* 38(8): 915–938.

Black, D. (1948) 'On the rationale of group decision-making', *Journal of Political Economy* 56(1): 23–34.

Bolleyer, N. (2008) 'Inside the cartel party: party organization in government and opposition', *Political Studies* 57(3): 559–579.

Budge, I. (1994) 'A new spatial theory of party competition: uncertainty, ideology and policy equilibria viewed comparatively and temporally', *British Journal of Political Science* 24(4): 443–467.

— (2000) 'Expert judgements of party policy positions: uses and limitations in political research', *European Journal of Political Research* 37(1): 103–113.

— (2001) 'Validating party policy placements', *British Journal of Political Science* 31: 210–223.

Budge, I., Ezrow, L. and McDonald, M. D. (2010) 'Ideology, party factionalism and policy change: an integrated dynamic theory', *British Journal of Political Science* 40: 781–804.

Budge, I. and Klingemann, H.-D. (2001) 'Finally! Comparative over-time mapping of party policy movement', in I. Budge *et al.* (eds) *Mapping Policy Preferences: Estimates for parties, electors, and governments 1945–1998*, Oxford, Oxford University Press, pp. 19–50.

Budge, I., Klingemann, H.-D., Volkens, A., Bara, J. and Tanenbaum, E. (2001) *Mapping Policy Preferences: Estimates for parties, electors and governments 1945–1998*, Oxford: Oxford University Press.

Budge, I. and Meyer, T. M. (2012a) 'Validated estimates versus dodgy adjustments', Typescript.

— (2012b) 'Face validity: From estimating to explaining party movements with the left-right scale', Typescript.

Budge, I. and Pennings, P. (2007) 'Do they work? Validating computerised word frequency estimates against policy series', *Electoral Studies* 26(1): 121–129.

Butler, D. and Butler, G. (2000) *Twentieth-century British Political Facts, 1900–2000*, Basingstoke: Macmillan.

Butler, D. and Kavanagh, D. (1997) *The British General Election of 1997*, Houndmills, Basingstoke: Macmillan.

Campbell, A., Converse, P., Miller, W. and Stokes, D. (1960) *The American Voter*, New York: Wiley.

Carrubba, C., Gabel, M. and Hug, S. (2008) 'Legislative voting behavior, seen and unseen: a theory of roll-call vote selection', *Legislative Studies Quarterly* 33(4): 543–572.

Carty, R. K. (2004) 'Parties as franchise systems: the stratarchical organizational imperative', *Party Politics* 10(1): 5–24.

Castles, F. and Mair, P. (1984) 'Left-right political scales: some "expert" judgments', *European Journal of Political Research* 12(1): 73–88.

CDU-CSU-FDP coalition contract (2009) Wachstum. Bildung. Zusammenhalt. Koalitionsvertrag zwischen CDU, CSU und FDP [Growth. Education. Unity. Coalition contract between CDU, CSU and FDP]. October 2009.

Chappell, H. W. and Keech, W. R. (1986) 'Policy motivation and party differences in a dynamic spatial model of party competition', *American Political Science Review* 80(3): 881–899.

Chong, D. and Druckman, J. N. (2007) 'Framing public opinion in competitive democracies', *American Political Science Review* 101(4): 637–655.

Clark, M. (2009) 'Valence and electoral outcomes in Western Europe, 1976–1998', *Electoral Studies* 28(1): 111–122.

Clarke, H., Sanders, D., Stewart, M. and Whiteley, P. (2005) *The British Election Study 2005: Face-to-face survey*, Colchester, Essex: UK Data Archive [distributor].

Clarke, H. D., Sanders, D., Stewart, M. C. and Whiteley, P. F. (2011) 'Valence Politics and Electoral Choice in Britain, 2010', *Journal of Elections, Public Opinion and Parties* 21(2): 237–253.

Clinton, J., Jackman, S. and Rivers, D. (2004) 'The statistical analysis of roll call data', *American Political Science Review* 98(2): 355–370.

Converse, P. (1964) 'The nature of belief systems in mass publics', in D. E. Apter (ed.) *Ideology and Discontent*, New York, Free Press, pp. 206–261.

Crewe, I., Robertson, D. and Sarlvik, B. (1981) *British Election Study, February 1974, October 1974, June 1975, May 1979; Panel Survey*, Colchester, Essex: UK Data Archive [distributor].

Crotty, W. J. (1968) 'The Party Organization and its Activities', in W. J. Crotty (ed.) *Approaches to the Study of Party Organization*, Boston, Allyn & Bacon, pp. 247–306.

Curini, L. and Zucchini, F. (2012) 'Government alternation and legislative party unity: the case of Italy, 1988–2008', *West European Politics* 35(4): 826–846.

Dachs, H. (2006) ,Grünalternative Parteien', in H. Dachs *et al.* (eds), *Politik in Österreich: Das Handbuch*, Wien, Manz, pp. 364–388.

Dahl, R. A. (1971) *Polyarchy: Participation and opposition*, New Haven: Yale University Press.

Dalton, R. J. and Wattenberg, M. P. (eds) (2000) *Parties without partisans: political change in advanced industrial democracies*, Oxford: Oxford University Press.

Damgaard, E. (2000) 'Denmark: The life and death of government coalitions', in W. C. Müller and K. Strøm (eds), *Coalition Governments in Western Europe*, Oxford, Oxford University Press, pp. 231–263.

de Boer, B., Lucardie, P., Noomen, I. and Voerman, G. (1999) 'Overzicht van de partijpolitieke gebeurtenissen van het jaar 1998', in Documentatiecentrum Nederlandse Politieke Partijen (DNPP) (ed.) *Jaarboek 1998*, Groningen, DNPP, pp. 14–94.

de Marchi, S. (1999) 'Adaptive models and electoral instability', *Journal of Theoretical Politics* 11(3): 393–419.

Denver, D. (1988) 'Britain: centralized parties with decentralized selection', in M. Gallagher and M. Marsh (eds), *Candidate Selection in Comparative Perspective: The secret garden of politics*, London, Sage, pp. 47–71.

Deschouwer, K. (1992) 'Belgium', in R. S. Katz and P. Mair (eds) *Party Organizations: A data handbook on party organizations in Western Democracies, 1960–90*, London, Sage, pp. 121–198.

—— (1994) 'The Decline of Consociationalism and the Reluctant Modernization of Belgian Mass Parties', in R. S. Katz and P. Mair (eds) *How Parties Organize: Change and adaptation in party organizations in Western democracies*, London: Sage, pp. 80–108.

—— (2002) 'The Colour Purple: The end of predictable politics in the Low Countries', in P. D. Webb, D. M. Farrell and I. Holliday (eds) *Political Parties in Advanced Industrial Democracies*, Oxford, Oxford University Press, pp. 151–180.

de Swaan, A. (1973) *Coalition Theories and Cabinet Formations*, Amsterdam: Elsevier.

Detterbeck, K. (2005) 'Cartel parties in Western Europe?', *Party Politics* 11(2): 173–191.

Deutscher Bundestag (1992) Bekanntmachung von Rechenschaftsberichten der politischen Parteien für das Kalenderjahr 1990. 12/2165.

—— (1995) Bekanntmachung von Rechenschaftsberichten der politischen Parteien für das Kalenderjahr 1994. 13/3390.

—— (2000) Bekanntmachung von Rechenschaftsberichten der politischen Parteien für das Kalenderjahr 1998. 14/2508.

—— (2004) Bekanntmachung von Rechenschaftsberichten der politischen Parteien für das Kalenderjahr 2002. 15/2008.

De Winter, L. (1988) 'Belgium: Democracy or Oligarchy?', in M. Gallagher and M. Marsh (eds) *Candidate Selection in Comparative Perspective: The secret garden of politics*, London, Sage, pp. 20–46.

Die Grünen (2005) Satzungen der Partei 'Die Grünen'.

Diermeier, D. and Feddersen, T. J. (1998) 'Cohesion in legislatures and the vote of confidence procedure', *American Political Science Review* 92(3): 611–621.

Dinas, E. and Gemenis, K. (2010) 'Measuring parties: ideological positions with manifesto data a critical evaluation of the competing methods', *Party Politics* 16(4): 427–450.

Downs, A. (1957) *An Economic Theory of Democracy*, New York: Harper & Row.

Dumont, P. and Caulier, J.-F. (2005) 'The "Effective" Number of Relevant Parties: How Voting Power Improves Laakso-Taagepera's Index', CEREC-FUSL Working paper 2003/7. http://centres.fusl.ac.be/CEREC/document/people/caulier/enrp.pdf.

Dutch Ministry of the Interior and Kingdom Relations (undated) 'Herijking Wet subsidiëring politieke partijen'.

Duverger, M. (1954) *Political Parties: Their Organization and activities in the modern state*, New York: Wiley.

The Economist (2010) 'Take a punt on me', http://www.economist.com/world/britain/displaystory.cfm?story_id=15912978 (accessed 15 April 2010).

Election Resources on the Internet (2010) www.electionresources.org

Elvert, J. (2003) ,Das politische System Irlands', in W. Ismayr (ed.) *Die politischen Systeme Westeuropas*, Opladen, Leske and Budrich, pp. 263–300.

Enelow, J. M. and Hinich, M. J. (1984) *The Spatial Theory of Voting*, Cambridge: Cambridge University Press.

Epstein, D. and O'Halloran, S. (1994) 'Administrative Procedures, Information, and Agency Discretion', *American Journal of Political Science* 38(3): 697–722.

— (2006) 'A Theory of Efficient Delegation', in D. Braun and F. Gilardi (eds) *Delegation in contemporary democracies*, London, Routledge, pp. 77–98.

Epstein, L. D. (1967) *Political Parties in Western Democracies*, New York: Praeger.

Erikson, R. S. and Romero, D. W. (1990) 'Candidate equilibrium and the behavioral model of the vote', *American Political Science Review* 84(4): 1103–1126.

Evans, S. (2008) 'Consigning its past to history? David Cameron and the Conservative Party', *Parliamentary Affairs* 61(2): 291–314.

Ezrow, L. (2010) *Linking Citizens and Parties: How electoral systems matter for political representation*, Oxford: Oxford University Press.

Ezrow, L., De Vries, C. E., Steenbergen, M. and Edwards, E. E. (2010) 'Mean voter representation and partisan constituency representation: do parties respond to the mean voter position or to their supporters?', *Party Politics* 17(3): 275–301.

Falter, J. W., Gabriel, O. W. and Rattinger, H. (2002) *Political Attitudes, Political Participation and Voter Conduct in United Germany 2002*, Köln: GESIS.

Farrell, D. M. (1992) 'Ireland', in R. S. Katz and P. Mair (eds) *Party Organizations: A data handbook on party organizations in Western Democracies, 1960–90*, London, Sage, pp. 389–457.

—   (1994) 'Ireland: Centralization, professionalization and competitive pressures', in R. S. Katz and P. Mair (eds) *How Parties Organize: Change and adaptation in party organizations in Western democracies*, London, Sage, pp. 216–241.

FAZ (2009) 'Kernenergie: Geschichte eines Realitätsverlusts [Nuclear power: Losing grip of reality]'. http://www.faz.net/aktuell/wirtschaft/wirtschaftspolitik/kernenergie-geschichte-eines-realitaetsverlusts-1829454.html (accessed 19 October 2012).

Feldkamp, M. F. (2005) *Datenhandbuch zur Geschichte des Deutschen Bundestages 1994 bis 2003*, Baden-Baden: Nomos.

Finnish Ministry of Justice (1998 [amended 2004]) Finnish Act on Parliamentary Elections 1998.

Finnish Voter Barometer 1975 (2002) Tampere: Finnish Social Science Data Archive [distributor].

—   1979 (2002) Tampere: Finnish Social Science Data Archive [distributor].

—   1983 (2004) Tampere: Finnish Social Science Data Archive [distributor].

—   1984 (2000) Tampere: Finnish Social Science Data Archive [distributor].

—   1986 (2000) Tampere: Finnish Social Science Data Archive [distributor].

—   1987 (2000) Tampere: Finnish Social Science Data Archive [distributor].

—   1990 (2006) Tampere: Finnish Social Science Data Archive [distributor].

—   February 1995 (2006) Tampere: Finnish Social Science Data Archive [distributor].

—   January 1999 (2006) Tampere: Finnish Social Science Data Archive [distributor].

Fiorina, M. P. (1981) *Retrospective Voting in American National Elections*, New Haven: Yale University Press.

Fowler, J. H. and Laver, M. (2008) 'A tournament of party decision rules', *Journal of Conflict Resolution* 52(1): 68–92.

Franzmann, S. and Kaiser, A. (2006) 'Locating political parties in policy space – a reanalysis of party manifesto data', *Party Politics* 12(2): 163–188.

Gabel, M. J. and Huber, J. D. (2000) 'Putting parties in their place: inferring party left-right ideological positions from party manifestos data', *American Journal of Political Science* 44(1): 94–103.

Gallagher, M. (1988a) 'Introduction' in M. Gallagher and M. Marsh (eds) *Candidate Selection in Comparative Perspective: The secret garden of politics*, London, Sage, pp. 1–19.

—   (1988b) 'Ireland: the increasing role of the centre', in M. Gallagher and M. Marsh (eds) *Candidate Selection in Comparative Perspective: The secret garden of politics*, London, Sage, pp. 119–144.

Gallagher, M. and Marsh, M. (eds) (1988) *Candidate Selection in Comparative Perspective: The secret garden of politics*, London: Sage.

Gay, O., White, I. and Kelly, R. (2007) 'The funding of political parties', *Parliament and Constitution Centre – Houses of Commons Library*.

Gelman, A. (2006) 'Multilevel (hierarchical) modelling: what it can and cannot do', *Technometrics* 48(3): 432–435.

Gelman, A. and Hill, J. (2007) *Data Analysis Using Regression and Multilevel/ Hierarchical Models*, Cambridge: Cambridge University Press.

Gemenis, K. (2012) 'Proxy documents as a source of measurement error in the Comparative Manifestos Project', *Electoral Studies* 31(3): 594–604.

German Federal Elections Act (1993 [amended 2008]).

Gidlund, G. and Koole, R. A. (2001) 'Political Finance in the North of Europe: The Netherlands and Sweden', in K.-H. Nassmacher (ed.) *Foundations for Democracy*, Baden-Baden: Nomos, pp.112–130.

Gilmore, T. N. (1988) *Making a Leadership Change: How organizations and leaders can handle leadership transitions successfully*, San Francisco: Jossey-Bass Publishers.

Green, J. (2007) 'When voters and parties agree: valence issues and party competition', *Political Studies* 55(3): 629–655.

Green, J. and Jennings, W. (2012) 'Valence as macro-competence: an analysis of mood in party competence evaluations in Great Britain', *British Journal of Political Science* 42(2): 311–342.

Grofman, B. (1985) 'The neglected role of the status quo in models of issue voting', *Journal of Politics* 47(1): 230–237.

Groseclose, T. (2001) 'A model of candidate location when one candidate has a valence advantage', *American Journal of Political Science* 45(4): 862–886.

Groß, H. and Rothholz, W. (2003) ‚Das politische System Norwegens', in W. Ismayr (ed.) *Die politischen Systeme Westeuropas*, Opladen, Leske and Budrich, pp. 131–166.

Gschwend, T. and Pappi, F. U. (2003) *Vorwahlbefragung Belgien 2003*, Köln: GESIS.

Hammond, J. S., Keeney, R. L. and Raiffa, H. (2006) 'The hidden traps in decision making', *Harvard Business Review* 84(1): 118–126.

Hansen, M. E. (2008) 'Back to the Archives? A critique of the Danish part of the manifesto datase', *Scandinavian Political Studies* 31(2): 201–216.

— (2009) 'The positions of Irish parliamentary parties 1937–2006', *Irish Political Studies* 24(1): 29–44.

Harmel, R., Heo, U., Tan, A. and Janda, K. (1995) 'Performance, Leadership, Factions and Party Change: An Empirical Analysis', *West European Politics* 18(1): 1–33.

Harmel, R. and Janda, K. (1994) 'An integrated theory of party goals and party change', *Journal of Theoretical Politics* 6(3): 259–287.

Hazan, R. Y. and Rahat, G. (2010) *Democracy Within Parties: Candidate selection methods and their political consequences*, Oxford: Oxford University Press.

Hazan, R. Y. and Voerman, G. (2006) 'Electoral systems and candidate selection', *Acta Politica* 41(2): 146–162.

Heath, A., Jowell, R. and Curtice, J. K. (1998) *The British Election Study 1992–*

1997, Colchester, Essex: UK Data Archive [distributor].

— (1999a) *British Election Panel Study, 1983, 1986 and 1987*, Colchester, Essex: UK Data Archive [distributor].

— (2001) *The Rise of New Labour*, Oxford: Oxford University Press.

— (2002) *British Election Panel Study, 1997–2001; Waves 1 to 8*, Colchester, Essex: UK Data Archive [distributor].

Heath, A., Jowell, R., Curtice, J. K., Brand, J. and Mitchell, J. (1993) *British General Election Panel Study, 1987–1992*, Colchester, Essex: UK Data Archive [distributor].

Heath, A., Taylor, B., Brook, L. and Park, A. (1999b) 'British national sentiment', *British Journal of Political Science* 29(1): 155–175.

Hecking, C. (2006) 'Das Parteiensystem Belgiens', in O. Niedermayer, R. Stöss and M. Haas (eds) *Die Parteiensysteme Westeuropas*, Wiesbaden, VS Verlag für Sozialwissenschaften, pp. 41–65.

Heidar, K. and Koole, R. A. (2000) 'Parliamentary Party Groups Compared', in K. Heidar and R. A. Koole (eds) *Parliamentary Party Groups in European Democracies: Political parties behind closed doors*, London, Routledge, pp. 248–270.

Helander, V. (1997) 'Finland', in P. Norris (ed.) *Passages to Power: Legislative recruitment in advanced democracies*, Cambridge, Cambridge University Press, pp. 56–75.

Hellwig, T. (2012) 'Constructing accountability: party position taking and economic voting', *Comparative Political Studies* 45(1): 91–118.

Hippe, J., Lucardie, P. and Voerman, G. (2003) 'Overzicht van de partijpolitieke gebeurtenissen van het jaar 2002', in Documentatiecentrum Nederlandse Politieke Partijen (DNPP) (ed.) *Jaarboek 2002*, Groningen, DNPP, pp. 18–180.

— (2004) 'Overzicht van de partijpolitieke gebeurtenissen van het jaar 2003', in Documentatiecentrum Nederlandse Politieke Partijen (DNPP) (ed.) *Jaarboek 2003*, Groningen, DNPP, pp. 15–137.

Hirschmann, A. O. (1970) *Exit, Voice, and Loyalty*, Cambridge: Cambridge University Press.

Hix, S., Noury, A. and Roland, G. (2005) 'Power to the parties: cohesion and competition in the European Parliament, 1979–2001', *British Journal of Political Science* 35: 209–234.

— (2006) 'Dimensions of politics in the European Parliament', *American Journal of Political Science* 50(2): 494–511.

Holsti, O. R. (1969) *Content analysis for the social sciences and humanities*, Reading, Mass.: Addison-Wesley.

Hooghe, L., Bakker, R., Brigevich, A., De Vries, C., Edwards, E., Marks, G., Rovny, J., Steenbergen, M. and Vachudova, M. (2010) 'Reliability and validity of the 2002 and 2006 Chapel Hill expert surveys on party positioning', *European Journal of Political Research* 49(5): 687–703.

Hooghe, M., Stolle, D. and Stouthuysen, P. (2004) 'Head start in politics: the recruitment function of youth organizations of political parties in Belgium (Flanders)', *Party Politics* 10(2): 193–212.

Hopkin, J. (2001) 'Bringing the members back in?: Democratizing candidate selection in Britain and Spain', *Party Politics* 7(3): 343–361.

Hotelling, H. (1929) 'Stability in competition', *The Economic Journal* 39(153): 41–57.

Huber, J. D. (1989) 'Values and partisanship in left-right orientations: measuring ideology', *European Journal of Political Research* 17(5): 599–621.

Huber, J. D. and Inglehart, R. (1995) 'Expert interpretations of party space and party locations in 42 Societies', *Party Politics* 1(1): 73–111.

Huber, J. D., Shipan, C. R. and Pfahler, M. (2001) 'Legislatures and statutory control of bureaucracy', *American Journal of Political Science* 45(2): 330–345.

Hug, S. (2006) 'Selection Effects in Roll Call Votes', *CIS Working Paper* 15.

—— (2010) 'Selection effects in roll call votes', *British Journal of Political Science* 40: 225–235.

Hug, S. and Schulz, T. (2007) 'Left-right positions of political parties in Switzerland', *Party Politics* 13(3): 305–330.

Humphreys, M. and Laver, M. (2010) 'Spatial models, cognitive metrics, and majority rule equilibria', *British Journal of Political Science* 40: 11–30.

Infratest dimap (2000) *DeutschlandTREND Juli 2000. Umfrage zur politischen Stimmung im Auftrag von ARD/ "bericht aus berlin" und 8 Tageszeitungen.*

Interparliamentary Union (2010) 'PARLINE database'. http://www.ipu.org/parline/

Irwin, G. A., van Holsteyn, J. J. M. and den Ridder, J. M. (2005) *Dutch Parliamentary Election Study 2002–2003*, Amsterdam: Steinmetz Archive [distributor].

Jackman, S. (2001) 'Multidimensional analysis of roll call data via Bayesian simulation: identification, inference, and model checking', *Political Analysis* 9(3): 227–241.

Jahn, D. (2003) 'Das politische System Schwedens', in W. Ismayr (ed.) *Die politischen Systeme Westeuropas*, Opladen, Leske and Budrich, pp. 93–130.

Janda, K., Harmel, R., Edens, C. and Goff, P. (1995) 'Changes in party identity: evidence from party manifestos', *Party Politics* 1(2): 171–196.

Jenkins, R. W. (1999) 'How much is too much? Media attention and popular support for an insurgent party', *Political Communication* 16(4): 429–445.

Jenny, M. (2006) 'Programme: Parteien im politischen Wettbewerbsraum', in H. Dachs *et al.* (eds) *Politik in Österreich. Das Handbuch*, Wien, Manz, pp. 305–321.

Jones, B. D. and Baumgartner, F. R. (2005) *The Politics of Attention: How government prioritizes problems*, Chicago: University of Chicago Press.

Karvonen, L. and Paloheimo, H. (2003) *Finnish National Election Study 2003*, Tampere: Finnish Social Science Data Archive [distributor].

Katz, R. S. (2001) 'The problem of candidate selection and models of party democracy', *Party Politics* 7(3): 277–296.

Katz, R. S. and Mair, P. (eds) (1992) *Party Organizations: A data handbook on party organizations in Western Democracies, 1960–90*, London: Sage.

—   (1993) 'The evolution of party organizations in Europe: the three faces of party organization', The American Review of Politics 14(4): 593–617.

—   (1994) (eds) How Parties Organize: Change and adaptation in party organizations in Western democracies, London: Sage.

—   (1995) 'Changing models of party organization and party democracy: the emergence of the cartel party', Party Politics 1(1): 5–28.

—   (2009) 'The cartel party thesis: a restatement', Perspectives on Politics 7(4): 753–766.

Katz, R. S., Mair, P., Bardi, L., Bille, L., Deschouwer, K., Farrell, D. M., Koole, R. A., Morlino, L., Müller, W. C., Pierre, J., Poguntke, T., Sundberg, J., Svåsand, L., van de Velde, H., Webb, P. D. and Widfeldt, A. (1992) 'The membership of political-prties in European democracies, 1960–1990', *European Journal of Political Research* 22(3): 329–345.

Kedar, O. (2005) 'When moderate voters prefer extreme parties: policy balancing in parliamentary elections', *American Political Science Review* 99(2): 185–199.

—   (2009) *Voting for Policy, Not Parties: How voters compensate for power sharing*, Cambridge: Cambridge University Press.

Keman, H. (1994) 'The search for the centre: pivot parties in West European party systems', *West European Politics* 17(4): 124–148.

Kiewiet, D. R. and McCubbins, M. D. (1991) *The Logic of Delegation: Congressional parties and the appropriations process*, Chicago: The University of Chicago Press.

King, G., Keohane, R. O. and Verba, S. (1994) *Designing Social Inquiry: Scientific inference in qualitative research*, Princeton: Princeton University Press.

King, G., Murray, C. J. L., Salomon, J. A. and Tandon, A. (2004) 'Enhancing the validity and cross-cultural comparability of measurement in survey research', *American Political Science Review* 98(1): 191–207.

King, G., Tomz, M. and Wittenberg, J. (2000) 'Making the most of statistical analyses: improving interpretation and presentation', *American Journal of Political Science* 44(2): 341–355.

King, S. and Gillespie, G. (1998) 'Irish political data 1997', *Irish Political Studies* 13(1): 211–279.

Kirchheimer, O. (1966) 'The Transformation of the Western European Party Systems', in J. LaPalombara and M. Weiner (eds) *Political Parties and Political Development*, Princeton, Princeton University Press, pp. 177–200.

Kitschelt, H. (1989) *The Logics of Party Formation: Ecological politics in Belgium and West Germany*, Ithaca: Cornell University Press.

—   (1994a) 'Austrian and Swedish Social-Democrats in crisis: party strategy and organization in corporatist regimes', *Comparative Political Studies* 27(1): 3–39.

—   (1994b) *The Transformation of European Social Democracy*, Cambridge: Cambridge University Press.

—   (2000) 'Citizens, politicians, and party cartelization: political representation and state failure in post-industrial democracies', *European Journal of Political Research* 37(2): 149–179.

Klemmensen, R., Hobolt, S. B. and Hansen, M. E. (2007) 'Estimating policy positions using political texts: an evaluation of the Wordscores approach', *Electoral Studies* 26(4): 746–755.

Klingemann, H.-D., Volkens, A., Bara, J. L., Budge, I. and McDonald, M. D. (2006) *Mapping Policy Preferences II: Estimates for parties, electors, and governments in Eastern Europe, European Union, and OECD 1990–2003*, Oxford: Oxford University Press.

Klotzbach, K. (1996) *Der Weg zur Staatspartei. Programmatik, praktische Politik und Organisation der deutschen Sozialdemokratie 1945 bis 1965*, Bonn: Dietz.

Knutsen, O. (1995) 'Value orientations, political conflicts and left-right identification: a comparative study', *European Journal of Political Research* 28(1): 63–93.

Kollman, K., Miller, J. H. and Page, S. E. (1992) 'Adaptive parties in spatial elections', *American Political Science Review* 86(4): 929–937.

—   (eds) (2003) *Computational Models in Political Economy*, Cambridge, Massachusetts: MIT Press.

Koole, R. A. (1994) 'The Vulnerability of the Modern Cadre Party in the Netherlands', in R. S. Katz and P. Mair (eds) *How Parties Organize: Change and adaptation in party organizations in Western democracies*, London, Sage, pp. 278–303.

—   (1997) 'Ledenpartijen of staatspartijen', In Documentatiecentrum Nederlandse Politieke Partijen (DNPP) (ed.) *Jaarboek 1996*, Groningen, DNPP: 156–182.

—   (2001) 'Political Finance in Western Europe: Britain and France', in K.-H. Nassmacher (ed.) *Foundations for Democracy*, Baden-Baden, Nomos, pp. 73–91.

Koole, R. A. and Leijenaar, M. (1988) 'The Netherlands: The predominance of regionalism', in M. Gallagher and M. Marsh (eds) *Candidate Selection in Comparative Perspective: The secret garden of politics*, London, Sage, pp. 190–209.

Koole, R. A. and van de Welde, H. (1992) 'The Netherlands', in R. S. Katz and P. Mair (eds) *Party Organizations: A data handbook on party organizations in Western Democracies, 1960–90*, London, Sage, pp. 619–732.

Koopmans, R. (2007) 'Who inhabits the European public sphere? Winners and losers, supporters and opponents in Europeanised political debates', *European Journal of Political Research* 46(2): 183–210.

Krasner, S. D. (1984) 'Approaches to the state: alternative conceptions and historical dynamics', *Comparative Politics* 16(2): 223–246.

Kreps, D. M. (1990) *A Course in Microeconomic Theory*, New York; London: Harvester, Wheatsheaf.

Krippendorff, K. (2003) *Content Analysis: An introduction to its methodology*, Newbury Park: Sage.

Krouwel, A. (1999) *The Catch-All Party in Western Europe: A study in arrested development*, Amsterdam: Vrije Universiteit.

— (2003) 'Otto Kirchheimer and the catch-all party', *West European Politics* 26(2): 23–40.

Kuitunen, S. (2002) 'Finland: Formalized procedures with member predominance', in H. M. Narud, M. N. Pedersen and H. Valen (eds) *Party Sovereignty and Citizen Control*, Odense, University Press of Southern Denmark, pp. 63–104.

Laakso, M. and Taagepera, R. (1979) '"Effective' number of parties: a measure with application to West Europe', *Comparative Political Studies* 12(1): 3–27.

Labour Party (1997) *New Labour: Because Britain deserves better*, London.

— (2006) *The Labour Party: Financial statements for the year ended 31 December 2005*: Electoral Commission.

Lacewell, O. and Werner, A. (2012) 'Coder training: key to enhancing reliability and validity', *Typescript*.

Lau, R. R. and Redlawsk, D. P. (1997) 'Voting correctly', *American Political Science Review* 91(3): 585–598.

Lau, R. R., Andersen, D. J. and Redlawsk, D. P. (2008) 'An exploration of correct voting in recent US presidential elections', *American Journal of Political Science* 52(2): 395–411.

Laver, M. (1997) *Private Desires, Political Action*, London: Sage.

— (2005) 'Policy and the dynamics of political competition', *American Political Science Review* 99(2): 263–281.

— (2006) 'Legislatures and parliaments', in B. R. Weingast and D. A. Wittman (eds) *Oxford Handbook of Political Economy*, Oxford, Oxford University Press, pp. 121–140.

Laver, M. and Budge, I. (eds) (1992a) *Party Policy and Government Coalitions*, London: Macmillan.

— (1992b) 'Measuring Policy Distances and Modelling Coalition Formation', in M. Laver and I. Budge (eds) *Party Policy and Government Coalitions*, London, Macmillan, pp. 15–40.

Laver, M. and Hunt, B. W. (1992) *Policy and Party Competition*, New York, London: Routledge.

Laver, M. and Shepsle, K. A. (1996) *Making and Breaking Governments: Cabinets and legislatures in parliamentary democracies*, Cambridge; New York: Cambridge University Press.

Laver, M. and Schofield, N. (1998) *Multiparty Government: The politics of coalition in Europe*, Ann Arbor, Mich.: The University of Michigan Press.

Laver, M., Benoit, K. and Garry, J. (2003) 'Extracting policy positions from political tests using words as data', *American Political Science Review* 97(2): 311–331.

Leijenaar, M. (1993) 'A battle for power: selecting candidates in the Netherlands', in J. Lovenduski and P. Norris (eds) *Gender and Party Politics*, London, Sage, pp. 205–230.

Levi, M. (1997) 'A model, a method, and a map: rational choice in comparative and historical analysis', in M. I. Lichbach and A. S. Zuckerman (eds) *Comparative Politics: Rationality, culture, and structure*, Cambridge, Cambridge University Press, pp. 19–41.

Liberal Democrats (2006) *Reports and Financial Statements for the Year Ended 31 December 2005*: Electoral Commission.

Liegl, B. (2006) 'Kleinparteien', in H. Dachs *et al.* (eds) *Politik in Österreich: Das Handbuch*, Wien, Manz, pp. 402–411.

Lijphart, A. (1999) *Patterns of Democracy: Government forms and performance in thirty-six countries*, New Haven; London: Yale University Press.

Lin, T.-M., Enelow, J. M., and Dorussen, H. (1999) 'Equilibrium in multicandidate probabilistic spatial voting', *Public Choice* 98(1–2): 59–82.

Lipset, S. M. and Rokkan, S. (1967) *Party Systems and Voter Alignments*, New York: Free Press.

Lowe, W., Benoit, K., Mikhaylov, S. and Laver, M. (2011) 'Scaling policy preferences from coded political texts', *Legislative Studies Quarterly* 36(1): 123–155.

Lucardie, P. (2006) 'Das Parteiensystem der Niederlande', in O. Niedermayer, R. Stöss and M. Haas (eds) *Die Parteiensysteme Westeuropas*, Wiesbaden, VS Verlag für Sozialwissenschaften, pp. 331–350.

Lundell, K. (2004) 'Determinants of candidate selection: the degree of centralization in comparative perspective', *Party Politics* 10(1): 25–47.

Lupia, A. (2003) 'Delegation and its Perils', in K. Strøm, W. C. Müller and T. Bergman (eds) *Delegation and Accountability in Parliamentary Democracies*, Oxford, Oxford University Press, pp. 33–54.

Lupia, A. and Strøm, K. (2008) 'Bargaining, Transaction Costs, and Coalition Governance', in K. Strøm, W. C. Müller and T. Bergman (eds) *Cabinets and Coalition Bargaining: The democratic life cycle in Western Europe*, Oxford, Oxford University Press, pp. 51–83.

Luther, K. R. (2006) 'Die Freiheitliche Partei Österreichs und das Bündnis Zukunft Österreich', in H. Dachs *et al.* (eds) *Politik in Österreich: Das Handbuch*, Wien, Manz, pp. 364–388.

McDonald, M. D. and Mendes, S. M. (2001) 'The policy space of party manifestos', in M. Laver (ed.) *Estimating the Policy Positions of Political Actors*, London, New York, Routledge, pp. 90–114.

McDonald, M. D., Mendes, S. M. and Kim, M. (2007) 'Cross-temporal and cross-national comparisons of party left-right positions', *Electoral Studies* 26(1): 62–75.

Macdonald, S. E. and Rabinowitz, G. (1998) 'Solving the paradox of nonconvergence: valence, position, and direction in democratic politics', *Electoral Studies* 17(3): 281–300.

Macdonald, S. E., Rabinowitz, G. and Listhaug, O. (1998) 'On attempting to rehabilitate the proximity model: sometimes the patient just can't be helped',

  Journal of Politics 60(3): 653–690.

— (2001) 'Sophistry versus science: on further efforts to rehabilitate the proximity model', *Journal of Politics* 63(2): 482–500.

Mair, P. (1997) *Party System Change: Approaches and interpretations*, Oxford: Clarendon Press.

— (2008) 'The challenge to party government', *West European Politics* 31(1&2): 211–234.

— (2009) 'Representative versus Rsponsible Government', *MPIfG Working Paper* 9(8): 1–19.

Mair, P., Müller, W. C. and Plasser, F. (eds) (2004) *Political Parties and Electoral Change: Party responses to electoral markets*, London: Sage.

Mair, P. and van Biezen, I. (2001) 'Party membership in twenty European democracies, 1980–2000', *Party Politics* 7(1): 5–21.

Mancini, P. (1999) 'New frontiers in political professionalism', *Political Communication* 16(3): 231–245.

Manifesto Project Database (2012). https://manifesto-project.wzb.eu/.

Manin, B., Przeworski, A. and Stokes, S. C. (1999) 'Elections and Representation', in A. Przeworski *et al.* (eds) *Democracy, Accountability, and representation*, Cambridge, Cambridge University Press, pp. 29–54.

Maravall, J. M. (2008) 'The Political Consequences of Internal Party Democracy', in J. M. Maravall and I. Sánchez-Cuenca (eds) *Controlling Governments: Voters, institutions and accountability*, Cambridge, Cambridge University Press, pp. 157–201.

Marsh, M. and Sinnott, R. (2002) *The Irish National Election Study 2002*.

Meguid, B. M. (2005) 'Competition between unequals: the role of mainstream party strategy in niche party success', *American Political Science Review* 99(3): 347–359.

— (2008) *Party Competition Between Unequals: Strategies and electoral fortunes in Western Europe*, Cambridge: Cambridge University Press.

Merrill, S. III and Grofman, B. (1999) *A Unified Theory of Voting: Directional and proximity spatial models*, Cambridge: Cambridge University Press.

Meyer, T. M. and Jenny, M. (2012) 'Measuring error for adjacent policy position estimates: dealing with uncertainty using CMP data', *Electoral Studies* forthcoming.

Michels, R. (1915) *Political Parties: A sociological study of the oligarchical tendencies of modern democracy*, New York: Hearst's International Library.

Mikhaylov, S., Laver, M. and Benoit, K. (2012) 'Coder reliability and misclassification in the human coding of party manifestos', *Political Analysis* 20(1): 78–91.

Mill, J. S. (1846) *A System of Logic, Ratiocinative and Inductive: Being a connected view of the principles of evidence and the methods of scientific investigation*, New York: Harper.

Miller, J. H. and Stadler, P. F. (1998) 'The dynamics of locally adaptive parties under spatial voting', *Journal of Economic Dynamics and Control* 23(2): 171–189.

Miller, S. (1974) *Die SPD vor und nach Godesberg*, Bonn: Verlag Neue Gesellschaft.

The Ministry of Government Administration and Reform (2005) Act on certain aspects relating to the political parties (The Political Parties Act), Norwegian Ministry of Government Administration and Reform.

Mitchell, P. (1993) 'The 1992 General Election in the Republic of Ireland', *Irish Political Studies* 8(1): 111–117.

Mjelde, H. L. (2009) *Explaining Membership Growth in the Norwegian Progress Party (Frp) from 1973 to 2008*, Köln: Lambert Academic Publishing.

Müller, W. C. (1992) 'Austria (1945–1990)', in R. S. Katz and P. Mair (eds) *Party Organizations: A Data handbook on party organizations in Western Democracies, 1960–90*, London, Sage, pp. 21–120.

— (1997) 'Inside the black box: A confrontation of party executive behaviour and theories of party organizational change', *Party Politics* 3(3): 293–313.

— (2000) 'Political parties in parliamentary democracies: Making delegation and accountability work', *European Journal of Political Research* 37(3): 309–333.

— (2006) 'Die Österreichische Volkspartei', in H. Dachs *et al.* (eds) *Politik in Österreich: Das Handbuch*, Wien, Manz, pp. 341–363.

Müller, W. C. and Meyer, T. (2010) 'Meeting the challenges of representation and accountability in multi-party governments', *West European Politics* 33(5): 1065–1092.

Müller, W. C., Plasser, F. and Ulram, P. A. (1999) 'Schwäche als Vorteil, Stärke als Nachteil. Die Reaktion der Parteien auf den Rückgang der Wählerbindungen in Österreich', in P. Mair, W. C. Müller and F. Plasser (eds) *Parteien auf komplexen Wählermärkten*, Wien, Signum, pp. 201–245.

Müller, W. C. and Strøm, K. (eds) (1999) *Policy, Office, or Votes?: How political parties in Western Europe make hard decisions*, Cambridge: Cambridge University Press.

— (2000a) 'Coalition Governments in Western Europe: An introduction', in W. C. Müller and K. Strøm (eds) *Coalition Governments in Western Europe*, Oxford, Oxford University Press, pp. 1–31.

— (eds) (2000b) *Coalition Governments in Western Europe*, Oxford: Oxford University Press.

Munzinger Online (2010). www.munzinger.de.

Murphy, R. J. and Farrell, D. M. (2002) 'Party Politics in Ireland: Regularizing a volatile system', in P. D. Webb, D. M. Farrell and I. Holliday (eds) *Political Parties in Advanced Industrial Democracies*, Oxford, Oxford University Press, pp. 217–247.

Nannestad, P. (2003) 'Das politische System Dänemarks', in W. Ismayr (ed.) *Die politischen Systeme Westeuropas*, Opladen, Leske and Budrich, pp. 55–92.

Nassmacher, K.-H. (ed.) (2001a) *Foundations for Democracy*, Baden-Baden: Nomos.

— (2001b) 'Comparative Political Finance in Established Democracies', in K.-H. Nassmacher (ed.) *Foundations for Democracy*, Baden-Baden, Nomos, pp. 9–33.

Neuendorf, K. A. (2002) *The Content Analysis Guidebook*, London: Sage.

Niedermayer, O. (2009) 'Parteimitglieder in Deutschland: Version 1/2009', *Arbeitshefte aus dem Otto-Stammer-Zentrum* 15: 1–21.

Norris, P. (ed.) (1997) *Passages to Power: Legislative recruitment in advanced democracies*, Cambridge: Cambridge University Press.

Obler, J. (1973) 'The role of national party leaders in the selection of parliamentary candidates: The Belgian case', *Comparative Politics* 5(2): 157–184.

— (1974) 'Intraparty democracy and selection of parliamentary candidates: the Belgian case', *British Journal of Political Science* 4(2): 163–185.

OECD (1999) 'Classifying educational programmes: Manual for ISCED-97 implementation in OECD countries',

Olson, M. (1965) *The Logic of Collective Action*, Cambridge: Harvard University Press.

Orwell, G. (1949) *Nineteen Eighty-Four*, Signet Classic edition from 1996, New York: Signet Classic.

Panebianco, A. (1988) *Political Parties: Organization and power*, Cambridge; New York: Cambridge University Press.

Parties and Elections in Europe (2010). www.parties-and-elections.eu.

Pedersen, M. N. (2002) 'Denmark: The interplay of nominations and elections in Danish politics', in H. M. Narud, M. N. Pedersen and H. Valen (eds) *Party Sovereignty and Citizen Control*, Odense, University Press of Southern Denmark,pp. 29–61.

Pelinka, A. (2003) 'Das politische System Österreichs', in W. Ismayr (ed.) *Die politischen Systeme Westeuropas*, Opladen, Leske and Budrich, pp. 521–552.

Pelizzo, R. (2003) 'Party positions or party direction? An analysis of party manifesto data', *West European Politics* 26(2): 67–89.

Pennings, P. (1999) 'The Consequences of Candidate Selection for Policy-Making in Western Europe', presented at 27th Joint Sessions of Workshops of the European Consortium for Political Research, in Mannheim.

— (2011) 'Assessing the 'Gold Standard' of party policy placements: is computerized replication possible?', *Electoral Studies* 30(3): 561–570.

Peters, B. G. (2005) *Institutional Theory in Political Science*, London: Continuum.

Pettitt, R. T. (2007) 'Challenging the leadership: the party conference as a platform for dissenting membership voice in British and Danish parties of the left', *Scandinavian Political Studies* 30(2): 229–248.

Pfeffer, J. and Salancik, G. R. (1978) *The External Control of Organizations: A resource dependence perspective*, New York: Harper & Row.

Pierce, R. (1999) 'Mass-elite issue linkages and the responsible party model of representation', in W. E. Miller *et al.* (eds) *Policy representation in Western democracies*, Oxford, Oxford University Press, pp. 9–32.

Pierre, J., and Widfeldt, A. (1992) 'Sweden', In Richard S. Katz and Peter Mair (eds), *Party Organizations: A Data Handbook on Party Organizations in Western Democracies, 1960–90*, London, Sage: 781–836.

Pierre, J., Svåsand, L. and Widfeldt, A. (2000) 'State subsidies to political parties: confronting rhetoric with reality', *West European Politics* 23(3): 1–24.

Pierson, P. (2000) 'Increasing Returns, path dependence, and the study of politics', *American Political Science Review* 94(2): 251–267.

Plasser, F., Ulram, P. A. and Sommer, F. (eds) (2000) *Das österreichische Wahlverhalten*, Wien: Signum.

Plott, C. R. (1967) 'A notion of equilibrium and its possibility under majority rule', *The American Economic Review* 57(4): 787–806

Plümper, T., Troeger, V. E. and Manow, P. (2005) 'Panel data analysis in comparative politics: linking method to theory', *European Journal of Political Research* 44(2): 327–354.

Poguntke, T. (1994) 'Parties in a Legalistic Culture: The case of Germany', in R. S. Katz and P. Mair (eds) *How Parties Organize: Change and adaptation in party organizations in Western democracies*, London, Sage, pp. 185–215.

Poguntke, T. and Boll, B. (1992) 'Germany', in R. S. Katz and P. Mair (eds) *Party Organizations: A data handbook on party organizations in western democracies, 1960–90*, London, Sage, pp. 317–388.

Poole, K. T. and Rosenthal, H. (1991) 'Patterns of congressional voting', *American Journal of Political Science* 35(1): 228–278.

Powell, G. B. (2000) *Elections as Instruments of Democracy: Majoritarian and proportional visions*, New Haven: Yale University Press.

Proksch, S. O. and Slapin, J. B. (2009) 'How to avoid pitfalls in statistical analysis of political texts: the case of Germany', *German Politics* 18(3): 323–344.

Proksch, S. O., Slapin, J. B. and Thies, M. F. (2011) 'Party system dynamics in post-war Japan: a quantitative content analysis of electoral pledges', *Electoral Studies* 30(1): 114–124.

Przeworski, A. and Teune, H. (1970) *The Logic of Comparative Social Inquiry*, New York: Wiley-Interscience.

Rabe-Hesketh, S. and Skrondal, A. (2005) *Multilevel and Longitudinal Modelling Using Stata*, College Station, TX: Stata Press.

Rabinowitz, G. and Macdonald, S. E. (1989) 'A directional theory of issue voting', *American Political Science Review* 83(1): 93–121.

Rahat, G. (2007) 'Candidate selection: the choice before the choice', *Journal of Democracy* 18(1): 157–170.

Rahat, G. and Hazan, R. Y. (2001) 'Candidate selection methods: an analytical framework', *Party Politics* 7(3): 297–322.

Rahn, W. M. (1993) 'The role of partisan stereotypes in information-processing about political candidates', *American Journal of Political Science* 37(2): 472–496.

Ranney, A. (1981) 'Candidate Selection', in D. Butler, H. R. Penniman and A. Ranney (eds) *Democracy at the Polls*, Washington, American Enterprise Institute.

Ray, L. (2007) 'Validity of measured party positions on European integration: assumptions, approaches, and a comparison of alternative measures', *Electoral Studies* 26(1): 11–22.

Res Publica (ed.) (1988) Leuven: Acco.

— (ed.) (1989) Leuven: Acco.

— (ed.) (1992) Leuven: Acco.

— (ed.) (1993) Leuven: Acco.

— (ed.) (1997) Leuven: Acco.

— (ed.) (1998) Leuven: Acco.

— (ed.) (2001) Leuven: Acco.

— (ed.) (2002) Leuven: Acco.

— (ed.) (2004) Leuven: Acco.

— (ed.) (2005) Leuven: Acco.

Riffe, D., Lacy, S. and Fico, F. G. (2005) *Analyzing Media Messages: Using quantitative content analysis in research*, Mahwah: Lawrence Erlbaum.

Riker, W. H. (1982) *Liberalism Against Populism: A confrontation between the theory of democracy and the theory of social choice*, San Francisco: W. H. Freeman.

Riker, W. H. and Ordeshook, P. C. (1968) 'Theory of calculus of voting', *American Political Science Review* 62(1): 25–42.

Roberts, G. (1988) 'The German Federal Republic: The two-lane route to Bonn', in M. Gallagher and M. Marsh (eds) *Candidate Selection in Comparative Perspective: The secret garden of politics*, London, Sage, pp. 94–118.

Robertson, D. (1976) *A Theory of Party Competition*, London: Wiley.

Roemer, J. E. (1994) 'A theory of policy differentiation in single issue electoral politics', *Social Choice and Welfare* 11(4): 355–380.

Rohrschneider, R. and Whitefield, S. (2009) 'Understanding cleavages in party systems issue position and issue salience in 13 post-communist democracies', *Comparative Political Studies* 42(2): 280–313.

— (2010) 'Consistent choice sets? The stances of political parties towards European integration in ten Central East European democracies, 2003–2007', *Journal of European Public Policy* 17(1): 55–75.

Rosenthal, H. and Voeten, E. (2004) 'Analyzing roll calls with perfect spatial voting: France 1946–1958', *American Journal of Political Science* 48(3): 620–632.

Saiegh, S. M. (2009) 'Recovering a basic space from elite surveys: evidence from Latin America', *Legislative Studies Quarterly* 34(1): 117–145.

Sainsbury, D. (1993) 'The politics of increased women's representation: the Swedish case', in J. Lovenduski and P. Norris (eds) *Gender and Party Politics*, London, Sage, pp. 263–290.

Sánchez-Cuenca, I. (2008) 'How Can Governments be Accountable if Voters Vote Ideologically?', in J. M. Maravall and I. Sánchez-Cuenca (eds) *Controlling Governments: Voters, institutions, and accountability*, Cambridge, Cambridge University Press, pp. 45–81.

Sartori, G. (1976) *Parties and Party Systems: A framework for analysis*, Cambridge: Cambridge University Press.

Scarrow, S. E. (1996) *Parties and Their Members: Organizing for victory in Britain and Germany*, Oxford: Oxford University Press.

Scarrow, S. E. (2002) 'Party Decline in the Parties State? The changing environment of German politics', in P. D. Webb, D. M. Farrell and I. Holliday (eds) *Political Parties in Advanced Industrial Democracies*, Oxford, Oxford University Press, pp. 77–106.

Scarrow, S. E., Webb, P. D. and Farrell, D. M. (2000) 'From Social Integration to Electoral Contestation: The changing distribution of power within political parties', in R. J. Dalton and M. P. Wattenberg (eds) *Parties without Partisans: Political change in advanced industrial democracies*, Oxford, Oxford University Press, pp. 129–153.

Schattschneider, E. E. (1942) *Party Government*, New York: Farrar and Rinehart.

Schindler, P. (1999) *Datenhandbuch zur Geschichte des Deutschen Bundestages 1949 bis 1999*, Baden-Baden: Nomos.

Schlesinger, J. A. (1984) 'On the theory of party organization', *Journal of Politics* 46(2): 369–400.

Schmitt, H. (2006) *The Mannheim Eurobarometer Trend File 1970–2002*, Köln/Mannheim: Gesis/MZES [distributor].

Schnell, R., Hill, P. B. and Esser, E. (2005) *Methoden der empirischen Sozialforschung*, München: Oldenbourg.

Schofield, N. (2003) 'Valence competition in the spatial stochastic model', *Journal of Theoretical Politics* 15(4): 371–383.

— (2005) 'A valence model of political competition in Britain: 1992–1997', *Electoral Studies* 24(3): 347–370.

Schofield, N. and Sened, I. (2006) *Multiparty Democracy: Elections and legislative politics*, Cambridge; New York: Cambridge University Press.

Schumacher, G., de Vries, C. E. and Vis, B. (2012) 'Why political parties change their positions: Environmental Incentives & Party Organization', Typescript.

Schumpeter, J. A. (1942) *Capitalism, Socialism and Democracy*, New York and London: Harper and Brothers.

Seyd, P. (1998) 'Tony Blair and New Labour', in A. King *et al.* (eds) *New Labour Triumphs: Britain at the polls*, Chatham, NJ: Chatham House Publishers, pp. 49–73.

Seyd, P. and Whiteley, P. (2004) 'From Disaster to Landslide: The case of the British Labour Party', in K. Lawson and T. Poguntke (eds) *How Political Parties*

Respond: Interest aggregation revisited, London, Routledge: 41–60.

Share, D. (1999) 'From Policy-Seeking to Office-Seeking: The metamorphosis of the Spanish Socialist Workers Party', in W. C. Müller and K. Strøm (eds) *Policy, Office, or Votes? How political parties in Western Europe make hard decisions*, Cambridge, Cambridge University Press, pp. 89–111.

Shaw, E. (2002) 'New labour in Britain: new democratic centralism?', *West European Politics* 25(3): 147–170.

Sheafer, T. and Wolfsfeld, G. (2009) 'Party systems and oppositional voices in the news media: a study of the contest over political waves in the United States and Israel', *International Journal of Press-Politics* 14(2): 146–165.

Shikano, S. and Pappi, F. U. (2004) 'Ideologische Signale in den Wahlprogrammen der deutschen Bundestagsparteien 1980 bis 2002', *MZES Working Papers*.

Sickinger, H. (2000) 'Parteien- und Wahlkampffinanzierung in den 90er Jahren', in F. Plasser, P. A. Ulram and F. Sommer (eds) *Das österreichische Wahlverhalten*, Wien, Signum, pp. 305–331.

— (2009) *Politikfinanzierung in Österreich*, Wien: Czernin.

Slapin, J. B. and Proksch, S.-O. (2008) 'A scaling model for estimating time-series party positions from texts', *American Journal of Political Science* 53(3): 705–722.

Smirnov, O. and Fowler, J. H. (2007) 'Policy-motivated parties in dynamic political competition', *Journal of Theoretical Politics* 19(1): 9–31.

Somer-Topcu, Z. (2009a) Responsive Agents: party policy shifts in twelve Western European democracies. Prepared for presentation at the Comparative Subconstituency Representation Workshop at the University of Essex, October 21, 2009.

— (2009b) 'Timely decisions: the effects of past national elections on party policy change', *Journal of Politics* 71(1): 238–248.

— (2009c) 'Responsive Agents: Party policy shifts in twelve Western European democracies', Typescript.

Spiegel (2011a) 'Deutsche wenden sich radikal von der Atomkraft ab [Germans turn away from nuclear power]'. http://www.spiegel.de/panorama/umfragen-deutsche-wenden-sich-radikal-von-der-atomkraft-ab-a-750955. html (accessed 15 March 2011).

— (2011b) 'Deutsche finden Atomwende der Regierung unglaubwürdig [Germans consider the government's turn in nuclear energy to be unreliable]'. http://www.spiegel.de/politik/deutschland/umfrage-deutsche-finden-atomwende-der-regierung-unglaubwuerdig-a-751538.html (accessed 17 March 2011).

Standards in Public Office Commission (2010). http://www.sipo.gov.ie/en/.

Statistics Norway [Statistisk sentralbyrå] (2010).

Steenbergen, M. R. and Jones, B. S. (2002) 'Modelling multilevel data structures', *American Journal of Political Science* 46(1): 218–237.

Steenbergen, M. R. and Marks, G. (2007) 'Evaluating expert judgements',

European Journal of Political Research 46(3): 347–366.

Stimson, J. A. (1991) *Public Opinion in America: Moods, cycles, and swings*, Boulder: Westview Press.

Stimson, J. A., Mackuen, M. B. and Erikson, R. S. (1995) 'Dynamic representation', *American Political Science Review* 89(3): 543–565.

Stimson, J. A. (1999) 'Party Government and Responsiveness', in A. Przeworski, S. C. Stokes and B. Manin (eds) *Democracy, Accountability, and Representation*, Cambridge, Cambridge University Press, pp. 197–221.

Stokes, D. E. (1963) 'Spatial models of party competition', *American Political Science Review* 57(2): 368–377.

— (1992) 'Valence Politics', in D. Kavanagh (ed.) *Electoral Politics*, Oxford, Clarendon Press, pp. 80–100.

Stokes, S. C. (1999) 'What do Policy Switches Tell Us About Democracy?', in A. Przeworski, S. C. Stokes and B. Manin (eds) *Democracy, Accountability, and Representation*, Cambridge, Cambridge University Press, pp. 98–130.

Stone, W. J. and Simas, E. N. (2007) 'Candidate Valence and Ideological Positioning in the 2006 House Elections', Berkeley: University of California, Davis.

— (2010) 'Candidate valence and ideological positions in US House elections', *American Journal of Political Science* 54(2): 371–388.

Strøm, K. (1990) 'A behavioral theory of competitive political parties', *American Journal of Political Science* 34(2): 565–598.

Strøm, K., and Müller, W. C. (1999) 'Political parties and hard choices', in W. C. Müller and K. Strøm (eds) *Policy, Office, or Votes?: How political parties in Western Europe make hard decisions*, Cambridge, Cambridge University Press, pp. 1–35.

Strøm, K., Müller, W. C. and Bergman, T. (eds) (2003) *Delegation and Accountability in Parliamentary Democracies*, Oxford: Oxford University Press.

— (eds) (2008) *Cabinets and Coalition Bargaining: The democratic life cycle in Western Europe*, Oxford: Oxford University Press.

Sturm, R. (2003) 'Das politische System Großbritanniens', in W. Ismayr (ed.) *Die politischen Systeme Westeuropas*, Opladen, Leske and Budrich, pp. 225–262.

Süddeutsche (2011) 'Brüderle und das Moratorium. Merkels Glaubwürdigkeits-GAU Brüderle and the moratorium. Merkel's credibility worst case scenario]'. http://www.sueddeutsche.de/politik/atompolitik-bruederle-merkel-und-das-moratorium-es-ist-nun-ja-wahlkampf-1.1076912 (accessed 25 March 2011).

Sundberg, J. and Gylling, C. (1992) 'Finland', in R. S. Katz and P. Mair (eds) *Party Organizations: A data handbook on party organizations in Western Democracies, 1960–90*, London, Sage, pp. 273–316.

Svåsand, L. (1992) 'Norway', in R. S. Katz and P. Mair (eds) *Party Organizations: A data handbook on party organizations in Western Democracies, 1960–90*, London, Sage, pp. 732–780.

—   (1994) 'Change and adaption in Norwegian Party Organizations', in R. S. Katz and P. Mair (eds) *How Parties Organize: Change and adaptation in party organizations in Western democracies*, London, Sage, pp. 304–331.

Swyngedouw, M., Billiet, J. and Frognier, A.-P. (1999) *Belgium General Election Study 1999*, Amsterdam: Steinmetz Archive [distributor].

Tavits, M. (2007) 'Principle vs. pragmatism: policy shifts and political competition', *American Journal of Political Science* 51(1): 151–165.

Thomassen, J. (ed.) (2005) *The European Voter*, Oxford: Oxford University Press.

Thorlakson, L. (2009) 'Patterns of party integration, influence and autonomy in seven federations', *Party Politics* 15(2): 157–177.

Totten, K. and MacCárthaigh, M. (2001) 'Irish political data 2001', *Irish Political Studies* 16(1): 287–351.

Tsebelis, G. (2002) *Veto Players: How political institutions work*, Princeton: Princeton University Press.

Ucakar, K. (2006) 'Sozialdemokratische Partei Österreichs', in H. Dachs *et al.* (eds) *Politik in Österreich: Das Handbuch*, Wien, Manz, pp. 322–340.

UNESCO (1997) *International Standard Classification of Education, ISCED 1997*: UNESCO Institute for Statistics.

Valen, H. (1988) 'Norway: decentralization and group representation', in M. Gallagher and M. Marsh (eds) *Candidate Selection in Comparative Perspective: The secret garden of politics*, London, Sage, pp. 210–235.

Valen, H., Narud, H. M. and Skare, A. (2002) 'Norway: Party Dominance and Decentralized Decision-Making', in H. M. Narud, M. N. Pedersen and H. Valen (eds) *Party Sovereignty and Citizen Control*, Odense, University Press of Southern Denmark: 169–215.

van Biezen, I. (2003) *Political Parties in New Democracies: Party organization in Southern and East-Central Europe*, Basingstoke: Palgrave Macmillan.

—   (2004) 'Political Parties as Public Utilities', *Party Politics* 10(6): 701–722.

—   (2008) 'State intervention in party politics: the public funding and regulation of political parties', *European Review* 16(3): 337–353.

van der Brug, W., van der Eijk, C. and Franklin, M. (2007) *The Economy and the Vote: Economic Conditions and Elections in Fifteen Countries*, Cambridge: Cambridge University Press.

Voerman, G. (1996) 'De ledentallen van politieke partijen, 1945–1995', *Jaarboek 1995 Documentatiecentrum Nederlandse Politieke Partijen*, Groningen, pp. 192–206.

Volkens, A. (2007) 'Strengths and weaknesses of approaches to measuring policy positions of parties', *Electoral Studies* 26(1): 108–120.

Walecki, M. (2001) 'Political Finance in Central Eastern Europe', in K.-H. Nassmacher (ed.) *Foundations for Democracy*, Baden-Baden, Nomos, pp. 393–415.

Walgrave, S. and Nuytemans, M. (2009) 'Friction and party manifesto change in 25 Countries, 1945–98', *American Journal of Political Science* 53(1): 190–206.

Ware, A. (1996) *Political Parties and Party Systems*, Oxford: Oxford University Press.

Webb, P. D. (1992) 'The United Kingdom', in R. S. Katz and P. Mair (eds) *Party Organizations: A data handbook on party organizations in western democracies, 1960–90*, London, Sage, pp. 837–870.

—— (1994) 'Party Organizational Change in Britain: The Iron Law of centralization?', in R. S. Katz and P. Mair (eds) *How Parties Organize: Change and adaptation in party organizations in Western democracies*, London, Sage, pp. 109–133.

—— (2002) 'Political Parties in Britain: Secular decline or adaptive resilience?', in P. D. Webb, D. M. Farrell and I. Holliday (eds) *Political Parties in Advanced Industrial Democracies*, Oxford, Oxford University Press, pp. 16–45.

Whitefield, S., Vachudova, M. A., Steenbergen, M. R., Rohrschneider, R., Marks, G., Loveless, M. P. and Hooghe, L. (2007) 'Do expert surveys produce consistent estimates of party stances on European integration? Comparing expert surveys in the difficult case of Central and Eastern Europe', *Electoral Studies* 26(1): 50–61.

Wiberg, M. (1991a) 'Introduction', in M. Wiberg (ed.) *The Public Purse and Political Parties*, Helsinki, Finnish Political Science Association, pp. 7–12.

—— (ed.) (1991b) *The Public Purse and Political Parties*, Helsinki: Finnish Political Science Association.

Wickham-Jones, M. (2005) 'Signaling credibility: electoral strategy and New Labour in Britain', *Political Science Quarterly* 120(4): 653–673.

Widfeldt, A. (1999) *Linking Parties with People?: Party membership in Sweden, 1960–1997*, Aldershot, UK and Brookfield, USA: Ashgate.

Wilson, F. L. (1994) 'The Sources of Party Change: The Social Democratic Parties of Britain, France, Germany and Spain', in K. Lawson (ed.) *How Political Parties Work: Perspectives from within*, Westport, Praeger, pp. 263–283.

Wittmann, D. (1983) 'Candidate motivation: a synthesis of alternative theories', *American Political Science Review* 77(1): 142–157.

—— (1990) 'Spatial strategies when candidates have policy preferences', in J. M. Enelow and M. J. Hinich (eds) *Advances in the Spatial Theory of Voting*, Cambridge, Cambridge University Press, pp. 66–98.

Woldendorp, J., Keman, H. and Budge, I. (1998) 'Party government in 20 Democracies: an update (1990–1995)', *European Journal of Political Research* 33(1): 125–164.

Wooldridge, J. M. (2002) *Econometric Analysis of Cross Section and Panel Data*, Cambridge: MIT Press.

World Political Leaders (2010). http://www.terra.es/personal2/monolith/00index2.htm

Wuffle, A., Feld, S. L., Owen, G. and Grofman, B. (1989) 'Finagle Law and the Finagle Point, a new solution concept for 2-candidate competition in spatial voting games without a core', *American Journal of Political Science* 33(2): 348–375.

Young, L. and Cross, W. (2002) 'The rise of plebiscitary democracy in Canadian political parties', *Party Politics* 8(6): 673–699.

Zaller, J. R. (1992) *The Nature and Origins of Mass Opinion*, Cambridge: Cambridge University Press.

Zaller, J. R. and Chiu, D. (1996) 'Government's little helper: US press coverage of foreign policy crises, 1945–1991', *Political Communication* 13(4): 385–405.

Zaller, J. R. and Hunt, M. (1994) 'The rise and fall of Candidate Perot: unmediated versus mediated politics-Part 1', *Political Communication* 11(4): 357–390.

— (1995) 'The rise and fall of Candidate Perot: the outsider versus the political-system-Part 2', *Political Communication* 12(1): 97–123.

Zárate, R. (2009) 'World Political Leaders, 1945–2008'. http://www.terra.es/personal2/monolith/00index2.htm.

| index

Page numbers in italics indicate information in tables and figures.

Abney, R. 86
acceptance of party policy shifts *see* voter policy shift perception model
Adams, J. 18, 19, 20, 21, 23, 59 n.1, 70, 79, 86, 88, 90, 92, 133, 137, 160, 165 n.25, 180, 187, 205, 209, 214
Aldrich, J. H. 18, 82, 92, 174
Alvarez, R. M. 22, 23, 57, 59, 77, 220, 221
Austria 36, 39, 229, 231, 232
    intra-party structure analysis 179, 182
    party funding 173
    party position placement and 36–7
    Social Democrats 175
    voter perception analysis 136, 143
        data sources 140
Axelrod, R. M. 80

Bartels, L. M. 22, 77
Bartolini, S. 181
Baumgartner, F. R. 88, 174
Beck, N. 180, 225, 227
Belgium 37, 136, 149, 229, 231, 232
    intra-party structure analysis 179, 182, 184, 185
    party position placement and 140
    voter perception analysis 136, 143
        data sources 138, 140, 143
Bendor, J. 21
Bennett, W. L. 81
Benoit, K. 30, 31, 32, 33, 34, 35, 36, 37, 40, 43, 44, 45, 46, 47, 49, 50, 52 n.18, 91, 92, 104, 137, 229, 230 n.4
Bergman, T. 93
Berlusconi, S. 26
Best, H. 30
Best, R. 33

Bille, L. 25, 179, 184 n.6
Birnir, J. K. 179
Black, D. 17
Blair, T. 5, 107, 109, 111, 130–1, 210
Bolleyer, N. 26, 176
Brehm, J. 22, 23, 77, 221
Brown, G. 106
Budge, I. 20, 21, 29, 30, 31, 34, 36, 41, 87, 95, 102, 104, 137, 180, 186
Burke, E. 16
Butler, D. 102, 105, 140
Butler, G. 102, 140

Cameron, D. 5
campaigning 11, 170, 171, 177, 193, 212
    capital-intensive and labour-intensive forms of 172–173, 212
    party resources for *see* under voter policy shift perception model
Campbell, A. 17 n.2, 19, 88
Carrubba, C. 31
cartelisation of party systems 176
Carty, R. K. 24, 181 n.2, 186
Castles, F. 30, 32, 91, 92, 142
Chapel Hill expert survey 35
Chappell, H. W. 18, 19
Chiu, D. 81
Chong, D. 97
civil society 170, 171, 176 n.1
Clarify 107 n.7, 109 n.8, n.9, 111 n.11
Clark, M. 19, 86
Clarke, H. 19, 138
Clinton, J. 29
coalition government 19, 24, 80, 81
Comparative Manifestos Project (CMP) 29, 33–53, 102, 136, 137, 180, 186, 229, 231
    history of 33

left-right scale 100, 102, 112, 137, 142, 157, 192, 196
Manifesto Project Database 33
validity and 136, 137, 179
Comparative Study of Electoral Systems (CSES) 30
content analysis of political texts *see* party policy shifts, measurement of
Constitutional Change and Parliamentary Democracies project 140
Converse, P. 133
credibility *see* under party policy shifts
Crewe, I. 97, 100
Cross, W. 181 n.2
Crotty, W. J. 24, 183
Curini, L. 30, 32

Dahl, R. A. 15
Dalton, R. J. 27
Damgaard, E. 91, 93, 230 n.3
de Marchi, S. 21
Denmark 181, 229, 231, 232
intra-party structure analysis
data sources 180, 182, 185
party system in 91, 93
voter perception analysis 136, 138, 153 n.18
data sources 138, 140
Denver, D. 184 n.7
Deschouwer, K. 182, 184
de Swaan, A. 80
Deutscher Bundestag 185–6
De Winter, L. 184 n.7
Die Grünen 184
Diermeier, D. 136
Dinas, E. 31
Downs, A. 3, 7, 16, 17, 18, 19, 22, 23, 33, 34, 77, 85, 86, 214
Economic Theory of Democracy 18, 86
spatial models and 3
see also party competition
Druckman, J. N. 97
Dumont, P.

Dutch Ministry of the Interior and Kingdom Relations 186
Duverger, M. 24, 26, 172
dynamic representation 90, 214

The Economist 5, 49 n.15
education *see* under voter policy shift perception model
electoral systems
multiparty 3, 75
single-party majority 80
two-party 3, 17, 75, 80
see also party competition; party systems
Enelow, J. M. 22, 23, 59 n.1, 60, 79
Epstein, D. 173
Epstein, L. D. 24, 172
Erikson, R. S. 19
Eurobarometer surveys 97, 138, 143 n.9
trend file 138, 161
European Parliament 30, 32
European Voter Project 102, 138
Evans, S. 5, 21
Ezrow, L. 21, 90, 133, 160, 166, 205, 214

Farrell, D. M. 182, 184
FAZ 4
Feddersen, T. J. 136
finance of parties *see* intra-party structure, party finance
Financial Times 106
Finland 37, 136, 229, 231, 232
intra-party structure analysis 173, 179, 182, 186 n.10
voter perception analysis 136
data sources 138, 140
Finnish Ministry of Justice 184
Fiorina, M. P. 17 n.2
Fowler, J. H. 21
France 39, 136
Franklin, C. H. 22, 77
Franzmann, S. 34, 38, 39–40

Gabel, M. J. 38, 40
Gallagher, M. 24, 25, 183, 184
Gay, O. 186
Gelman, A.180, 226
Gemenis, K. 30, 31, 34
Germany 229, 231, 232
  Christian Democrats (CDU) 4, 92, 93
    CDU-CSU-FDP 2009 coalition 4
  Federal Elections Act 1993 184
  Greens 4, 184, 229
  intra-party structure analysis 173,
    179, 182, 184
    data sources 185–6
    party funding and 185
  Liberal Party (FDP) 4, 92, 93
  nuclear power debate in 4
    party position change and 4
  party placement/ranking and 37, 39,
    92, 140
  Social Democrats (SPD) 4, 83, 92,
    93
    policy shift 1959 and 82
  voter perception analysis 136, 153
    n.18
    data sources 138
Gidlund, G. 26 n.9, 186
Gilmore, T. N. 85, 214
González, F. 5–6, 175
  government party see under voter
    policy shift perception model
Great Britain see United Kingdom
Greece 136
Green, J. 19, 97, 100
Grofman, B. 59 n.1
Groseclose, T. 18 n.4, 19, 86
Gyurcsány, F. 36 n.6

Hammond, J. S. 6 n.1
Hansen, M. E. 30, 32, 34
Harmel, R. 21, 25, 85, 214
Hazan, R. Y. 24, 183, 184
Heath, A. 83, 97, 100, 106
Heidar, K. 136
Hellwig, T. 21
Hill, J. 180, 226

Hinich, M. J. 22, 23, 59 n.1, 60, 79
Hirschmann, A. O. 11, 25, 174, 199
Hix, S. 30
Holsti, O. R. 30
Hooghe, L. 30, 31, 32, 34, 35
Hooghe, M. 171
Hopkin, J. 25, 184
Hotelling, H. 17
Huber, J. D. 30, 32, 38, 40, 47, 91, 92,
  93, 142, 229
Hug, S. 30, 32
Humphreys, M. 59 n.1
Hunt, B. W. 30, 32, 81, 91

ideology 16, 18, 85, 91–3, 94
  see also left-right placement of
    political parties
Infratest dimap 4
Inglehart, R. 30, 32, 91, 92, 93, 142,
  229
intra-party structure 10–12, 16, 21,
  23–5, 27, 141, 169–77
  decision making rules and 24–5, 27,
    169, 173–5, 177
    candidate selection and 183–4,
      189, 195
    elite and 11, 12, 24, 170, 171,
      173
    history of party and 170, 174
    party leadership and 11–12, 24,
      152–3, 169–70, 171, 173–4
  party finance 11, 12, 13, 23, 25–7,
    170, 171, 172–3, 175–7, 193
    'plutocratic' financing 26
    public funding of 26–7, 169, 170,
      173, 176, 177, 193, 212
    resource dependence theory 25,
      212
    vote maximisation and 176
  party membership 11–12, 170–3
    basic party role of 170–1, 172,
      173, 189, 193
    costs of participation 174
    decision making, role in 24, 25,
      174–5

mass membership, effect on
  party policy shifts 11, 24, 25,
    170–3, 180–1, 183, 184, 189
organisational needs of 170, 172
principal-agent relationship in
  24, 169–70, 173–4
public funding, effect on 173,
  176, 177, 185
veto players and 11, 13, 25, 64,
  170, 175, 195, 204
IntUne project 30 n.1
Ireland 32, 136, 229, 231, 232
  intra-party structure analysis 179,
    182, 184, 185 n.8, 186
  voter perception analysis 136, 143
    data sources 140, 143
Italy 32, 36 n.7, 37, 39, 44, 136, 179

Jackman, S. 29
Janda, K. 16, 21, 25, 85, 214
Japan, Fukushima disaster (2011) 4
Jenkins, R. W. 81
Jennings, W. 97
Jenny, M. 29, 46, 230 n.1
Jones, B. D. 88, 174, 180, 226

Kaiser, A. 34, 38, 39–40
Katz, R. S. 11, 24, 26, 170, 172, 174,
  176, 179, 180, 181, 182, 183, 184,
  185, 215, 225, 227
  Party Organizations 179, 185
Kedar, O. 17
Keech, W. R. 18, 19
Keman, H. *182*, 186
Kiewiet, D. R. 24, 173
King, G. 33, 34, 44, 51, 75, 107 n.7
Kirchheimer, O. 24, 172
Kitschelt, H. 25, 175, 176, 187
Klemmensen, R. 31, 34
Klingemann, H.-D. 30, 137, 180, 186
Klotzbach, K. 83
Knutsen, O. 92
Kollman, K. 21, 209
Koole, R. A. 26 n.9, 136, 182, 184,
  186

Koopmans, R. 81
Krasner, S. D. 88
Kreps, D. M. 64
Krippendorff, K. 30
Krouwel, A. 24, 179

Laakso, M. 140, 149
Lacewell, O. 51
Lau, R. R. 213
Laver, M. xi, 17, 21, 30, 31, 32, 34, 35,
  36, 37, 40, 43, 44, 49, 50, 59 n.1,
  63, 80, 91, 92, 104, 137, 142, 169,
  180, 192, 209, 229, 230 n.4
left-right placement of political parties
  91–3, 186
  see also Comparative Manifestos
    Project (CMP), left-right scale
Levi, M. 20, 87
Lijphart, A. 80
Lin, T.-M. 19
Lipset, S. M. 82
Lowe, W. 34, 40, 41, 43
Lundell, K. 25, 184
Lupia, A. 64, 80, 173

McCubbins, M. D. 24, 173
McDonald, M. D. 31, 33, 35, 36, 91
Macdonald, S. E. 17, 18 n.4, 19
Mair, P. 11, 24, 25, 26, 27, 30, 32, 91,
  92, 142, 170, 171, 172, 174, 176,
  179, 182, 183, 184, 185, 186, 215
  Party Organizations 179, 185
Mancini, P. 172
Manifesto Research Group (MRG) 33
  see also Comparative Manifestos
    Project (CMP)
Manifesto Research on Political
  Representation (MARPOR) 33, 34
  see also Comparative Manifestos
    Project (CMP)
Manin, B. 62
Maravall, J. M. 5, 25, 175
Marks, G. 30, 32, 34, 35
Marsh, M. 24, 25, 138, 184
measuring party policy shifts *see* party

policy shifts, measurement of
media
  party positions, presentation of 3,
    11, 59, 171
    campaigning and 173, 177
    government and oppositional
      parties 80–2
    'relevance' of parties and 80
  policy shifts, role in 75, 76, 80
    magnitude of shift and 84
    party coverage and 76
  political awareness/interest, role in
    101
Meguid, B. M. *182*, 186, 187
Mendes, S. M. 33, 91
Merrill, S. III 19, 21, 59 n.1, 86
Meyer, T. M. 29, 41, 46, 173
Michels, R. 181 n.2
Mikhaylov, S. 31, 34, 40, 44, 50, 51,
  104
Mill, J. S. 135
Miller, J. H. 21
Miller, S. 83
Müller, W. C. 17, 19, 26, 140, 142,
  170, 171, 172, 173, 176, 182, 184,
  229
Murphy, R. J. 182

Nassmacher, K.-H. 26, 176 n.1, 185,
  201, 215
Netherlands, the 37, 229, 231, 232
  intra-party structure analysis 179,
    182, 184, 186
  party position placement and 37,
    142
  party system in 92, 229, 231, 232
  voter perception analysis 136, 138
    data sources 138, 140
Neuendorf, K. A. 30
New Labour (UK) policy shift analysis
  5, 9, 12, 21, 83–4, 87, 97–112, 113,
  128–9, 130–1, 132–3, 210
  data used in 97, 99
    British panel election studies and
      97, 99–100, 102, 219

    policy issues/dimensions and
      99–100
  measurement/method and 97–8,
    99–105, 222 n.2
    as two-stage model 111–12, 113,
      116
    CMP left-right scale 100, 102,
      104
    covariates used 98, 100–1, 116
    party ideological territory and
      104, 131, 134
    policy scales and 100, 101
    regression models and 98, 107,
      113, 125
  1993 Labour conference 105–6
    Clause IV and 106
  1997 election policy position 87,
    104, *128*, 130–1, 134, 210
  trade union influence, change of
    105–6
  2001 policy shift and 130–1, 134
  voter perception (acceptance/recep-
    tion) covariates 98, 101–112,
    116, 125, *128*, 130–1, 132–3
    age and gender *103*, 104, *107*,
      108, 109, 128, 130
    education level 101, *103*, 107,
      108, 109, 112, *128*
    government party 102, *103*
    leader's prestige 102, *103, 107,
      108*, 109, 125, *129*, 134
    leadership change 102, *103*, 107,
      125, *129*, 130, 134
    magnitude of shifts and 102, *103,
      107, 108*, 109, *110, 128*, 130
    party identification 102, *103*,
      107, 110–11, 112, 125
    past shifts and direction of 102,
      103, 107, *108*, 110–11
    personal policy preferences and
      111, 112, 116
    political awareness 101, *103*,
      107, 109, 112, 113, *128*
    position shifts 101, 102, *103*,
      104, 106–7, 125, *129*

see also United Kingdom, party
 position shifts analysis
niche parties 21, 160, 186–7, 189, 192,
 197, 198, *199*, 201, 205, 214–15,
 232
see also parties political, types of
Norris, P. 25
Norway 136, 138, 229, 231, 232
 intra-party structure analysis 179,
  182, 184, 185, 186
 party position placement and 142
 Political Parties Act 2006 185
 voter perception analysis 136, 138
  data sources 138
Nuytemans, M. 21, 64, 84 n.4, 88, 175

Obler, J. 25, 184
O'Halloran, S. 24, 173
Olson, M. 174
 opposition party *see* under voter
  policy shift perception model
Ordeshook, P. C. 79
organisation of parties *see* intra-party
 structure
Orwell, G. 8–9
 Nineteen Eighty-Four 8–9

Panebianco, A. 16, 172
Pappi, F. U. 92, 138
Parties and Elections in Europe 140
parties, political 15, 169
 definitions of 15–16, 27, 209
 democracy, role in 3, 15, 90
 government/opposition roles 80–2
 rival parties 15, 16, 21, 27, 209
 trust in 62, 73, 94
 types of 24
  cadre 24
  cartel 24, 26, 170, 172, 176, 201
  catch-all 24, 83, 172
  elite 24, 170
  franchise 24
  mass 24, 26, 170, 172, 175, 212
  niche 21, 160, 186–7, 189, 192,
   197, 198, *199*, 201, 205,

   214–15, 232
party activists 18, 25, 169, 170–1
 see also intra-party structure
party competition 59, 209, 215
 Downs proximity voting model 17
 policy shift analysis and 140, 149,
  177
 spatial models and 3, 4, 18, 20, 133
  left-right dimension and 59
 static models and 7, 8, 17–18, 20,
  27, 209
 time dimension and 7, 15, 20, 21,
  27, 209
party identification 10, 19, 27, 84–5,
 88–9, 176
 policy shifts, perception of and 10,
  17 n.2, 57, 84–5, 94, 95, 97
party leaders 18
 changes in 85, 140, 152–3, 214
 policy shifts and 85–6, 97, 98, 131,
  140, 152–3, 212, 214
 prestige of 19, 140
 see also party policy shifts; voter
  policy shift perception model
party manifestos
 as indicator of change 37
 CMP data and 29, 33–53
 decision making processes and 181
 length of 49
 party policy goals and 49
 policy shift analysis and 29, 30,
  33–53, 91
  coding methods and 30–1
  measurement error and 36
  underlying assumptions of 47,
   49–50
 see also Comparative Manifestos
  Project (CMP)
party policy shifts 3–6, 16, 29, 30–1,
 63–73, 209–15
 acceptance/reception of 9, 11, 12,
  57–64, 66, 73, 75–6, 84–96,
  210–11, 213–14
  causes/consequence for shifts
   and 75, 135

complexity and 75
magnitude of shift and 76, 94, 130
party reaction to 63, 66, 135
see also voter policy shift perception model
concept/definition of 15
constraints faced by parties in 4, 7–8, 10, 12, 15, 27, 64, 73, 85, 135, 169, 209, 215
see also intra-party structure; voter policy shift perception model
costs of 6, 7, 22, 64, 73, 76–7, 171
cost-benefit argument and 64, 73, 77, 78
credibility loss and 21–2, 130, 157, 213
government/opposition parties and 19, 80–2, 139
incentives and 15, 17, 21, 23, 27, 71
intra-party structure *see* intra-party structure
leader prestige and 19, 102, 131, 132, 155–7, 171, 210
leadership and 169–70, 210, 214
change of and 140, 152–4, 214
magnitude of policy shifts and 154–5
measurement of *see* party policy shifts, measurement of
media, role in *see* media
niche parties and 21, 160, 186–7, 189, 192, 197, 198, *199*, 201, 205, 214–15
party income *see* intra-party structure, party finance
policy space, concept of 32–3
status-quo trap of 6, 7, 8, 9
uncertainty and 7, 22, 23, 49, 77
electoral market and 7–8
higher information costs and 77
voter misperception, consequences of 62–3, 213
voter preferences, shift towards and

65, 69, 78, 82, 85, 87, 89, 95, 111, *117, 121, 124, 126*
party policy shifts, measurement of 12, 29–53, 133, 135–6, 217–233
assumptions of 47–9, 53
comparability of position and 32, 223, 226–8
centrist bias, effect of 46–7, *48, 52*
left-right positions and 32, 33, 34, 35, 38–44, 46–7, 49, 50–1, 223
policy space and 32–3, 38
content analysis (political texts) 29, 30, 33, 52
cross-national comparability and 33, 34. 35, 36–7, 38, 40, 135–6, 138, 225, 226, 227
expert judgements, use of 35, 35–7, 38, 43, 49, *50,* 92
left-right placement and 92, 99, 141–2, 231
CMP left-right scale 100, 137, 142
MRG/CMP/MARPOR data 33–53
coding process 34, 35, 44, 50–2
data validity/reliability 34–6, 38, 50–2
left-right (RILE) scale and 34, 35, 36, 37, 38, 40–4, 45, 47, 50–2
uncertainty, estimates of 44–6, 49–50, 52–3
valence issues and 38, 39
policy dimensions, use of 99–100
position and valence issues 38–9
roll call analyses 29–30, 31, 32
survey-based approach 30, 31, 32, 33
time-series data 29, 31, 33, 35, 38, 52
see also Comparative Manifestos Project (CMP)
party systems 10, 82, 230 n.3
complexity of 82–3, 136
government-opposition divide and

134
  left-right axis description and 91
  policy change, perception of and 75,
    82, 127–30, 136, 141
Pedersen, M. N. 184
Pelizzo, R. 34, 37, 44, 136, 137, 179
Pennings, P. 30, 31, 184
Perot, R. 80–1
Peters, B. G. 87
Pettitt, R. T. 181
Pfeffer, J. 25, 175
Pierce, R. 59
Pierre, J. 26, 173, 179, 182, 184 n.6,
    185
Pierson, P. 20, 87
Plott, C. R. 17 n.2, 19
Plümper, T. 226–7
political awareness see under voter
  policy shift perception model
Poole, K. T. 29
Portugal 136
Powell, G. B. 80
Proksch, S. O. 31, 34, 137
Przeworski, A. 135
public opinion
  media, role in 80
  niche parties and 187
  policy shifts and 10, 12, 21, 27, 73,
    79, 85, 90, 96, 130, 134, 141,
    147–8, 160–1, 209, 214, 215
    benign and harmful shifts 70–1,
      73, 147, 160–1
    left wing parties and 187
    see also voter policy shift
      perception model
  voter predisposition and 23, 57

Rabe-Hesketh, S. 180, 226
Rabinowitz, G. 17, 18 n.4, 19
Rahat, G. 24, 183, 184
Rahn, W. M. 23, 88–9
Ranney, A. 24, 183
Ray, L. 31
reception of party policy shifts see
  voter policy shift perception model

Redlawsk, D. P. 213
resources of parties see intra-party
  structure
Riffe, D. 30
Riker, W. H. 62, 79
Robertson, D. 17 n.1, 174, 175
Roemer, J. E. 19
Rohrschneider, R. 34
Rokkan, S. 82
Romero, D. W. 19
Rosenthal, H. 29, 30

Saiegh, S. M. 30
Sainsbury, D. 184
Salancik, G. R. 25, 175
Sánchez-Cuenca, I. 18, 23
Sartori, G. 16
Scarrow, S. E. 25, 26, 182, 184
Schattschneider, E. E. 15, 16, 24, 90,
    183
  Party Government 16
Schlesinger, J. A. 25, 174
Schmitt, H. 138
Schnell, R. 101
Schofield, N. 17, 18, 19, 63, 86, 169
Schulz, T. 30, 32
Schumacher, G. 25
Schumpeter, J. A. 16, 22
Sened, I. 18, 19, 86
Seyd, P. 83, 106
Share, D. 5, 25, 175
Shaw, E. 24 n.7, 83, 181
Sheafer, T. 81
Shepsle, K. A. 21, 80
Shikano, S. 92
Sickinger, H. 185
Sieberer, U. 49 n.14
Simas, E. N. 19, 86
Skrondal, A. 180, 226
Slapin, J. B. 31, 34, 137
Smirnov, O. 21
Somer-Topcu, Z. 21, 137, 160, 165
    n.25, 180, 187, 209, 214
Spain 136
  1982 general election 175

party position change in 5–6, 175
Social Democrats (PSOE) 5, 175
UCD 175
Spiegel 4
Stadler, P. F. 21
Standards in Public Office
Commission (Ireland) 186
Statistics Norway [Statistisk sentral-
byrå] 186
Steenbergen, M. R. 30, 32, 34, 35,
180, 226
Stimson, J. A. 89–90, 97, 214
Stokes, D. E. 19, 38 n.8, 86
Stokes, S. C. 62
Stone, W. J. 18, 86
Strøm, K. 17, 19, 25, 26, 64, 80, 140,
142, 170, 172, 173, 174, 176, 229
Süddeutsche 4
Sweden 229, 231, 232
intra-party structure analysis 179,
184, 185 n.8, 186
political parties in 37, 93
Riksdag 186
Social Democrats 175, 229, 231
voter perception analysis 136, 138,
153 n18
data sources 140
Switzerland 32

Taagepera, R. 140, 149
Tavits, M. 21, 137, 180
Teune, H. 135
Thatcher, M. 5
Thomassen, J. 92, 102, 138, 142
Thorlakson, L. 25, 184
Truman, Harry S. 10
Tsebelis, G. 25, 64, 174

United Kingdom 37, 39, 229, 231
Conservative Party 5, 10, 49 n.15,
102, 104–5, 229
policy shifts analysis *115, 116,
119, 120, 122, 123, 128–9*
2005 elections 5
Labour Party 5, 21, 197–134, 181,

182, 229
ideological territory of 10, 104,
130
New Labour policy shift *see*
New Labour (UK) policy
shift analysis
policy shifts analysis *115, 116,
119, 120, 122, 123, 128–9,*
130–1
Liberal Democrats 93, 102, 104,
105, 183, 229
Alliance 1987–1992 104
1992 policy shift 130, *131*
policy shifts analysis 113 n.12,
130
panel election studies and 97, 99,
132, 137, 138, 209–10, 217–19
party policy shifts analysis
104–105, 109, 112–34, 136, 138,
149, 210
data used in 112, 138, 140, 184,
185 n.8, 186, 217–19
expected party shifts and 130–2
government parties and *115,* 117,
119, 122, 124, *125,* 127, 134,
210
intra-party organisational
strength analysis 179, 184,
185 n.8, 186
magnitude of shift and 114, *115,*
117, 118, *119,* 120, 122, *123,*
124, *125, 126, 128–9,* 130,
132, 134
Nationalisation vs. Privatisation
scale 100, 101, 102 n.4, *103,*
106, 113–18, *126, 128–9,*
130, 133
party ideological territory and
130–2
party leadership and 114, *115,*
117, 118, *119,* 122, *123, 126,
129,* 130–2, 133, 210
party placement 142
political awareness/interest
and 113–14, 118, *119,* 120,

121–2, 124, *125,* 126, *128,*
132, 133, 210
size of policy shift and 127,
129–30
Taxes vs. Services scale 99, 100,
101, 102 n.4, 103, 106, 107,
113, 118–120, *126, 128–9,*
130, 133
two-stage model and 116–17,
121–2, 133
Unemployment vs. Inflation
scale 99, 100, 101, 102 n.4,
103, 106, 107, *113,* 120–4,
126, 128–9, 130, 133
voter age and gender *115, 116,*
119, 120, 123
voter education and 114, *115,*
118, *119, 122,* 124, *125, 128,*
132, 133, 210
voter expectations and 104,
130–2
voter party identification and
114, *115,* 117, 118, *119,* 121,
123, 126, 127, *132,* 133–4,
210
voter perception of 112–13,
116–17, 210
voter preferences and 114, *116,*
117–18, *120,* 121, *123,* 127,
129, 132, 133, 210–11
party system in 92, 93, 117, 127
United States 179
Congress 29
media, political role of 101
party policy shifts and
roll call analyses 29–30, 31
presidential campaigns 80–1
primaries and 24, 183
Republican Party 52

Valen, H. 184
valence issues 19, 38, 39, 86, 87
van Biezen, I. 25, 26, 27, 171, 172,
176, 179, 182, 185, 186, 215
van der Brug, W. 17 n.2

van der Eijk, C.
Voeten, E. 30
Volkens, A. 31
Vote World project 32 n.3
voter policy shift perception model 9,
22–3, 27, 57–74, 210–12
as a spatial model 58, 72, 73
as a two-stage process 12–13, 57,
61, 72–3, 98, 111, 116–17, 210,
219–21
acceptance/reception criterion
9–10, 57, 58, 60–1, 62, 66,
67, 69, 72, 73–4, 75–95, 98
covariates and 75–84, 85, 86–95,
210, 211
complexity of political market and
82–3, 94
education and 138
effect on party position shifts 70–4
benign and harmful shifts 70, *71,*
147–8
party incentives for change and
71–2
government/opposition party
differences 80–2
ideological territory and voter
expectations 91–93
interest/awareness, role of 9, 22–3,
27, 57, 61, 75, 76–7, 78–9, 94,
101, 144
leadership and personnel changes
84, 85–7, 94, 97, 102, 140,
152–4
prestige of and 84, 86–7, 94, 102,
140, 152, 155
left-right dimension and 38, 59, 79,
85, 90, 91, 99
country differences and 92
ideological constraints 85, 91–3
personal preferences and 90
voter expectations and 91–3, 130
magnitude of shift and 83–4, 94,
102, 141, 144, 210
party credibility and 5, 9, 22–3, 27,
60, 73, 130, 152

constant changes and 84, 87–8
past behaviour and 87–8, 157
valence issues and 86–7
party identification and 88–9, 97,
141, 159
political awareness 76–77
public opinion shifts and 70–72,
78–79, 89–90
time dimension and 57, 58, 72
voter misperception/non perception
and 62–3, 213
Zaller's RAS model and 57–8, 72,
75, 210
voters
decision-making strategies of 88–9
education level of 9, 22, 75, 77–8,
94
information costs and 77–8
policy shifts, reception of and 78
policy issues, importance of 99–100
political awareness of 22–3, 57, 75,
76–7, 78, 94, 125, 133
concept of 76
sociodemography of 19
turnout of 176
see also party identification
voting
Michigan model 88
probabilistic/deterministic 19–20
stochastic 19
perception of policy shifts see voter
policy shift perception model

Walecki, M. 179
Walgrave, S. 21, 64, 84 n.4, 88, 175
Ware, A. 26, 170
Wattenberg, M. P. 27
Webb, P. D. 183, 184
Werner, A. 51
West European countries, policy shift
analysis 13, 36, 45, 47, 52, 72 n. 3,
82, 136–66, 211–12
case selection 136, 179
covariates of voter perception
137–45, 211

education 138
government party 139–40, 143,
148–9, 164, 165, 211
ideological territory and voter
expectations 139, 162–3,
164, 165, 166, 212
leadership change 139, 140, 143,
151, 152–5, 164, 165–6
leadership prestige 139, 140–1,
143, 155–7, 164, 165, 166,
212
magnitude of shift 139, 141, 144,
145–8, 149, 154, 157–9,
164, 212
parties, number of 139, 144, 149,
150, 164
party identification 139, 141,
143, 157, 158, 165
past shifts 139, 143, 144, 157,
164, 166
political interest 137–8, 139,
143, 144, 145–8, 149, 164,
165, 211
public opinion shifts 160–1, 165
voter direction 139, 141, 143,
145–6, 156, 157, 161, 164,
165, 211
data and sources 136, 137, 138,
139, 140–1, 143–4, 165, 229,
231, 232
intra-party structure analysis
179–205, 212–13
covariates and control variables
182, 183–9
data availability and measurement 179–83, 185–7
decision-making rules and 182,
184, 187, 188, 189, 195–9,
204, 205, 212, 213
left and right wing parties and
182, 187, 188, 189, 191, 196,
197, 198, 201, 202, 205
mass organisational strength
and 180–1, 182, 187, 188,
189–94, 203, 204, 212, 213

member inclusiveness and 184,
    195–9, 204, 212
niche parties 186–7, *188*, 189,
    191, 192, *194*, 196, 197, 198,
    201, *202, 203*, 205
party size *182*, 186, *188*, 189,
    191, 192, *194*, 196, 198, 201,
    202, 203, 205
public funding/subsidies, effect
    of *182*, 185, *188*, 193,
    199–203, 204, 205, 212, 213
time effects and *182*, 186, *188*,
    189, 192, 197, 201, *203*, 205
measurement of 136–7, 140–4, 165,
    180–1
left-right scale and 136, 137,
    138, 141–2, *143*, 144
magnitude of shift and 137, 141
public subsidies 185, 187
voter expectations 142, 145
see also under names of individual
    countries
Whitefield, S. 30, 31, 32, 34
Whiteley, P. 106
Wiberg, M. 26, 185
Wickham-Jones, M. 21, 83, 106
Wilson, F. L. 7
Wittmann, D. 18
Wolfsfeld, G. 81
Wooldridge, J. M. 98
Wuffle, A. 21–2, 23

Young, L. 181 n.2

Zaller, J. R. 9, 22, 23, 57–8, 72–3, 75,
    76, 81, 101, 138
    *The Nature and Origins of Mass
        Opinion* 23
    Receive-Accept-Sample (RAS)
        model 57–8, 75, 210
Zárate, R. 102
Zucchini, F. 30, 32

www.ingramcontent.com/pod-product-compliance
Lightning Source LLC
Chambersburg PA
CBHW072057020426
42334CB00017B/1547